TACTICAL PERIODIZATION

VITOR FRADE CLARIFIES

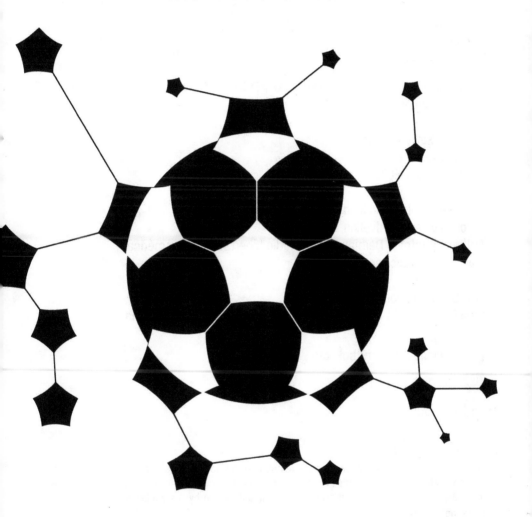

XAVIER TAMARIT

Foreword: Mauricio Pellegrino

Translation: Francisco Fardilha

Tactical Periodization Vs Tactical Periodization / Xavier Tamarit - 1a ed. -
LIBROFUTBOL.com, 2021.
282 pages; 15,2 x 22,9 cm.

ISBN 978-987-8370-45-3

1. Football
CDD 796.33409

TACTICAL PERIODIZATION VS TACTICAL PERIODIZATION
by Xavier Tamarit

Cover design: Luciano Medvetkin
Layout: Luciano Medvetkin
Author's photo: © Demian Alda, Estadio Libertadores de América.
Translation: Francisco Fardilha

LIBROFUTBOL.com
Olga Cossettini 1112 - office 8F - City of Buenos Aires - Argentina

ediciones@librofutbol.com

+54 9 11 2215 1982

@librofutbol

1st edition: July 2021
ISBN 978-987-8370-45-3

ISBN 978-987-8370-45-3

9 789878 370453

> A TAILOR-MADE SUIT

Xavier Tamarit

> Foreword

....

Mauricio Pellegrino

Technical Director

While looking for arguments that support the foundations of my beliefs and trying to order my ideas with a minimum of sense, I faced an instigator of truths, that suddenly turned my faith upside down.

I heard at some point that "it is more difficult to drop an old habit than to adopt a new one". How difficult it is to see things from a different perspective, with a different lens. We find excuses not to leave behind what is so deeply rooted in our habits. How powerful is domestication with universal truths, how comfortable we feel in them.

Although I don't want to generalise this personal feeling, I believe that in many occasions we don't want to see something different or something that has taken a different path to get to the same place.

Through his research, Xavi provides us with tools that have been thought and articulated to provide each of us with the ability to create a *tailor-made* plan. One that never expires, because its horizon is always beyond. It carries the weight of tradition, while being contemporary. It as a start, but it can never be finished. He provides us with the best of his work to understand any logic, "the one of the way of playing we carry inside", that renews those nooks from yesterday to help us being alert in the present.

The richness of this material is just like a bookshelf or a library that allow you to organise your ideas and concepts, ordering them, taking them out to get some fresh air, and trade them by others if you see it fit. There will be new shelves, bigger or smaller, with endless details to be made sense of. But without this shelf, they would perhaps have never seen the daylight.

The organisation of a TEAM is too complex to ignore the whole. It tells us about MODEL-MA-TRIX-IDEAS-CONCEPTS-CULTURE and other topic that will arouse the curiosity of those who have invested so much time and an intense calling to continue giving us questions-answers and even more doubts, but always aiming at improving the COLLECTIVE ABILITY of a FOOTBALL TEAM.

Thanks to all those who keep the fire burning on the search for something better.

With gratitude.

Mauricio Pellegrino

....

> Introduction

When I first travelled to Oporto after my experience in Greek football – in March 2010 – I had a clear goal: speaking with Vítor Frade about my new project, even if we had already spoken about it on the phone. The idea was to write a new book, my second, about Tactical Periodization, providing a fresh perspective on this methodology with the intention of making it easier to understand.

The primary intention was to observe training sessions conducted by certain coaches who were operating in different realities, all of them with a certain adherence to Tactical Periodization. I planned to interview them, and orientate the book based on that. Professor Frade was quick to suggest me some names and we decided rapidly who would be the most appropriate: coaches who were working at the elite level, academy coaches...

So, I started working and starting to pack and unpack my suitcases, taking off from some airports, landing on others, crossing the peninsula from east to west by car, staying in hotels - in Oporto I mostly stayed with friends – visiting 'sporting cities', training grounds, pre-match hotels, sports faculties...I was accumulating valuable information that I would then analyse and organise back home.

We soon realised that there was something missing, because despite the higher or lower level of alignment of those coaches with Tactical Periodization, there was still room for confusion. We found a solution: basing the book on an interview with the creator of Tactical Periodization himself, from which the other themes would arise. The interview lasted many hours. At a point, it crossed my mind that Professor Frade would kick my...But it wasn't like that, what he ended up giving me was a masterpiece with his answers.

I started to create the book and little by little it came to life. A Matrix to which I kept giving identity, modifying its contour bit by bit, through the emergences that would happen 'here and now' and through the reflection on everything that was happening.

And once again new trips, this time with sketches fulfilled with hope which would be fulfilled with corrections on the way back...and so on until the day in which I decided to end the book.

It is possible that by the time you are reading this sentence I have already changed all those that come after – excluding those of the interviewees, those in the forewords or those of authors cited -, as I did so many times when I found others that were more satisfying...making it hard for this book to see the daylight.

As we all know, thought is not static and so is not a book, even though it may seem like, because one cannot change what is printed. A book is a beginning but never an end, even when it carries the abyssal zone!

1

> The Game Model as Previous Intention + the Methodological Principles

"Right content in a wrong context is really misinformation that will lead us either off course or on a dangerous course"

(Lipton & Bhaerman, 'Spontaneous Evolution', 2009, p.1)

Index

(...) that that is why I systematically talk about two levels and always high-lighting the indispensability of the Methodological Principles! Because it can only be Tactical Periodization if you have an idea for playing and if you make it systematic. And the operationalisation is something very complex, the possibility of you being concerned with the sectoral, intersectoral, intrasectoral and even individual improvements. Imagine this, you are not able to do a tumble, and I get you to do tumbles, and you say: "that is not Tactical Periodization!". It is, because the diversity side of it, you are improving something that then, when you perform a bicycle kick or some other kind of kick, leads you to an improvement! So, the training is finished, and it is really hot outside, you drink what, is that not Tactical Periodization? Is it no longer Tactical Periodization because you drank water? But some players did not drink water, are you going to force them to drink? All those things are part of diversity.

What Tactical Periodization is, depends on what you are doing as a pattern. If it directs the Process for everyone while simultaneously allowing each one to improve individually so that they can interfere with the Process. And for it to work that way you need to have a way of playing, a systematised way, and so this diversity is as good as the idea and depends on it being achievable through experiencing the Methodological Principles. That is why I ask, what means playing well? People should worry about that! And after that sometimes you can achieve it, sometimes being more concerned with some things that make that idea, sometimes with others, but the sense of direction must be present, with a specific hierarchy, and the loss of that sense of direction can only be avoided if they have a previous idea about the collective matrix, if it is in their minds already, and then the same thing occurs regarding the tumble for example! It is not a punishment. And then the whole Process, considering one or considering ten, twenty, thirty-five, it always abides by the logic of the Methodological Principles, otherwise it is not Tactical Periodization!

Now, the guy performed a tumble, those are complementary exercises. Not really complementary, they are complementary but with small case. Like drinking water. What directs the Process is a matrix, an idea of playing and operationalising, because Specificity is only guaranteed...it is not guaranteed by the macro level, it is guaranteed by the intervention you are able to have in all the details, in the sense that they contribute to the whole, because otherwise it is not Specificity. Because if you do not realise that Joaquim is different from Manuel, and this is different from that...So, Specificity is also there, if the parts improve, the whole improves. Now, how to improve?! That needs to be done through the logic of Methodological Principles, it is not easy, no-one should think it is easy (...)

(...) and notice that for a long time, 90% of the people that talked about Tactical Periodization, did not even mention the Methodological Principles which is the point I highlight the most with students, because everyone has an idea for playing, for playing in a certain way, then making it more or less systematic, but how do you build that?

[1]Vítor Frade (1)

---

1 Vitor Frade: interviewed by Xavier Tamarit in 2010

To put Tactical Periodization in practice, it is necessary to have a clear Game Idea, defined, structured, and coherent in all its Game Moments. It should be operationalised through certain Methodological Principles – Principle of Propensities, Principle of Complex Progression, and Principle of Horizontal Alternation in specificity – that differ from the conventional methodological principles.

Only if the following conditions are met – systematisation of a Game Idea together with its operationalisation through the Methodological Principles abovementioned – can we say that we are doing Tactical Periodization. It is an objectivable methodology, with Methodological Principles that must be respected and that allow us to clearly evaluate if someone is working in accordance to Tactical Periodization.

The coach's Game Idea, that will end up being the Game Model[2] when it meets a reality and when it is performed (the Game Model is what exists in structural and functional terms, and what allows a team to reveal certain regularities that identify. This is the result of a certain operationalisation, which leads the players' bodies to become structurally conditioned at all levels), it should support the Moments that form the Game. It should also help dealing better with the particularities of the Game's instants – Offensive Moment, Defensive Moment, Attack/Defense Transition and Defense/Attack Transition – through its Game Principles, Sub-Principles, and Sub-Sub-Principles, which will orientate the whole Process from the beginning of the season until its end, looking to produce a desired way of playing. This orientation will occur through a higher emphasis on some areas of the way of playing at a given time, and on some others at a different moment, without ever losing track of the objective.

There will be no losing track of the objective, among other things, when there is a previous idea regarding the collective reference (Game Idea) from both staff and players. There lies the importance of a global idea of the game that is desired since the beginning of the Process.

Tactical Periodization will therefore be directed by a Matrix that shall be both conceptual and methodological – a Game Idea and its operationalisation based on some Methodological Principles – trying to achieve a Collective Organisation with quality, and focusing thereafter on individual improvement, in such a way that the evolution of each player within the collective will interfere with the latter's improvement. Like this, we show that Tactical Periodization is not only concerned with the collective, as many claim, but also with the individual. Therefore, the Specificity can only exist when the intervention of the coach does not focus solely on the Macro level of playing, but also on the Micro level, meaning the particularities. The Plano Meso must be considered as well, aiming at the interactions between those particularities, not only among themselves, but also between them and the whole, contributing to the whole.

We are therefore talking about a systemic methodology that as such cannot understand the parts if they are not part of a whole. And I am referring to all levels.

Also, the Methodological Principles must be understood through their interaction and inter-relationship, because if understood in isolation *"they lack an adjusted and coherent Articulation of Meaning, because they are embedded and implicated in an interactive and independent way in the same process. Just by themselves, they have no value"*,[3]Jorge Maciel (1)

---

2 **Game Model: is what happens as a pattern during the regular playing of a team and what identifies it. A qualitative evolution may occur. In this book, with the objective of clarifying what it means within Tactical Periodization, we will mention the Game Model as Previous Intention, Game Model as Intention-in-Action and Game Model as a whole.**

3 **Jorge Maciel (1): 'Pelas entranhas do Nucleo Duro do Processo'. Unpublished article, 2010.**

1.1. The Loop of the Game Model created within the Previous Intention, Operationalisation, and Reflection.

(...) one thing is the Game Idea and the other is the Game Model. It might seem a paradox, something weird, but first comes the Game Idea and only after the Game Model. The Model is also submissive to the circumstances. The Model is everything because it is the Game Idea plus the circumstances, and the circumstances can relativize what I would do in different circumstances, but in terms of pattern it's the same! I want to play more or less like that. (...)

Now, the Game Idea is something, the creation of the Idea has to do with the circumstances and that is the Game Model, that also implies the existential dynamic of the Methodological Principles. And the Model is everything, even sometimes something unknown to me, something that 'promotes' modelling, because if I didn't take it into account, I blew it! Now, in general terms, the way a guy understands the game, it does not make sense that he doesn't look for the same things, but he needs to adapt that to the circumstances. (...)

That is why it works better if you have a previous idea, a Previous Intention, which is the Game Conceptualisation, the Game Idea, and that should be showcased already in the beginning, so that the people that you will work with can already familiarise themselves with it. Some may say "but this is not how it should be!". But those are the setbacks that you will have to deal with and overcome with time.

Vítor Frade (1)

1.1.1. The Game Model as Previous Intention (the team's Game Idea – collective matrix – already considering the context)

We must, at this point, and to avoid confusion at a later stage, distinguish between Game Idea and Game Model. As Vítor Frade says, **"first comes the Game Idea and only after the Game Model"**.

The Game Idea is the type of football that the coach (and each player) has in his mind and would desire his team (any team) to play. It is a Game Conceptualisation that each coach has and that depends on his previous experiences in football — played, watched, studied...or even, why not, invented. Therefore, this Game Idea belongs to the Axiological Level, to the level of values. It is fundamental that each coach reflects on the way of playing he desires, structuring it in a logical and coherent manner (but never unmounted due to the non-linearity of the Process), creating the Game Principles and Sub-Principles in accordance to his Game Idea.

Jose Tavares (1)[4] cannot *"understand how you can train without having that well-defined group of ideas, that group of Game Principles: how we want to attack, how we want to defend, how we want our transitions from one to other, and vice-versa".*

Therefore, each coach should have his Game Idea and systematise it. He must define what he wants his team to do in each of the Game Moments and in their instants, he must structure his way of playing using Game Principles and Sub-Principles. When this coach, with his Game Idea, arrives at a certain context: a country, a club, a history, some players...this Game Idea is strongly influence by these surroundings, having the coach to be intelligent and model it according to the circumstances, keeping the Matrix of his Game Idea but being coherent – with the intention of promoting efficacy and efficiency – with the context in which he will be embedded.

With these factors interacting, the coach's Game Idea and the context, a collective Game Idea is formed, a collective reference for all those taking part in the Process. So, already having in mind the reality in which we find ourselves, and that consequently is not abstract. To this, I have decided to call it Game Model as Previous Intention, with the objective of, firstly, distinguishing it from that abstract Game Idea, not considering a certain reality, that the coach has in his mind before being hired by a club, and secondly, so that we understand that the Game Model is a whole formed by parts that interact continuously in what I have called 'The loop of the Game Model'.

Jose Tavares (1) explains us that the Game Model (as Previous Intention) is *"that group of ideas, Principles, Sub-Principles and Sub-Sub-Principles that we build, that we create as a basis that will orientate all of our daily, weekly, and future work, so that we always know where we are and where we want to go".* This, in a way that, as I mentioned before, cannot result in a loss of direction.

When a coach arrives at a team, he must consider certain things that will change, or may change, certain aspects of his Game Idea – on its contour, but not in his Matrix.

To that refers [5]Marisa Gomes (1) when clarifying that the construction of the Game Model (as Previous Intention) is influenced by the context we face: *"first you need to get to that context and see what you have, trying to know the reality, and to do that you need to know the past. Knowing what you have presently and what happened in the past. What has led to your arrival, what is expected of you. Then you see the conditions of the club, the players, the league, and the macro-context in which the Process will be developed. From there you try to hierarchise your way of playing, to make it the most efficient possible. If you were fighting for promotion you would see a higher number of offensive aspects, maybe, and you need to defend in a way that allows that predominance. If you were trying to avoid relegation, maybe the defensive organisation should be your main strength because you will spend a lot of time in defensive organisation and so the other moments will depart from that hierarchisation. Then you need to understand several contextual things related with the players' minds, which is what they have, what they did until now, what allowed them to get there, and the dimension of the context. Like that, you can direct the project and the expectations of those involved and making the game always what you want it to be".*

---

4 Jose Tavares (1): Interviewed by Xavier Tamarit in 2010.

5 Marisa Gomes (1): Interviewed by Xavier Tamarit in 2010

Moreover, our interviewee adds that *"another important thing is the fact that, even though we may want to be distant from the issues of the board, the issues of the exterior context...it is very difficult because you are inserted in a reality, you are part of a context. You may want to play in a certain way, but that way is conditioned, consciously or unconsciously, by what surrounds you. You may even not be able to understand why, but that is present anyway. (...) In a professional team even worse, because the people are bigger, the beliefs are bigger, rooted deeper, and the contexts are different, you must be conscious that you must give primacy to the circumstances, to what you have, and only then, adjust that to what you think. The conceptual side exists only to help making the reality better. (...)"*.

As we see, Marisa Gomes pays special attention, among other things, to what the players believe and have in their minds. Our intention is that the players understand the desired way of playing, making them have in their minds and bodies our way of playing — collective Game Idea or collective reference — and for that it will be essential to have that previous idea, a global idea of the game, and since the beginning, that will allow them to be identified with a certain way of playing. Also, the players have beliefs that not only are related to the way of playing, but also with the way of training. Tactical Periodization does not overlook this, as we can see in the chapter that discusses the 'cappuccino' strategy.

For [6]Carlos Carvalhal (1) the context and the circumstances also gain a fundamental relevance when trying to build a Game Model (as Previous Intention). Firstly, it is crucial to *"understand the environment well, to understand the type of football player, having a good knowledge of the league in general terms, having a particular knowledge of the team you have available, what your team is capable of doing...Having a cultural knowledge of the environment where you are, knowing what were the best years of that team, the system it used, how it played, what the players and supporters are used to... We can say that we are talking about habits and also of an habituation that ends up being cultural. Knowing the culture of the club, the culture of the football and then, having considered and having analysed all this, having a perspective or having a plan where you will integrate your ideas and realise in what way there may be a conflict between your ideas and what seems to be the reality. We must meet the reality, bringing our ideas to it, and not the other way around"*.

Furthermore, the interviewee clarifies that: *"we must live with the reality, the reality is what we have, what is presented to us, and then we have our ideas. Therefore, between the reality and our ideas there is a difference that we must try to diminish at all times on the benefit of our ideas, but we must never ignore the reality in itself, the football that was played back in their golden years"*.

So, it is essential when creating and building the Game Model — as Previous Intention — to consider the environment in which find ourselves, and then, trying that it does not modify our Game Idea too significantly. A change that, usually, will occur within the contours of the Game Idea without affecting its Matrix.

[7]Jose Mourinho assures that *"the (Real) Madrid that I want is, obviously, a Madrid that is aligned with the objectives and the culture and the tradition. Objectives: winning (...). Culture and tradition: attacking football and with good quality. I want that. I*

---

6 Carlos Carvalhal (1): Interviewed by Xavier Tamarit in 2010.

7 Jose Mourinho (1): Informe Robinson, Canal + in 2010.

want to win, I want attacking football, and I want good quality football", highlighting the importance of knowing the culture and the objectives of the club where you will work.

As we can observe, the interviewees pay great importance to the culture of the club, its history, and the type of game that is in the heads of those surrounding them, the league where they will compete, the players available, the objectives proposed…and what is expected of them as coaches. All this together with your Game Idea will end up becoming the Game Model.

It becomes clear that the Game Model is not something natural, but something that is built. It is not something that you can just transfer from one place to another, from one team to another. It depends on the context and the circumstances. Later, we will see that this construction never stops. As Vítor Frade says, the Game Model is something that does not exist anywhere, because it is never finished.

As such, we can say that the Game Model as Previous Intention is formed by the interaction between the different 'factors', among which we can highlight:

- <u>Country's culture:</u> Everyone will agree with me that the football played in England, Spain, Italy, Portugal, Netherlands, Norway, Brazil, Argentina, Nigeria…is different. The football played by the children on the streets of these countries is different too. [8]Mourinho (2) refers to that, saying that *"I would like to see certain coaches working and coaching players with totally different characteristics. The richness of my job, the richness of my career, is having managed in Portugal, leaving Portugal and going to England, leaving England and moving to Italy, leaving Italy and going to Spain. For me this has a richness that a coach that works all his life in the same culture, in the same league, can never have".*

- <u>Culture of the Club/History of the Club:</u> Even in the same country the clubs have great cultural and historical differences. The philosophy, the values, the past…and the type of football produced by Athletic Club has nothing to do with Sevilla FC's, or that of FC Barcelona, Real Madrid CF, nor that of Valencia CF, or Club Atletico de Madrid; nor Manchester United FC with Arsenal, AC Milan with FC Internazionale Milano, etc. Jose Tavares (1) gives us an example: *"a coach that comes to FC Porto, before arriving here, must be a 'strong' coach that can put the team playing 'strongly' in attack, that is very 'strong' in the transitions, getting the team to be dominant because that is what the members want. The coach of FC Porto must meet that, if not he won't last long here. Therefore, when he arrives, he must understand the reality of the club, what the people of the club want. And as I said earlier, not in the sense of conditioning but in the sense of adapting his Idea".*

- <u>Structures of the Club/Aims of the Club:</u> It won't be the same being in a club with one structure or another. And it won't be the same in a club that aims to win every match in every competition or being in a club with the objective of avoiding relegation. For Jose Tavares (1): *"playing to become a champion is different from playing to avoid relegation. All these details, in my opinion, must be part of what I mentioned in the beginning. That is why the Model is so complex and has to be continuously constructed, re-constructed, with new things, dropping others that no longer make sense".* For us the Game Model is something that is under permanent construction – and that, therefore, will never be finished, as we will discuss in the next point of this chapter.

---

8 Jose Mourinho (2): Interview published in the daily newspaper AS on the 11th October 2010.

- <u>Coach's Game Idea:</u> The club, 'according to its philosophy' must also consider what kind of coach it hires, even if not always it happens that way. As coaches, we represent 'ideas', and it won't be the same hiring Fabio Capello and Louis Van Gaal; hiring Hector Cuper or Marcelo Bielsa, etc.

- <u>Game Structure(s) or System(s):</u> The Game System that we will use (1.4.3.3; 1.4.4.2; 1;3.2.3.2, etc.). This is a very important aspect to consider when creating the Game Model. A Game System that is alternative to the usual one can also be used. Attention must also be paid to when we play in numerical inferiority or superiority, final minutes with a favourable or a negative result, etc., which can lead to changing the Game System.

"

Those guys who usually say that (that Tactical Periodization is extremist) have no clue of what they are saying, because for them everything in football has been invented. And that allows them to speak so arrogantly. Mourinho told the four guys who went to him to write their book ('Mourinho: why so many wins?'): "guys, consider this, the majority of those individuals that are coaching at the national level, even after reading this 50 times, will still not get the essential.

I insist a lot in Mourinho, I highlight Mourinho because those who doubt Tactical Periodization's capacity are either stupid or have a bad intention. I am not saying that there are no other ways that lead you to victory, but what I know is that you win by constructing the game!

Any of these ways of playing can be built better by using Tactical Periodization and the evidence is in Mourinho, who beyond his genius is able to build his own which is then expressed in a way of playing that is even athletic, with players of a certain age, and being able to compete in all cups and league, and winning in all of them by playing only football!!!

If you don't know and you want to understand something you don't know, usually it's a fuck up! And that is what these guys want, they want to regulate something, problems, that they know nothing about.

So, a guy that talks about something he doesn't know about is either stupid or insolent, and I have no pity for people like that.

I realise that the main problems, or one of the main issues of Tactical Periodization for people is considering the Methodological Principles. People run away from them as a cat runs from hot ashes...

And people pass by Training Theory and Method-ology, which is a key module, they memorise that and end up knowing nothing. Then because they have less time to spend in the specialisation, it's only about "Game Model" here, drills over there...

It pleases me that more and more people are interested in Tactical Periodization. I recognise that there are people with different capacity to think about it.

So, what I can tell you is that Tactical Periodiza-tion is complete, it's plentiful, if the individual is able...let's say, if he is minimally intelligent

- Characteristics and Ability of the Players: Another very important aspect to consider, if not essential, is the players that we have. Their ability and individual characteristics will lead us to or may lead us to vary the Game Model. This is something very important in the creation of the Game Model and something that all methodologies agree upon, although it is something that must be understood according to different perspectives. An initial one, because the coach will consider at the time of shaping the Game Model as Previous Intention, and one posterior, from match to match, because depending on which player will take part in the match, the other players will have to recognise his particularities and support them within the way of playing, and that is something that can only be achieved through the operationalisation. This means, if the player experiences this way of playing during training and assimilate it together with the details that occur depending on the particularities they find by their side. And this is something that occurs in Tactical Periodization throughout the whole session. Jose Tavares (1) explains that *"it is very different if one player is playing or other, it is different. The game that will emerge from there is different, his behaviour will make it different, what will support that player? An order, the organisation of the team. If the team recognises it is different with the player, it will execute the Principle in a different way, but the Principle will remain the same, the team knows that we need to continue played in the creation of spaces, in the circulation of the ball, in the transition in this or that way. Now, how we will do it will be different, new, creative, because it's different. What creates that condition? It's the team recognising that it is different in that way, and it does not have to be the coach saying that. So, that is why you need to invest time in getting the team to know what it is doing, so that when things change in the game, the team knows it is different, keeping the identity, keeping the Principles".*

- Others: other factors that can influence the Game Model like the moment of the season you arrive at a team, if at the beginning or already with the season ongoing; the circumstances that lead you to managing that team, etc. ⁹Jorge Maciel (2) gives us other examples of things that can influence the Game Model, like: *"religious beliefs (Ramadan), other types of beliefs or superstitions, schedules (there are countries where, for example, the players do not train at certain times), climate, pitch condition, availability of a training ground, the influence of the medical department, commercial pressures…".* According to the author *"while some of these aspects may not impact the Game Idea, they interfere with the Process and with its operationalisation".* And the Game Model is everything!

---

9 Jorge Maciel (2): Conversations between Jorge Maciel and Xavier Tamarit in 2010 and 2011.

As Jose Tavares (1) says, *"when we arrive in a new place we cannot be autistic and insist on imposing our ideas and that's it. For me, we need to be able to understand what is our reality, which historical context we are facing, what are the realities of the club, the objectives of the club, what are the people who hired us wanting to happen and that not in a sense of conditioning us, but in the sense of being able to adapt our ideas for the game better".* Just like he says, it's about the coach adapting the ideas better to meet the reality.

[10]Mara Vieira (1), referring to some of the factors already mentioned, guarantees that *"the Game Model does not end in the way of playing but involves everything that encapsulates that way of playing. We cannot forget that the players are in a certain culture. When we talk about Italian players, for example, the majority grew up within Italian football, so they have themselves a Game Idea. If they move to another country, they take time to adapt. The Italian football has a certain pattern that we all know, and it is different from that of other countries. You talked about a country, but if we are in Europe, Latin America, or Africa, it works the same way. The playing patterns valued are different, depending on what those people know. Therefore, you must consider all that in the Game Model: the culture of the country, the culture of the club, the culture of the player. If you arrive at FC Porto, the idea that you always play to win is incorporated, the 'political issues' North-South as well,*

---

10 Mara Vieira (1): Interviewed by Xavier Tamarit in 2010.

the rivalry between Porto and Benfica...It is not something that is isolated from the game, it is something that is part of the Model and that must be considered".

However, this Game Model that we have been discussing will only be the Previous Intention, the way of playing that we hope to create, taking into account everything that we mentioned before: our Game Idea plus the circumstances of the context; and, consequently, belonging to the Axiological Level. This will be joined by what happens in its execution, which relates to the 'Here and Now', what emerges in training, in the matches, in all that happens during the Process and that will make us vary the so-called Game Model in its contours, giving it a unique configuration. I will call this the Game Model as Intention-in-Action.

Like Vítor Frade says, when we talk about the Game Model, we should move away from the level of words and move into the level of somatisation, into the level of operationalisation, because when the development of the Process there are repercussions in the athletes at all levels.

To end this point, an answer by [11]Mourinho (3): *each manager has his way of working and it is equally respectable. I like to consider the idiosyncrasy of a country, speaking in football terms, and of a club. The football culture is very different in England, Italy, and Spain. To win different leagues you need to adapt to the cultural characteristics of the leagues you play in. Thinking like that allowed me to win in Portugal, England, and Italy, in the first season I arrived. You need to know your opponents well and their characteristics. How would I ignore such an important tradition like Real Madrid's, the club that has won more Champions League trophies?!".*

1.1.2. The Game Model as Intention-in-Action

By operationalising this Previous Intention, meaning training the Game Model on the pitch and making it an Intention in Action – action that happens in the 'here and now' -, we will see Actions and Interactions that we did not expect and that may lead us to partially modify such Previous Intention. This will also happen during matches. Why do I say, 'may modify' and not 'will modify? Because some of these Actions and Interactions that emerge throughout the operationalisation may seem important for our way of playing and we will include them in the collective Game Idea. Others may not be so important, and we will have to supress them. I repeat that these changes will be produced at the level of the contours but never at the level of the game Matrix.

Something that becomes essential is the Reflection of the coach between what is the Previous Intention and the Intention-in-Action, which will make us decide between one or other direction. The coach must have, as Vítor Frade suggests, a sense of Divine Proportion, which we discuss in other area of this book. The coach must be very focused and have great sensitivity towards what is happening, because the smallest detail can mean going from success to failure and vice-versa. Moreover, it will be his responsibility that the existing relationship between the Previous Intention and the Intention-in-Action is consistent. To ensure that, good intervention skills will be fundamental, through the manipulation of

---

11 Jose Mourinho (3): Interview published in the daily newspaper AS on the 22nd November 2010.

exercises and the creation of [12]emotions and feelings in the 'here and now', something crucial in Tactical Periodization.

Through the emergence that occurs in the 'here and now', the Game Model evolves constantly without losing the Matrix that identifies it. According to Jose Tavares (1) "at the level of the Idea, the reflection on the Idea that is performed daily is fundamental because that is what will allow us to adjust our practice (…). We cannot forget that the players are the ones who play, they are the ones thinking during the match, so we have to invest in that to understand how they do that, why that is happening".

We must consider that the same Game Idea will be performed differently by different individuals, even if it is still the same Previous Intention. Therefore, one thing will be the Previous Intention and a different one the Intention-in-Action, which will allow this Previous Intention to evolve constantly, without modifying the Matrix.

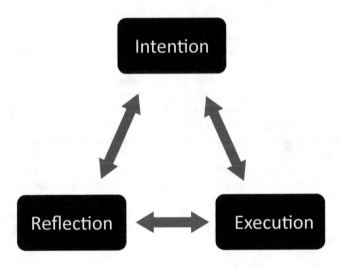

Game Model Loop.

So, the Game Model, although it does not lose its Matrix, will be rebuilding itself continuously, entering in a loop between the Previous Intention, its Intention-in-Action, and a Reflection that will lead us to a [13]new Previous Intention plus the new circumstances that may be created with the development of the Process, and so on.

I repeat that the importance of the 'here and now' in the Process is fundamental, so the coach must be very attentive to everything that happens in the training sessions and during the matches. Mara Vieira (1) refers to this when suggesting that the Game Model as Previous Intention *"is a theoretical idea, but when put in practice there are always other things arising. I keep taking note of some particular things, at a more micro level, for example: how two players*

---

12 Topic that has been more widely discussed in my first book: 'What is Tactical Periodization?', Bennion Kearny, 2015.

13 The intention is kept the same in general terms. Although it has to be permanently readjusted at the level of detail, it is still the same idea.

interact with each other, how they understand each other, how they contaminate each other". Here is, once again, the intervention in the individual, in the particularity, something essential, but always departing from a collective reference.

Therefore, the focus of the coach on the 'here and now' will be fundamental to understand those particularities, those interactions that occur between the parts, and that may – or may not – become part of our way of playing, according to our evaluation. And not only due to that, but also because we know that the exercises that focus on systematic repetition support acquisition. For example, if your goal during the exercise is that we produce the acquisition of X, which is an important aspect for our way of playing, but at the same time, if we are only focused on X, we prevent Y from happening, something that is also essential to that way of playing. We will be producing a systematic repetition of something that we don't want, meaning the non-emergence of Y, and that is consequently a non-intended acquisition.

The interviewee gives us an example that allows for a better understanding of what she is referring to: *"I have ideas, that I systematised on the paper, but then who brings these ideas to life are the players, because they recreate that same idea. We orientate, but in reality, they are the ones who play and interpret, and being them the ones interpreting, that has a meaning for each one, being expressed in a common sense. So, that is a Principle, because then each player will interpret it in a 'certain' way and, when relating with the whole, the playing is expressed by this incorporation. That is the importance of the reality that we have, the characteristics of the players, and from there, what they can provide to our ideas. For example, forgetting the ages, in my women's team that number of skilled players is different from the one I have in the youth team. In the youth team I am working with the best. So, the way of playing is different in both teams, but both have the same Principles. However, they execute them differently. What you can expect from one team or the other is very similar, except in how they execute it".* Mara Vieira talks about a similar Game Idea in her two teams, which keep that Idea of quality that she is looking for – Previous Intention – but they execute it differently, even if both in accordance to the Previous Intention, because they have different players with different particularities.

[14]Vítor Frade (2) warns for the importance of these particularities or individualities, which will lead to the emergence of things that we had not considered, evolving that Game Model into [15]'another' Game Model. *"(…) the organised and coordinated relationship between the players of a team leads to the emergence of something that is beyond the sum of the parts, and consequently, that also leads to the evolution of the way of playing, of the identity. This results from the exponentiation of the Great Principles, but it is related with the increasingly better articulation between the Sub and the Sub-Sub Principles, and that is achieved daily. And many times, this potentiation arises from having faced opponents and having overcome them, from having won with that. This allows inclusively the emergence of capacities that the coaches and themselves had not known about, and all this is what makes the Model".*

---

14 Vitor Frade (2): Interviewed by Fabio Moura. Dissertation: 'O Periodo Preparatorio como espaco privilegiado para a 'plantacao' do nosso jogar, de forma a podermos cultiva-lo, enraiza-lo...dentro da logica da Periodizacao Tactica!', 2010.

15 The Game Model will never be a different one, because the Matrix remains unchanged. What will occur is a new configuration of its contours.

The interviewee adds that *"the Model is something that does not yet exist anywhere, and I keep trying to find it, it even seems like a paradox! It does not exist anywhere like it is because it is being built, but it is not modified in its Matrix. Previously, I spoke of linear and non-linear causality and this is related because this way of thinking has to do with systemic modelling, the mathematical modelling is something else. The systemic modelling is different: I am modelling an operationalisation based on certain values and principles, but the eventual system also allows emergence, otherwise we would not say that the whole is bigger than the sum of the parts. But it is also different in these because they are not parts anymore, like when they are just parts by themselves, they become parts due to their relationship with the whole. That is why I usually say that the primacy is in the individual, but he needs to evolve in relation to the others, that is why I call self-eco-hetero".*

During the operationalisation of a collective Game Idea, just like during it execution in matches, unexpected things will emerge due to the eventual system in which they are developed, allowing for the modification of contours of the Game Model (at the level of details). That is why training is focused on the players, but on the players within a collective, being no longer isolated parts to become parts due to their relationship with the whole, and that is why Tactical Periodization becomes self-eco-hetero.

For Jose Tavares (1), the criterium will always be *"our team, which is composed by players, and the better our team is the easier the individualities will appear. And we believe that our players will grow there, within the context of our team. That is why it is important to observe and see what our team is so that we can recognise where our team is not so well".*

As I pointed out, the intervention of the coach before, during, and after, becomes essential in shaping the Game Model. Before, he should have clear objectives, belonging to the way of playing, for each training session and create exercises, contexts that are prone to the desired, and it will be his responsibility that the players understand it within the Whole. During the exercises the coach must intervene so that the intended actions and interactions occur, and emotions are generated among the players. He must also pay attention to the emergences that are produced in the 'here and now' and that may lead to trimming the Game Model after the posterior reflection.

1.1.3. The Game Model as a whole...that does not exist anywhere!

Arrived at this moment, I recall once again something that we have been mentioning since the beginning of the book: we should understand the Game Model as a whole. Not only the way of playing that we want and that is modified into 'other' ways of playing, but everything that happens throughout the Process. How we train, the relationship that we have with our players and the relationship between them, the climate among the staff, the results that are being achieved...

Professor [16]Vítor Frade (3) tells us that *"the Model is everything! We should understand the Model as the Intention (intention of the coach, the desired 'way of playing') that is developed and executed in all moments, from the Planning (Intentionality) to the execution (emergence that is visible in the 'here and now', but that does not end here) until the Reflection on what has happened, considering what is wanted".*

Therefore, initially the coach will have a Game Idea, that has created throughout his experiences and through his creativity. This Idea should be well-defined and structured in every moment. Then, when he gets inserted in a certain reality, he must analyse it well, understanding the culture of the place, its history, the objectives to be achieved, the players he has available...building a Game Model as Previous Intention, a collective reference. Through practicing this Game Model and its execution by the players, things will emerge that should lead the coach to reflect, trimming the Game Model in a regular way. To this he must add everything else that happens during the Process. And, of course, this is not easy, so knowledge is necessary and so is sensitivity. Divine Proportion is required.

For Jose Tavares (1) *"football because it is so complex, needs the coach's modelling. The coach will build that game that he wants to see played. When we try to build our game, for our team, it makes sense to support it with our Principles, adjusted to the reality, to our players, to our objectives...but where the coach defines the Game Model. That does not die there, that does no end, it's never static, but continuously constructed. It is built throughout time. From certain moment, we start realising if that Idea is appropriate or not. If everything is well, we keep perfecting and improving it. When we find some difficulties, some moments in which it is not adequate, we must reflect again. Something that is not static, that daily and weekly reflection that we keep doing to understand if the Idea is adjusted to our reality or not, or if it is our operationalisation at the level of the Idea that is not working".*

Jose Tavares adds a very important aspect to consider: not always is in the Idea – the collective Game Idea – that we got wrong (when things are not working out well), but sometimes, or even most times, it is its operationalisation that has not been adequate. That is why, once again, we highlight how essential the intervention of the coach is.

As our interviewees have suggested along this chapter, we must understand that each player, due to his culture, the place in which he developed, and other things, will have his own Game Idea – he will always have one regarding training. What we seek is that all have the same game – collective Game Idea or collective reference – from head to feet, first at a conscious level and then subconsciously, and therefore somatised. The Game Idea that the coach desires, and that, when meeting the reality and being executed, gives birth to the Game Model. For that, we should dismiss the usual response patterns of our players and try to create new, common ones, Principles or intentionalised criteria that will form the Principles and Sub-Principles of our Game Model.

Therefore, it will be crucial to decode the context successfully. Vítor Frade (2) explains that *"the better my ability to take a picture of my environment, the better I will create the training contexts. Now, if I am less identified with some players or with the environment, naturally I will take a picture that does not match the reality. It is in this sense that I suggest that the Model is always being shaped, not always*

---

16 Vitor Frade (3) as cited in 'What is Tactical Periodization', Xavier Tamarit, Bennion Kearny, 2015.

being created, because the Model must also be supported by a Matrix, and the Matrix is always the same. It's its complexity that we are acculturing".

This creation of common habits or acculturation in a playing Matrix will only be achieved through the operationalisation or experiencing of that playing and that is why it is so important to acculture since the grassroots. For that to happen training should be in accordance to what Tactical Periodization proposes, being therefore required some Methodological Principles, those of our methodology, that interact between them in a collective manner.

[17]Guilherme Oliveira (1) refers that *"many coaches know what they want. However, it is not simple to create the Process, build that way of playing and make it appear during the match in an effective way. And the value of Tactical Periodization is exactly having found a group of Methodological Principles that, when considered, will allow that the team expresses those ideas of the coach. Now, if they play well or badly, that's another thing. Because the ideas of the coach can be shitty ones and they play badly. Or they can be excellent ideas, and they play well".*

We should recall that the problem is not always in the Game Idea but, at times – many – it can be in the operationalisation. Because it is not easy to operationalise in accordance to this methodology and even less if you don't know much about it. Moreover, it is not easy to lead, it is not easy to manage well our knowledge considering the circumstances and the context. For that, the coach needs a great sensitivity that allows him to understand what to priorities, what is the right measure of progression of the way of playing, how to dosage the times of execution, recovery, etc.

For the interviewee, *"more than having good ideas, there are several other aspects that are crucial for success: the permanent interaction between coach and players, a permanent vision of things, being able to keep the players happy with what they are doing, feeling identified with that way of playing. There should be a group of positive interactions in which the emotional aspects should be deeply involved…".*

There are many aspects, not only these but many others, that are determining for success, also making part of the Game Model, because as we have already emphasised, the Model is everything. Isn't it possible that some coaches understand this concept, of the Game Model as a whole, using press conferences and the media, to foster conflict, creating climates or environments that they believe can benefit them?

As we can see the Game Model is shaped throughout the Process. As put by poet [18]Antonio Machado, *"walker, there is no path/the path is built by walking",* but we need to know in which direction we are heading. So, even if we keep modelling, the Matrix remains unchanged. This is essential. It is a systemic modelling, meaning that when operationalising the Game Idea, unexpected things will happen and emerge, leading us to trimming the Idea in its contours. That is why the whole is bigger than the sum of the parts, as the latter are no longer isolated and become parts related with other parts and with the whole they allow for the emergence of things that we didn't know. This will make us reflect and continuously rebuild the Model, which will never be finished, and therefore, will never exist anywhere.

And this only occurs through experiencing that way of playing, the whole and the parts, the parts and the whole, and the whole that it implies. It refers to the Specificity of our way of playing, a Specificity with capital S, that is present at all levels, and that is only possible due to a correct understanding and use

---

17 Guilherme Oliveira (1): Interviewed by Xavier Tamarit in 2010

18 Antonio Machado: 'Proverbios y cantares', Campos de Castilla, 1912.

of Tactical Periodization's Methodological Principles. That is why the 'cappuccino' strategy, although necessary at times, can become dangerous if the 'blending' process is conducted by someone who does not know 'how to prepare the mixture'.

1.2. The importance of aesthetics in playing

(...) because I think that training and playing to win, and that is why I say that I am constantly focused on efficacy and efficiency, but also continuously concerned and even disturbed by the aesthetic problem! I watch again that 19Brazil of 1980, 1982 and even of the 1970s, and I love watching that. But is that transferrable to our time? In terms of attack yes, but now I have to worry about the balance within the team, something they didn't worry about back then, if I want to win. So, I am interested in the aesthetics! That is why I say that the next revolution must be structural.

(...) aesthetics is very relevant with regards to the attack, when looking at defense maybe the global side, the formal side may be rich, but the individual cannot, otherwise...in attack, it can be the opposite!

(...) you can only reach the Top if you are systematically concerned with objectivity, with efficiency, with efficacy. Bearing in mind what football is, I need to be permanently disturbed, I need to be concerned, I need to be permanently concerned with the aesthetics of the game. And the aesthetics are the finest thing in terms of allowing objectivity to be objectivity. If I exaggerate in terms of the loss of aesthetics, I will lose there, if I exaggerate in the improvement of aesthetics I will lose there, and that is not for anyone. Because many times, at a Top level, the simple fact of diminishing the aesthetic range, let's put it this way, will lead to less fatigue, because it is less complex, and people cannot understand that! Now, Mourinho can, and that is why he is who he is, and others are not.

Vítor Frade (1)

Much has been said about the game in this chapter, and it has even been mentioned that it should have efficacy and efficiency. A new concern emerges now: the aesthetic side of the game.

As Spanish National Team manager, [20]Vicente del Bosque, suggests: *"we should not forget that people are not only going to the stadium to watch their team winning. Although that is a priority, it is not the only important thing. The crowd also expects to*

---

19 In 1970 the Brazilian National Team won the World Cup with a team considered by many as one of the best in the history of football. Their third title was achieved with the contribution of legends like Tostao, Rivelino, Pele, and Carlos Alberto.

20 Vicente del Bosque (1): Interview published in the daily newspaper AS on 17th November 2010.

have a good time, enjoying some good football, and being happy in that little bit. This is a philosophy that I have always had".

Football is the 'king' of sports and the supporters always expect to witness a great show. The 2010 World Cup in South Africa has proven that this show is increasingly less of a show, at least with regards to what is football in its pure state. National Teams that until now invested in a certain style of playing with great aesthetics have let everyone down. Luckily, for those 'romantics' of the sport, the Spanish National Team was crowned World Champion for the first time in history, displaying an aesthetic style in all its Moments and Instants. This philosophy had also led them to winning the 2008 European Championship, played in Austria and Switzerland two years earlier. Also, an 'unknown' German National Team, if we look at its recent past, offered brilliant football from an aesthetic point of view, reaching the semi-finals in South Africa 2010 and being a finalist in Austria and Switzerland 2008. The Germans were defeated, in both occasions, by the Spanish. This allows us to keep alive the belief that it is possible to reach success with this way of playing, concerned with the aesthetic side, that has already been developed by other National teams with different nuances in previous years.

There are several important things to clarify regarding aesthetics. We must not confuse it with playing well or badly. A style of playing can be less aesthetic but better than other that is more aesthetic. How can we tell if a way of playing is aesthetic or not? This is something highly subjective and normally it has been the attacking moment carrying all the plaudits and recognition. So, is there no aesthetic in defense? And what about transitions? Or are we seeing a single part of that game?

Jorge Maciel (1) claims that *"the great problem is that the aesthetic notion of the game is not rarely circumscribed to the aesthetics of attacking. We ignore the aesthetics of defense, we only see half of the game, or not even that, because we don't recognise the entire nature of the phenomenon".* Put simply, one must understand that aestheticism in defensive terms should be seen as something more collective and not so much individual – even if the latter can occur – as Professor Vitor Frade mentioned earlier.

Recognising the aesthetic side as an important part of playing, it will be important that the coach has a great dose of intelligence and sensitivity – 'Divine Proportion' – to know until when or where he can increase or diminish the aesthetics of his way of playing. This is because, as we could read earlier, *"if I exaggerate in the loss of aesthetics I will lose something here, if I exaggerate in the increase of aesthetics, I will lose there".* Let's not forget that higher aesthetics implies higher complexity, what in turn will require more expenditure of energy, especially at an emotional level, something that must be considered in High Performance, where the density of matches is increasingly higher. So, it is fundamental to have a good understanding of Recovery, as proposed by Tactical Periodization.

Caring about the aesthetics does not mean caring less about winning. It is also important to realise that aesthetics implies subjectivity and that, therefore, it will be strongly related with individual and cultural tastes.

No matter how our way of playing looks like, we will need a Process that can foster its operationalisation. Tactical Periodization is composed by Methodological Principles that allow for the latter through a Logic that has nothing to do with the conventional logic.

1.3. The Methodological Principles that allow for the operationalisation of a way of playing (and that must be understood as a single Principle)

The Principle of Propensities is actually a term coined by [21]Popper that I use, that I got from Popper, because the propensities have to do with the <u>context</u> being more prone to X than to Y, because normally people say, "I want you to do this or that". No! I want him to do depending on a certain context. So, I need to give birth to a context, not to the behaviours, and that confuses people badly. One if the Principle of Propensities, I must articulate depending on how I play, defending in a certain way to attack in a certain way, for example, I am concerned with the defensive transition, and with the attacking transition (...)

So, I need to create conditions for that to be organised in a more preferential way, so that there is a certain familiarity with a certain logic.

So, the Principle of Propensities is that, the eventual context. (...)

Then there is the Principle of Complex Progression because the Complex Progression relates, on the one hand, with the growth of the way of playing, with the weekly distribution, with who I am going to play, with this guy that entered the team...it is complex because progression is not linear and involves several things! It has to do with these principles that were "solidified" but now fail to appear with regularity for 3 or 4 times....and therefore we have... that is why it is complex! That is why I say: the fundamental is the pattern of connections between all of this. (...)

That's why it is complex, non-linear, it goes back and forth, and that means that all aspects, all circumstances enter your domain, and it is in that sense that I keep highlighting what Mourinho says, that the Model is everything.

The Model is everything because...what is the Model?! It is the picture, or maybe the echography that you take of reality so that you can model, it is in this modelling that the approximation between the model and what you are looking for happens. But if you neglect relevant aspects you are modelling badly. That is why the Model is everything, what ends up being a completely different logic from that one that leads people to say that the model is 4-3-3 or something like that. Look, if a guy...a context, when it is experienced, leads to some postures, attitudes, behaviours, many of them resulting from a habit that might even be sub-conscious, we might not be aware of it, so it is very complex. What I want is an affinity of emotions, an affinity of affection, conceptual affinity, of a playing idea, and that is achieved through a context, but it cannot be an empty context, like "it's 11v11 and this and that!". No! No! These are fractioned contexts in relation to a hierarchisation of what I conceive, which is not mandatory, it depends on my deviations, on my circumstances, on my intelligence, that's it. But it needs to be like this, without losing

---

21 Karl Raimund Popper: Austrian philosopher (Vienna, 1902 – London, 1994). Earned his bachelor's degree at the University of Vienna and was a lecturer at the University of Canterbury and at the London School of Economics, in London. Among his works, we must highlight 'The logic of scientific research' (1934) and 'The open society and its enemies' (1945).

meaning. That is why I emphasise the Articulation of Meaning. This is complex. You cannot go like that. You cannot have a pre-made road map. No. That is why I say that the 'here and now' is extremely important, and then alright, organisational levels like Marisa does in the book about Ze Guilherme...otherwise you are alienating!

And then we have the 'heaviest' Methodological Principle, the Principle of Horizontal Alternation in Specificity...even more at the top level, because...I defend that it is absurd to train what is trained and how much it is trained...if we see [22]Germany playing, only if we are contaminated by what I referred earlier can we say that they run a lot. No, they stop, exchange the ball, and the same with Spain. [23]Portugal ran more than Spain! So, I need to train less than usual, my pattern is 90 minutes, more than that is unnecessary! But playing every Sunday, it is a waste if I don't use more than one day for training, but I can only do that if I have the guarantee that I am training in accordance to my way of playing, but not always working on the same contents of my way of playing! That is what alternation is about. And that is only guaranteed if I am able to, relatively to a certain objective that is non-discussable, ensure than I am trimming here, and trimming there, but always trimming the same object!

So, what did I imagine, if the effort arises from having to contract muscles, having to move them, there are three indicators that characterise the way muscular contractions are expressed. And it is also different the way in which the extension of its expression or of its fatigue.... then we must work on calibration there. It is about bringing to the extreme or maximising, let's put it this way, one indicator on one day, the other on another day, and so forth. (...)

So, that so-called more physical side, is important and is considered by the Horizontal Alternation in Specificity. That is the side the allows me to be fresh to play. And people pass by Training Theory and Methodology, which is a key module, they memorise that and end up knowing nothing. Then because they have less time to spend in the specialisation, it's only about "Game Model" here, drills over there, Biochemistry and all that...What is that? Maybe it's shit.... And just a few are interested on what is essential, the others don't even notice it. (...)

So, the core Methodological Principles are these, then if we want to talk about Specificity it is a 'categorical imperative'...these three, for the methodological core, these three are enough.

Vítor Frade (1)

Tactical Periodization is supported by three Methodological Principles that allow — and only these allow — a Logic that is different from the conventional: The Principle of Propensities, the Principle of Complex Progression, and the Principle of Horizontal Alternation in specificity. I emphasise, once again,

---

22 Professor Frade is referring to the German National Team, finalist of the 2008 European Championship in Austria and Switzerland, and semi-finalist in the 2010 World Cup in South Africa. Germany, managed by Joachim Low, has portrayed a different way of playing in comparison to some of the country's historical teams.

23 Referring to the match between Spain and Portugal, during the 2010 World Cup in South Africa, which Spain won 1-0.

that all Principles nominated here occur together, allowing for the Articulation of Meaning. They must be understood as a single Principle, having a connective pattern that leads them to existing in a certain way. Jorge Maciel (1) warns that *"the Methodological Principles need to be expressed inter-dependently"*.

Therefore, Tactical Periodization is formed in its methodological Matrix by three Methodological Principles whose names are those mentioned above and not others that have been coined as a product of misinterpretations. However, there is a Principle of Principles (Supra-Principle), or as Vitor Frade calls it, a 'categorical imperative', intrinsic to all of them, and that emerges from their interaction. This is Specificity. This Supra-Principle is the one enveloping everything that is done, at all levels, subordinated to the way of playing that we want to achieve. From the operationalisation of the latter, as we explained earlier, unexpected things will emerge and shape that way of playing into 'another' without losing its conceptual Matrix.

As [24]Guilherme Oliveira, Nuno Amieiro and Vitor Frade (1) defend, *"in Tactical Periodization, Specificity (...) contextualises everything that is done"*. The authors add that *"something is considered Specific when it is related to the Game Model that is being created"*.

Moreover, its operationalisation *"should assume several dimensions/scales: Collective dimension, Intersectoral dimension, Sectoral dimension, Group dimension and Individual dimension"*. We should add here the Intrasectoral dimension as well. Once again, we express the Tactical Periodization's concern with both the Macro and Micro levels, and consequently, with the Meso-level as well.

As these authors suggest, for an exercise to contain Specificity, other than this relationship with the Game Model, it should have the following characteristics:

- <u>Players should understand the aims and objectives of the exercises within the whole game:</u> to achieve this is will be fundamental that they have a global knowledge of the desired way of playing, through mental pictures and their experience. Something that, as we will see in the next chapter, Tactical Periodization fosters since the first week of training, trying to transform a 'knowing how' into 'knowing about knowing how'.

- <u>Players should be focused throughout the whole exercise</u>: with this we will be able to execute the whole drill at Maximum Relative Intensity, which is the same as Specific Tactical Concentration, something indispensable in this training methodology.

- <u>The coach should intervene adequate and purposefully when seeing the interactions that emerge during the exercise:</u> through his intervention, the coach will create and potentiate the desired contexts. He should also try to create emotions and feelings – positive or negative – depending on the interactions his players show during the operationalisation stage. So, it will also be fundamental that the coach is fully focused during the whole session so that the desired acquisitions are achieved, at the Macro, Micro, and Meso levels.

In such a way we see that *"exercises are only <u>potentially Specific</u>"*. That is why I have always thought that it made no sense to put exercises in my books and why I never minded that someone would observe my training sessions, taking notes of what I was doing (except when the Strategic dimension is

---

24 **Guilherme Oliveira, Nuno Amieiro and Vitor Frade (1):** 'Tactical Periodization: a training model', translated and presented in Barcelona by Xavier Tamarit, in 2008.

involved, for obvious reasons). An exercise is not only its structure and functioning. It includes the dynamics and sub-dynamics that occur throughout it, and how we got to them (through Complex Progression). It is the sense they make within our way of playing for my players. It is about the circumstances that lead us to do it in that day and in that Morphocycle and not in other(s). It is my intervention during its execution, etc., etc., etc.

Therefore, this Specificity based in the contextualisation towards a way of playing, this Tactical Specificity that impregnates the whole Process will allow that Specificity to occur, consequently, at all levels and dimensions: Physical, Technical, Psychological and sometimes Strategical. For that to happen in a coherent and beneficial manner for what we desire – preparing our team for competition – it is necessary to understand and to know how to operationalise according to the three Methodological Principles that are fundamental in this methodology. The execution of the Game Model as Previous Intention, through the Methodological Principles, is what allows the emergence of a Specificity, and this is only achieved through the weekly expression of the Morphocycle.

1.3.1. The Principle of Propensities

The Principle of Propensities is about achieving, through the creation of a contextualised exercise (with the desired way of playing, either at a more Macro or more Micro level), the appearance in great quantities of what we want our players to experience and acquire, at all levels. It is about modelling the exercise towards the desired context. For that, the intervention of the coach will be important. It should span from the creation and manipulation of the exercise before its execution, creating suitable environments, to the intervention that occurs in the 'here and now', and include the posterior Reflection. This Principle is what allows for Systematic Repetition to happen, something essential in all learning processes. According to [25]Nuno Resende (1), *"learning (the assimilation and incorporation of certain Principles of the Game Model) is the result of systematic repetition"*. Jorge Maciel (1) adds the repetition should be based on *"[26]non-mechanical mechanisms, through experiencing open-ended contexts, probabilistic and not deterministic"*. The true 'Systematic Repetition' is achieved through the execution-experiencing of the Morphocycle.

As Professor Vítor Frade mentioned, is about giving birth to the context and not to the behaviours, as in Tactical Periodization it is essential that learning occurs through discovery and not via reception. Understanding this is key for understanding this methodology.

According to Jorge Maciel (1), this Principle has the objective of *"creating rich contexts, that allow players to experience, while performing, a high number of Inter-Actions that are relative to our way of playing, and especially relative to the nuances expressed in our way of playing throughout the different days of the Morphocycle"*.

25 **Nuno Resende (1):** 'Tactical Periodization: a methodological conceptualisation that is a trivial consequence of the (specificity of our) football game. A case-study of a pattern Morphocycle of FC Porto's First Team'. Unpublished dissertation. Oporto, 2002.

26 **Non-mechanical mechanisms:** concept that is widely discussed in my first book.

The author adds that *"Systematic Repetition (crucial for the acquisition of a Collective Intentionality) of the parts of the way of playing that we want to experience in the different days, like the respective patterns of performance and configurations of the exercises, occur by the convenient consideration of this Methodological Principle".*

Thanks to the Principle of Propensities we will achieve the Systematic Repetition of the desired specific experiences, of the Actions and Inter-Actions of our way of playing, and of those of each player's way of playing within the whole, which will depend on the day of the Morphocycle — due to the Principle of Horizontal Alternation in specificity — at the Tactical, Physical, Technical, Psychological, and sometimes Strategical levels. With this, I mean that this Systematic Repetition during the Pattern Morphocycle, will be more related with some Sub-Principles and <u>especially with some Sub-Sub-Principles</u> on one day, and will be more related with others a different day. On another day, that will be in between these two, it will focus more on the Macro Principles and Sub-Principles. And the same will occur from the perspective of effort/performance, for example with the Systematic Repetition of Actions and Inter-Actions with a dominance of high tension of muscular contraction in one day, other with actions with a dominance of high speed of muscular contraction...but always supported by the same metabolic web.

As Jorge Maciel (1) explains, *"the aim is not quantifying actions, but instead to create exercising contexts that lead to a certain dominance of Inter-Actions relative to our way of playing, always considering the performance and effort patterns that characterise that day of the Morphocycle".*

To guarantee that in each day of the Morphocycle the Systematic Repetition occurs as we desire, at all levels, it is key to produce a 'Reduction without Impoverishment', which will be simultaneously qualitative and quantitative.

Jorge Maciel (1) refers to this when he proposes that *"it is due to the Reduction without Impoverishment that we can ensure the desires dominances for each training unit. A reduction that, while being qualitative, because it refers to the complexity of a way of playing, is also quantitative (...) because the configuration of the training exercises and the way how playing is experienced (without a loss of Specificity) requires that the coach manipulates and articulates parsimoniously the following variables: space, number, and time. These, while quantifiable, should not be taken as universal, not for different teams, not for different ways of playing. They must also respect the Principle of Complex Progression".*

So, the coach must create propense contexts, exercises that promote Systematic Repetition, which can allow the acquisition of Actions and Inter-Actions that will shape the desired way of playing, through a Reduction without Impoverishment, without the loss of the identifying pattern of 'its' nature. To apply correctly the Methodological Principles of Tactical Periodization, the coach will have to deal correctly with three variables: number of players, playing space, and exercising time. The correct manipulation of these three variables will make the exercise propense, at all levels, to what is desired on that day. We will also use these variables to increase or decrease the complexity of our exercises, as contemplated by the Principle of Complex Progression. And we will also use them for the correct alternation of Specificity.

1.3.2.   The Principle of Complex Progression

The Principle of Complex Progression makes sense due to the NON-linearity of the Process. It occurs at least at two different levels, which interact together.

At a more long-term level, it is about prioritising what we consider more important, hierarchising the Game Principles and Sub-Principles in the evolution of our way of playing. That will highly depend on the circumstances. In Tactical Periodization, during the first week one will see a global idea of the desired way of playing. Then, values or criteria will be prioritised, meaning that Game Principles and Sub-Principles will be hierarchised, in what will become the evolution of that way of playing, which, as this Principle suggests, will travel from a less complex way of playing to a more complex. As we already know, this is not a linear evolution, so there will be deviations, 'U-turns'…but always consistent with the playing Matrix, without a loss of direction.

It is about having first a Game Idea, an image of the way of playing we want, and then asking ourselves how are we going to get there? So, we should prioritise the Game Principles and Sub-Principles, starting with the more fundamental in a less complex manner to allow the players to absorb them. Then, we will be able to progress toward a higher complexity.

It must be considered that this is something complex and that requires training certain things, evolving into others, returning into some that for some reason we stopped doing, not being able to move on because we did not manage to acquire what we wanted, respecting the different nuance that a player provides in comparison to another, etc. Because of all these reasons, it is so important that the coach has a systematic and clear Game Idea, as is his ability to adapt it as well as possible to the reality in which he finds himself. Otherwise, he will risk being lost in that path that is built while walking.

Referring to having to return to some important things, Jose Tavares (1) explains that *"if you don't practice some important things for a while – and that can be three or four days or two weeks – and you don't return to that, they will lose those behaviours (intentionalised interactions)"*.

Now, I repeat, in this Complex Progression the circumstances of the moment will be fundamental, being able to change what would happen under other circumstances. When we arrive at a team, the priorities will be much different to those of other teams. If the season is already ongoing or if it just started, why that club signed you, what is the culture of the place you went to, etc. Inclusively the way of playing that the other coach had. When you analyse the way how the team played, you will have to decode the things that you think are important to change straight away, and others that you can maintain a little longer, and that you can change later depending on the development of the Process. We know it is not possible to learn everything we want from one day to the other, so we will have to prioritise what is most important considering the moment of the team.

At other level, more short-term, we should take into account the control and regulation of the complexity of the exercises during each session of the Morphocycle. So that a coherent tactical effort-recovery is accomplished according to our Logic. Beyond this weekly regulation of complexity, we must also hierarchise Principles and Sub-Principles, defining priorities depending on the circumstantial needs, always determined by our idea.

It is clear the importance that Tactical Periodization attributes to the correct dosage of effort/performance and the concern for emotional recovery, although not exclusively. Regulating it through the complexity of the exercise to be executed is something essential, so that the players can get to the next match in the best possible shape. To achieve that, we must understand that the complexity of an exercise depends on the relationship between several variables, among which we can highlight the following:

- The complexity of the Principle(s) and Sub-Principle(s) or of the articulation between Principle(s) and Sub-Principle(s) that we are experiencing;

- The dominant regimen of the 'effort' and of the dominant pattern of muscular contraction that are implicated;

- The number of players performing the exercise.

- The size of the area where the exercise is being performed.

- The time duration of the exercise.

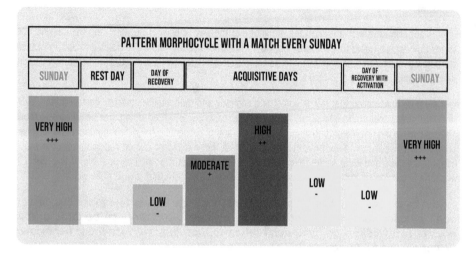

In this graph we see how to regulate the emotional demand and, therefore, we witness the importance of the manipulation of the exercises, with regards to complexity, in the training sessions of a Tactical Periodization Pattern Morphocycle with a match every Sunday.

As we can see, during the matches the emotional demands are very high, due to the complexity involved. Naturally, there will be matches with much higher complexity than others and this is something that we should also consider when planning the Morphocycle. What the Principle of Complex Progression tries, in a short-term level, is to prioritise the Principles and Sub-Principles to be trained, and to control the complexity of the exercising during the Morphocycle so that the players can get to the next match in the best possible shape and at all levels. This without producing acquisition in those days destined to it.

The teams, mostly those involved in High Performance settings, find themselves immersed in Process in which most weeks they will play more than one match. Therefore, the Morphocycle will be modified in all its aspects — even in the one we are mentioning — without, however, losing its Logic, as we can see in the following graph. Therefore, we will label this as the [27]'Exceptional Morphocycle'.

---

27 I will explain why this is the 'Exceptional Morphocycle' in chapter 3.

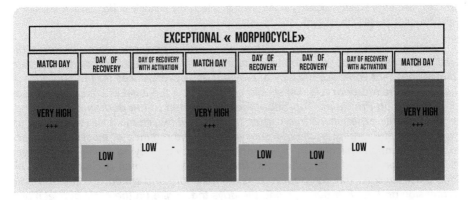

Obviously, we are referring to the group of players that took part in last match and that will play the following one. In chapter 3, 'a tailor-made suit', we will explain in more detail the differences between those players who play and those who do not. Their process, at a shorter or longer-term, will develop in a different context and in different circumstances, which are not invisible for Tactical Periodization. After all, it is a tailor-made suit.

1.3.3. The Principle of Horizontal Alternation in Specificity

Lastly, but not independent of the rest, we have the Principle of Horizontal Alternation in Specificity. I will recall a quote cited earlier by Professor Vítor Frade, that I consider fundamental to understand, at least partially, the essence of Tactical Periodization with regards to the Physical Dimension, differentiating it from the 'physical' of the conventional logic: *"(...) the effort arises from having to contract muscles, having to move them, there are three indicators that characterise the way muscular contractions are expressed. And it is also different the way in which the extension of its expression or of its fatigue.... then we must work on calibration there. It is about bringing to the extreme or maximising, let's put it this way, one indicator on one day, the other on another day, and so forth".*

Moreover, Tactical Periodization has other physical concerns - biochemical, bio-energetic, neural, etc. which will be discussed in the chapter 'The abyssal zone of Tactical Periodization'.

It becomes clear, therefore, that tension of muscular contraction is not the same as strength, that duration of muscular contraction is not the same as resistance, and that speed of muscular contraction is not the same as 'speed' (these are parameters of the expression of muscular contraction, nothing to do with the conventional and abstract concepts of strength, speed, and resistance). We will also see later that recovery is not equal to 'recovery'. IT is also clear that the conventional logic, even in those so-called systemic methodologies, has a concept of 'physical' which is different from Tactical Periodization. Those who keep seeing it in that way, with 'conventional lenses', will be far from understanding its Logic, and I don't refer exclusively to the physical aspect. The Principle of Horizontal Alternation in specificity, goes beyond this aspect.

According to Jorge Maciel (1) *"the differentiation of the performance regimens invol- ved in the different days is done having in mind the fractalization of the different dimensions that compose the way of playing. As key references for the operationa- lisation of the Morphocycle, we should consider: 1 – the level of complexity (Great Principles, Sub-Principles, Sub-Sub-Principles) related to the portion of our way of playing that is experienced in a certain training unit (which must be understood as part of something bigger, the Morphocycle); 2 – the regimen of muscular contrac- tion dominantly implicated in experiencing the way of playing along the different days that compose the Morphocycle. The contraction regimen is characterised by and must consider three variables: tension, duration, and speed; 3 – the strategic dimension and its distribution along the days that make up the cycle between two matches is another dimension to consider".* It is important to remind that the metabolic web implicated should be the same in every day.

We know that for training to exist, there must be fatigue. We must fatigue and recover – correctly – so that we can fatigue again, and this is achieved uninterruptedly through the alternation of the specificity that allows us a correct recovery of the different structures. The alternation of specificity allows for the maximisation of some structures in certain days and their recovery in others, without ever abandoning the specificity, and with the intention of not over-fatiguing them.

So, the alternation occurs at different levels. And the physical is not any kind of physical, it is a Specific physical of a way of playing, which is characterised according to the variables of the [28]muscular contrac- tion and the bioenergetic mixture required by such way of playing. It steps away from the 'physical', as conventionally presented.

The mode of expression of the muscular contractions is characterised by the interaction between its tension, duration, and speed. Even though we know that throughout the whole exercise all these para- meters or indicators interact together and systemically, meaning that all are present, we also know that some increase the dominance of one in relation to others, depending on the Actions and Inter-Actions (football-related in this case) that are performed. Through this Methodological Principle, together with the other two, we may be able to privilege one of these indicators, the one that we want to promote on that day. Our goal is allowing it to be the dominant and achieving its maximisation on that day, but always subordinated to a way of playing, and to its recovery in other days. Through patterning, we will maintain our team well-prepared and fresh to compete.

No matter which indicator we favour, there will always be incidence in the faster muscular fibres, being these the dominant in our contraction pattern.

---

28 **Muscular contractions of the muscular chains that are predominantly involved.**

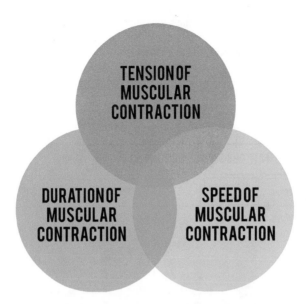

It can be argued that this Methodological Principle consist of training always with Specificity in mind, without remaining at the same level of specificity. This means, training always our way of playing, but at different levels, both at the level of muscular contraction and the alternation between Game Principles and Sub-Principles, in such a way that the emotional recovery (which I discussed in the previous Methodological Principle) is respected, and a recovery of the effort/performance within the different expressions of muscular contractions, etc.

Jorge Maciel (1) explains that *"it is a horizontal alternation because it refers to the need of variation of the contours of the way of playing and the management of the dualities Effort/Performance and Effort/Recovery, which should be monitored along the different days that compose the Morphocycle. The existence of a horizontal alternation tries to avoid that, in the different days that make up the Morphocycle, there is a confusion of many things, with no clear dominances nor priorities. Even worse if they are not patterned, which can lead the teams to reach incapacitating states of fatigue. States that result from the way the process is conducted and that leads the team to feel tired for one of the reasons: because they trained too much, or because they trained too little. Both reasons have the same cause, a lack of adjustment in the training process"*.

As the author has mentioned, it is about provoking an alternation of dominances at all levels during the different days of the Morphocycle, ensuring that there is no pattern dominance, what could lead to excessive fatigue of certain structures and with that, to incapacity. However, there should be a dominance on each day. It will also be fundamental, within this alternation, and to avoid reaching the referred excessive fatigue, even if not only because of it but also due to the 'fuel' involved, the correct understanding of the continuity that each training unit should have. Depending on the day of the Morphocycle we should allow higher or lower discontinuity. There should always be a level of discontinuity, something that we will explore further in chapter 3, 'A tailor-made suit'.

Also, this Methodological Principle becomes fundamental to the correct manipulation of the three variables abovementioned (number of players, size of the playing area and exercising time) to create in each exercise the desired dominances, and at all levels.

The Morphocycles, depending on the number of days between matches, would be as follows:

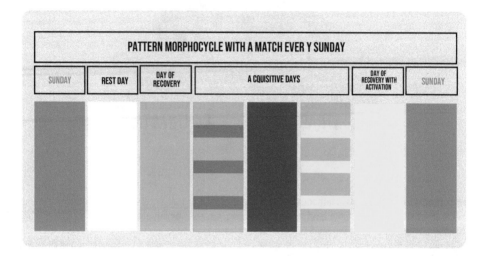

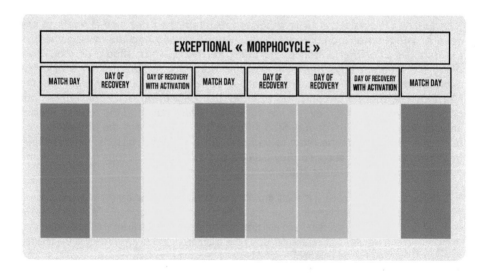

PICTURE – Xavier Tamarit Valencia Champions League

Once again, I emphasise how important it is to understand these Methodological Principles (Principle of Propensities, Principle of Complex Progression, and Principle of Horizontal Alternation in specificity) in an harmonious manner during all the exercise and throughout the whole Process, in such a way that a functioning pattern can be created – the Morphocycle – to which the Whole organism should be adapted since the beginning.

As a conclusion for this chapter, Jose Tavares (1) warns us that *"the coach will only improve if he can know the game better, or if he knows the game, so he needs to invest much time in knowing and understanding the game. At the same time, if we believe that we construct the game, with our ideas, then we must learn a lot about training too. We need to know our training, we need to know the Methodological Principles, the methodology we use to make that way of playing become a reality"*.

2

> The way of playing: driver of the Process since the beginning of the season until its end

"*Our subconscious mind directs the show 95% of the time. Therefore, in reality, our destiny is controlled by several recorded programmes, or habits, derived from the instincts and the perceptions that we acquire in our vital experiences*"

(Lipton & Bhaerman, 'Spontaneous Evolution', 2009)

Imagine that you are going to coach a new team, you have all the interest that it identifies with your general ideas, macro, how you want them to play. And understanding if this is more or less complex than training a transition or something else...That is why I say that hierarchisation must be...and on the first session, look, you don't know what you will find, but they must know since the beginning how you want them to play in general terms. So, the hierarchisation starts from the macro level, from the object, from the acquisition of the contours of your way of playing. It's [29]Gestalt, do you understand?!

Vítor Frade (1)

Along this book it has already been mentioned that the idealised way of playing, whose nuances will be trimmed with time, will direct and orientate the Process, since the beginning until the end of the season. From the first to the last training session. First, we will have to expose our players to a global idea of the way of playing we want them to perform – as I have already mentioned in chapter 1, it will be formed by the interaction produced between the Game Idea of the coach, and the context, together with other possible circumstances, leading to a collective Game Idea, or to a collective reference, the Game Model as Previous Intention -, the Macro Principles of what will be our game, so that after we define priorities with regards to the evolution of our way of playing, hierarchising the Game Principles and Sub-Principles.

However, as I have mentioned in the previous chapter, we must remember that these Game Principles and Sub-Principles, although already acquired, should be put in practice regularly, otherwise we risk that our team stops reproducing them (Complex Progression).

This global idea of playing that I am referring to, and that will be exposed and operationalised since the beginning of the Process, accompanying it to its end, will be crucial for the evolution of our way of playing.

Carlos Carvalhal (1) mentions the importance of the way of playing as director of the whole Process. He tells us that his work follows two areas, with the beginning of the season being slightly different from the competitive period, due to the need of incorporating the Strategic level, considering the opponent. This may occur already during the non-official matches, when our team is identified with our way of playing and has already incorporated it. At the beginning of the season, Carvalhal explains that *"we orientate all our work towards the acquisition of Game Principles that will identify our Matrix, our identity. In the competitive period we join our Matrix and our Principles with the [30]Strategic side of the game. Therefore, the Process is developed since the first day of work until the end with the intention of connecting what we do with our Game Idea. We also adjust the strategy that we have for the next match".*

The interviewee continues explaining how he looks at the beginning of the season with his team and how, at the start of competition, he starts considering not only his desired way of playing but also the way of playing of the next opponent, which may modify the contours of our way of playing. That will be fundamental when deciding which Principles and Sub-Principles should be prioritised over others during

---

29 Gestalt: German word that has no literal translation. It can be understood as 'shape' or 'figure', among others. It has a holistic focus. From this focus has resulted the Gestalt Psychology.

30 The relevance of the Strategic Dimension in Tactical Periodization lies in how it is incorporated in the weekly process, making it a complement and never a foundation. The Strategic Dimension is explored further in a different chapter of this book.

the Morphocycle: *"At the beginning, we have a hierarchisation of the Game Principles that aims to evolve the complexity, to achieve what we are looking for. It is different in the beginning of the season, because when we enter the competitive period, we will discuss more the Strategic domain. And when we enter this domain we will be talking about the specificity of each match, the difficulties of each match, what we are doing, what we should be doing and cannot do, what difficulties the opponent can pose, and what we can take advantage of, regarding the opponent".*

Therefore, training should be oriented and directed by the way of playing in different scales – the Macro, Meso, and Micro levels. In certain moments, we will have to consider the opponent we will face – the Strategic Dimension – in the competitive period. However, this can happen earlier, or can even be overlooked in some moments of that competitive period. Our way of playing should be privileged, with some small changes, always in the contours and never in the conceptual Matrix, with the intention of taking advantage of the opponent's weaknesses while mitigating our weaknesses and avoiding the expression of their core strengths. In such a way, the training should always be subordinated to the Tactical Dimension (Tactical Supra-Dimension, as I have mentioned in my first book), and sometimes, to the Tactical-Strategical Dimension.

I will discuss the Strategic Dimension in further detail with the progression of the topic, and deeper in a chapter that is fully dedicated to it. But I can say, in advance, that in order to reach it, our team must be firstly identified with our way of playing – without having a pre-defined time. I refer here to both the conscious and sub-conscious because we risk creating a great confusion among the players, as they may not clearly identify our way of playing.

The words of [31]Vitor Pereira (1) reflect this idea that within Tactical Periodization the Process will be oriented by the Tactical Dimension, and sometimes by the Tactical-Strategical: *"I cannot design any exercise that is not related to what I am looking for in terms of my team's behaviours (intentionalised interactions). Even the initial activation (warm-up) must be directly related to what I will do after (…). I direct the training in order to promote a certain type of behaviours (intentionalised interactions), every bit of the exercise will be direct towards those behaviours that I want to contemplate on that day".*

To achieve that identification between player and the way of playing, either conscious and sub-consciously, the operationalisation of that way of playing will be essential. It will allow the acquisition of certain behavioural patterns at the individual, group, sectoral, intersectoral, intrasectoral or collective levels, therefore, its IncorporAction. This should, according to Tactical Periodization, direct the Process since the first training session. As referred, we should start by exposing the players to the global idea of playing, using images and making them try it out on the pitch. The existence of a global understanding is very important for a later understanding of the parts. As Professor Frade says, **"the hierarchisation starts from the macro level, from the object, from the acquisition of the contours of your way of playing. It's Gestalt."**

---

31   Vitor Pereira (1): Interviewed by Xavier Tamarit, in 2010.

2.1. The beginning of the season: a concept that differs from the so-called 'pre-season' and 'preparatory period'

The Logic of Tactical Periodization does not understand the initial period – labelled as 'pre-season' or 'preparatory period' in the conventional logic – like other methodologies. According to Vítor Frade (2), *"people even call it pre-season and I don't know what that is, because pre- is always before the season and if they say it is preparatory it is already part of the season"*. The interviewee adds that *"in Tactical Periodization, the preparatory period is not preparatory of anything, that period before the beginning of official competition is not preparatory of anything because the competitive period is also preparatory, because there is a permanent concern with preparation"*.

Does it make sense to call it 'pre-season'? Isn't it part of the season? Some teams even play official matches in this 'pre-season' period! And what about preparatory period? Maybe according to a conventional logic, it makes sense, because according to this perspective this period is used to prepare everything that will come after – with the preparation being oriented by the Physical Dimension. Tactical Periodization sees it differently, so the wording used must be different too.

According to Vítor Frade (2), this initial period, **with regards to Tactical Periodization, is the first moment in which you start training to make possible reaching a certain goal. So, as you are starting, you need to have certain methodological precautions, let's put it that way, but not because it should be a different period in comparison to others. The difference is in the gradation and fundamentally in the absence of a competitive framework. That period, and I don't mind at all if you call it preparatory, but with a different meaning. It prepares indeed, it prepares the first match"*.

A period that should consider from the first day a pattern of trainability-competition that is like the one that will occur when the official competitions start. Vítor Frade (2) clarifies that *"in the Logic of Tactical Periodization, what is essential is to create patterns that regularise, the regularities that consider the framework that will be face during the competitive period. So, if there are competitive matches each Sunday, or Wednesday and Sunday, if there is a dominant pattern or other. What makes sense is to then create an adaptation to a similar pattern"*. So, there must be common sense in bringing that people to adapt to an increasing demand gradually. But having already in mind that they can deal with a type of effort and rest that looks like the one that will become their usual pattern of demand, that I called the Morphocycle"*.

Therefore, already since the beginning we must training with the intention of finding an adaptation of the organism to what will be a pattern of demand (having concerns in terms of achieving this correctly, in a gradual manner, because the players are coming back from a period of inactivity, or perhaps even worse, of an uncontrolled period of activity): this period should be as similar as possible to the competitive one. An adaptation oriented by the Specificity of a way of playing. Being so, in our Logic the so-called 'preparatory period' does not exist. However, there is a preparatory period that happens throughout the whole year, with the intention that our team displays a Game Matrix from match to match, including an ability to insert adequate nuances to each match. In summary, the way of playing will be equal from a Macro level, but different from a Micro perspective.

2.2. The first week: presentation of the Game Model (as Previous Intention) and the adaptation to effort that it requires

Xavier, you start, and you don't know how they will turn up, they can even say that they have done some activity every day, but can they measure well? Do they know what it was? So, as a precaution, and for other reasons...if it is the same team or if it is a new team, it makes all sense for you to identify the players, the group... (...)

You need to adapt, you need to go from low to high, but from the low-high to the high-high, and the low-high is the 'less football'. But it's only because of that, so, in the beginning, for example if the guys are used to a different logic, we can even do some light running so that they think they ran. (...)

It is a matter of general adaptation to effort. And if in that time I say "Look, we will look to play like this and that...!". But that is about common sense, that is Tactical Periodization. Tactical Periodization requests the best possible common sense. You may have 2 days in which you are not worried, or just a week, for the players to spend in a more diversified activity. Normally they return from being sedentary and you do several different things, some fun stuff, that is all positive...and, they can identify with the formal aspect, with the way I they are going to play, as you want, as you will coach. I am a strong believes in creating straight away a great resemblance with the Morphocycle we will face! I don't have a match? I can create one, that may even be...it will be in a smaller space, or three quarters of the pitch...rest, Tuesday, Wednesday, Thursday, Friday training and then Saturday and Sunday, to create in the organism the adaptability to the configuration of the Morphocycle. We are an animal of habit, an organism in habituation, so we should create an identification with the Morphocycle since the beginning. (...)

The initial adaptation does not mean that you are working outside the Morphocycle. (...) it's just like watching a match in a normal speed and then watch it in slow motion! (...) Tactical Periodization must contemplate the circumstances, so, if you know that people just returned from doing nothing, from holiday, progression has to do with that. It's a matter of common sense, but that can be perfectly framed under the Morphocycle.

(...) that is how we build that hierarchy, how are we going to start? First by the macro, articulating defense with attack or the attack with the defense, it's that, hierarchisation is that, and then depending on the week "what is not working so well?". (...)

Vítor Frade (1)

Within Tactical Periodization, the first week is not the 'Adaptation Week' as proposed by some authors. To allow an easier understanding, they label it like that to suggest that this first week is one of adaptation to a way of playing and to a new work methodology. However, the designation can also be misleading due to the meaning this word has in the conventional logic — in our methodology every week is a week of adaptation. The first week is in fact a week in which these must be special caution, as the players are returning from a period of inactivity, something that is already accounted for in the Principle of Complex Progression, even if not only at a physical level.

This first week is aimed at, in accordance to the Principle of Complex Progression, exposing the players to the Game Model as Previous Intention, providing them with a global idea of the way of playing we want to implement. It is a week of bonding between the players, although it should continue throughout the season. It is a week of gradual adaptation to what will be the posterior effort, Specific of course, going from low-high to high-high as Vitor Frade says. It is a week of adaptation to a Logic of training, even if sometimes there must be a little 'disguising' (the 'cappuccino' strategy), but even here respecting...the same Complex Progression.

In this week we already can — or should — train emphasising a similar Morphocycle to the one we will use during the season. Depending on the circumstances and on the context, this week may be 'different' in its contours, but not in its matrix. The Process always depends on the context and on the circumstances.

Guilherme Oliveira (1) explains that he starts "already in the first week like in the rest of the season. The only difference is that in this first week I want them to understand the Great Game Principles (Macro Principles), so that after I can start articulating the great with the smaller, the Sub-Principles. My first week is one of identification with my Game Model in global terms. At the end of the first week they must know what they need to do in global terms when they are defending, when they are attacking, when they are in offensive or defensive transition, they need to know that globally. This is useful for them to then understand everything that we will do. Because one of my concerns as a coach is that they realise that all exercises are designed to improve a certain aspect of our game. There is no exercise that is not intended at improving our way of playing.

Jose Tavares (1) agrees, adding that "since the first day I am going to invest time in having my players starting to think of playing in a certain way, that we are going to play in a certain way. So, during that week we have some basic ideas to make that happen, so that the players start understanding the things that the coach wants, that the team will playing a certain manner, and so we start creating that mental picture in the players' minds, so that they interiorise how we are going to play, but we start from a basic idea, a global idea".

In the same direction, Vítor Pereira (1) explains that "the first week is almost a re-adaptation (...) When I start working, there are many players that are not yet identified with my work and that first week is used to start sharing a common terminology, so that they can understand when I am referring to a certain moment, when I articulate a moment or other (...). For them to understand my language. And our work is very similar globally. It starts being tactical, it requires assimilation of behaviours that we are looking for (intentionalised interactions), although with a lower degree of complexity.

As we can see through the examples provided by our interviewees, since the first week there is a respect for Specificity, contextualising everything that is done according to the Game Model. There is respect for the Principle of Propensities, because if we want to produce the acquisition of certain Actions and Inter-Actions, the context should be prone to their emergence. There is also respect for the Principle of Complex Progression, as they refer to going from a 'low-high' to a 'high-high', starting with a lower degree of complexity. And there is respect for the Principle of Horizontal Alternation in specificity, because they say that we should train since the beginning with a Morphocycle that is like the one we will use during the season, even if we must consider the circumstances of the moment. <u>Tactical Periodization has a pattern from beginning to end (methodological matrix).</u> The first week will serve to adapt the organism to this pattern – even if there must be a certain precaution, as the players are returning from a period of inactivity, or at least of non-supervised activity – and to make our players identified with a Macro level of our way of playing, a global idea of our way of playing, which will continue to be present with the season unfolding. Even when we perform exercises at the Micro level, more individualised or more targeted, allowing therefore the Articulation of Meaning and the Reduction without Impoverishment. As I mentioned earlier, this is an indispensable requirement for the existence of Specificity, for the players to understand the parts within the whole game.

Mara Vieira (1) reports her concerns during the first training week: "I want to show them the great principles (Macro Principles that will orientate our work throughout the season. The whole (...) Then, from the second week, we operationalise in accordance to the Pattern Morphocycle. We must show what we want and gradually reinforce it, continuously, along the Process. It is important to recall with certain regularity what we discussed on the first day, especially when we feel that something essential is missing".

This global idea of our way of playing, those Macro Principles that will direct the whole season, must be constantly reminded, because there are certain periods that are more prone for deviation, even if unconsciously, from the Game Model. And in those exercises more 'micro', the players must recognise that portion of the way of playing as part of the whole, in such a way that there is no loss of intentionality. I repeat, because this is crucial, understanding the parts within the whole is fundamental to avoid a loss of direction.

In this first week we will need to consider many variables and circumstances.

For Vítor Frade (2) **"the players are returning from holiday and they may return to the same team, with the same coach and the same Game Idea, the same framework. They can also return from 10 or 20-day holidays, which is not the same thing. But for me there is no problem, it becomes the same thing. Another issue is if we have players with varying vacation times, that arrive completely out of tune with the context they will integrate. The adaptation happens at two levels, let's put it that way: a more 'macro' level, that I label as conceptual – which is getting in tune with the Principles, with the Game Idea that we seek – and another more 'micro', which is motor or 'bodily' – and if all this is not foreign to them, there will be no major problems as long as there is common sense".**

So, the adaptation does not occur only at a conceptual – 'macro' – level, related to the identification of the players with the Game Model, but also at a methodological – more 'micro' – level, expressed as motor adaptation, and everything else that the desired way of playing requires.

The interviewee also explains that through this adaptation **"what the training will give them is an enhanced speed of recovery, or it may give, if just like the training the recovery is not something abstract. This is very objective. Therefore, if the individuals are returning and already have the way of playing in their minds, in their minds and in the toe nails, in the conscious and in the subconscious...if they are not stupid, it is not hard at all that the 'new' way of playing becomes part of the conscious, but this is not enough. It is the whole body who plays, with an affective and emotional dimension incorporated, and those relate to** *the acquired habits, they have to do with what has not been changed yet! This requires time and that is why it is not the same if the players are not familiar with the way of playing and return from 10 or 20 days of holiday. It is not the same thing, and therefore you should be able to design that progression more gradually and better".*

What Tactical Periodization tries to ensure is that our players incorporate our desired way of playing at both the conscious and subconscious levels. That means a simultaneous development of 'knowing how' with 'knowing about knowing how'. At a conscious level it takes less time, but the possibility of expressing that spontaneously – subconsciously – will require a longer period. It implies the creation of habits through emotions and feelings. That is why, as Vítor Frade suggests, it will make a difference having players that worked with the coach during the previous season, and that, therefore, are already identified with that way of playing, Similarly, the number of days available for the players to familiarise themselves with the intended way of playing will also be important, as we may need to do it in a more gradual manner, for a longer period.

As we see, the circumstances can bring changes to the Process, reason why Vítor Frade says that there is a large difference between our Logic and the conventional one: *"the other framework is what you would call a 'ready-to-wear' (pret-a-porter) suit, meaning that is already built and is one-size-fits-all. No! Tactical Periodization is nothing like that. It is about tailor-made suits. It is different if, for example, I have less time available, if I have the same players or not, if it is the same club, the same team, the same coach".*

2.2.1. Importance of a global idea of playing in the posterior hierarchisation of the Game Principles and Sub-Principles

Yes, the earliest and the deepest the better.

So, I need to lead the players to understanding the game, to understanding the way of playing, that is why I say that Tactical Periodization associates the 'knowing how', which is something that you can even learn by yourself, with 'knowing about knowing how', in coexistence, since the beginning. It has to do with getting the players to identify, since the beginning, the Game Principles that I want, which in the end is my Game Idea. And that since the beginning, and even with the kids. Now, obviously there needs to be a 'lower' degree of complexity for the kids, it must be different. I need to understand that a kid 'doesn't have' capacity for abstraction, I need to find metaphors to use with the kids, I have to... (...)

I often use two concepts, one is the understanding of the game, and even more appropriately, the understanding of the way of playing, because that is the one I am looking for, but the generic understanding of the game is also culture e it is already something important. And many times, the generic knowledge of the game that they have can be an obstacle for the understanding of the way of playing that I seek. (...)

I think that the better that player understands our game, the better he will be. That is why I should care, as soon as possible, about the identification of the players that I will work with, with the way of playing that I am looking for. That is why I say that Tactical Periodization, since the beginning, is simultaneously a knowing about knowing how. It is about the players identifying the Game Principles that I want, what in the end is my Game Idea. And that since the beginning, even with the kids.

I often say that drills have potential information, so if it is possible to impose a certain dynamic on the drill, the information will be converted into ability, meaning that is allows for the assimilation of certain things. And one of the requirements to make it happen, is that who performs the drill is identified with what we are looking for, and what we look for in training is not always, and most of the times it is not the whole game, it is just a part of the game. So, it makes sense that they know to which part that part belongs to, and they will only know it if in the meanwhile they know that we are concerned with an intersectoral problem for example, and that that is related to... They are not mentally retarded, clearly there are some more intelligent than others but... Now, understanding does not lead them to do better but it certainly helps, it helps because many of our behaviours, against what many things, they belong to the sub-conscious sphere. But due to what? Due to habits! So, if they are used to a different logic, it is fundamental that it is dismantled. But depending on what? On the assimilation of the logic that we look for, and when it becomes a habit then it becomes spontaneous. The habit is an intention acquired in action, let's put it that way. It is through action that you get there. Every neuro-scientifically or neurobiologically it is not the same thing, I even say that only the intentional action is educational. So, the birth of the action as a previous intention, being a conscious realisation of what it is, when it doesn't...but the relationship after that, and even the subsequent feedback is different regarding the intervention of different elements of the brain and nervous system, depending on the existence – or not – of a previous intention!

Vítor Frade (1)

It is fundamental that our players have, since the beginning, a global idea of the way of playing that we want to implement, a Previous Intention. They must be understanding what we are doing at each moment and why they are doing it, associating that 'knowing how' with the 'knowing about knowing how'. And this since the beginning of the season, inclusively since the grassroots (having in mind their singularities). In such a way, when we perform a 6v4, trying to implement some Game Sub-Principles, for example, if they understand the exercise as part of that globality, as part of our way of playing, we will be provoking an intentional learning and not an abstract learning. And this results in the learning process having different implications in the brain, so this is more relevant than it can seem at first sight. This is what Tactical Periodization is about: "*bringing to life an Intentional Process oriented by a way of playing*" (Jorge Maciel (2)).

This global idea of playing, the identification with the Macro-Principles of our way of playing, is converted in something essential for the development of the whole Process, as it is fundamental for habit assimilation and creation, just like we desire. Those performing the exercise must be identified with what we are looking for. This understanding allows the action to be intentional, and that identification will lead to the creation and integration of habits. As Vitor Frade says, even the elements of the brain and nervous system are involved differently in relation to posterior feedbacks, depending on the existence – or not – of a Previous Intention.

However, the occurrence of this global understanding of our way of playing does not require that we always practice it as a whole. Many times, or even the majority of times, we will only practice parts of this way of playing.

Carlos Carvalhal (1) considers that we must depart "always from a global ideal. We don't particularise at the beginning, we do the opposite, starting from a global idea that we try to define from the first working days; exactly what we are looking for in global terms for our team, so that the player can have in his mind exactly what we are looking for with our Game Idea (…)".

The interviewee reinforces this perspective, guaranteeing that what he does is "starting from the global and moving to the singular. That is our idea for the first days. I believe it is essential to have a global idea of what we seek with regards to the Great Game Principles (Macro Principles). Making the players feel what we want, which will be our Game Matrix, what will be our identity card, what will identify us as a team…and then from the existence of that understanding, which is relatively easy, we move towards the path to get to those Principles, and that path is made of Sub-Principles, and Sub-Principles of those Sub-Principles, which we will have to hierarchise and adjust on a weekly basis (…)".

So, we move from the global idea to the particular, having to hierarchise, as previously explained, the Game Principles and Sub-Principles. What does this mean? Starting from what we consider more important, which will depend on the context, because we cannot expect them to learn everything at once. So, for example, if you arrive at a team with players that have great quality and much attacking power, but that last year conceded a lot of goals and lost many 'one-off' matches it will perhaps be convenient to start by improving the defensive aspect. This without disconnecting from the rest, because with the quality of your players you can generate scoring opportunities without having such a great attacking organisation. And once this is sorted, you can focus more on the attacking organisation, without practicing the rest in an articulated manner. This is an objective and contextualised example that relates to the coach's ideas, who will try to improve his team's defensive aspects starting from the attacking style that the team uses.

Carlos Carvalhal (1) explains that "therefore, there is a hierarchisation of the Principles and Sub-Principles to get us to where we want to go".

For the interviewee, the beginning of the season serves exactly for that, to *"place the cement and create solid foundations for those Tactical Principles that we want during the whole season. Knowing that along the season we will lose some things, which will have to be recovered, and others that need to be maintained as well"*.

I highlight, once again, the importance of, during the hierarchisation of the Game's Principles and Sub-Principles, and the acquisition of more individual, sectoral or intersectoral aspects, not losing sight of the whole picture. Doing so will mean that the learning process will no longer be contextualised, and therefore, it will lose its intentionality, and the necessary Specificity that allows for the emergence of the Logic of Tactical Periodization.

Guilherme Oliveira (1) considers that intentionality as *"fundamental, and many times the coaches do not explain why they do certain things, they are not able to…or the players are not able to see why this 3v3 or 4v4 situation will benefit them during* the match. *They do that because they like it, but the maximisation of their quality is not achieved because they cannot transfer it from one side to the other*". This means that the exercises are only potentially specific, as I explained in the previous chapter.

As all our interviewees claim, the understanding of the way of playing we desire is crucial to associate the 'knowing how' with the 'knowing about knowing how', which becomes essential for the creation of Intentionalised Interactions. And that understanding must be promoted since the beginning, through a global way of playing, that will then allow for the hierarchisation of its Game Principles and Sub-Principles without a loss of meaning.

I could answer you with my own case, and give you examples of players I have worked with, even though I cannot say I was applying Tactical Periodization 100% (...). But I don't even want to go down that road... I just need to give you the example of Mourinho. Mourinho's teams are usually said to be very athletic. So, if they are, they are due to training the 'athletic' without training the athletic. That is because Tactical Periodization does what you are referring to.

There are several preconceived ideas about what strength, speed, and others are and I like to make fun of that. I really like good cycling, especially on the mountains. I like watching Contador and Schleck leaving everyone behind when they go up, even those with a more athletic morpho-type. Why do they leave the rest behind? Do they use a lift? And with that more or less 'weak' musculature, even looking like that shirt is riding by itself. Do they not have strength? Then how the hell did they climb it? If they don't need muscular hypertrophy is because it is related to something else! That has nothing to do with strength, because in conventional terms strength is nothing like that.

Look at the African teams, except for Ghana they are all huge guys, really impressive guys, proper 'beasts'! Resistance machines are everywhere, and those guys impress us...should we buy them? But, all together, they are just like a 'herd of elephants'! Look how hard it is for them, they cannot be anyone. Now, look at the South American teams, they are all skinny, small guys, and that sometimes miss the collective support, but at least...look at the European teams, all formatted excepted for Germany, Spain...this, just by itself should deserve...! I mean, the richness, the variety of Italian football, the variety of French football, the variety of English football...it all fits in just two pages. You can't do that with Argentina, you need a textbook and all that. People should reflect on these things!

Now, with that strength training shit, those guys with big chests, they will be running around for 90 minutes 'carrying' 90kg on their backs! That is why you don't see any marathon runner with the body type of a sprinter, and these guys want to play for 90 minutes with bodies that are increasingly looking like those of sprinters. This is being stupid, this is being stupid!

This is key to unmount the former playing logic that the players followed – just like the methodological logic -, removing the habit of playing in a certain way to create other habit. Complex Progression is very important here, as going too fast or too slow can be fatal. Having sensitivity and intelligence is fundamental, knowing how to manage the coach's knowledge in relation to the context and to the circumstances. As Vítor Frade says, having a sense of Divine Proportion, both conscious and subconsciously, something that can only be achieved through experiencing that way of playing. That is why the way of playing directs the whole Process.

Once this global idea is exposed to our players, we should be able to read the context to create a hierarchisation of Principles and Sub-Principles which is the most adequate possible to our reality. It is about recognising which are the most important things for our team in that moment, and where we should start building our way of playing, without disconnecting it from the whole!

According to Jose Tavares (1), *"the coach will then adapt, depending on the management of effort, depending on the management of time, considering the first competitive match, considering a number of things that make part of it. The coach will speed it up or not, will suggest or not, will create a context of propensity for certain Principles – more important than others – because that hierarchisation of Principles and behaviours (intentionalised interactions) must happen. I don't want them to do everything perfect at first, I need to recognise what is the most important for my team in that moment. (...) Now, the essential is that they understand where we are, how we want to play".*

2.2.2. The images and practicing the global idea of playing so that no-one sees 'y' when I say 'x'

Look, if we run a test now, there are 20 people here and you go to the first one and whisper him a secret and ask him to pass it on to the other and so forth, when it gets to the last one...you have said nothing like that, so if I want precision, objectivity...it is in that sense that I talk about object, object of study. And our object of training is the way of playing. Why object? Because for me, in scientific terms, it can be objective. I have to make it objective in its key aspects, in its fundamental areas that when in interaction, interact and produce an infinity of those things, and those things, when they happen, can be beneficial or not.

Vítor Frade (1)

It is important that players can see images of that way of playing, as the [32]brain relies heavily on images to work. Often, we explain to the players what we expect from them in a certain situation, and

---

32 "In complex organisms such as ours, the apprehension of any object (in this case a group of ideas associated to a playing pattern that is designated as Game Model) is represented in our brain in the form of images". (Simao de Freitas, 'A especificidade que esta na 'Concentracao Tactica' que esta na ESPECIFI-

then during the match or training, they cannot perform it. It can be the case that the players are not listening to us, but it can also mean the player has not understood what we are requesting. We may not be in the same level of understanding.

I can also be due to other circumstances. For example, although the player understood it, having been used to doing something different for many years in the same situation, may lead him to keep doing the same thing when he loses focus, when he stops being conscious under situations of stress and higher pressure, when the subconscious 'drives' us. Bruce H. Lipton (1) explains that although we may try to overcome our subconscious programming, "such efforts face different degrees of resistance, because the cells are obliged to follow the subconscious programme". The author warns that in the battle against subconscious programming there is "a great expenditure of energy". That is why in Tactical Periodization we train and experience constantly the way of playing we want to achieve, so that the player 'loses' previous habits from a former way of playing and becomes familiar with the new way of playing at both the conscious and subconscious levels. Because we know that most our behaviours are dictated by the subconscious and not the conscious. "Cognitive neuroscientists have found that the self-conscious mind contributes only %% to our cognitive activity, which means that 95% of our decisions, actions, emotions, and behaviours derive from the unsupervised processing of our subconscious mind". However, it has little capacity for creativity. It is the conscious mind which has the ability to promote creativity and only through consciousness can we "examine the behaviours that are occurring. When a reprogrammed behaviour is developed, the surveillant conscious mind can intervene, stop such behaviour and create a new response". Let's imagine therefore what means for a team changing many habits simultaneously. It will be a terrible battle against the subconscious, an energy expenditure that will 'play' against us. That is why we must hierarchise and, knowing that we cannot change everything at once, prioritise what we want our team to incorporate first. Once those initial priorities are incorporated, we can move on with the complex progression of our way of playing. When our way of playing belongs already in its majority to the subconscious sphere, there will be more energy and they conscious mind, less active in its battle against the subconscious, will have further capacity to pay attention to detail, including creativity. And this energy saving, produced by a well-functioning conscious/subconscious, will lead to a fresher team at all levels, because the organism works as a whole. That is why, at times – and I repeat, at times! – and facing a lack of time due to the density of matches, a less aesthetic and less complex way of playing may lead to better results.

As Guilherme Oliveira (1) suggests when referring to the importance of images for the presentation of the global idea of playing, *"it is fundamental to show it through pictures, because through pictures they can see straight way what we are looking for. Images are a very strong way to transmit certain type of ideas"*.

Vítor Pereira (1) explains how he does it with his teams, with images not only of his own team, but also showing pictures of teams that perform similar intentionalised interactions to those he wants to see. *"We often use our own matches to see that it is possible to play with quality behaviours (intentionalised interactions) at this level as well, playing with behaviours of great teams (...) so that they believe, it is important the they believe! (...). If I want a defensive transition with high pressure on the zone of the ball, it is important that we show them that it is possible to do it, with images, either from our team in previous years or using images of elite teams so that they clearly understand that if those players can perform that behaviour, our players also can. We may not have such a high degree of quality when performing it but doing it can lead us to success. And that is the way. It is through audio-visual resources and then moving*

CIDADE...no que deve ser uma operacionalizacao da Periodizacao Tactica', 2005.

on to the pitch, and being completely coherent with what we are acquiring, with what we are seeing (...). Results are the most important because without results there is no belief. But if the results go together with us, if we believe in what we are doing, if we don't have deviations – today we do it one way, tomorrow a different way – I sincerely believe that at a certain point we will have an identity, we will have a playing identity".

However, as our interviewee tells us, this presentation of the global idea of playing cannot be done exclusively through images. It must also occur on the field of play. The players must see it visually and then perform it on the pitch during training. IT will be essential that they believe in what we are trying to do, and the results are the most important to guarantee that. The coach should also be sensitive with regards to the instants chosen to identify and reinforce the images shown – as a pattern -, to enhance the chances of these occurring in training and during competition.

Carlos Carvalhal (1) also refers to the importance of bringing those images to the field of play when he mentions that he goes beyond the use of pictures. The author prefers to support his ideas *"with the work on the field, putting them into practice. I can do a 11v11 situation, explaining what I want in each moment, what will be our identifying Matrix, if we will be a team with more ball possession, if we will favour more fast transitions, if we will defend with a lower line, medium line, a higher line, what will be the Matrix that we want, what we want for each Moment, if we want to recover the ball quickly, if we prefer to reorganise in our own half...all this leads us to a more global identification".*

When questioned about this topic, Jose Tavares (1) indicates that he would present his players *"not only concepts and words, but also images of something I would like to see happening. If possible, something already with the identity of the club, images related to the club, old or not, so that the players recognise, once I speak to them, that we have to play in a certain way".*

Tavares proceeds, mentioning the importance of bringing that to the pitch and incorporating it: *"that will always by a basic assumption for me, the introduction is only that, an introduction. For me it is important that they understand straight way that what they have in their minds, and that is not yet a part of them, is what the coach wants to see happening. So, we go and practice. And then the coach explains why he practices in that way. That is the ambition, and from a certain moment, what they saw, what they talked, is not as important because in practice they already feel that this is how we want to play, this is how we will have success, and so the mental picture is different because they have incorporated it: 'oh, this is part of us'. And the mental picture is no longer the most important. Instead, it is what they feel, what they create in the action, what they create with their team-mates, the success or the problems they faced...later, that image will emerge with an emotion associated to it. So, that moment of introduction was merely an introduction. Now we have new behaviours (intentionalised interactions), new actions, new things that are much more important, that make sense (...). What they players have in their minds will be important for what we want, for them to anticipate, but it is a mental picture that is different from the one we had in the beginning, it belongs to them. They must believe that is important to them, they must see that it has a meaning for them".*

So, what we try is to create a mental picture of the way of playing we want to perform and incorporate it gradually, somatising it: making that mental picture emerge among our players with an emotion associated to it, bringing it then to the field of play. Firstly, in a more global manner and then with the hierarchisation of that way of playing in Game Principles and Sub-Principles following a Logic (Pattern Morphocycle) that allows for a Horizontal Alternation in specificity at all levels. It must always respect that interconnection of Methodological Principles. We must consider that when bringing that mental picture to 'life', the emergence of new things relative to the 'here and now' will modify the contours of our way of playing, transforming it in 'another' way of playing, modifying that mental picture, which becomes closer to the one we desire.

The embodiment of a new way of playing in our players will require the creation of habits, which, as I have already mentioned, will imply the elimination of previous habits. This is something important to consider. As is understanding that it takes time to operate this 'disassembling and re-assembling' of habits. In the beginning – the necessary time will depend on several factors – our players, both during training or during matches, when they start to feel tired and lose focus, may resort to their old way of playing, directed by the subconscious. When this happens, we must intervene, allowing them to rest, because this goes against our objectives. As we mentioned before, when experiencing a context, we acquire behaviours, postures, attitudes and when these are not the ones we desire, we will be drifting away from our Previous Intention.

Mara Vieira (1) reports an experience related to this topic: *"I arrived and presented the idea of what I was looking for. I used images, Power Point, videos. Collective references and then intersectoral and sectoral relationships...But it was interesting because it was so different (to what they did before) that the players found it weird and I got the feeling they understood very little. I realised that on the pitch, when I saw what they understood from those initial pictures. In the first couple of friendly matches, the team was able to play well for 20 to 25 minutes. When they were still comfortable thinking. From that moment, when they started feeling tired, they went back to their old habits. The body took control. But it was important to acknowledge this, to know that we would gradually improve. They were in conflict. So, the idea of the 'whole' is key, because otherwise they tend to go back to their old habits"*.

The interviewee highlights the importance of that global idea at the beginning, so that after they players can understand the parts. This initial idea should be visual, but it should especially be experienced on the field of play since the beginning.

Although we consider images to be essential for the identification with a way of playing, Jose Tavares (1) guarantees that "the key is on the training session, in practice".

2.3. The beginning of the season: adaptation of the organism to the effort and the non-adaptation of the effort to external aid

When I started as a football coach, I did everything I could to avoid that in the pre-season players were given multivitamins or got massages, or something like that! You cannot imagine how long it took to reach an agreement. Because what I am seeking is the adaptation of the organism, so I cannot be giving it aid. During the season is different, due to the impossibility of controlling everything, because if you have a match three days after the previous one and the other team has had four resting days, there are some players that you will need to use more than others, so some levels of overtraining or tiredness or fatigue may emerge – or not – but there you need to think in the possibility of providing massages, vitamin supplements, etc., etc...! But not initially.

I even think further, for example, I have been thinking a lot on several of these things, for example, when a player has a sprain and the blood vessels 'leak', is it really advisable to use ice? Because the inflammatory reaction is a defensive reaction from the body. Now, if it goes past certain limits I need to stop it with a tourniquet or whatever, but initially I don't think so, I don't think so in order to defend the body. So, that idea of taping the feet or similar, these are cultural issues, which are (un)necessary and so you have it...the Game Model is everything, it is everything that the players have in their minds. (...)

I am talking about an injury with a leak from the blood vessels, because the inflammation is not allowed! Because the inflammation is a positive reaction... and what do you want...? I am convinced that today many people's immunological deficiencies are due to the antibiotics and others...! For example, those sudden deaths that have been occurring with extraordinary frequency, today there are even scientific studies that point that it may be due to the excessive use of anti-inflammatories. And because there is an increasing competitive density, then sudden deaths...it's not me telling it, these are scientific studies, so the reasoning is the same! (...)

Vítor Frade (1)

The beginning of the season is important to create a mental picture of our way of playing and to start incorporating it in our players, within a determined pattern – inside a methodological logic. Such pattern will demand a determined Effort/Performance-Effort/Recovery relationship.

Therefore, there should also be an adaptation of the organism to the duality Effort/Performance-Effort/Recovery. This should not be abstract, but instead Specific, as required by our way of playing.

Moreover, for different reasons but especially because the game requires confrontation, regularities, but also unexpected events, we should prepare our team to respond to patterns of problems that may arise in competition. And that is possible through experiencing in anticipation potential problems that the opponents may pose us. This can be achieved through game-related contexts, because only these will provide us with the necessary adaptability to answer the competitive challenges.

This adaptation of the organism to the abovementioned Specific duality stops occurring, in the most adjusted manner, if we seek multi-vitaminic supplements and other resources. The organism stops adapting to recovering as it should, for example, because those external substances start doing it in its substitution, so we are not achieving what we wanted to. It is possible that in other methodologies where the logic is increasing the volume in an unmeasured way in a period in which the players return from being inactive, has some logic (!?), but the understanding of Tactical Periodization is different, not only in terms of football but also in terms of training and with regards to the Human Being in general.

For Guilherme Oliveira (1), providing external aid at the beginning of the season *"is not advisable because the organism needs to adapt to it all (…). At the beginning of the season we are undergoing a process of adaptation to the effort by the organism. If we are helping the organism with substances to make recovery faster, the organism is not really adapting to it. So, at the beginning of the season, I don't think that is very important, but from a certain point of the season I would recommend it, because the organism will be so debilitated that if we manage to…"*.

As our interviewee points out, this refers to the beginning of the season. After, when the season unfolds, this type of aid may be beneficial (!?) for certain players with great tiredness or with certain deficiencies, helping them to recover better from one match to the next. It is also possible that at the beginning of the season some player will need it due to exceptional circumstances. The problem is when this aid starts becoming the norm, and not a circumstantial aid.

Our organism, if it does not have any kind of disfunction, produces everything that we need to function in the context in which it operates. If we provide it external aid it will no longer produce it, with the intention of saving energy or due to atrophy…Moreover, as Bruce Lipton suggests[33], when introducing external substances with the intention of correcting a function, we will be altering others without intending to. *"Every time a substance is introduced in the body to correct a function A, then functions B, C or D are inevitably changed too"*.

Carlos Carvalhal (1) considers that *"the vitamins are used fundamentally to treat or supplement some foundational deficiencies that the players may have and, if so, they should take them. Or if there is a player that may have a problem in a given moment, that is how I see it. Nothing more than that"*.

Vítor Frade (2) explains that ***"what I care is that it is the organism and not these 'crutches' who is adapting. Now, what makes them adapt in a way that they don't stop or get injured and keep evolving is the ability that I have, it is the quality of football training. Because the players may also feel the need, but it is our job to explain them why things are like that. But I am sure that it works the other way around, even in the grassroots. Some people, when an important match or a play-off is approaching, advise their players to take a reinforcement of magnesium"***.

It is important to make our players understand why this kind of 'aid' — e.g. multi-vitaminic, anti-inflammatories — may not be beneficial in certain situations…so that they, even when feeling the need (because we got them used to), end up deciding not to take them. So, the adaptation will depend of a high-quality training Process that respects the Logic of Tactical Periodization.

---

33 Bruce H. Lipton & Steve Bhaerman, 'Spontaneous Evolution' (2009).

Professor Frade (2) adds that *"there was a time in which everyone said we should take creatine to become more powerful, faster, etc. And this makes no sense at all levels, but above all if it is the individual that does the work, that works to gain power, dynamism, to a model that is fast in the intermittence of events. Therefore, our organism (due to the desire that the game is dynamic), the body, must go, 'physically' or biochemically, the body adapts. The creatine or the phosphocreatine also improve their reserves, and its re-synthesis also improves, but if it is the product of work, and that is what a high-quality game must be – he is already like that and I will give him more creatine? It's just like giving more salt to someone with hypertension"*.

This applies not only to multi-vitaminic supplements and other external aid, but also to anti-inflammatories, ice (used as anti-inflammatory after a sprain for example), bandages…the reasoning is the same. It is important to understand how the body works and its ability to adapt, etc., to at least doubt of some absolute or imposed 'truths' (cultural reinforcers). A good example is the excessive use of antibiotics, which makes the immune system progressively less efficient. Moreover, there are unintended consequences. *"Antibiotics are indiscriminate killers, they kill bacteria that are important for life in the same way they kill the harmful ones"* (Bruce H. Lipton).

3

> A(n) (II)Logical Process within an imposed logic

"*Just like you and me, the cells adapt to where they live. In other words, it's the environment, you fool!*"

(Lipton & Bhaerman, 'Spontaneous Evolution', 2009)

Let's divide it into parts. There are people saying that, but those people do not have a clue about Tactical Periodization, because it does not care about it. And I am the 'only one' who know about Tactical Periodization as Tactical Periodization!!! And those who want to talk about Tactical Periodization must talk about it as I do. Otherwise, they can talk about something else. People who talk like that are maybe thinking of working, and maybe putting it on Wednesday and putting resistance on Thursday and then at certain times, hurdles on a Wednesday, do some runs on Thursday or increase the time playing with the ball...that is not Tactical Periodization because Tactical Periodization does not care about any of that! Tactical Periodization is concerned with getting the players, on a Wednesday, to develop game objectives, Sub-Principles that are related to the details that I am looking for in my way of playing, more at an individual level or in combinations of two, or whatever. When these occur on a Wednesday, because there are some that do not require increased tension, those I move them to Friday. So, the team is powerful, the guys are powerful and resistant, but they are so in a different way. Because when I am concerned with the details of some guy that plays as a winger, I am also concerned with the one that plays as a centre-back, but in a different way, because one is in a certain space, and the other occupies a different one and uses different combinations from the other, even with increasing tension. What strength? He is being capable of playing with contraction and relaxation in the way that I seek, proactive and spontaneously.

That has nothing to do with strength because in conventional terms strength is nothing like that. Now, do they get stronger? Yes, maybe they do. If that is what strength is about, no-one does more strength training than myself. And that implies several other things, protecting the 'finetuning' of the organism. That is why, in the sphere of recovery, I have daily concerns with tightening 'nuts and bolts'. The same way the guy that is under the sun will have to drink, the guy that also does certain things will need to stretch the body so that it doesn't shorten. Because if I do this here to my limit, and you only need to do a single contraction, it will be shorter straight away. So, I need to know and take that into account, but none of this is complementary. Complementary in the sense of complementarity that they talk about! This is part of Specificity. I care about tightening 'nuts and bolts' Specifically, depending on the Specificity of consequences.

I already told you, it's like someone punches me in the testicles when someone talks about "the tension day, the resistance day, and the speed day"! Because it's nothing like that. Perhaps I also have some responsibility regarding that, and why? When I did, and I think I only did it back then...I had never worked with [34]Fernando Santos, and he made me responsible for preparing the training sessions, and he wanted me to capture the logic embedded in all that, so I would tell him: "look, here is the kind of strength-session, here is the kind of resistance-session". And because I gave that, as you know I don't hide anything, I give it all, I gave that to the students and maybe because it was easier, they...! But Jose Guilherme is also responsible for that to some extent, because sometimes, also trying to make things easier...'it's the tension day...'.

---

34 Fernando Manuel Costa Santos: Lisbon, 1954. Portuguese football coach, current Portuguese National Team Manager. As a football player, represented SL Benfica, CS Maritimo and GD Estoril-Praia. As a coach, worked with clubs like FC Porto, AEK Athens, Panathinaikos, Greek National Team, SL Benfica, Sporting CP, PAOK Thessaloniki. He was the first Portuguese coach and the third overall to manage the three biggest clubs of his country.

It's not the tension day!!! Is there no tension on the other days?! Yes, there is, but it's not maximal. But there is tension. On Friday it's the day of tension if I do some bursts...when you do a burst, initially there is high tension, but because of what I am interested in after that is the speed of contraction, then it's not. People don't have a clue about these things!

(...) That is why I feel outraged when people talk about training the tension, it's nothing like that. It is not the day of tension, it's not about doing something with tension, and that's it! Because that leads people to become concerned about tension, so they do something that involves tension, and that's it done. No! It's the day of details, of "small" principles, small things, the micro-levels and all that...in attack or in defence, but with the guarantee that there is a significant number of eccentric contractions, so, there is an increase in tension, but in details of the bigger picture of playing! I need to be concerned with providing variability to my sessions, inventing and going through those game situations, that are what I care about regarding my desired way of playing. So, I have two things, I need to invent that, and I need to know that there is increased tension. It is not the day of tension. Otherwise, I would just put some shit out, doing some leg skipping, and it is nothing like that, it's precisely the opposite! And the next day, let's say it's more about the Macro-principles, there are other references, space... but not necessarily using the full pitch, but it makes more sense that the training is not so intermittent. But if I manage to include some intermittence in the non-intermittence even better. This means, that if I am able to do four or five 10-minute times instead of 2 times 20 minutes or 3 times 15 minutes, that's even better! Because there are breaks and that is what ensures the logic.

But where I am again radical, because look, I say that we need to train much less than people usually train, because most teams are training, playing, relatively fatigued, and I think that you can train being fresh, (...)I say that in recovery....great, they rest or they do nothing, but it doesn't make sense! So, I have 3 days, and they will be 3 days off? Then, they will go there and do 'nothing'! Or even better, they will keep doing 'nothing' due to the length of breaks that I need to provide. But I need to act over (in energetic terms) the bioenergetic 'wool-ball' that is involved there and that supports the adaptability, and it is tired. So, it's only about playing 3v3 and shooting for example, and they stopped, and then they play again but for a very short time only! Because, what will make him rest 'is not' that, it's about resting from there, the different breaks! So, he goes there and trains, but trains without training, keeping the stimulation of the essential, but without getting tired, but I can only do that if I rest properly...people seem to have a tendency not to rest, and they keep saying that "having 7 breaks is the same as having 3!", or 3v3 is the same as 6v3, but 3v3 and 6v6 are not the same things. The ideal is, in reality, going there to train 'without training'! If you put it this way: "I have a match with maximum demand, and my team can only play another maximum demand match in four days", then why you think about it from Sunday to Wednesday and don't think the same from Thursday to Sunday?! It's the same! Or almost the same, because the demanding match and demanding training are different. And regarding that, I have no doubts that only Tactical Periodization, well-understood Tactical Periodization, solves the issue (...).

Vítor Frade (1)

Since the publication of [35]'Mourinho, why so many victories?', followed by other [36]books that focus on the same topic, a great number of people became interested in Tactical Periodization. These books tried to explain, in different ways, a different methodology. Even more importantly, they tried to explain a Logic that is different from the conventional and institutionalised logic. And when we talk about a different logic, it has nothing to do with training with or without the ball, making more game-related and analytical drills...Even with experiencing our way of playing, whole or partially, on the training ground. Instead, it is related to a different way of seeing the Human Being and his functioning, and therefore, a different way of conceptualising his training. And, sometimes, we may believe that some training sessions look like Tactical Periodization, but only in their shape. The root remains conventional. Nonetheless, the great majority of readers and even some non-readers have understood Tactical Periodization from a 'conventional perspective'. They have not captured, in depth, what this revolutionary methodology proposes.

The conventional 'lenses' that most people have used to read those books, together with the complexity of the topic, have resulted in misinterpretations. These misinterpretations, based on a preferential logic, promoted by cultural reinforcers, has firstly distorted it and then expanded it in many locations – forums, conferences, articles...and even books. In the end, another methodology was 'created', one that has nothing to do with Frade's Tactical Periodization.

It must be said that sometimes, to allow more people to understand this methodology, some of us, Frade's 'disciples', have tried to present Tactical Periodization less complexly. Our goal was to make its Logic understandable for those who had never heard about it. In some cases, we have even adopted some conventional terminology to promote its comprehension among the traditional 'football-society'. For those who were not able to leave behind, subconsciously, their popular beliefs, this has resulted in a deeper anchoring of their (un)movable beliefs, and consequently, an understanding of this methodology through the 'lens' of 'their' logic. In such a way that makes no sense. And for those who do not wish to adhere consciously to this new Logic, and hope it is unsuccessful, it has allowed them to criticise it conventionally, making it sound incomplete due to the lack of some 'conventional-dependencies'. This added to the fact that many want to sound like they are 'experts' in Tactical Periodization, with some even offering seminars and writing articles and books about it without first understanding it, has led to a problem of misinformation and deformation of the methodology.

Therefore, we could say that Tactical Periodization has been erroneously publicised. By people that talk about it superficially without understanding it in depth. By people that talk about theories without discussing the game. People that talk about the methodology without mentioning the Methodological Principles coherently. People that talk about Tactical Periodization without understanding its Logic. People that talk about the Game as something 'systemic' but referring only to its globality...people that talk about something that they call Tactical Periodization. A 'Tactical Periodization' that has nothing to do with Frade's Tactical Periodization. To which they add some things, remove others...making it conventional!

However, Tactical Periodization has its Logic, which is (il)Logical at the eyes of conventionality. This Logic created by Vítor Frade is based on the creation of a Pattern Morphocycle: 'Morpho' because it

35 'Mourinho, why so many victories?' [Mourinho, porque tantas vitorias?]. Book written by Nuno Amieiro, Bruno Oliveira, Nuno Resende, and Ricardo Barreto. Published by Editorial Gradiva in 2006.

36 'What is Tactical Periodization?', Xavier Tamarit, Bennion Kearny, 2015; 'O desenvolvimento do jogar, Segundo a Periodizacao Tactica', Marisa Silva, MC Sports, 2008; 'A justificacao da Periodizacao Tactica como uma fenomenotecnica – A singularidade da INTERVENCAO DO TREINADOR como a sua impressao digital', Carlos Campos, MC Sports, 2008.

relates to the shapes, supported on the previously mentioned Methodological Principles, allowing for the operationalisation of a way of playing. A Morphocycle that will be contextualised and that, therefore, can vary depending on the circumstances – depending, for example, on the training days the team has available – but that cannot escape from its Logic.

Within the Logic of Tactical Periodization, the main concern is to bring the players to develop purposes of the game that we expect our way of playing to express – in all dimensions – alternating Game Sub-Principles and Sub-Sub-Principles that demand high tension of muscular contraction, with others that demand high speed of muscular contraction in another day, with the day of the Macro Principles and Sub-Principles in between. All this supported by the metabolic web of our way of playing, respecting our Methodological Principles if what we look for is that our players are able to play with the muscular contraction and relaxation that we are interested in, clever and spontaneous while keeping freshness. Recovery (also understood from another perspective) is also considered. In the end, everything emerges as Specific and [37]individualised.

We are discussing a Logic that is new and different from the other methodologies, searching for stabilisation of performance throughout the whole season. This will be achieved with the Pattern Morphocycle. This training structure demands Maximum Relative Intensities – understood from the Specificity – since the first day, understanding the duality Intensity-Volume in a way that is different from the conventional.

As Jorge Maciel (1) clarifies: *"Tactical Periodization is a methodological rupture with what is being done currently. The attention is focused since day one on the Intensity (high-quality intensity, meaning the performance that is expressed through experiencing and acquiring a way of playing) and not on the volume (as a conditional capacity). Within Tactical Periodization, the Volume only makes sense if it is one of high-quality, a Volume of Intensities (different levels of a certain Intentionality), which must inclusively assume a relative weight since the beginning, either weekly or in the cycles between matches, and next to the one that should be present throughout the whole season. This makes the existence and the respect for the Pattern Morphocycle something fundamental. In this way of conceptualising training, there is no search for 'performance peaks', but for levels of high performance, levels of performance that allow the team to maintain a level of functionality, adaptability, and interaction with high efficacy and efficiency, without jeopardising the expression of the matrix that identifies it as a team, doing it successfully. In that way, it is expected that certain Intentionality is regular, stable, without important variations throughout the season".*

---

37 Individualisation as understood by Tactical Periodization has nothing to do with the conventional understanding. Throughout this book there are several examples that explain this difference, inclusively a sub-chapter entirely dedicated to it.

3.1. The Pattern Morphocycle: A Logic that allows for the adaptation and stabilisation

(...) It is a cycle that resembles the next cycle, depending on what? On the shape of dynamism that causes repercussions! Because what you want to happen is for certain geometrical configurations to emerge but depending on the way that you want players to interact. That is a shape, Morpho because of that, a morphology, the logic of dynamics. So, it has nothing to do with the micro level, which is even less micro if you play midweek...but it doesn't lose the essential shape, because you need to guarantee the uninterrupted, constant presence of the pattern. And the pattern is related to the Idea (...). That is why it makes sense to speak about fractals. Otherwise, it doesn't! You fractionate, but without losing the configuration.

Why is it the Morphocycle? How do you identify it? Why do you say "look, that team is Barcelona, and that one is...whatever team"? You say it due to the geometric expression of teams, due to the identification of patterns. So, they play like that, the drills that you need to use to create must resemble the suggested geometrical expression, and then there are the possible dynamics which lead to the adaptation of teams, there is the construction of an adaptation of individuals and teams. For example, good teams, when the match is progressing through the right side, for example, you can see them progressing like this or like that, and you can see the adjustments. They are not thinking, I need to go here or there, they adjust depending on the habituation, and that is identifiable straight away... so, what happens is not only relative to the guys near the ball. It's not only those who show the team is organised, but you can see it also in the guys that are far from the ball, how they move and adjust.

Vítor Frade (1)

"Either you understand why the Morphocycle was created, and what it aims to be, or if you don't understand it, there is always the chance of making mistakes".

Most coaches, especially those operating at the TOP, agree that four days are needed after a match (effort of maximum demand) to play another match (effort of maximum demand) without a drop in team performance. This 'rule' of the four days is essential to understand the Logic of Tactical Periodization. Because admitting this represents the need for a single 'training' day (effort of maximum demand, even if we know that a training session has a lower demand in comparison to a match, so only three days will be needed before the next effort of maximum demand) in a Pattern Morphocycle with a match every Sunday due to a need of recovery between efforts of maximum demand. Therefore, the Morphocycle will look like this: match, rest, recovery, recovery with the acquisition, 'training', recovery with acquisition, recovery with activity, match.

So, this understanding of a single 'training session', which is further explained in chapter 4, makes us concerned with an all-encompassing intervention.

Now, knowing that the 'whole' is made of parts, we must guarantee that the parts don't get worse, and even improve. And that only occurs if we are also concerned and intervene in the parts. So, we must ensure that the players are recovering without losing possibilities of acquisition and improvement, and this happens in the days before and after this 'training session'.

Therefore, as the specificity of performance, in the case of our way of playing, results from the emergence of the expression of: 1) eccentric contractions of the muscular chains involved and 2) that the functionality of these chains is expressed at the maximum speed of contraction, we must work on them, with one being dominant in one day and the other on another day. The intention is maximising and recovering them, ensuring acquisition in everyone, without a loss of recovery in the Morphocycle. And, I repeat, we achieve this by focusing on the individual, with many intermittences and high recovery times between repetitions and exercises.

The way of playing emerges from Actions and Inter-Actions that are based on those emergences and among them the player walks, jogs, stops...Now, the ones that determine playing with high-quality (the TOP teams are characterised by an ability to perform a great number of actions of 'maximum intensity' and our intention is adapting the organism for that) are these two and they are supported by a metabolism with an anaerobic alactic dominance and by a dominance of the faster muscular fibres. That is why training should focus on these Actions and Interactions with one or other type of expression that appears between them and not in a disconnected way. And that is what Tactical Periodization achieves. And the horizontal alternation allows us to maximise and recover them.

And why Morphocycle? Morpho has a Greek origin, meaning shape. A shape that is the same from one Morphocycle to the other, because it is created depending on the playing patterns, of how we want our team to play. Therefore, it does not refer to the shape of the cycle but above all to the shape of the exercises according to the same Logic and to a certain way of playing.

The Pattern Morphocycle is the organisational structure of the Process. It is the same since the beginning of the season until its end (with regards to its Logic), varying due to the context and its circumstances – the moment in which the Morphocycle occurs; number of days between matches; number of daily training units, etc. – but that do not lead it to losing its shape, its morphology, which is the **"constant and uninterrupted presence of the pattern"**, as Vitor Frade explained earlier.

"The Pattern Morphocycle must be understood as a fractal of a more macro level of a certain Tactical Periodization, due to it being a more short-term periodization (cycle between two matches) it must also have a matrix configuration the constant presence of a Collective Intentionality, a way of playing that one wishes to express as the identity of the team", Jorge Maciel (1).

It will be through the existence of this Pattern Morphocycle – in permanent respect for the Methodological Principles – during the whole Process, from the beginning until the end, that we will reach the adaptation and stabilisation which will allow us to express the desired way of playing on each match. The latter will continue evolving towards 'another' way of playing due to the 'Loop of the Game Model' while keeping the conceptual Matrix.

Jorge Maciel (1) explains that *"it is in this paradox, promoting the evolution of a reality that we desire to be stable, where the Pattern Morphocycle plays a central role. On the one hand, it promotes the stabilisation of a way of playing and on the other its progression, even along different time-scales. The operationalisation of a way of playing, which takes into account the weekly pattern the players experience, allows for the maintenance of the integrity of an intensity (Tactical) without blocking its evolution. This is a spiralled evolution, leading to the emergence of several dimensions initially unknown, without a loss of identity due to the evolution of this process based on a Matrix (conceptual – the way of playing, the collective Identity, the Tactical) that is supported by the Great Game Principles and due to the process being operationalised supported by yet another matrix (the methodological – Tactical Periodization) that relies on the Methodological Principles and on their application in relation to a Pattern Morphocycle".*

The habituation that we seek in our players does not only regard the way of playing but also the operationalisation of that way of playing – the methodological matrix that is used.

However, the fact that the Morphocycles may be similar in their shape since the beginning of the season until its end does not mean their content will be identical. The Pattern Morphocycle has *"a configuration that while keeping its matrix, varies at the level of its essence, at the level of the content that is experienced in the different training sessions, even if this occurs only at the Micro level and without the loss of references in relation to the Macro level of our way of playing. It is a reduction without impoverishment, where the small changes throughout the days will provide the operationalisation of the process with a higher emphasis on different organisational levels of our way of playing"*, Jorge Maciel (1).

Once again, we refer to the importance of the existence of a playing Matrix and its consistent operationalisation. That is why in Tactical Periodization there are no typical weekly, monthly, or annual plans, etc., like in the conventional methodologies. The latter plan at length without realising which direction the Process may take due to the circumstances. That is also why – because the Process can change depending on the circumstances – that our methodology works differently.

Carlos Carvalhal (1) refers that *"we prefer to work in small time-frames. And why? Because the circumstances vary. The circumstances linked to what we achieve are also the result of players' assimilation and of the obstacles that many times we face along the way. We know what we want to do, but we don't know what is going to happen".*

As we can read, the interviewee plans short cycles regarding time, considering that the circumstances can change the direction of the Process, although they cannot change the Matrix.

The Pattern Morphocycle therefore, is created having in mind different variables, depending on the time of the season that we are in, the way of playing we want to achieve, how we played in the last match, the number of days between one match and the next, the opponent we will face, who may lead us to observe the strategical Dimension and change – or not – certain marginal aspects, etc. All this together with the Methodological Principles gives us that shape that we have discussed.

Vítor Pereira (1) comments on the impossibility of planning training and his objectives long-term: *"I keep planning every day. For example, today I plan tomorrow's session. At the beginning of the week, depending on the observation I make depending on the reports I get, on my analysis of the opponent, on the video I watch, the highlights I watch, I structure the training sessions for the week, but I don't get into much detail, I work generally considering what I want (...) then I plan from one day to the next, and tomorrow I will see if what I wanted is well 'digested' or if I need to change it, depending on what I planned at the beginning of the week. If I need to change it, there is no problem at all, I change it, and I keep planning from one session to the next".*

Therefore, with the example provided, the interviewee shows how he hierarchises the weekly priorities to consider within the Morphocycle at the beginning of the week. Then he builds the sessions daily, adjusting the general planning to the circumstances that direct the Process.

If the circumstances can make us change our planning from one day to the other, how is it possible to create monthly, and even yearly plans? How can we know what they will need to practice — at any level — a team, a player, within a month?

Mara Vieira (1), when questioned about her planning habits, explains that *"there is no such thing as an annual plan, I only plan from week to week, or put differently, from match to match"*.

There is no long-term planning in Tactical Periodization. We must have a goal, a general draft of our way of playing — conceptual Matrix — that we want to achieve, but the Process will be redirected from match to match, taking one path or another, according to the circumstances, but keeping the collective Game Idea as a reference.

Depending on the number of days between two matches, the Morphocycle can be diversified, with the following example as a variable permanently dependant on the circumstances. So, the Pattern Morphocycle with a match each Sunday would look like this:

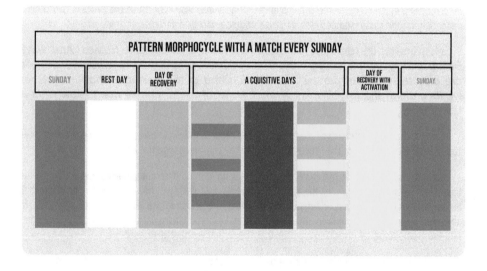

We can now understand that the creation of the Pattern Morphocycle generates the need for a routine in both shape and Logic. A conceptual and methodological routine. We will intend to provoke that routine without making it 'business as usual' so that everyone involved in the Process feels a continuous attraction for the same.

Jorge Maciel (1) suggests that *"the existence and operationalisation of the Pattern Morphocycle should always consider two aspects. One regards the need for this routine, which is Specific, being able to express itself without becoming 'business as usual' and without a loss of Specificity. (...) We need to make small changes in the experiencing of a way of playing along with the various Morphocycles of the season while preserving the respect for our processual matrix. This is another fundamental aspect to ensure the progression of our way of playing, the Complex Progression. A non-habitual routine, without a loss of the relationship with the essential at the methodological and conceptual levels, prevents the process from being just more of the same. It becomes a process that is keen for discovery and exploration, where the way of playing is constructed and emerges, and in which although the pillars are defined since the beginning (Great Principles), the unfolding of the process is still open-ended, with an unknown configuration (at a more Micro level). That creates in the different participants of the process a sensation of attraction for the apparently unknown, a natural attraction that is felt when one sees something growing, and not less important, the need to keep supporting that qualitative growth".*

A crucial aspect – but now the only one, as highlighted throughout the whole book – for the evolution of the team and for avoiding a nefarious routine will be the presence of competition in our training drills. As Jorge says, "*it is about promoting competition with Specificity, linked to a configurative matrix that is the team's intentionality*".

3.1.1. The Exceptional 'Morphocycle' (when there is more than one match per week): diversified without losing its shape and its Logic

It is a Morphocycle that is expressed in a diversified way because you have two matches in one week, that's it. But you cannot think about the drills differently. They must be identifying, they have to be identified with your intended way of playing, and the same with resting. It has to do with the shape, with the Morphology. Morphology is, in fact, the science of Dynamics, let's put it that way. How do you identify the teams? By certain patterns, and these patterns have a shape, and it is the dynamic that provides it with...you can to create that dynamic in training, then you must do it through those shapes. So, the exercises you invent may be less complex, they may resemble the micro dimension, but they need to contain the way in which you want to play, they have to have that dynamic correspondence. Therefore, that is what directs the adaptation, the same shapes, and in those shapes are involved all elements required to create them – the physical, technical, tactical... more or less complex, depending on the different days, and that is why Tactical Periodization talks about Complex Progression. The fact that you are giving more priority with issues that are more 'micro' in one week does not mean that you are not respecting the Complex Progression as you should. Because causality is a spiral, if you prefer, it is non-linear.

Vítor Frade (1)

As we can realise through the words of Vítor Frade, although the 'Morphocycle' contains more than one match per week, it does not lose its Logic – training according to the way of playing we want to display.

Even though we will be under a regime of recovery (the ones that have played), the exercises must have the shape of our way of playing. These forms will always direct the adaptability, being implicated in all dimensions.

Now, the Morphocycle must have a direction with regards to the dynamics of effort, at an acquisitive level and regarding the recovery that does not occur here. So, this is not a Pattern Morphocycle. Instead, we call it 'Exceptional Morphocycle'. For the Morphocycle to happen, there must be an orientation of the effort/performance and of the recovery and acquisition during training. They must be 'under control'. In this objective context, with more than one weekly match, we are able to control the recovery, but there is no longer an orientation of the effort/performance nor of the acquisitive side (at least for the players that played, and that will be under a recovery regime, which therefore is not an acquisitive one). These will be dependent on the match, being consequently random. We can no longer 'control them, and that is why Professor Frade called it 'Exceptional Morphocycle'.

An 'Exceptional Morphocycle' could look like this:

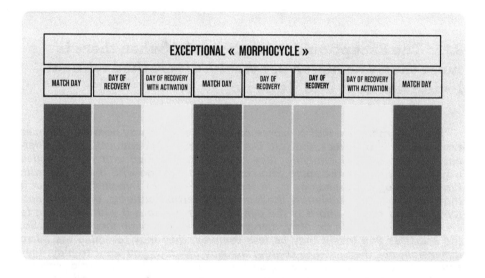

EXCEPTIONAL « MORPHOCYCLE »							
MATCH DAY	DAY OF RECOVERY	DAY OF RECOVERY WITH ACTIVATION	MATCH DAY	DAY OF RECOVERY	DAY OF RECOVERY	DAY OF RECOVERY WITH ACTIVATION	MATCH DAY

When this situation occurs for extended periods, it is fundamental to reinforce the orienting Matrix continuously throughout theoretical (images, conversations, etc.) resources or through exercises that, without disturbing the recovery, can assist us with recalling the Macro Principles, even if these should not be dominant. During extended periods without control of the acquisitive side, our team will be highly dependent on the circumstances that occur during the match. The Macro Principles may be demanded during the match – if we are able to impose our way of playing – or not – if the way of playing of the opponent prevents us from unfolding our way of playing. The latter can become a very negative aspect for the acquisition of our way of playing, interfering with and inclusively blocking it (and provoking the acquisition of unintended things, because as we have said before the experiencing of contexts leads to postures, attitudes, behaviours), so our intervention and the reinforcements of that game Matrix will be fundamental.

I must stress, before explaining each day of the Pattern Morphocycle, this time through the words of Vítor Frade (1), why it is so vital to creating within the players an understanding of the Process that we will follow so that they can understand its Logic.

"Usually the first thing I would do was 'automating' the guys, saying "look, today is Wednesday, but it's like if it was Tuesday or today is Thursday, but it's like Friday". And depending on that they would know, and they would end up saying "Professor, today is Wednesday, but it's Tuesday, or today is Tuesday, but it's in fact Wednesday...". All that is related to the Articulation of Meaning, with an understanding of the Process, with the complexity of the Process (...)"

3.1.2. The days of the Pattern Morphocycle: training while recovering, and recovering while training

As we have been discussing throughout this book, and more specifically in this chapter, Tactical Periodization follows a different Logic from the conventional one. Therefore, it is fundamental that from this moment onwards we stop 'reading' strength when we mention tension of the muscular contraction, resistance when we mention the duration of the muscular contraction, and 'speed' when we mention the speed of the muscular contraction. Even 'recovery', when we refer to recovery, among many other things. We should turn off the switch of conventional reasoning and start making sense, once for all, of the Logic that belongs to this training methodology, with the intention that Tactical Periodization is no longer the 'Tactical Periodization'.

It is very important to recognise that training and competition are inseparable in Tactical Periodization. As I have mentioned previously, during training, there should be competition, with the objective of increasing the motivation of our players, so that they can be in a routine without it simply meaning 'business as usual'. Moreover, everything that we practice relates to the wish of expressing a certain way of playing in competition. The competition will serve as a crucial test, even as training – a special kind of training – of what we are doing (let's not forget that competition produces acquisition, produces the adaptation, etc.). It is a fundamental day of the Process, to evaluate the evolution of the team – a qualitative and not quantitative evaluation, even if the latter is also present. This competition will be a starting point, together with other factors, to build the next Morphocycle. Jorge Maciel (1) explains that *"the competitive moments, play, as I have already mentioned, a central role in the structuring of the Morphocycle, because it is constructed having the previous competitive match (experienced demands, need to recover, correct and relive intentionalised Inter-Actions...) and the next one (type of demands predicted, at the Macro-level, that end up occurring)".*

In some of the Morphocycle's days, except perhaps in weeks without competition – such as the first training week – there will be different groups: the players who have played and the ones who haven't. Even within the group of those who haven't played, there will some that were named on the team sheet and others who have not.

3.1.2.1. The match day

Matches are fundamental for the structuring of the Morphocycle, from the latest to the next. I have explained how the Morphocycle is formed, and how it depends on several variables, like the number of days between competitions, how we played in our last match, what we aim to do in the next one…This will lead us to a hierarchisation of the Game Principles and Sub-Principles in accordance to our needs.

The match produces great expenditure at all levels: physiological, emotional, etc. That is why the Morphocycle has as its goal to allow the team to recover so that the players can be fresh for the next match, while simultaneously acquiring new levels of response. It is important to remember that there are players that have not taken part in the match and that need different things – not with regards to the Logic – from the ones who have. This acquisition in performance (commitment) must promote fatigue over the whole, the quasi-whole, the 'slightly-above-the-individual' and the individual, and all this over recovery.

It must be highlighted that now all matches have the same level of demand. It is also important to notice that in some matches we will be able to express our way of playing better than in some others. These aspects will influence the creation of the Morphocycle, requiring, therefore, different things. And, although we cannot be secure of what will happen during the next match, we have the ability – some coaches more than others – of predicting how the match may unfold, with regards to regularities. This is also relevant for the design of the Morphocycle.

So, when building the Morphocycle, other than considering what we have mentioned until now, it will be relevant to analyse our last match as precisely as possible: if it was more, or less demanding, if we managed to express our way of playing or if the opponent prevented us from doing so, obliging us to unexpected behaviours, that may affect what is still to come. Also, a preview of what can be the next match: if, for example, we will play against a team that presses high or low, the situations to be experienced during the week will be different. Or, in another example, if the opponent likes playing in the counter-attack, we will have to work more on the offensive organisation, the balances, the transition attack-defence, etc. This will influence which Principles and Sub-Principles will be prioritised during the week – the hierarchisation.

Jorge Maciel (1) explains it further: *"although it is important to plan and prepare, it is important to highlight that in this management, in this Phenomenon-Technique that requires much science (Methodological support), but also much intuition (a sense of Divine Proportion), we deal permanently with something that we effectively know - performance expressed in the previous competitive moment. But we also deal with something that we cannot know in detail (the demands of the upcoming match), although we hope it gains a certain configuration and meets our game Matrix. We can say that with regards to the previous match, we can decode, with more or less rigour, with which tonality it was painted[38], if darker or lighter.*

---

38 "It is important to explain the symbolism of the colouring of the Pattern Morphocycle, so that even colour-blind people like myself. The green colour corresponds to the complexity that is intrinsic to the Game (competition). For a convenient understanding of the meaning of the algorithm connected to the symbolism of colours, which in reality is 'something that provides a rhythm' to the construction of a way of playing, it should be understood that the emergence of the green results from what this collective dimension encapsulates – the yellow and the blue that when appropriately mixed and alternated, allow for the qualitative expression of a way of playing – the green. "So, we divide the way of playing (the whole = green) in different levels of organisation that are composed by all the represented parts: white + light green + blue + dark green + yellow + light yellow = green" (Marisa Silva, 2008 pp.94-95). It

So, there will be some people claiming that "there are no two equal matches". Or that "matches are like melons" - only after opening and tasting them can one find out how good they are. These are common sentences, so it is important to clarify and decode them. As Professor Vitor Frade usually says 'all generalisations are dangerous, including this one'. I do not ignore that matches are like melons because the Game has that dimension of unpredictability. However, we know that when we cut a melon open, it will more or less look like and taste like a melon (Macro level) and not like a pumpkin. But if it is an [39]Almeirim melon (Micro level), it will have a different configuration and essence from a melon [40]Casca de Carvalho. With this analogy I want to show that independently of unpredictability being a dimension that is present in the competitive moments, there are aspects (with regards to the Tactical, we refer to the Game Principles) that will be identifying and differentiating of certain qualitative realities (not hybrid or undefined), like for example a certain way of playing. We will never know in advance how the melon will taste or how the match will unfold, but we can predict that they will potentially have a certain configuration and will abide by a Matrix, with different articulations and expressivities in the various dimensions that compose them (Great Principles, Sub-Principles, Sub-Principles of the Sub-Principles). This is what gives them their own essence, an identifying, differentiating print. It is what allows us to distinguish a melon from a pumpkin, and even more, an Almeirim melon from a Casca de Carvalho one. This is what allows us to separate football from futsal, the different types of football, and the different ways of playing that compose the Game with a capital G".

Although we can predict something, it does not mean it will happen. And a match that we initially thought would be less demanding can end up being more demanding than expected.

Jorge Maciel adds that *"the impossibility of knowing, rigorously, which will be the effective demands of the upcoming match, reinforces the need for the process and its configuration, in a cycle that is comprised by the two competitive moments, to demand even more urgently the accomplishment of the Principle of Horizontal Alternation in specificity, in a precise and parsimonious manner. So that, even with relative fatigue, the team is fresh and able to keep the integrity and fluidity of its identity, its Collective Intentionality. So that it continues to express green tones, from our green".*

During the match day, there can be a group that trains, with the players that won't be included on the team sheet. And the group of players that will take part in the match (including substitutes) can do some mobility with stretching of short duration in the morning.

---

is nonetheless relevant to highlight that the white, each person paints it at her pleasure (without going 'crazy') and that the light yellow refers to the need of training and recovering in a more recreational way, but always in Specificity, so that it continues to be yellow, and continues to represent a certain level of organisation of the way of playing. It is from the correct calibration of the suggested colours that results the appropriate operationalisation of the Methodological Principles of Horizontal Alternation in specificity", Jorge Maciel.

39 Almeirim melon: type of melon cultivated in the Tagus Valley, Centre/South of Portugal.

40 Casca de Carvalho melon: type of melon cultivated in the Sousa Valley, North of Portugal

3.1.2.2. The rest day

In Tactical Periodization, the day after the match is usually the rest day. And I say usually because depending on the circumstances it can vary. For example: if the team has been subjected to a very high effort, we may give the players two rest days…with this, what we look for is that there is absolute rest during this day because the match leads to very high levels of tactical and mental/emotional fatigue.

Vítor Pereira (1) reflects on his own experience: *"after the Sunday match, I would train on a Monday to accelerate (?!) the recovery process. The problem is that I started to realise that on a Monday I was not at my best regarding work, I felt tired. After the match, I needed to forget about football, relax a bit, thinking about other things, so that I could get to Tuesday with a different…and I started realising that the same happened with players. The players also feel that need. Essentially from a certain moment they feel the need for…if they played today, forgetting about football for a day, spending time with their families. I need it too. And I started feeling that need, and if I had it, the players had it too. So, I changed my plan and stopped training on Mondays to resume training on Tuesdays instead"*.

In a Process that requires high levels of Tactical Concentration at all moments, there is great tactical fatigue (and as a result at all levels), so it is fundamental to consider Tactical Recovery. So, it makes sense to rest on the day after the match. For players to leave the environment in which they are immersed, to forget football for a day. It is necessary for them to understand the Principle of Complex Progression, just like the other Methodological Principles that compose Tactical Periodization and its inter-relationship. We have seen that at a mental/emotional level the highest amount of fatigue is produced on match days. So, for a true recovery, it is important to regulate it during the Morphocycle. Especially because this is a process that requires Maximum Relative Intensity (the same as concentration) all the time.

For Carlos Carvalhal (1) "we must pay a lot of attention, when we are in a Process where there should be a systematic concern with focus levels, to be cautious with the tiredness it involves. We need to contemplate this kind of tiredness too. So, we need to double our attention".

Normally in those methodologies that follow a conventional logic, the rest day occurs two days after the match, because the day right after the match is devoted to active recovery. This is due to *"strictly physiological reasons, centred exclusively in the energetic dimension and therefore not considering the attentional aspect which is submitted to great demands. We need to contemplate this type of fatigue too. We must double our attention"*, Jorge Maciel (1).

Is it right that from the physiological perspective it is more beneficial recovering two days after? Is that higher feeling of tiredness experienced by the player 48 hours after the match a reflection that he is really in a worse condition that the day before? Does the brain not require a certain time to recover from the match events? And what kind of weaknesses does the organism have after such a great effort, which we can only find out after?

So, given the reasons provided, in Tactical Periodization the rest day, in a Pattern Morphocycle, will normally be the day after the match. Jorge Maciel (1) suggests another justification for this: *"another reason for the rest day to be the Monday and not the Tuesday is that after a match the players, very tired and excited, will struggle to sleep. For this reason, and due to the trips, which may be relatively long and not very comfortable, or if they sleep later than usual and the quality of sleep is not ideal. So, they feel the need to extend their resting periods during the next day, if possible in a context of increased affectivity and tranquillity, in their own homes, without having to worry about going out for training. What would mean having to work".*

There will be weeks in which we may not give a rest day due to the tight, competitive schedule. But when this becomes a pattern, with various consecutive weeks of double commitments, it will be imperative to have rest periods.

3.1.2.3. The day of Recovery

This recovery must involve the bio-energetic web, the metabolic pattern, the canvas that is created between the different metabolisms, integrated in our way of playing, Specific of each way of playing and therefore fatigued. I mean that to promote recovery, this web must be activated. It is formed by the inter-relationship of the different energetic metabolisms that are activated when we play, and that is Specific of each way of playing, together with the commitment to each instant of the match. Only by doing this will we achieve adequate recovery in accordance with our Logic. So, we must promote exercises where there is a high level of commitment to the instant but for a short period, and with a lot of rest. This is a systemic understanding that goes way beyond the other 'systemic' methodologies.

This day will start to produce the so-called 'tightening nuts and bolts', which we discuss in further detail on a different chapter, and that must be present in every – or at least in most – training session, with higher relevance in some days than others.

This recovery may be different depending on the previous match, because as I have already mentioned, a match can have different demands from another, due to the circumstances. As Jorge Maciel (1) refers *"the configuration of this training session should equally consider the emotional state of the team. Training after a defeat is different from training after having won. It can also be different to have a recovery training in a period of high competitive density or during a low-density cycle"*. We also must consider who our next opponent is, we are always dependant on the circumstances, on the context.

The Recovery day (for the group of players that took part in the competition) will, therefore, include exercises of low complexity, but which demand maximum – and instantaneous! – commitment, without any acquisitive intention. It will be a session with a lot of discontinuity and with very high recovery time. There will be 3v3 small-sided matches with goalkeepers, for a minute, promoting this way the emergence of maximum commitment for an instant, allowing the activation of specific biochemistry, the emergence of the specific bio-energetic support and allowing for the dominance of the desired muscular fibres, the fastest ones. After there will be 6 to 8 minutes of recovery that we will use to tighten 'nuts and bolts'.

On this day, the muscular contraction for these groups of players will be characterised by 'high' tension and 'high' speed, but very low duration. So high, with no density, a small percentage, circumscribed or reduced to a 'few instants'!

Clearly, for the group of players who have not played, or who have played very little time, this won't be the Recovery day. They will have a different session, which will also depend on the number of days before the next match. Usually, they will do a kind of training session with demands that should be as similar as possible to those of a match at all levels. Even if we know that although similar, the level of demand will always be inferior to the one in competition.

In this day, we can also organise friendly matches, but with a smaller duration, because the next day they should train with the rest of the group, even if there may be exceptional cases.

For Vítor Pereira (1), the groups of players that played, in a Morphocycle with a match every Sunday, *"will be recovering on Tuesday, totally recovering. We will promote movement from one place to other, in a fun way (…) At a certain point, the recovery is fun, a match between them, they play a bit, but without tactical concerns, the idea is to get a bit away from what was the match"*. The interviewee adds that at an earlier stage of his career, his *"concern was to work tactically on a Tuesday, a recovery drill 10v0 in defensive terms, in attacking terms…But there is something fundamental: I started realising that at some point my teams would display tactical fatigue, there was such a big demand for concentration that we got to a certain stage, and the players would be begging…Sometimes we need to slow this down and forget a bit. So, I started feeling that the Tuesday session should be more fun"*.

For those players who played on the previous match, there should be no expectation of acquisition, but respect for recovery, especially at a mental/emotional level. Something that is referred to in the Principle of Complex Progression.

Regarding the session performed by those players who have not played at all or that played very little time, the interviewee explains that they must *"get a bit of what was the match"*. He adds that considering the training sessions of the following days, *"this practice should last more or less one hour"*.

When asked about the recovery in an 'Exceptional Morphocycle', Vítor Pereira (1) replies that in those days between two matches, all they do is recover, even if they review aspects that may be important for the next match. Always under a regime of recovery! *"We recover, but we try to work tactically, although with short repetitions, short things, intense but short, and contemplating the recovery because we are preparing the upcoming match"*.

Moreover, the interviewee gives us an example of how the context and the circumstances may lead us to vary and about the sensitivity that one must have to understand that at times change is necessary: *"when I came to work in the [41]Azores, we had to travel by plane and bus every two weeks. Here it is always raining, so the pitches are very heavy (…). So many trips, heavy pitches, that was almost like playing the Champions League, where you just need to do an exercise too much during the week and they won't be fresh. And I felt the team reaching that limit, and so we must clearly understand that (…) these are contextual issues"*.

Mara Vieira (1) develops her Process in a different context, with different circumstances, to which she must be sensitive and adaptable. Her team only practices three times a week. Therefore, although the match is played on a Saturday or Sunday, *"Monday will be a recovery session with the players that played the whole match or almost all of it. All the other players who haven't played will play in the training session. They will do a different session from the starting XI. I create a competitive context so that they play among them depending on the number of players available on that day. The ones who did not make the team sheet and the substitutes had no possibility of playing, and all enjoy playing. Of course, it won't be the same, because they will be playing in*

---

41 Azores: an autonomic region of Portugal located in the Atlantic Ocean, approximately 1,500km from Lisbon. It is composed of 9 islands and part of Macaronesia.

training, but anyway I create a competitive context because I think it is important for their evolution".

Nonetheless, because she doesn't have assistant managers that can help her, and her group is not able to self-organise, she usually cannot separate the players who have played from the ones who haven't. Otherwise she will lose control of the session. So, her exercises involve both groups, performing recovery with the players who played and giving the group of players who haven't played a session that is more similar to the match: *"I try to involve everyone. While some are playing the others are in support roles to those in possession of the ball, allowing for a pattern of muscular contraction that resembles the match but with a lot of rest time. Like this, they recover, and I can control everything".*

As we see, we must be sensitive to our context and adapt to the circumstances that surround us. As Vítor Pereira (1) claims, *"everything depends on the context we are working in, and we must be intelligent and decode that context well".*

Given the importance of Recovery in Tactical Periodization, and above all its correct interpretation, I will continue talking about it before finishing this chapter.

3.1.2.4. The day of Sub-Principles and the Sub-Sub-Principles with increased tension of muscular contraction

It is important to realise that the team is not yet fully recovered three days after the match. However, this is the first so-called acquisitive day, and it must not disturb recovery. We can say that it is the last day of recovery before the session of maximum demand. Most people involved in High Performance agrees that four days are needed in between matches so that the players can be totally recovered. As [42]Vítor Frade (3) warns *"after a match with high intensity, only after four days I can play another safely. Even though it becomes easier to achieve it in three instead of four if since the beginning of the season I plan considering the habit of training, for example, on a Wednesday, in a more Specific and intense way".* Once again, here is reflected the importance that the Morphocycle is as similar as possible to the competition since the beginning of the season, allowing for the necessary adaptation of our players to this type of effort/performance-effort/recovery.

The main concern on this day is to practice Sub-Principles and fundamentally <u>Game Sub-Sub-Principles</u>, in an <u>individual</u>, sectoral, intersectoral and intrasectoral way, prioritising muscular contractions with a significant increase of tension, without forgetting recovery. There should be a high number of eccentric contractions that are related to Actions and Inter-Actions of our way of playing.

On this day and on the days of the Sub-Principles and <u>Sub-Sub-Principles</u> with the increased speed of muscular contraction, <u>we must guarantee the promotion of individual consequences</u> (structural-functional)!

This is the day that represents the 'strength day' proposed by people belonging to other logic. Nonetheless, the Logic of Tactical Periodization is different. And it is also different regarding physical aspects.

---

42 **Vítor Frade (3): cited by Jorge Maciel in "Pelas entranhas do Nucleo Duro do Processo", Unpublished article, 2010.**

It characterises the muscular contraction by its degree of tension, duration, and speed. Although we know that during any exercise the muscular contraction expresses these three characteristics simultaneously (meaning that in any contraction there is tension, speed, and duration), we can, through the manipulation of the exercises, highlight more one or other. We can increase the tension in comparison to speed or duration on day x, maximising it while recovering the structures used during the other days (intervention on the parts, allowing for acquisition without loss of recovery). This day is about creating contexts that are prone to determined Actions and Inter-Actions, where the dominant contractions have high tension.

The manipulation of the training session on this day will attempt to prioritise Sub-Principles and Sub-Sub-Principles with a great amount of jumping, shooting, clashes, acceleration, braking, changes of direction...with the emergence, therefore, of a high number of eccentric contractions.

As Professor Vítor Frade explained in the introduction to this third chapter, to make things 'easier' and more understandable, this day has been designated by some as the day of increased tension of muscular contraction. Although on this day it is fundamental that the dominance of Actions and Inter-Actions where the tension of muscular contraction is increased in comparison to its other indicators, through a great density of eccentric contractions (according to the Principle of Horizontal Alternation in specificity), the training and the exercises on this day are directed by portions of our way of playing, by the shapes that we mentioned earlier. Intentionalised Actions and Inter-Actions at a more micro-level.

Jorge Maciel (1) clarifies that *"the dominance observed in this session has, therefore, in mind that on this day, three days after the competitive match, most players are not yet totally recovered. It is, however, the first dominantly acquisitive training session of the Morphocycle, with the intention of allowing for a convenient horizontal alternation. The playing experience on this day is characterised by intermediate levels of complexity, not very high, which focus on the Sub-Principles and on the Sub-Principles of the Sub-Principles, aspects that are attributed to the sub-dynamics that compose our way of playing. Through the experiencing of these assumptions, the strategical dimension is also considered, but not yet performed within a Collective dimension, but fundamentally at the Sectoral and Intersectoral level"*.

So, this will be a day in which, at least for those who played (because everyone trains together) the exercises will have more complexity than the day before, the Recovery day, but less than on the next day, the day of the Macro-Principles and Sub-Principles, because the team is not yet fully recovered (at all levels.). This is an intermediate complexity. We will practice Sub-Principles and fundamentally Sub-Sub-Principles, in small-sided areas, with a small number of players and short duration. This can be done by playing, although it should not be the dominant format – not on this day and not on the day after the day of the Macro Principles and Sub-Principles (which is the day of Sub-Principles and Sub-Sub-Principles with an increased speed of muscular contraction). There should be a dominance of repetitions concerning each player, individually. There should be many breaks so that there is an opportunity for a good recovery that allows us to exercise always at Maximum Relative Intensities, and always with the dominance of the desired metabolism – anaerobic alactic, as we believe this is the most differentiating metabolism of high-quality ways of playing. However, it is not disconnected from the others, shaping a bio-energetic mixture that is specific to the way of playing, and which may lead this session to be longer than usual, due to the higher quantity of rest periods that offer more time for recovery between exercises. This will favour the recovery of such metabolism so that it becomes once again dominant when the exercise is restarted. There can be strategic training, aspects with low complexity, but the Strategic Dimension within the Logic of Tactical Periodization should be well understood. This is discussed throughout the book.

On this day, due to the needs for muscular expression that involve the type of effort/performance to be promoted – dominance of muscular contractions with high tension, high speed, and short duration – and also, because of that, although not only, the higher number of existing breaks, attention should be paid to other specificities, that will have higher impact on this day and also on the following – acquisitive days – that belong to the Morphocycle, like stretching, abdominals…which means tightening 'nuts and bolts'.

This will be the most discontinuous day of those integrating the acquisitive part of the Morphocycle.

It is also very important to promote the emergence of many disturbances in the exercises to be performed during this session, requiring permanent readjustments. Jorge Maciel (1) explains that *"in order to accomplish the Methodological Principle of Propensities, respecting the regimen required on this day, we should create exercising contexts with significant disturbances, with contextual interference (why not recreating the match and placing obstacles on the exercising space?) that require adaptability and permanent readjustments (at the level of displacements and of the Inter-Action between players). The configuration of the exercises, aimed at presenting a great propensity, allowing for a high density of this type of actions and Interactions, should have a small number of players involved in Inter-Action and in a confrontation in a small exercising space, that promotes a very high exercising intensity. This is why the exercising times should be short"*.

Carlos Carvalhal (1) adds that on this day *"we are talking about a session in shorter spaces, not very prolonged duration, high tension, promoting certain aspects that we believe to be important for our way of playing"*.

Enquired about this day, Guilherme Oliveira (1) says he proposes *"relatively reduced exercises, training Sub-Principles, many times focusing on the aspects of transition during these days, on the aspects of the sectors and inter-sectors, exercises in which there is much activity, they stop, and again much activity (…) Always training the Sub-Principles that we want to work on, always focusing on the particular aspects"*, and therefore working fundamentally on the micro, on a day in which the Sub-Sub-Principles should be trained.

According to Vítor Pereira, this day is about performing *"short exercises with high tension, high intensity, short displacements with high tension in muscular terms with solicitations especially at the level of eccentric contractions and fractioned. So, exercises with a shorter duration, with recovery normally even in an alternated way, a team working and the other recovering, a team working and the other recovering (…)"*

So, on this day we should train Sub-Principles and Sub-Sub-Principles at a sectoral, intersectoral, intrasectoral, and especially individual level. There is a focus on the micro levels of our way of playing. With regards to the effort/performance, the training session seeks a great density of eccentric contractions, through the manipulation of the exercises, in a small-sided space, low number of participants, and short duration, producing an increase of the tension of muscular contraction, fundamentally on…each individual. Moreover, the exercises should be performed with a Specific bio-energetic support[43] and not just any, and this must be done every day, which requires a need for total recovery between exercises,

---

43 **Specific Bio-energetic support: this topic is widely discussed by Professor Vítor Frade in the chapter 'The abyssal zone of Tactical Periodization'.**

<u>and inclusively within the same exercise, in order to impact the same metabolic web with dominance of the anaerobic alactic, which would not occur if the recovery was insufficient.</u>

There is a fundamental aspect on this day, and why not saying, on the others, which is the need for training to be competitive, something that I have mentioned previously. This makes the training as similar as possible to the reality, among other things.

Vítor Pereira (1) believes it is crucial that training is *"competitive. That aspect for me is essential, always competitive with tournaments, imposing behaviours (intentionalised interactions) but always with a competitive component present. Sometimes they bet money, and it is very important because you only need one cent, one cent and everything changes. It is not about winning some money, it is about getting the money from their team-mate".*

To end this section, I leave you with a reflection by Jorge Maciel (1) on the day of the Sub-Principles and Sub-Sub-Principles with increased tension of muscular contraction, where he refers some things that I have mentioned previously, and others that we will discuss ahead. The understanding of the muscle and all the locomotor structure involved as Intelligent and Sensitive structures is very important to understand Sub-Logics of our Logic. *"On this day, the muscle and all the locomotor structure are stimulated in all their dimension not exclusively as producers of strength or effectors of movement, as they are conventionally conceptualised. In Tactical* Periodization, *these are Sensitive and Intelligent structures, that we shall imprint with the emotivity and sentimentality of our way of playing. On Wednesdays, the proprioception, the plasticity and the adaptability of these tissues are brought to the extreme, due to the need for permanent adjustments and readjustments. It is a session that involves the whole body. The others do as well, but this one does it very effective and intensely. The reason why it is important to manage this session very well, dosing and intervening conveniently on possible problems verified on the different structures involved. This accentuated demand, especially with regards to the physical dimension (because the dimension of our way of playing being experienced is not very complex), and due to the need to continue stimulating the recovery process due to the demands of the previous match, together with the need to ensure the quality of performances and allow the accomplishment of the desired regimens for this training unit, transform this session into the most discontinuous of the Morphocycle. In this session, the exercises performed should respect the relationship performance-recovery, promoting significant and successive recovery periods, because there will also be actions and Interactions with 'significant instantaneous intensity'. Also because of this, due to this need of considering the recovery during the training session itself, the duration of the session could go beyond the usual, but never with the intention of 'training more'. On the contrary, the goal will be to divide the exercising times further, so that the quality of performances, or if we prefer, so that the Intensity of the exercise is high and so that more resting times can be given, to tighten 'nuts and bolts'. For the same reason, if the coach prefers, there can be two sessions on this day, although with significantly smaller length in comparison to when a single session is scheduled. That may also depend on the context surrounding the training and the team. For example, if the board of directors demands that the team practices twice a day, due to cultural habits, or if the results are not helping to show that it can be done with just one daily session...It can be one of the strategies used to make them have a 'cappuccino'".*

3.1.2.5. The day of the Macro Principles and Sub-Principles with a high density of expression of the pattern of muscular contraction of your way of playing

This day has been erroneously designated as the day with an increased duration of muscular contraction. However, the muscular contraction is not prolonged in time. Otherwise, we would not be focusing on the dominance of the faster muscular fibres as we want to, but instead, on the slower ones. This would lead us to change not only the pattern of the desired muscular contraction but also the bio-energetic web. Over time, we would be modifying that acquisition that is produced and therefore provoking a different adaptation from the one we seek. Moreover, this would lead to changes in the Specificity.

If we have mentioned that a team is only ready to play a match of maximum demand, without a loss of its functional fluidity, four days after the previous match, it will also need four days until being able to face a training session with maximum demand. Always considering that a training session, even if it involves maximum demand, won't demand as much as the competition, excluding some rare exceptions. That is why Thursday, in a Pattern Morphocycle with a match every Sunday, will be the session with more similarities to the competition. This includes both interactions and demands because four days have passed and there are still three for the next match. A training session with maximum demand does not require four days of recovery, because the demand is lower in comparison to a match.

On this day we practice the Macro-Principles and the Game Sub-Principles together with the articulation among these. So, we will train in a more 'macro' way, with all, or almost all sectors connected, and with the parts that form the specificity of performance. Therefore, this is the session that implies more emotional demand, with the exercises of higher complexity. It is also the day that resembles more the match at the effort/performance level, because the exercises unfold in bigger spaces, with a higher number of players, and high duration times. There are fewer intermittences during the session. However, as we read earlier, Professor Vítor Frade suggests that we create a training session with intermittences within the non-intermittence, allowing us to train at Maximum Relative Intensities in every moment (and guaranteeing that exercising is being produced under the Specific bio-energetic support).

Also, on this day we can train over the Strategical Dimension with higher complexity than the required on the day before and on the day after.

Therefore, this is the training session that resembles competition the most. This does not mean that we need to play a match, nor that we must train using the whole pitch...even if this may happen as well. It is about performing exercises that are more 'macro', manipulated to promote the Systematic Repetition of what we desire, respecting the Principle of Propensities.

According to Jorge Maciel (1), *"the configuration given to exercises on this day must contemplate the experiencing of great portions of our way of playing in smaller spaces than the effective space of the game during competitive moments (...). From this configuration, a pattern of performance and effort emerges one that is very similar to what we wish to see in competition"*.

As we can observe, this is the most demanding training day at all levels, not only with regards to complexity. For the author, also in physical terms (and I am not only referring to the muscular contraction), "the demand is high because the dominant regime of contraction requests the solicitation in a high density of higher percentages of muscular mass, over-demanding in this mode the so-called organic structure". That is why this is the furthest day from the previous match and the upcoming one, allowing therefore for recovery. This enables us to practice with higher demands on this day, while simultaneously allowing for appropriate recovery before the next match.

Jorge Maciel highlights that "only by respecting conveniently four days of recovery, considering which day in the Morphocycle should have a higher presence of the acquisitive dimension, reflecting sensibly what will be done over the following days, is it possible to provide a satisfactory response inclusively in regimens of relative fatigue, to the demands posed by the upcoming match, without a loss of Collective Adaptability, Organisation and fluidity". In other words, with a Dynamism of the Collective dynamic.

For Carlos Carvalhal (1), on this day the exercises will always have higher complexity, *"even due to the characteristics of the exercise itself (…), with a higher number of players, more space, more duration, and the attempt to frame the exercise within a higher number of moments".*

Vitor Pereira (1) is aligned with Carvalhal, and also tells us about the incorporation of the Strategical Dimension (that I have already mentioned and that will only occur under certain circumstances) when he guarantees that, on this day *"we train Great Principles – Macro Principles – already with a strategical component well present the opponent, what we seek in terms of game, normally using a full pitch".*

Mara Vieira (1), due to her circumstances (having only three training days with her team), must do a 'non-mixed mixture', prioritising first Sub-Principles and fundamentally Sub-Sub-Principles with an increase of the tension of muscular contraction and after Macro Principles and Sub-Principles with high density of expression of the pattern of muscular contraction of the way of playing. The interviewee clarifies it: *"on Wednesdays, I practice the sectoral and intersectoral levels. Now, with regards to the predominance of the pattern of muscular contractions I have to make a mixture in the same session. We start with exercises that prioritise 'tension' with a sectoral organisation, and then we move into a configuration of the intersectoral exercise that prioritises the 'duration'. Sometimes, on this day, I only have a quarter of a pitch".*

Therefore, the Pattern Morphocycle is adaptable to the context: to non-professional teams, with less training days, creating a 'non-mixed mixture' that allows us to respect the Principle of Horizontal Alternation in specificity and the Logic; teams that practice with space limitations; teams that need to have two daily training sub-units as we will see ahead – for different reasons, etc.

3.1.2.6. The day of the Sub-Principles and Sub-Sub-Principles with an increased speed of muscular contraction

Being a day that is nearer to the match, it is important to consider the recovery (at all levels) again. Not only due to this, but also because we are in the day that follows the most demanding session. We are talking, therefore, about a day with decreased complexity (also from a strategic perspective) of the exercises in comparison to the previous day. So, we train Sub-Principles and Sub-Sub-Principles at a sectoral, intersectoral, intrasectoral and especially at an individual level, that must above all prioritise an increase of the speed of muscular contraction, respecting the Principle of Horizontal Alternation in specificity.

For Jorge Maciel (1), "this is a training session that while being acquisitive must also consider the fatigue arising from the previous session and the proximity of the next match. So, there should be a caution to avoid that the team experiences regimes of high fatigue. It justifies that on this day we experience small portions of our way of playing, Sub-Principles and Sub-Principles of the Sub-Principles, and aspects of low complexity relative to the strategical dimension. To accomplish these objectives, it is important to consider the more Micro levels of the team (Individual, Sectoral and Intersectoral).

On this day, the exercises will be manipulated so that there is high speed of displacement, being this a central concern with regards to the individual.

It is about creating exercises where muscular contractions with very high speed prevail, with increased tension at the beginning of the action — and not after — and with very short duration.

To do this, we will practice using exercises without much opposition that, other than allowing us that speed of contraction, will not require much tension, reducing their complexity as well. We will usually focus on the sectoral, intersectoral, intrasectoral and especially on the individual level. Therefore: dominance of medium spaces, not very small nor full pitch, few players and short duration. Also, with the intention of reducing complexity, without preventing acquisition, this should be a day in which we dominantly practice aspects that have already been internalised, that already belong to the subconscious. This is because, as I referred to the previous chapter, the conflict between the conscious and the subconscious generates high levels of tiredness. Bruce H. Lipton (1) even guarantees that "when the conscious mind is in conflict with a previously apprehended 'reality', stored in the subconscious mind, the intellectual conflict is expressed through the weakening of the corporal muscles".

Jorge Maciel also reflects on the topic, claiming that "the propensities on this day should lead to the occurrence of actions that dominantly involve the solicitation of 1/3 of the time used in which action destined to the so-called execution (effector dimension of the movement), avoiding a focus on the other 2/3 destined to decision-making and conscious apprehension (cognitive dimension of the movement). This is because these 2/3, or the quest for a 'knowing about knowing how' is most present on the previous days, so it is important that on this session we do not insist on overusing the structures that allow its expression, and which will be necessary involved during the upcoming competitive moment. It is important that it is expressed without fatigue so that within our way of playing creativity can emerge and be expressed".

If we do not follow this advice, we will have teams with low levels of mental preparedness during matches and much more. So, it is fundamental to seek the comprehension of this day of the Morphocycle without deviations, just like with the others. Training Actions and Inter-Actions of our way of playing that have already been internalised (embodied) and belong to the subconscious becomes necessary on this day.

In summary, it is a session in which there must be plenty of discontinuity, plenty of breaks between exercises that allow us to recover and practice at Maximum Relative Intensities without inducing fatigue and accelerating recovery, as well as focusing all the time on the metabolic web that supports our way of playing.

According to Jorge Maciel (1), "the dominant regime of contraction on this day is characterised by the presence of a high speed of contraction, short duration and non-maximal tension. On this day we want the exercises to present a high pro-

pensity to the occurrence of Actions and Inter-Actions that allow for a maximum contractile speed of muscular fibres, while simultaneously seeking a reduced density of eccentric contractions. To make this possible, the exercises are performed in small spaces, with few players involved and during equally short periods. Another important aspect to consider on this day, and in contrast with what must happen on Wednesday, is that the exercising contexts should not contain much 'noise'. There should be little contextual interference, little unpredictability, reason why the opposition should not be very significant".

The author adds that this should be a day of *"racing on a straight-line, without jumps, changes of direction, accelerations, braking...the exercises must be as 'clean' as possible, without disturbances, because that is what increases the tension of muscular contractions, preventing, therefore, the possibility of expression of initial maximum tensions and consequently, of maximum speeds of contraction, according to what we want for this day".*

Therefore, although we practice Sub-Principles and fundamentally Sub-Sub-Principles just like on Wednesday, the concerns will be considered differently.

For Carlos Carvalhal (1) on this day we practice *"actions of short duration, very quick actions that we can plan and usually plan on playing situations as well (the playing situations should not be dominant on this day) seeking, as I said, the acquisition of Principles or also the Strategical side".* He adds that *"the training normally continues to be intense, following a regime of speed. Even though there are two days left, the intensity is still high, although we don't allow it to last very long".*

Vitor Pereira (1) reveals that on this training day he focuses especially *"on speed, but normally with an attacking dynamic, also with a strategical component (...) these are exercises with lower complexity, without much opposition (...) and already considering recovery".*

On this day, Mara Vieira (1) also uses a 'non-mixed mixture', once again adapting to her circumstances because this is the only day she has a full-pitch available and must take advantage of it: "On a Friday I focus on the relationship between sectors but with higher resting time. I only have a full pitch available on this day, for them to experience the real dimensions. Also because of that, I use bigger spaces (...) I do such a mixture because of the spatial limitations. So, it is a Morphocycle that is adapted to my reality".

The Strategical Dimension during this training session must have low complexity due to all the reasons expressed.

3.1.2.7. The day of Recovery with Activation

It is the day before the match, so special attention must be paid to recovery, so we will only use very small scales of our way of playing. But at the same time, and also because it is the day before the match, there should be activation of the organism at the level of effort/performance-effort/recovery, and not only, that will be required on the following day.

This is a day for reviewing, from the Tactical-Strategical perspective, what has been practised during the other days of the Morphocycle and of the dynamic automatisms of the team. We perform exercises that do not require great complexity, that require maximum performance but in very short periods.

There should be a great number of breaks that make this a discontinuous session, so many think that this is a good day to recall set-pieces, which, in my opinion, should not only be practised on this day.

According to Jorge Maciel (1), *"the dominant regime of contraction to be experienced on this day should be characterised by high tension and speed, but little density and short duration. The exercises have a short duration and can vary on the number of players involved and on the size of the areas used, depending on the scale of Collective organisation (Individual, Sectoral, Intersectoral, Collective) on which the coach wants to focus during a given exercise".*

The author explains that on this day *"the exercises have a more informal character due to the lower acquisitive demand they possess, due to the need for recovery and to having to prepare the players for the competition without getting them fatigued. The contexts of exercitation on this day must present situations that contain a bit of everything the game contains, but on a smaller scale and with the minimum fatigue involved. These are exercises that recreate the game, having as a background a way of playing and the possibility that that way of playing is expressed on the following day. The central objective of this day is to act over the players on the sense of activating and leaving imprinted some of the dynamic automatisms of the team, reminding them of what we worked on throughout the week".*

For Carlos Carvalhal (1), the day before the match is used to perform a *"Tactical-Strategic session to review what we worked on during the week"* and to practice *"set-pieces: throw-ins, corners, free-kicks, penalty kicks…".*

On this day, during some exercises or in some part of the session we can practice in separate groups, with the starting XI on one side, and the others on the other. It is important to remember that although some players will not be part of the starting XI and go to the substitutes' bench, there may be some unexpected situations which can lead us to change our line-up.

3.1.3. The Morphocycle with friendly matches at the beginning of the season

The first concern is to create habituation to the Morphocycle, training in a way that resembles the competitive period (...) Now, it is not the same, having four training days, to play 45 or 90 minutes!

Vítor Frade (2)

You may have doubts now about the Morphocycles at the beginning of the season, due to the 'friendly matches' or non-official matches to be more precise. During this period there will be weeks in which we will have to play two matches. So, should we practice as if we were on an 'Exceptional Morphocycle'? Or should we use the Pattern Morphocycle as usual even though we have a mid-week match, facing this match 'as if' we were merely practising the Macro Principles and Sub-Principles?

We can face such week at our convenience but always following the Logic of Tactical Periodization, respecting the structure of the Pattern Morphocycle or instead of the Exceptional Morphocycle, depending on what we have decided. The key is to always consider the circumstances and the type of schedule we will have during the season.

For Guilherme Oliveira (1) *"many times these matches are part of the preparation. What we do is avoid playing 90 minutes because they are not prepared to play for 90 minutes. Instead, we play 45 with eleven players and other 45 with others. And then, the match becomes part of the preparation. We often choose the match as if it is the day of the Great Principles – Macro Principles".*

In my opinion, even if sometimes the context and the circumstances prevent it, at the beginning of the season the players should play for 45 minutes, or, if possible, for two halves of 25 minutes each. That may be even better. So, a group of eleven players plays the first half, the other group plays the second, and little by little we increase the playing minutes, gradually, as the friendly matches unfold.

And this is not only due to aspects connected with the physical – although also for that reason and very importantly – but also for the creation of new habits as we have discussed previously. Our players have not yet embodied the way of playing we want to perform, it is not yet part of their subconscious. So, from a certain moment, they would stop playing as we wish, resorting to their subconscious, to their old habits, with the match no longer having the desired acquisitive side present at all levels, and perhaps even promoting non-desirable acquisitions.

In the beginning, to make the player dispose of certain habits to acquire others, he must be very focused on the new ones, until being able to transfer them into the subconscious sphere. When a player must perform intentionalised Actions or Inter-Actions that are different from the ones he used to do, due to fatigue, he will no longer be focused. Instead, he will resort to the habits he has previously internalised, the old ones, which disturbs the creation of new habits. This is something coaches must consider and prevent at all cost.

Slowly, as the players acquire these new Game Principles, Sub-Principles and Sub-Sub-Principles, and these become part of the subconscious sphere, they will stop performing the old ones. They will no longer consume such high concentration quantities, which also require very high energetic expenditure, being able to focus more on details. Moreover, our team will become gradually more prepared from an effort/performance perspective to face an activity with a higher duration.

3.1.4. The Morphocycle with two training sub-units per day: no more 'working' time, more recovery time instead

(...) Many times, it is even advisable in certain circumstances, on a Wednesday for example (in a Morphocycle from Sunday to Sunday), if instead of one, but these are not two training units, it is one but divided, you have a bigger break let's put it that way. In conventional terms, you have two sets, a set that you perform in the morning, then the break, the food, and then the second set. And instead of 1h30 or 2 hours, because in the morning the session can sometimes last 2 hours due to the breaks, because it is necessary, especially earlier in the season, to give very long breaks, and then you do one hour and then another hour in the afternoon. You can, but that is why I told you a while ago, there were coaches that would say "See, we could do three training sessions and...", And I would reply "We can even do 5!". Maybe by doing 5, I treat them better than others doing just three, it depends on what I do in those 5!

There are those who train fatigued so that...because there it is, they think that training fatigued they will make better use of energy, improve lactic acid and tolerate lactic acid in circulation and more. I don't defend any of that, I defend precisely the opposite. What I really look for is a certain 'date' that then allows for a 'marriage', and an ever-lasting 'marriage' with all energetic sources, depending on the fundamental response type.

Vitor Frade (1)

Usually in Tactical Periodization, as we have already seen in the Pattern Morphocycle, there is a single training unit per day. However, due to the circumstances and the context, we might find ourselves having to perform two daily training sub-units. This means, one session divided in half.

Even so, as we will prove through the words of our interviewees, the Logic of these sub-units, which I repeat, is a single unit but divided, will have nothing to do with the conventional. The latter usually promotes higher 'work-load' or to perform two units with different 'physical' objectives. By performing two training sub-units in a day, our Logic seeks, or put differently, takes the opportunity to promote higher recovery time to be able to train always at Maximum Relative Intensities...focusing on the same structures. This is something that may occur at the beginning of the season (because the team needs more time of recovery between exercises to train at Maximum Relative Intensities but mostly due to the 'cappuccino' strategy) or in some special occasions when the competitive period has already started.

Either motivated by one or other reason, if we decide to have two training sub-units, it may be more beneficial to do it in some days of the Pattern Morphocycle than in others. These will be the days in which we want to emphasise the acquisition of Sub-Principles and <u>fundamentally Sub-Sub-Principles</u>, because of the higher intermittence, where the recovery times between exercises should be higher. And even more on the day in which these Sub-Principles and Sub-Sub-Principles have an increased tension of muscular contraction.

For Carlos Carvalhal (1), *"at the beginning of the season, we divide the work more"*. The interviewee explains that this is because *"we need more time to recover. Not because we want to work more but fundamentally because we need to recover more"*.

According to the author, during the season, exceptionally and not as a pattern, there can also be two training sub-units, especially on a Wednesday (the day of Sub-Principles and Sub-Sub-Principles with increased tension of muscular contraction), as it requires more recovery between exercises "On that day we feel the need to rest a bit more". Another possibility is Friday (the day of Sub-Principles and Sub-Sub-Principles with an increased speed of muscular contraction) where, for example, "we can do fractioned work, prioritising the strategical side or set-pieces during the afternoon).

Now, I repeat that performing two training sub-units does not mean having two training units. It is about having one session divided by two, training 45 to 60 minutes in the morning and other 45 to 60 minutes during the afternoon. The intention is always to allow or take advantage of the increased recovery to exercise at Maximum Relative Intensities, even if this is due to cultural, contextual, or circumstantial needs (the 'cappuccino' strategy).

Carlos Carvalhal (1) adds that in those days in which we have two training sub-units these should not be extended in time – *"these should be the shortest sessions of the week"*.

Vitor Pereira (1) adds that *"at the beginning, to avoid having 90 consecutive minutes of training, we do 45 in the morning and 45 in the afternoon. Why? So that they can recover and to maintain the behaviours – intentionalised Actions and Inter-Actions – from one session to the next (...)"*.

Like this, a Pattern Morphocycle with two training sub-units could look like the following graph:

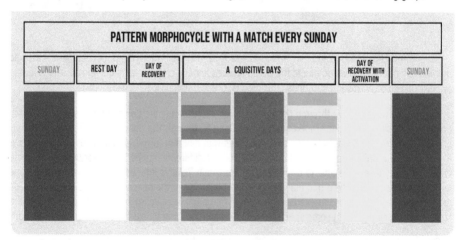

This is an example of a Pattern Morphocycle with two training sub-units on the days of the Game Sub-Principles and Sub-Sub-Principles, Wednesday and Friday. Although this unit is divided into two sub-units, we continue to prioritise intentionalised Actions and Inter-Actions at the individual, sectoral, and intersectoral levels, with an increased tension of muscular contraction in one case and an increased speed of muscular contraction in another. The sub-dynamics of the effort/performance will be the same in both training sub-units.

Here we have an example provided by Guilherme Oliveira (1) that may improve our understanding: *"let's imagine the following – beginning of the season, sometimes this happens with a certain regularity, we go for eight days to a certain place, and I have a pitch available whenever I want. I could easily train twice a day, but I wouldn't do two training sessions, <u>it would</u> be one session divided by two. Because if I train 1h30 in the morning and 1h30 in the afternoon, it is brutal, it is violent, three hours of training is too much. But if I divide the session I usually do, which has 90 minutes, in one hour plus one hour, or 45 minutes plus 45 minutes, or one hour plus 45 minutes...if you divide the session, what does this allow you? IT allows for a much higher recovery, which means training always at relatively maximum intensities. What happens at the beginning of the season is that players take longer to re-cover, some have physical deficits that are completely normal because they were inactive. And half-way through the season in one situation, I can do four times ten minutes, the same situation with the same intensity...I can only do it three times six minutes at the beginning of the season (...) I always do the same sub-dynamics, but I achieve superior intensities because they have more recovery time. Now, during the season I never train more than once a day"*.

In my opinion, what leads us to organise two training sub-units per day, in Tactical Periodization, normally has to do with the culture, the development, with what the players and those who surround them have in their minds and in their bodies, what they believe is essential to being well. Not because we think it is better. We move to the 'cappuccino' strategy, we take advantage of this situation to in-crease recovery. However, if we practice in the afternoon, we must alert that there will be fewer hours of recovery until the training session the next morning, something that we will need to consider when doing our planning.

According to Vítor Frade (2), *"I can train twice a day. Now, I need to know that training twice, because there are people who train twice and saying that it is important for the player to be tired so that he is working with lactic acid in his blood, but that is another logic...Within the Logic of Tactical Periodization, it doesn't work like that! You go to <u>a club,</u> and that club has <u>the habit</u> of going eight days to a certain place. It makes a lot of sense, even if you don't need to train twice a day, that you do so to keep the players busy, <u>because</u> when people lose their routines they <u>don't even remember what they have to do</u>, and they usually end up doing foolish things, what they do is harmful. So, you can fulfil the schedule like that. <u>You can even have five sessions per day, and that can be better than having just one in the Logic of Tactical Periodization.</u> You have <u>one training unit,</u> and you <u>divide it in two</u>, what is the problem? Now, if you trained two hours in the morning, and then want to train another two hours in the afternoon, that cannot happen. If you have the chance, it even makes more sense to train less time in the morning so that the players are effectively fresh to train in the afternoon. That is why I say that training is <u>a tailor-made suit"</u>.

3.2. Goalkeeper training: A very special Sub-Specificity within the Specificity of playing

We shouldn't need to write a section devoted to goalkeeper training if we have understood the Logic of Tactical Periodization. However, I imagine that many of you will be questioning if the training of goalkeepers also abides by a logic that is different from the conventional. It is obvious that the goalkeeper training in Tactical Periodization is also integrated with the Logic that I have mentioned along this chapter and throughout the whole book. Its exercises must always be specific to his playing within the Specificity of the way of playing we want to promote. Many times, he will practice individually, others intersectoral, and in other occasions, he will be with the whole group. As we see, its Specificity results from the Logic of the Process.

Goalkeepers, just like the other players, must understand the game and internalise it. They must experience it so that it becomes a part of their subconscious. According to Jose Tavares (1), *"our players have to know the game, our goalkeeper has to know the game"*.

Carlos Carvalhal (1) adds that the preparation of the goalkeeper *"depends very much on the training unit, on what we will prioritise. Many times, they are a little apart, many times they don't have a lot of time to warm-up and enter already with the team, we try to unite them as much as possible"*.

Obviously, goalkeeper training, like the training of the rest of the team, will also be promoted at times by the Strategic Dimension, depending on the characteristics of the opponent, without leading to changes in the way of playing, in its Matrix.

The goalkeeper training respects the Horizontal Alternation in specificity of the efforts/performances (and of everything else as well) because it follows the same Logic as the rest of the group. So, in a Morphocycle with a single weekly match, the goalkeeper that played should recover on the first training day. The other goalkeepers will do a session with similar characteristics to the match in which they did not participate. Then, the next day, they will practice Sub-Principles and Sub-Sub-Principles with increased tension of muscular contraction. The next day the Macro-Principles and the Sub-Principles, and so on.

As we can notice, in Tactical Periodization the training of goalkeepers follows the Logic, being contextualised at all moments with regards to the way of playing we seek, and in accordance to the Methodological Principles that work as its foundations.

It is possible that there will be times in which the goalkeepers train separately. When the day requires a more micro-level, they will have fundamentally individual exercises, even if not only. Other days they will practice collectively, on a macro-level...So, the Logic is the same, training a way of playing within a way of playing, bringing the individualisation to its maximum, contextualised with regards to an objective Collective Organisation.

"

Since many years I have been saying that any kind of test is only convenient and necessary for those who don't need them! Tests are like bikinis, they show many things but hide the essential.

I have never used heart-rate monitors, in 28 consecutive years on the field, I have never used a stop-clock. And I have always been well paid, 'won' leagues, I was in Champions League, 'won' cups! So...!

FC Porto should hold a Guinness record, because in FC Porto, with Bobby Robson as a manager, we played 72 matches in one season (official and non-official), 55 consecutive matches without being defeated, Robson 'culturally' did not like to do substitutions , so we used 13 players, won the league, were kicked out of the Champions League in the semi-finals, by Barcelona, won the Super Cup and the Portuguese Cup, using just 13 players, practising once a day. So how? We had no injuries because otherwise, we could not have used only 13 players, and Robson's way of playing, everyone knew it as high-pace or whatever.

Look at how stupid this is, people, saying that Mourinho's team is defensive! So, the guy wins leagues, has the team that scores the most and the team the concedes the least! How can it be defensive? And they win! People do not know what means being an attacking team. Attacking means scoring systematically and not necessarily scoring seven goals. Portugal beat Korea by 7 goals and was kicked out. They did not score on the other matches.

Transition and that is another confusion, have you seen what people say transition is? It is when...already in attacking already, if you are fast or not, no, no, that is a way of attacking. The transition is passing from one moment to the other, so I say the moment is one thing and the instant is another. So, what helps me deal with those in-

stants to take better advantage of the moments is the understanding of the game and the ability to anticipate, that is psychological! The transition is that. It's switching from a mental configuration to another and if maximally qualitative, it is collective, that's what it is, and depending on this or that it is performed faster or slower.

The reality does not end with language, in the terminology that we use.

3.3. The Recovery: such an important topic in Tactical Periodization that requires yet another reflective moment

Recovery does not occur in one single day. A few moments ago, I told you that after a game with maximal demand we know that you need 4 days to be ready to face an identical situation, so it's a space of 4 days at least. Even in those days in which I am training before a match, how do I consider recovery? Even on a Wednesday, maybe, that is why I have so many breaks! But it is essential that the recovery is achieved by not going there, not training, because if it is a recovery, getting out of the environment works as a mental recovery, it is very important and very necessary, indispensable! But then when I go back to training, still needing to recover, I can recover in many ways, even dancing I can recover! I can, yes, I can, why not? I have there 10 guys that played, doing some light movements, but making sure that at least that will alert them for the strategic aspects relative to the opponent we will play next, or to our own team, is that a waste of time? But that is not how the recovery, especially the biochemical, will work! Because the 'specific' biochemistry needs to be activated, and especially if I am feeling slow, I don't activate it! The activated is, in fact...I can only guarantee it if I am doing an 'objective' 3v3, only like that I can know that the three, in the minute they are there, are back and forth, there's a shot and it stops! Am I making myself clear? So, they can spend three days recovering, doing 'nothing'. But maybe they can go there 'doing nothing either', doing something else that can benefit recovery even further! How? Through the solicitation of the same bioenergetic things, but within a very short timeframe. I don't know if I am making myself clear?! Diversifying the organisational scales of our way of playing throughout the week. Because I need the same singular bioenergetic support, which is what supports my performance. And only through what? Through an action that represents a fractal of that, and it is only a fractal if it is in fact a tiny fraction, with a very short duration. If you are standing for one hour, you will feel tired, because those depth muscles, the posture muscles, will be activated. Even those guys that used to do continuous running stopped doing it and took up the bicycle, for example, and that's not too bad, it's better than continuous running. Because if you want to activate the circulation, that can do it and it won't put too much pressure on the body. Now, with that strength training shit, those guys with big chests, they will be running around for 90 minutes 'carrying' 90kg on their backs! That is why you don't see any marathon runner with the body type of a sprinter, and these guys want to play for 90 minutes with bodies that are increasingly looking like those of sprinters.

(...) The importance of Tactical Periodization relates to its ability to install a logic of adaptation. And in recovery, I must act on what is responsible for the same logic of adaptation! But if you are fatigued, I will not overload you. I will wake you up! That is what guarantees the maintenance, and because when I do that (the 3v3), in order to protect rest, I will only need to repeat it a little later, if I do it 5 or 6 times, I will have fulfilled 1 hour or 45 minutes, and I was doing something very easy for 4 or 5 times, and it promotes the two sides of the coin: Adaptability and Recovery.

You can do those 3v3 in a fun way, you just need to say "whoever loses has to pay a juice to the others, or piggyback them, or will have to get all the balls…" it must always have that fun side, involving emotions. (…)

That is why I recommend a maximum of 3v3, in a small-sided space, so that during the minute or 1m30 that they spend there provides them with the possibility of having acquired the same pattern of demand of the match! (…)

Now, when you have a match on Saturday and another on Wednesday, everything is very tight. You have 4 days to rest, but you will want to do something, then you will do something following the logic of recovery that can simultaneously rest and revive! So, it needs to be just a little! But if you do this straight after the match, maybe it's a mistake.

And then recovery is also about that. If I am tired due to a mixture of the relationship between 3 or 4 energetic sources, or the one that we want, then I act on one, and I recover everything?! Don't play with me, I am not that stupid. I need to recover, but not only one of them.

Vitor Frade (1)

In Tactical Periodization, Recovery does not occur exclusively during the so-called day of Rest and day of Recovery, as we can notice by reading the words of Professor Vítor Frade, and as we referred earlier. All this shows how important Recovery is for Tactical Periodization. A Recovery that is not exclusively physical, but that happens at all levels. A Recovery that should develop, understanding the 'rule' of the four days, from Sunday to Wednesday and from Thursday to Sunday when in a Pattern Morphocycle with a match every Sunday. The concern is that our players can approach the next match with great freshness and fluidity at all levels.

Even if we consider that four days should be enough to recover the team, achieving it successfully or not will depend on what we do in training. We have already explained that during the Morphocycle, although same days are acquisitive, they should not disturb the recovery.

Jorge Maciel (1) refers to this when he guarantees that being able to recover a team in four days is something that *"highly depends on what is done during those four days. It depends on the quality of the process and how the horizontal alternation is performed. Unfortunately, the way as recovery is usually planned and operationalised has nothing to do with what Tactical Periodization proposes. Most coaches, to recover their players, submit them to abstract efforts, with a pattern of demand that is completely different from the one they find in the competition. They have a single objective, the so-called physical recovery, ignoring, therefore, the global tiredness (Tactical Fatigue) of the players. Almost every coach considers the recovery to be fundamental in football, with an increasing discussion regarding this problem. However, although some recognise the 'physical' and 'mental-emotional' fatigue that results from the expression of a way of playing, not rarely is what coaches say very different from what they do".*

So, despite the majority of coaches recognising the need for four days of recovery between matches with great demand, they only use two days to recover, the rest day and the day of 'active recovery', doing it inclusively in the opposite order. As their concern is exclusively physical, what they do is practice on the day after the match and then rest on the following day, with the intention of practising with 'heavy loads' on Wednesday...So, although they claim that four days are needed to recover, on the third day they are already not respecting that recovery. Then they design sessions with a predominant 'physical' component, including double sessions. Many discuss the need for emotional-mental recovery, but only a few really calibrate the emotional-mental expenditure during training sessions.

Moreover, the day of Recovery within the Logic of Tactical Periodization has nothing to do with the conventional understanding – as I have mentioned before, ours is a transgressive conceptualisation. We consider that this day consists on the activation of that biochemical and bio-energetic mixture that we use during the match (and also of the emergence regarding the dominance of a type of muscular fibres – the fastest and not others) and that, furthermore, will be Specific to our way of playing. Therefore, it is about awakening that bio-energetic web, that 'Specific' biochemistry and stop, reawaken it, and stop again...This activation should have a short duration, followed by large periods of rest, where the aerobic metabolism will act dominantly, without disconnecting from the others, just like during the match.

And how can we awake this web? Through the 'acquisition'-in-movement of the same pattern of demand of the match, through a fractal of our way of playing.

For Jorge Maciel (1) in the so-called day of recovery, *"the dynamic of the exercises should be very similar to what we observe during competition. Therefore, the performance of the exercises during this session should be characterised by high Intensities, like those of the competition. This is a transgressive aspect in comparison to what is conventionally recommended, and with the way, recovery is traditionally conceptualised in football. In Tactical Periodization, recovering means focusing on the same matrix that is implicated when we compete. Only in such a way can we act on and activate, to consequently recover, the same structures that were involved in the competition. Now, to make this happen conveniently, it is important to manage the necessary dynamic appropriately between the exercising and recovery times. On this day, the dosage and fractioning of the exercising and recovering times are fundamental aspects. In this training unit, the exercises should be executed at high intensity, but should have short duration, with substantially larger rest periods, which we can use to tighten 'nuts and bolts', and over which the aerobic metabolism will act significantly, with the objective of reducing the metabolisms produced during the match (and in the meanwhile 'stored'). These were 'liberated' by the required stimulation, on this day, in those exercising periods of high intensity"*.

According to the conventional logic, present not only in those traditional methodologies but also in the so-called 'systemic', recovery means performing continuous running, or more recently, riding the bicycle, or even through exercising tactical aspects but with low intensity, requesting therefore the dominance of the aerobic metabolism and the dominance of the slowest muscular fibres...at all levels!

As Jorge Maciel (1) says, *"conventionally, recovery is not understood like this because there is an assumption that the different metabolic pathways operate separate and concurrently. That is a mistake, there is plenty of evidence that they (although depending on the type of effort promoting different dominances) act interconnected and influence each other. Only having this in mind is it possible to recognise that a session with a higher intensity that focuses immediately on the anaerobic metabolisms can have non-immediate and more significant implications at the aerobic level when compared to a typical aerobic recovery training"*.

To achieve the Recovery that we have been discussing, relative to our Logic, the ideal exercise is 3v3 games in a very small space, leading to the emergence, as Professor Vítor Frade says, *"of the same*

pattern of demand of the match!" However, it is very important that the training unfolds in an enthusiastic environment so that we can get our players to involve emotionally with it. To do that, there is nothing better than the competition, something that I have emphasised earlier, but that is very important to remind.

Guilherme Oliveira (1) talks about the type of Recovery that we have been discussing and tells us that his team, in day of Recovery, perform *"very quick exercises in very short moments, and then we rest for long periods; very fast things with plenty of resting time, just to activate some structures that were demanded, but without tiring them out".*

If we can understand how the organism works as a whole and the need for Specificity to promote adaptation, and — excuse me for the redundancy — for its better functioning in the context in which it develops, many other 'needs' linked to the conventional logic will no longer make sense. They will no longer be necessary. As an example, Jorge Maciel (1) points out something promoted by the conventional logic that he believes does not make sense: *"there is something usually done during the festive season when there is a great distance between two competitive moments. When this happens, the time is used for recovery, but how? 'Recharging batteries'. This means, submitting the players to continuous, low-intensity efforts, requesting the aerobic metabolism dominantly. It is the so-called period of oxygenation.*

Another example that this traditional perspective of training looks at the energetic sources erroneously, in isolation, sequential or by stages, disconnected. The dominant request of the aerobic metabolism, in a conventional way, means performing low-intensity activities, during prolonged periods and having associated a great amount of mobilised muscle mass. This movement pattern contrasts with what happens during the competition, where there is a demand for different intensities, and there is also great variability. However, verifying this 'recharging batteries' during a significant time-frame, what ends up happening is the habituation of the organism to that pattern of functionality, which due to being contrary to the one we want to express during the competition, becomes a 'parasite'. It prevents the team from expressing its identity with the desired fluidity. The players feel 'sleepy' as if they were under 'anaesthesia', they want to, but they cannot. And all this without even mentioning the damage of collective articulation that results from the team not having trained its Collective Organisation".

So, we create an adaptation of the organism, and with this, we end up losing Specific functionality and adaptability to our way of playing, decontextualised from its surroundings.

Moreover, the interviewee adds that *"the effort pattern involved in continuous running, dominant activity when we want to 'recharge batteries', has a great demand, due to the gesture repetition and due to the successive impact over the different structures that are responsible for the movement. This leads the muscle-skeletal structures to a 'repetition stress' that in turn is conducive to the saturation of those intelligent mechanisms that are responsible for the movement. The increased muscular fatigue leads to a loss of motor refinement and influences negatively the expression of proprioception and kinaesthesia, installing consequently higher joint vulnerability and a higher propensity for injuries".*

Does this only happen with continuous running when 'recharging batteries'? Doesn't it also happen during the 'pre-season'? And when recovering injured players?

Within this understanding of Recovery promoted by Tactical Periodization and amplified in this chapter, we must give emphasis to the so-called tightening of 'nuts and bolts', that we discuss in detail in another chapter of this book.

Professor Frade (2) provides yet another reflection on recovery: *"I dare to say, even if it may seem paradoxical, that at this TOP level, recovery is more important than training. We can say that training is as important as recovering, even if many people say that and then training a lot and do no recovery. But recovery is much more important than training because when you play at the TOP level, you have to play with a certain dynamism, with a certain ability to focus and in different areas. I say that it is important to be fresh, and I am only fresh if I am recovered, but if I haven't recovered I may even want to be fresh, but in fact, I haven't done it properly. That is why I say that recovery is the most important".*

According to Mourinho[44] (4), "the competitions are won with groups, not with eleven players. But a football player, with the science and the recovery methods, can play 50 matches per season if he trains and lives well from a social point of view".

Which recovery methods is Mourinho talking about? Is his understanding of recovery not the conventional one? Why do his teams seem fresher than the others by the end of the season? Couldn't this Logic of holding on well during the matches being fresh allow for a better coping in the long-term than holding on well during the matches being fatigued?

---

44 Jose Mourinho (4): Interview published on the daily newspaper AS, 10th November 2010.

> The abyssal zone of Tactical Periodization

After conducting all the interviewees, inclusively the one with Professor Frade: recording them face-to-face with the interviewees, transcribing to the computer, translating them into Spanish, analysing and detangled them for an appropriate use; I started connecting some words with others with the intention of making sense of them, I started adding the comments of the interviewees...definitely, I started bringing a new book to life.

That was when we felt (myself and Vítor Frade) the need to add one more question to his interview. He not only agreed but in facto 'obliged' me to meet him again face-to-face. Through his answers after the first interviewee, the analysis of the other interviews I performed an observation of training sessions of various teams (Portuguese Premier League) that we identify a lack of knowledge from a great number of people — even those linked to Tactical Periodization — about a crucial aspect of the Logic. The exercising times were often too large, and the recovery times between exercises normally too short, something that went against the Logic.

Vítor Frade's answer to the question "Professor, today many people are trying to train using Tactical Periodization, there are some people more identified with it than others, but in your opinion, which are the most common mistakes in the operationalisation of Tactical Periodization?", led me to understand even further this widespread lack of knowledge.

That is why I decided to call this chapter 'The abyssal zone of Tactical Periodization'. The abyssal zone or abyssopelagic zone is that zone of the ocean that goes from a depth of 3,000m down to around 6,000m. It is below the bathypelagic zone and above the hadal zone. It is characterised by extremely high pressure and total absence of light, among other things. It is said that the human being has explored more the outer space than the deep ocean, reason why this zone is mostly unknown to us.

This chapter is the integral translation of Professor Frade's answer, accompanied by footnotes and some clarifications that will try to help you understand it.

I don't know if the mistakes that we identify are not all caused by a single mistake: the understanding...

VF: It may look like I am going to give you an empty answer, but it is the understanding of what Tactical Periodization is. Because sometimes, due to the level of demands, to the existing reality, there may seem to exist an affinity with Tactical Periodization, but once the situation is more compatible or more corresponding with maximal demand, then a certain incoherence emerges. Because either you understand the way it started, and that implies that you study, that you identify yourself, but deeply, with what exists, with what is conventional. Or if that does not happen, then we are also possessed by much of that conventional, when we try to operationalise the process, or even when we try to identify it. So, there needs to be...because that...and sometimes it's even worse...! It is about what is essential regarding the conventional, but because there is a lower level of understanding or because it implies too much work and there is no capacity to identify that, that side is a very important gap, especially the metabolic processes, what we call bioenergetics[45].

---

45 Bioenergetics: one of Physiology's main themes, especially dedicated to the study of the various chemical processes that make cellular life possible from an energetic point of view. It seeks, among many other things, to explain the main chemical processes that occur in the cell and to analyse its physiological implications, mainly with regards to the way how those processes are framed in the global concept of homeostasis. The understand of what 'energy' means and how the organism can acquire, convert, store and use it, is key for understanding the organic functioning in both performance sports and recreational and leisure activities. The study of bioenergetics allows for the understanding of how the capacity to

So, I said that, in the first place, we need to understand the phenomenon as something complex and if it is complex we need to act upon it, reflecting upon it, acting upon it without never forgetting that complexity, it needs to be complex in a higher or lower degree. When I planned to do a PhD that was already the topic of my research, the problem of causality[46]. And many times, the lack of understanding of these things, and the rush to think they are experts in the area, leads them to...now, because this is the context, one that does not have maximum demand, it is not so obvious, and it is so that people's conceptualisation of learning is one of reception, instead of one of discovery. So, because this is not a framework of maximum demand, the problem of tiredness, for example, cannot be put the same way. Also, the problem of continuity of the same adaptability record cannot be set the same way, etc., etc., etc.... So, you need to face this reality, recognising it as non-linear, and all thought should have that foundation, non-linear.

And I see very often vertigo, for people that seem to be more or less identified, certain vertigo in building a catalogue of reality, and that has nothing to do with non-linear causality. On the contrary, it is a certain type of vertigo with linear causality. To answer your question, I used to think, until a short time ago, that a certain inability to deal with Tactical Periodization within the limits of possible was the result of – even though I continue to think that it is essential – the non-familiarisation of people with High Performance[47]. Because there is a very unique constraint there, where you either can deal with it, or you don't and end up drifting, right? It is indispensable to "play" on the borders of things. Those conditions, or those circumstances, if they don't exist, the degree of possibilities ends up changing, and it may look like we are better or worse and not as we really area. But as I was saying, until some time ago, I thought it was the result of that. I still do, and that's why I imagine that without the possibility of being at that level, it would be challenging for people, in what is related to dosing, which is an essential aspect, to detect and be conscious of the extreme sensitivity of these things to make it work. So, there are some key aspects, that may not be so easily understandable, but I have realised that in cases like Marisa, for example, who is not work-

---

perform work (exercise) depends on the successive conversion of one in other energetic elements.

46 Causality: the relationship between a certain event, usually designated as cause, and a second event designated as effect. In a linear conceptualisation, the latter is a consequence of the former. We can distinguish two types of causality: linear and non-linear. Gleick (1998, pp.23-24) clarifies that "linear relationships can be captured with a straight line on a graph. (...) Linear equations are solvable, which makes them suitable for textbooks. Linear systems have an important modular virtue: you can take them apart and put them together again – the pieces add up. Nonlinear systems generally cannot be solved and cannot be added together. (...) Nonlinearity means that the act of playing the game has a way of changing the rules. (...) That twisted changeability makes nonlinearity hard to calculate, but it also creates rich kinds of behaviour that never occur in linear systems". We can say that causality of determination of a phenomenon is the specific way in which events are related and emerge and that is why learning or trying to decode the general characteristics of causality of a phenomenon means understanding the relationships that are established and the amplification that may result from those relationships. This is what allows for an understanding of the global intelligibility of a system, even if, in the case of non-linear causality, as is the case of football, such intelligibility should stay away from the 'vertigo' of categorisation, because its details are not decodable. That is why Professor Vitor Frade claims that "there is no equation for the detail".

47 High Performance: the highest level of performance one can achieve. This is the performance level where the top teams and top football players operate. A high level of demand, high level of aspiration and high competitive density are its main characteristics.

ing at a top level, or recently Jorge, who understand it without needing this guarantee.

So, I go back to my initial question, to my initial answer, which is, in fact, the non-understanding of what is – or aimed to be – Tactical Periodization. This is situated in two levels, right? The first, the conceptual level, therefore theoretical and then, because of many insufficiencies at that level, the methodological level[48]. To be more objective, I could say that with a higher or lower degree of confusion, with a higher or lower level of understanding, I think we can say that in the end, the mistakes result from the lack of understanding of the Morphocycle. Because you either understand why the Morphocycle was created and what it aims to be, or you don't, even partially mistakes can always happen. So, we have in first place to agree, understand, feel, and because of that I sometimes imagine 'but if people are not at the top level, they cannot feel that". But that's not true, it is possible to feel it without having been there because people have a head to think. And if you ask a question to a hundred guys who have been at the top level, and are at <u>the top</u> level as coaches, independently of their answer being impossible to justify, if it proves within the current framework of science, it is <u>empirical evidence</u>. So, all of them, or 90 something percent of them, will say that after a maximum demand effort, a match with maximum demand, that team who had to perform that effort, will only be ready again to perform at the same level, without boiling, without seeing its usual functional flow disturbed, four days after. <u>So, this is the key, this is the key for everything else.</u> Either people recognise the validity of this claim, or they will not fully understand the essence of the Morphocycle, and consequently, the essence of Tactical Periodization. So, if this is true, if this is true, imagining that the <u>competitive framework</u> has, as a <u>pattern,</u> one match every week, that is why I say, Morphocycle as a Morphocycle is that period or that cycle that is identifiable by the presence of two matches separated by one week. All other conditions are exceptional, and that exceptionality can be more or less regular, but if they become a rule, we then need to change some fundamental things.

So, the Morphocycle is definable by the presence of one match on a Sunday and another on the other Sunday, for example. So, if I know, and I am convinced that, and I have no doubts that only after four days I will be able to perform an effort like that, then just after four days I will be able to demand a level of effort that requires maximum availability regarding the team's effort. So, there is very little time left to train, even if I say that a maximum demand in a match is different from a maximum demand in training, but even like that certainly I won't say that I need less than three days...if it is absolutely indispensable an effort of maximum demand. Because without tiredness there is no training, without fatigue there is no training, without fatigue, there is no

---

48 Conceptual and Methodological levels: these two levels are the great pillars, or matrixes, around which the whole process should develop, and they necessarily require a convenient Articulation of Meaning, so that what emerges from the process makes indeed sense, the sense we want to give to the Process. The Conceptual level also demands, at its internal level, an Articulation of Meaning so that the fluidity can be coherent and the way of playing represents a truly unbreakable wholeness. That is the level related to the Game Idea and includes the Game Principles that construct it in its different scales (Great – Macro; Sub – Meso; Sub-Sub – Micro). The Methodological level is what allows for the operationalisation of the Conceptual level, is what brings it to life, it is composed by Tactical Periodization's Methodological Principles. It also requires an Articulation of Meaning, since the process dynamic implies the dynamic interaction between the different Methodological Principles.

improvement, and with fatigue, there is an absolute need for recovery so that you can be ready, and with a certain time to allow for that to happen[49].

So, as I mentioned, having as a reference a Morphocycle of this kind, everything is played in this Morphocycle, so only half-way through it, I am able to perform an effort of the same type, half-way which is on a Thursday. Then I still have Friday, Saturday, and Sunday, only three days. Therefore, I say that if on Thursday we have the training of maximum demand, even if it is mandatory to have a maximum demand, it will be below, it will be below maximum demand in comparison to a match, also because there are only three days left for the next match. So, I know that this effort of maximum demand of my team, when in play, is characterised by a dynamic of the team that expresses a functionality. *But to make it happen, it is supported by certain bio-energetic adaptability, so only after four days, I can be sure that this bio-energetic support is ready to be activated again. Even if this is training and not a match, the conditions that need to be promoted will be analogous to those that as a team, the team reveals to work. Therefore, it's this logic that allows for continuity, and that is why I say that <u>systematic repetition </u>is the weekly expression of the respective Morphocycle[50]. But then, this type of work, let's put it this way, of trainability, focuses principally on the whole, but the whole is guaranteed as a whole if the elements that are part of it as a whole do not lose maximum possibilities of expression in the whole, when the expression of the whole is required! But because training, thought this way, is concerned with the whole, the probability of not everyone being stimulated in the same way is a reality.*

So, how can I prevent that?! That is why I operationalise the Morphocycle bearing in mind that "if he played here, he needs four days to rest, he will train there". This time that separates both matches should be a time of recovery. How can I, while protecting recovery, ensure that the individuals, as players, are not losing possibilities? I should ensure that I provide them with stimulation that leads them to evolve even under these conditions, do I make

---

49 Fatigue is also a need for Tactical Periodization, it is even one of its central aspects. It appears to be indeed one of the very few common points this methodology has with the others. However, this is just an illusion because there are highly significant differences, especially in what represents the stimulus that ignites performance, a qualitative and not quantitative stimulus, and not less relevant in the recognition of the need to recover from those constant performances and consequent states of fatigue, what does not happen with conventional methodologies, where the logic favours a quantitative emphasis and its objective is to perpetuate fatigue with the objective of allowing the organism a higher capacity of response under conditions of continuous and accentuated fatigue. On the contrary, in Tactical Periodization, inducing fatigue has to do with the possibility of aspiring to states of structural, functional and organisational re-organisation successively higher (even if not linearly), which are only possible if the recovery from those efforts is completed. The adaptability that emerges from there arises from a process that represents some kind of biological resilience and does not aim for a higher response capacity in a situation of heightened fatigue, but instead a higher quality of performance through a better management of fatigue, safeguarding its perpetuation.

50 Weekly expression of the Morphocycle and systematic repetition: that is the reason why the Pattern Morphocycle is the nucleus, the core of the process, a methodological matrix that assumes itself as an invariance through its continuous repetition throughout time, in terms of logic, and not necessarily in terms of content. It is this methodological regularity that allows for stabilisation without crystallisation – hopefully - of the team's way of playing.

libro
futbol
.com
AL GOL SE
LLEGA LEYENDO

109

myself clear or not? So, because the whole is made of parts, I need to ensure, or guarantee, that also the parts do not regress, and only working on the parts I can be sure of that[51]. So, imagining that the <u>bio-energetic algorithm[52]</u> may be, and so the colours...the symbolism of the colours, can be considered as having the need present, due to the specificity of the performance, of the eccentric contractions and also the need of muscular groups or muscular chains that are more involved, directly involved, required for the collective functionality, expressing themselves at the maximum speed of contraction. I thought that working on each of these aspects in those days that, if using a formal framework, would belong to the recovery period...by doing that without losing that recovery...working individually could contribute to the improvement and guarantee the individual development of the players.

So, this is <u>a logic that must be respected without interruption,</u> and that requires awarding significant importance not only to the duration of exercises as you mentioned earlier but also, and essentially, to the resting times between each exercise. And at this level of the Morphocycle, there can be many incoherencies, the dosing is something that I notice is often overlooked. Here it is, why? Because they are too influenced by the conventional, notice, you only need to practice once a week! In the eye of the conventional that is almost a crime, almost a crime. But when you are facing a framework of maximum demand, these conditions pose by themselves a need for this kind of attention and care. When it does not happen, of course, if you have sensitivity and intelligence you will have to admit "but, then..."...and that is why that it makes a lot of sense to highlight the importance of periods that emerge with two matches a week (with one match in the middle of the week), but even further, to highlight that the possibility of being in good conditions (without training) when that happens is something viable! Even if you have no control over the midweek match, so that is out of your control. But that does not happen when you have a normal Morphocycle. So, the biggest, let's say, confusion, lies here, and then it has to do with many other things, the lack of knowledge of the reality, also in what refers to...

---

51 Hologrammatic principle: one of the foundational principles of complex thinking, allowing us to understand what Professor Frade refers to when he discusses the issue of reciprocal implications between the parts and the whole. Morin (2003, pp.108-109) clarifies that "in a physical hologram, the smallest point of the hologram's image contains the almost entirety of the information of the represented object. It is not only the part that is in the whole, the whole is also in the part. The hologrammatic principle is present in the biologic and sociologic worlds. The idea of hologram overcomes, not only the reductionism, which only considers the parts, but also the holism, which only sees the whole". He adds that "then, one can increase the knowledge of the parts through the whole, and of the whole through the parts, in the same movement, producer of knowledge". What seems especially relevant for football, if we consider that, as Morin suggests, "the anthropo-social relationship is complex, because the whole is in the part, which is in the whole". It should be highlighted that from the relationship of the whole with the parts but result different states of complexity of the whole. The whole may be less than the sum of the parts, equal to the sum of the parts, or more than the sum of the parts. But only the organised whole can be more than the sum of the parts.

52 Algorithm: a number of rules and 'step-by-step' for mathematical procedures or to reach a conclusion (Stacey, 1995). It is therefore a finite sequence of instructions, clearly defined and non-ambiguous, that abide to logic commands overseen by an objective. It is important to highlight that although the concept of algorithm is commonly illustrated by the example of a recipe, there are algorithms whose essence and operationalisation is much more complex due to the dynamic of the process that they try to respond to, and by the consequent, constant need of 'revision and refuelling', even if paradoxically it has to be a processual regularity. Just like it happens with the Pattern Morphocycle.

For example, I gave away a few days ago, in a meeting I had with other coaches, a short text that must be around 40 years old. A key text for my colleague and friend Monge da Silva, who was the first person in Portugal to lecture things systematically in relation to Sport Training, that has to do with the understanding of two principles. <u>The principle of self-renovation of living matter and the principle or Law of Roux, Arndt-Schulz[53]</u>. And it strikes me that people who have a contemporary connection with faculties do not know any of that. The interpretation of the text, as it is, can be mutilating, but if you look at it through what we know from systems theory nowadays, you can understand how important that text is, and how it is a guarantee of what I told you earlier.

So, a little ago I was saying that facing the <u>need for some resting time </u>so that the team is again ready to develop the same dynamics, the same func-tionality and all that, it implied considering that the Morphocycle would be filled with effort, game performance, recovery, training on Thursday, recovery, match on Sunday. And having said that a formal framework would lead us to recognise the possibility of the existence of a single training session, even in what refers to training, without losing the profile or the adaptability matrix, and therefore, the specificity. This specificity, considering the way how we want to play, so the identity of our team even if still on a Thursday we can contemplate it, through repetitions with some intermittence, in the continuity that is independent of the central aspects, with the Principles or primary game criteria of the team being respected.

And I said that if something like this is presenting to most people, this sounds like sacrilege, how can you only train once a week?

But it is essential that regarding operationalisation that is recognised! So how can the Morphocycle emerge then with three acquisitive days, so it's not only one, it's three, and two days of recovery, and the Saturday also for recov-ery[54]? And this here is about solving an apparent paradox, like I had already mentioned to you, in what should still be a recovery period, to which extend, without losing that recovery, can I consider an acquisitive training, that can be acquisitive without at the same time compromising recovery? There are only two ways to do this. Knowing it is an essential aspect of the way of playing which we are interested in we have the guarantee that will affect an individ-ual, the individual more precisely. And we also have the possibility that that potential individual growth supported by an indicator, which are the eccentric contractions for example, but having in mind some aspects of how we want to play. These will happen with the use of a bio-energetic support that is similar to the bio-energetic backing of the web, the more global game matrix, which is...and we are able to make this happen under conditional circumstances,

---

53 Principle of Self-Renovation and Law of Roux, Arndt-Schulz: in this interview there are several ref-erences to this principle. So, for further clarification of these principles and laws, it is advisable to read the text mentioned by Professor Vítor Frade, titled 'The cycle of self-renovation and the Law of Roux, Arndt-Schulz'.

54 Dominantly: it is crucial that when we talk about acquisitive or recovery days we are not taking it too literally. This means that we are referring to what is dominant in those days, acquisition or recovery, hav-ing as a reference what is collective, but never exclusively one or other type, because there may be the possibility/need in days which formally are considered of recovery, to take into account the individual dimension of the acquisitive aspect. This is a call for attention that maybe be useful here but also later on this interview, especially with regards to the patterns of sub-dynamics implied on each Morphocycle day (pattern of muscular contraction, metabolic pattern, experienced complexity, etc.).

conditional circumstances that lead to this happening with a dominance[55] of the emergence of the mechanisms or the alactic anaerobic metabolism. So, these are the conditions on both Wednesday and Friday, and Thursday, that identify the presence of the same matrix or of the same so-called physiological pattern, or even better, bio-energetic. And therefore, it is the guarantee of this happening without interruption every week, that not only allows me to maintain the same bio-energetic profile but also concerning what I have to do, it gives me the possibility of improving or at least not regressing because I know that the individuals...that I am giving each of them the possibility of improving, but also, and this is a fundamental aspect, not emphasising for lack of respect for the conditions, or the conditional circumstances over the appearance as a dominant emergence, of the alactic anaerobic mechanisms, and that the adaptability, the direction of that adaptability changes. Therefore, it remains unchanged, as there is the need for all training to promote fatigue, but that fatigue must be the necessary condition, protecting the required time for the initial conditions to return without representing an anomaly. This will happen if I don't respect the breaks for the consecutive appearance of these conditions or of these conditional circumstances of alactic anaerobiosis. This leads me to say that the adaptability must be the consequence of the presence of the same bio-energetic pattern every day, because otherwise it is not specific. And this presence is only guaranteed with a perfect understanding of the Morphocycle.

For me this is essential, and then we can return to the first question you asked, that had to do with the exercising times and with the break times. Because if I don't allow for break times, so if I don't respect a profile of intermittence I have no guarantee that the dominant mechanism that is present to support the effort will be, in fact, the alactic anaerobic mechanism[56]. So, it

---

55 Propensities: those "conditional circumstances that lead to...", determined by the purposes of our way of playing, the emergence of a propensity that allows what we desire to effectively happen (criteria that support our Game Principles, and more precisely, those that we prioritise in a certain instant or training unit), and to happen as we want it to happen, respecting a determined eventual logic and abiding to the pattern configuration of the sub-dynamics of the specific day. As it can be verified in this explanation, we include in a connected way the three Methodological Principles of Tactical Periodization (Principle of Propensities – "conditional circumstances that lead to..."; Principle of Complex Progression – what in a certain moment is a priority; Principle of Horizontal Alternation in specificity – respect for the pattern of the training unit).

56 Metabolisms or Energetic Systems: reinforcing what it is said in the interview, Paulo Santos (undated) refers that "to understand the energetic needs of any sport, in terms of training and competition, it is essential to know the sport profoundly. The success of any motor task requires the conversion of energy to be performed efficiently, in a direct proportion to the energetic needs of the skeletal muscles involved in that activity. It will be important to mention that the energetic expenditure depends on various factors, among which we can refer the exercise typology, frequency, duration, intensity, dietetic aspects, environmental conditions for exercising (altitude, temperature, humidity), the athlete's physical condition, and her muscular composition with regards to fibres (type I and II)". We should remember that the metabolic systems are generally classified in three types: a) Anaerobic alactic system or phosphagen system (ATP and phosphocreatine – PCr): uses the immediate sources of energy supply, which are also the most powerful (highest energetic contribution per time unit), usually associated with performances that require high metabolic intensity and short duration); b) Anaerobic lactic system or glycolytic systems or glycolysis: uses carbohydrates as energetic source, with energy production being the result of glycogen unfolding (way of storing the carbohydrates in the cells) as lactic acid, in a process called glycolysis that occurs at the level of the cytosol without intervention of oxygen. In energetic terms, it is more efficient than phosphagens, because it provides a higher quantity of energy globally, but is less powerful, because it requires more time to act. It can be predominantly found in high intensity, while non-maxi-

is through the <u>breaks</u> that I guarantee that possibility of, once again, having the guarantee that the fuel will allow for a certain type of effort and no other. So, you have a formula 1 car, a way of playing like Barcelona, but that car, that way of playing, can only work if supported if having as a dominant support a certain metabolic mechanism and not any metabolism. Therefore, just like in a formula 1 car, if you use diesel as a fuel, there is no point having a formula 1 car. If you put fuel with little octanes,[57] it will also not serve you well, so the pattern of the physiological level, or of the bio-energetic level you are interested in, is guaranteed through the perfect understanding of the Morphocycle, which is something that in reality is not always, or very little respected. Because if you do not respect the possibility of providing enough time so that the metabolic web that is the result of the continuous demand of that metabolic coordination which is required for your way of playing, if you do not respect the time required to be again in good condition for it to emerge, what will happen, what will happen is that you may produce the effort, but you will do it at the expense of the dominance of the glycolytic mechanisms, and therefore with the presence of lactic acid in the circulation. <u>So, in the continuity, inclusively</u> the adaptability that will be generated will have to do with that, you keep producing the effort but not in the ideal conditions in which you would produce that effort it the support was the same. That is only possible depending on the <u>guarantee of an uninterrupted presence of the Morphocycle as I understand it.</u> So, on a Friday it is the same or even worse than on a Wednesday. I need to guarantee, I need to make sure that what I am doing...On the one hand, my interest is experiencing it. And that is why the situations are more small-sided, but notice that I say reducing without impoverishing. You will only not impoverish if you don't touch the met-

---

mal performances, with a relatively significant duration (even if short). Although it can generate a great production of energy, it has, as a nefarious consequence, the accentuation of metabolic acidosis due to the accumulation of lactic acid, which is counterproductive when the aim is to achieve quality performances. c) Oxidative or aerobic system: metabolic process that occurs at the level of the mitochondria, responsible for energy production with the intervention of oxygen (aerobic) through the mitochondrial oxidation of glucose (derivative stored as a result of carbohydrates), lipids (fatty acids) and also amino acids (proteins). It is the least powerful metabolic system, but at the same time the one that has more absolute capacity, being therefore commonly associated with efforts of a higher duration. It is essential to highlight that none of these systems operates in isolation, no matter what a type of performance requires predominantly. All systems are permanently involved, even if at different levels.

57 Fuel, Diesel, Octanes: this metaphor refers to the way how metabolic systems can interfere with performance. In Tactical Periodization, it is suggested that the metabolic system which is predominantly implicated in the emergence of a good way of playing (formula 1) in training and in competition, should ensure a great 'combustion' potential. There is a belief that what determines and differentiates the good ways of playing is the possibility of operationalising the desired action, adjusted to the circumstances, and that action can be operationalised through a variety of ways (with acceleration, slowly, in deceleration, at high speed, in the air, on the floor, static, changing speed, ...). Therefore, the metabolic support that 'feeds' such action, or better, that interaction, must allow for all this. And this variability is only allowed if the incidence or dominant stimulation in the training process aims at the alactic anaerobic metabolism., the only that respecting the recovery times will allow for the development of the other metabolic ways. The adaptability that the process should promote, through its continuous stimulation and consideration of the need of recovery, must potentiate and occur supported by the best fuel for the desired way of playing. And if the desired way of playing, just like a formula 1 car, requires curving, accelerations, braking, changing speed...if it encapsulates all that variability, then it demands the best possible fuel, in this case the more adjusted. And the more adjusted is petrol with many octanes (in football type formula 1 is the phosphagen system) without mixing other fuels when you have to fill the tank. A recurring and continuous need when one trains in the limit and that need for fatigue and recovery is recognised.

abolic coordination and if what I am doing is related with a possible gain of specificity. Here already with a capital S. Therefore, even using the analogy of fractal geometry, you can notice people proposing small-sided games without considering if the number of times that the individuals will intervene is related to the number of times those individuals will intervene during the match in their roles/positions.

And if it isn't, what does this lead to?

It results in, bringing this to a continuity, an expression that is not related to the fuel with higher octanes but in the use of the glycolytic mechanisms. To be fractal, what has to be dominant here (in the reduction) is the dynamic of the fractal[58]. Are you following me?! If so...that is why it is an important characteristic...the effort being followed by the necessary time for being fresh so that when it restarts the maximum fuel is anaerobic alactic. So, for me, this is key, essential, and this promotes inclusively the adherence to a certain type of playing. Therefore, where in fact the guarantee of what is essential to promote, by the spontaneity that is requires from me or any other, can be supported on the dominance of the request of anaerobic alactic mechanisms.

This is fundamental inclusively even, due to the following, because the energy is brought by the participation of triphosphate adenosine, but triphosphate adenosine, the ATP[59], can be implicated in the metabolic process A, or B, or C. It is clear that there is no energy if there is no ATP present, and its breakdown, its synthesis or re-synthesis. But we have seen that if I am working using the anaerobic lactic, the phenomenology involved is not the same, inclusively changing the participation of not only the ATP receptors but also of the enzymes involved in all this. The contextual alteration is fundamental not only because a certain adaptability is installed, but moreover, and nowadays we are certain of this, and this you will hardly hear in any sports faculty in the World being put like this...the ATP that exists in the interior of the cells, neural or non-neural, has two roles, one...So the one that exists internally in the cell has that role that is providing energy, but it has another that is related to signalling, transmitting information. Now see if it is not...it shouldn't be difficult to accept that the information to be brought in connection with other cells and with the external environment is not the same if the metabolisms involved are different. Once again, the relevance of specificity and more, when there is a need for tiredness, for fatigue in the cells so that there is self-renovation. And the self-renovation occurs bringing this particularity that has been acti-

---

58 Fractal: the propriety of fracturing in similar models. The fractal dimension measures the constant degree of irregularity of a chaotic model (Stacey, 1995, p.547). "Fractality propose an uncentred ethnocentrism (as it unveils the centre in the periphery), it claims the local-global, the micro-macro (a global built from the emergence of the local and a local built from the evidence of globality). The fractality predicts that the micro is not opposed to the macro, it knows the macro contains the micro, but it is the micro who identifies it, who provides identity to the macro" (Cunha e Silva, 1999, p.62).

59 ATP: Triphosphate adenosine. The cells need to possess mechanisms for energy conversion. Therefore, they need the presence of a substance that has the capacity to accumulate the energy that comes from exergonic reactions (reactions that release energy). It is equally mandatory that this substance is posteriorly able of providing that energy to the endergonic reactions (that consume energy). That substance exists in our cells and is called adenosine triphosphate, commonly known as ATP. ATP is a labile chemical compost that is present in every cell. It is a combination of adenosine, ribose, and three phosphate radicals. The two last phosphate radicals are connected to the rest of the molecule through high energy connections.

vated, when is gestation time is respected, so that they can again be...appear improved, so that is why I say that it is self-renovation that leads to self-generation. So, <u>through fatigue</u>...and therefore this is related to the Principle of Self-renovation and the Law of Roux, Arndt-Schulz.

Now see, if...they even say that this circumstantial collapse state of the functionality of any atom or any organ, is a state of parabiose[60]. Because it is a moment when the circumstances or the reality regresses regarding functionality so that it can restructure to perform in better conditions if there is respect for time to allow for a delayed effect. As this is played, there needs to be a significant stimulation, a strong stimulation! If I don't respect the conditions for this emergence, the fatigue that arises is not the same, it's another, and that has very negative consequences in the organism, and that is why it should lead us to <u>reflect</u>...and I usually joke, <u>the way people usually train</u>, not respecting this logic, does not lead to parabiose but instead to 'paranecrose'[61]. And the indicators of this are the constant inflammations of the body, the constant pain, and that is a symptom of, how can I put it...organic injury, an injury of the issues. When this injury of the tissues occurs, the body in order to react accordingly provokes changes in the way it works with the ATP, and the ADP that results from the emptying of the ATP due to the restructuration of what is weakened originates, for example, that in the bloodstream the ADP, adenosine diphosphate and the mono-phosphate end up also connecting to receptors and the result of this is, for example, the ADP being connected to the platelets and the platelets, for the need of, let's say, recomposing the wound that was generated, creates clots that obstruct something that should be free. See here how this is relevant, the <u>specificity!</u> But more, all this implies understanding <u>proprioception</u>[62] to its ultimate significance, including the

---

60 Parabiose: process that illustrate the merger of living elements. It is used here, as being motivated by the qualitative training stimuli, and aiming at the articulation that occurs with this phenomenon, after the de-structuration generated, merging a certain generation linked to the stimulus that motivated it. It is a process of self-organisation that conceptualises the organism and its constitutive parts as dissipative structures which can aspire to increasing levels of complexity. Cunha e Silva (1999) argues that the systems that constitute themselves far from the equilibrium, as they require continuous energetic and matter supply for maintenance purposes, are called dissipative structures. This author, in consonance with the idea, conceptualises the 'moving body' and the 'sporting body' as dissipative structures, suggesting that these use the hostility of the environment, and as such, of the disorder that the latter contemplates, to overcome itself. To create a new form of internal order with increased complexity. He further proposes that the thermodynamics of non-equilibrium (a key concept in the way Professor Vítor Frade conceptualises football training) establishes the connection between order and disorder and also the possibility of emergence of structures (resulting from the parabiose) in the systems that are away from the equilibrium. He adds, reinforcing the need for training to be operationalised at the borders of chaos, with the consequent need for states of parabiose, that far from the equilibrium, in 'excitable' environments, we can observe a type of essential solidarity, an associative intelligence that leads the elements of the system to cooperate, with the objective of creating more complex structures that can make it viable, presenting them with new opportunities.

61 Paranecrose: phenomenon analogous to the description of parabiose, but whose effects, due to the qualitative difference at the level of the stimulus, due to a lack of respect for the recovery time, promotes the death of living elements and consequent loss of complexity by the system. Laborit (1971) suggests that "the death of the organism results on the death of the organ, but the most usual is that the death of the organ results in the death of the organism".

62 Proprioception: involves several roles of the nervous systems from which result the sensation of balance, position and movement of parts of the limbs and body (Habib, 2003). Marisa Gomes clarifies that "proprioception is a beautiful word but...it has to do with what you said about the academy kid.

eventual problem of the different mechanoreceptors as well[63]. Therefore, the importance of this specificity being guaranteed, and guaranteed with regards to what?! The framing that I want to see. Aspiring to play in a certain way should not make me forget the present because I get to the future depending on the trainability that I promote, and this involves the circumstances that are complex as hell! That is why I find a quote by Mark Twain amusing, which says that when a person's favourite tool is a hammer, then for him all problems will be nails. So, if we realise at a bare minimum that this is something complex, the tool must be complex too, with different degrees of complexity, but it must be complex! So, I return to my initial question, that I referred was already in-cluded in my doctoral application, the problem of causality.

I will tell you a story that happened very recently: I was watching a match between Benfica and FC Porto, under-15s, seating next to many Porto coaches, and a goalkeeper coach. And during the match, because Benfica had scored, Porto was playing near the opposing box, and the goalkeeper would adjust and position himself regularly on the limit of his own box so he would move, adapting sub-consciously to the circumstances. And the goalkeeper coach that was standing next to me starts shouting the name of the goalkeeper until he finally acknowledges the coach, who tells him not to leave the goal so often, because if... And that has a lot to do with the fact that "we should have as-sistant coaches, goalkeeper coaches, this and that", and how that can be a problem and makes me question that necessity at times. So, what happened? That interfered with the goalkeeper's spontaneity. How did we concede the two goals? Balls played to the middle of the centre-backs, on their back, the goalkeeper had to move from where he was to fight for the ball with the strik-er, and in both cases, the striker got there first and scored. Now, I ask, what if the goalkeeper coach had not shouted from the stand? Probably he would be at least a metre ahead, and he would not have conceded any of those goals.

It is not enough to talk about extreme sensitivity to the initial conditions[64]. These are expressions that we get from somewhere else, like fractals, but the reality is complex. So, I need to take into account the circumstances, and I consider these circumstances more or less depending on how I understand the logic of life, in this case, or the logic of reality. Therefore, on the one hand for the acquisitive, it cannot be any acquisitive. It has to be 'the' acquisitive. And it cannot be the acquisitive without the conditions for the acquisition of the acquisitive because otherwise that assimilation is not performed, and the

---

Proprioception is a capacity of the game, of being able to play, even when static, but being static in such a way that the player can intervene in the context, that is another expression of proprioception and proprioception is not only touching the ball, it's knowing how to touch the ball, it's doing so while considering the circumstances".

63 Mechanoreceptors: specialised receptors that can be found in the most diversified structures of the body (skin, muscles, tendons, ligaments, joint capsules, and very likely, in the bones too) and have the task of continuously sending information to the nervous system about the status of the body in each moment. The neuromuscular spindle and the Golgi Tendon Organ (GTO) are muscular receptors. There are also joint receptors like the Pacinian corpuscles, the Meissner corpuscles (both of fast adaptation), the Ruffini corpuscles and the Merckel receptors (slow adaptation). It is also important to mention the existence of skin receptors in different layers, like the corpuscles of Meissner and Pacini.

64 Extreme sensitive to initial conditions: "amplifying property of non-linear feedback mechanisms, meaning that minor changes may increase until a long-term change of behaviour is reached" (Stacey, 1995, p.548).

conditions of the acquisitive imply that either in relation to the whole, or the quasi-whole, or the individual, lead them to fatigue, to exhaustion, and allow time for the recovery to happen, so that they can be ready for that.

Roughly, this is what both the cycle of self-renovation and the Law of Roux, Arndt-Schulz refer to. They say that in any activity – they say physical activity, but it happens in any activity -, when we invest in it, it influences the organs, the systems, and the roles. I would even add, the individuals and with regards to football, the <u>individual in co-relation and co-difficulty</u>, because there are the other guys, what makes it complicated. But it exerts on the individual, and if the activity has the symbolic side as significant, it has the side of previous intentions, of the intentionalised, meaning, the game criteria that we are looking for. Or, if you prefer, the Game Principles that we are looking for has over the Man as a psycho-biological unit, or even socio-psycho-biological because it is 'a society'. And what Tactical Periodization and the Morphocycle want is that this is considered, and that is considered <u>without excluding</u> the capturing sensitivity of the individuals concerning the circumstances. And therefore this has to do with the first timing of expression of the parts of the body involved, therefore in the co-contractibility[65] that has to occur so that the movement of the body is fluid, and in how this occurs depending on the need to adjusted the circumstances to the surroundings and that many times is decodable in anticipation. But to be that it needs...it's not the problem of decision-making, because it can be wrong. It's a problem of choices, and the familiarisation with a context gives me that advantage, predicting, anticipating the decisions that I need to make and that I will do better when the body is used to it or when a somatisation has occurred. And this has to do with the second timing.

So, what do the first and the second principle tell us about reinforcement? What is the role, they call it functional load because they say there must be a stimulation, but they always do it in individual terms, they do it inclusively with each metabolism, saying that each of them has a different time of replenishment, they talk about the delayed effect of loads. But what we care about is the delayed effect of performance, our performance. The performance is a performance that demands a certain 'romance' among metabolisms. I need to know in advance which 'romance' I am looking for, and after finding that out and having this knowledge, I can make it happen. Therefore, this stimulation is a metabolic acceleration, they even call it a 'metabolic turmoil', that lead those things implicated to de-structure and restructure and therefore reappear improved. But these are the responsible for a very significant involvement, very strong and critical in the consumption of oxygen, with the internal respiratory processes of the tissues and with the...therefore associated to the oxidative phosphorylation and this acceleration of the activation of these things allows the human organism that trains, training under certain conditions, to perfect itself and self-renovate.

In the end, what they say is that this <u>self-renovation</u>, is the way life and atoms exist, or those albuminoid bodies, as they say, the mode of existing or of existence consists in the constant renovation through themselves, of those implied bodies. Deep down, deep down, of the chemical components of their

---

65 Co-contractibility: mechanism of muscular contraction in which more than one muscle receive an innervation message to contract, but in which the excitation is more intense for the agonists than for the antagonists. A contractile coordination that involves very importantly the mechanoreceptors and similarly its desired acculturation.

bodies, and an alteration occurs...sometimes there is only the need for a proton (H+) to change or a calcium or sodium ion so that things change radically. This was proven a long time ago through the labelling or the method of atom labelling. So, we can say that the _atomic composition of our body_ renews itself endlessly and continuously or even perpetually. Now, that renovation is performed much faster that it was once thought, and that is why they say there is a kind of 'metabolic turmoil', but we have already seen, or we know that depending on the dominance of the metabolisms involved, a or b, time is not the same, we need to know when we do...That is why that I talk concerning recovery that I say that _recovery is achieved_ by recovering with intermittent points where this metabolism, this metabolic web that results from the romance and the continuous 'marriage', is also activated, although shortened in its length. Its nature is the same, but the duration is different when prodding the same metabolism.

What is claimed is the opposite, look, this makes no sense to me, so you got tired due to a complex whole, and now you are acting on the aerobic metabolism and you are recovered!! Rubbish! What happens is that, and that is why I mentioned earlier on than when maximal exertion happens with fatigue resulting from it because the ATP or phosphocreatine stocks are temporarily emptied, in this state the aerobic activation is high, after it, depending on the great need for oxygen. The residual side of the lactic acid is suppressed or swept depending then on the arrival of oxygen, so during the break, that due to this existence is designated of anaerobic exercise, I don't know if it is. For me, it is not, because, in fact, I don't die after, I am resting and at that time what is happening is something totally different. Therefore, the metabolic processes develop rapidly in everything that is living matter in a constant self-renovation and that in this case, because it aims to be oriented, self-generative, and is intentional, _it is therefore essential that one knows what it is meant when in Tactical Periodization we discuss the Tactical dimension._

The Tactical dimension only exists a priori as a theoretical configuration, a conceptualisation of what I aspire to, as a hypothesis. Because what is Tactical, what belongs to the Tactical, is what exists in Barcelona. Even when Barcelona is playing bad, you say that it is Barcelona playing, so it is _an intentionalised organisation_ because they want to be in a certain way when they have the ball. They want to do things in a certain way, and when they don't have the ball they want to...that is the Tactical Dimension. _That is nothing that exists a priori_, it exists after as an _emergence_[66]. That is why it is said, "oh, the game model..."! No, the Game Model is nothing that I can say, it's this, it's that, no. That sets the boundaries of the Model's moderation because _the_

---

66 Emergence: "emergence is a complex organisational structure that grows from simple rules. The emergence means unpredictability in the sense that small events cause great and qualitative changes in big events. The emergence is a law of nature to which human beings are submitted to" (Laughlin, 2005). Henry Atlan (2011) highlights that these phenomena can be observed in different scientific domains – epigenetic, physical-chemical, cognitive and in social sciences, because each cannot avoid an analysis to those complex systems. He adds that in these systems, a great number of elements interact with each other, in such a way that the global behaviour of the system cannot be predicted and understood from any of its elements. He classifies these as non-trivial emergence phenomena, characterised not only by the global results being larger than the sum of its constitutive properties, but also by the unpredictability of the result, at least in a detailed manner. Finally, he refers that it is a certain dose of serendipity, random disturbances, called noise by the theory of information and fluctuations in thermodynamics, that introduce an unpredictable novelty in those emergence phenomena.

Model is when you want Barcelona playing and say: "no, their game model is a line of three and one loose guy...", But _when they are doing it! It's a soma- tisation of certain values, certain categories, certain principles, certain criteria,_ and whatever.

Then, you can easily see that even within the Methodological Principles, and I get upset when some guys try to come up with more Methodological Principles, it's a lack of understanding that the Methodological Principle is one, but complexity is complex! And I must, without losing the unbreakable wholeness, 'breaking it down', keeping it present. And that is why I say that _Specificity_ is related to the conjecture, it belongs to the theoretical, the con- ceptual, the values, it's a _judgement of value,_ it's a way of playing that I choose. "No, we will play this way". It's an _idea of playing_ that I extract from the conceptualisation of the game of football. The conceptualisation of the game of football has to do with the rules that football has so that it can be football. Otherwise, it's rugby, that belongs to the conceptualisation. From there I extract...it belongs to the _axiology,_ it belongs to the _values,_ it belongs to the _judgement of value,_ it is a judgement of value that I have to make with regards to the way how I want to play. The Specificity is there but as a draft, because it is the only Specificity with a capital S when it happens as emer- gence. But even that way maybe with a capital S and between inverted com- mas, or better, with suspension points, because it won't stop growing at the level of the whole, at the level of quality uninterruptedly, and inclusively at the level of variability. That is why I say that the quality of the way of playing, then the option I have for the way of playing, occurs depending on the possibility of evolving at the same time the maximisation of redundancy. Or in other words, what is identifiable, what I said a while ago about Barcelona that even when playing badly, everyone can recognise that is Barcelona playing. With what? With the _variability,_ the maximisation of variability. That is why the _orienting principles_ must be present every week as _context,_ as the background theme that allows me to improvise. It belongs to the _meso_ and especially to the _micro;_ I never have two equal matches, at the _macro_ level, every match is the same because otherwise I...or almost the same, because otherwise, I cannot distin- guish Barcelona from Real Madrid, etc., etc., etc....

This means that...see...the importance or need for the Methodological Principle of Horizontal Alternation in specificity, I put specificity in lower case, because I alternate, giving contour to the Specificity, and inclusively having in mind the individual or considering the whole. But notice, _how do I do that?_ Us- ing what contents? Contents that refer to the way how I want to play, _contents that favour_ the emergence of what I am looking for, so they are propensities. And then, at the beginning of the season, I do it the same way as later? No. There is the Complex Progression. That is why I talk about a _connective pat- tern,_ and this pattern appears when I respect the weekly _Morphocycle_ without interruptions. So, this self-renovation or self-generation does not occur auto- matically as thought before, even if we know that a guy that spent two months sick or three in bed without walking when we finally got up, he could not manage to walk. Even if that was known, it was thought that it was some kind of natural law...no, you need..._the processes_ of self-renovation are actioned, they are put to work. And for them to be actioned in a more appropriate man- ner without..._there needs to be exhaustion,_ they _need to be fatigued,_ and that is what the Law of Roux, Arndt-Schulz says. It is the value of the load, they said, _the value of the stimulus is substantial,_ and it cannot be strong immedi- ately after without this happening. And it will only be achieved if the time for *parabiose, and the phase of exaltation as they call it, or overcompensation, occurs...Only through, they say the functional load, I call it performance. By the performance, or as they say, the functional load, resides the organism's excitation or, if you prefer, is the state of the whole organism. Again, the relevance of a correct understanding of the Methodological Principle of Horizontal Alternation in specificity, and it is so that nowadays everyone knows that what we have regarding neurological does not appear all at the same time, it is not born with us straight away. No, the neural plasticity, today we know that it is a reality, so what is happening is defining or influences that neural aspect. And today we know that even in the relationship between the myofibrils[67] and the neurons[68] and the information that passes to the brain, the heart, etc., etc... the glia[69] is very relevant, a kind of frontier of the nervous system, like the logic of participation and interference of the sympathetic and parasympathetic nervous systems. Therefore, the loss of specificity is the loss of all this.*

We can synthesise saying that either the glandular cell or the muscular fibre or the myofibrils or the nervous cell get worn when they work, when they are trained, when they are requested and especially when they are requested entirely, with an emotion linked to it. That is why the playing, the competition, is the essential nature of training. So, they are worn, exhausted, fatigued.

Even though for myself and for Tactical Periodization training means learning, it is about learning a way of playing, it is about learning in certain circumstances and only...that is why I initially told you about the conception people

---

67 Myology: the muscle is coated by a layer of connective tissue – epimysium – and there are fasciculi that, despite their small dimensions, are visible to the naked eye. Only microscopically can the functional units of the muscle be observed: the muscle fibres, which are also coated by sheath of the same connective tissue – endomysium. The muscular fibres may have different dimensions and each muscular fibre is enveloped in a membrane – the sarcolemma – and just like the other cells, it is composed by multiple organelles situated in the sarcoplasm (the cytoplasm of muscular fibres). This space is penetrated by a very dense net of small transversal tubules – t-tubules – that ensure the communication and transport of substances throughout the whole muscular fibre. The fibres possess a net of membranous channels as well – sarcoplasmic reticulum – whose main function is to release and store calcium (Ca2+) during all stages of muscle contraction and relaxation, respectively. The muscular fibres are also composed by numerous myofibrils, which are the contractile units of the muscle, and that are themselves composed by even smaller units – sarcomeres – with three bands (I band – light zone; A band – dark zone; H band – medium part of the A band). Within these bands we can also distinguish small protein filaments, ones thicker than others. The thinnest ones are actin and the thickest myosin. These are the two most important contractile proteins of the skeletal muscle. Myosin is composed by two intertwined filaments that end in a protuberance designated as myosin head. These structures, when in contact with actin, allow for the muscular contraction. Each muscular fibre is innervated by a motor nerve – motoneuron. The group of muscular fibres, together with the motor neuron that innervates them, is called motor unit. All the fibres of the motor unit have the same characteristics. They are all from the same type, which means that in one motor unit there are no different types of fibres. The skeletal muscle is characterised by the presence of different types of muscular fibres, that are usually classified in three types, depending on their metabolic profile and speed of contraction: type I (slow and oxidative), type IIa (fast oxidative-glycolytic) and type IIb (fast glycolytic). (Soares, 2005)

68 Neuron: "Main cellular unit for the transformation of information within the nervous system that normally is constituted by a cellular body (soma), dendrites and an axon" (Wolfe, 2004, p.183)

69 Glial cells: one of the two biggest types of nervous cells. The other is the neuron. The glial cells are present in a 10:1 ratio in comparison to the neuros and are also known as inter-neurons. They transport nutrients, allow for a rapid recovery of other nervous cells and can create its own communications network. Glia is the short term for 'neuroglia' (Jensen, 2002).

have of <u>learning,</u> either by reception or discovery, because by reception, it means that you...the primacy is in the frontal cortex, in the rationality, so the circuit to be established is very different if the primacy is in the brainstem[70]. The primacy is only in the brain stem when you are required to act, carrying the emotion with it, independently of you placing feelings in that after, or an understanding of the principles or the reasoning about this. So, the logic is not the same, and Damasio's recent book clarifies that well. This way of training and this way of playing <u>demand, when they occur,</u> the expenditure of highly energetic substances. The glycogen, for example, the phosphocreatine or creatine-phosphate and fundamentally the tri-phosphate adenosine acid (ATP). <u>Resting, recovery, the break is a sine qua non requirement,</u> and that is why I say that the break is more important than the effort itself, because only with the existence of the break, like I tried to explain, will I have the initial conditions for the desirable implication of the effort in this case.

That is why I told a while ago that understanding this is almost choosing a way of playing football. That is why I like Barcelona's way of playing so much. The resting after a drill, after exercising and...<u>but exercising what?!</u> With what?! And the <u>fatigue</u> that is not an ordinary resting state. It is, in fact, <u>a deliberate resting state.</u> It is not pragmatic, it's praxiological because the practice has logic and it is deliberate with regards to what we are looking for and depending on how it is brought to life. Therefore, the fatigued organ or organism <u>are converted during rest</u> in the accentuation of self-renovation if we

---

70 Brainstem: structure usually presented as a primitive brain which deserves the attention of author and neuroscientist Antonio Damasio in his recent book 'Self Comes to Mind' – especially with regards to the construction of human consciousness. In this book, Damasio inverts all the existing paradigms that surround the role of consciousness, by presenting the brainstem as the key unit. He explains that "the brain does not start constructing consciousness, the conscious mind, at the level of the cerebral cortex, but at the level of the brainstem" (Damasio, 2010, p.41). "But contrary to tradition and conventions, I believe that the mind is not made in the cerebral cortex alone. Its first expressions emerge at the level of the brainstem. The concept that the mental processing has at the level of the brainstem is so little conventional that it does not even suffice to say it has little popularity...This concept, and the one that claims that the primary emotions occur in the brainstem are interconnected" (2010, p.103). The author clarifies that the brainstem does not play an exclusive role but is clear in stating that the human consciousness needs as much the cerebral cortex as it needs the brainstem. "The grand symphonic piece that is consciousness encompasses the foundational contributions of the brain stem, forever hitched to the body, and the wider-than-the-sky imagery created in the cooperation of cerebral cortex and subcortical structures, all united harmoniously, propelled to the future, in a continuous movement that can only be interrupted by sleep, anaesthesia, brain function or death." (Damasio, 2010, p.44). This book reinforces also the need for a permanent interaction between the non-conscious and conscious levels to live. More objectively, and in what regards football, these ideas reinforce the possibility of the concomitant development of a 'know-how' and a 'knowledge about the know-how'. However, the relevance and the role of the brain stem highlights the need for a primacy of action in that aspiration, just like with survival. So, it is starting from the 'know-how' that players do, that we should trigger that knowledge about the know-how, the conscious realisation of what they are doing. In summary, it requires that in methodological terms the primacy is in the action, in doing, practicing, and not in the rationalisation, even if it does not ignore it at all. "There are two types of action control, conscious and non-conscious but the non-conscious control can be partially shaped by the conscious control. Human childhood and adolescence take the inordinate amount of time that they do because it takes a long, long time to educate the nonconscious processes of our brain and to create, within that nonconscious brain space, a form of control that may work, in a more or less reliable way, in accordance to intentions and conscious objectives. We can describe this slow education as a process of partial transfer of the conscious control to a nonconscious server, and not simply the offer of conscious control to the unconscious forces that can provoke chaos in human behaviour." (Damasio, 2010, p.332)

wish, or self-renovate, self-generate as I like saying and this leads them, if the process is well driven, to accentuating its capacities and its potential, so referring to the animated operations of renovation and of its components. That is why I mentioned parabiose and paranecrose. 'Paranecrose' is something I invented, you cannot find this...

We can say and notice how this is relevant because it considers the oxygen important connecting it with an indexation; therefore the fatigued organism absorbs willingly, avidly, the oxygen, but where it absorbs the oxygen more willingly is precisely after an alactic effort. Now, the alactic effort is only alactic, especially if its more in its power than in its capacity if its duration is short. And then the absorption of oxygen is in fact, further to the substances that are nutrients, that are needed especially after the effort. And with this assistance, the <u>fatigued body recovers itself, restructures itself, re-functionalises itself,</u> replacing inclusively the substances used by new ones. All this is achieved, produced, operationalised, <u>modelled,</u> under the de-toning effect of oxygen. Oxygen that is, in fact, a key element for the re-synthesis and the reconstitution of phosphocreatine and ATP that are exhausted when the effort is performed. The reconstitution occurs, and if the text is conventional, if it has an analytical reading it says all this, <u>you only need to put on a different pair of glasses.</u> Therefore, the <u>reconstitution</u> does not only occur at the starting level, like a kind of natural law, therefore regularly, <u>going beyond</u> that reconstitution, the structuralism, and consequently that functionality. <u>But a matching functionality,</u> one that protects a certain logic and certain principles that is what Tactical Periodization aims to achieve by leading to the presence of three Methodological Principles and the emergence of a connective pattern through the realisation, or as I prefer to say, through <u>the weekly expression of the Morphocycle.</u> So, a super-reconstitution is obtained, as they put it, or a super-compensation, or a phase of exaltation as they also say and during this circumstance, there is more glycogen, more phosphocreatine in the muscle, as they say, more nitrogenated albumin[71]. And what else?! <u>The acquisitive Specific. As this is done</u> conditioned to the dominance of the acquisitive Specific, <u>the way in which it is articulated is not any, it's one...!</u>

That is why I get agitated when people talk about "the tension day, the strength day and the speed day". No, it is about bringing the muscular units, or the essential muscular groups to operate under certain conditions, but with the objective of doing something in more individual terms or in more collective terms, that has to do with the way I intend us to play.

Now look, when you add all this together, when this happens, when the existence of this process is protected, especially this addition of ATP, of the ATP reserves, therefore of the adenosine triphosphate acid... Thanks to this accumulation of new energetic loads, let's put it this way, the improvement

---

71 Albumin: a protein with high biological value, the main protein of the blood plasma, synthesised in the liver through the hepatocytes. The replenishment of albumin is used, in the medicine, to treat severe burns and haemorrhages. It can also be used for the recovery of patients that underwent plastic surgeries like lipo-suction, because the albumin helps easing swelling. The normal concentration of albumin in animal blood is between 3.5 and 5 grams per decilitre and constitutes around 50% of plasmatic proteins. The albumin is fundamental for the maintenance of osmotic pressure, necessary for the correct distribution of bodily fluids between the intra-vascular and extra-vascular compartments located among the tissues. The main roles of albumin are related to the regulation of the following aspects: maintenance of osmotic pressure, transport of thyroidal hormones, transport of liposoluble hormones, transport of free fatty acids, transport of unconjugated bilirubin, competitive union with calcium ions and pH control.

of the fuel's octanes, _the exercising capacity is altered, and it is specifically changed, but during what?!_ During the stage that comes after the break time so that the reconstitution can occur, the _exaltation phase_ as they call it. This is the stage that brings the organism, or brings the organ, or brings the atoms, or brings the added ATP, improved. _So, it's in that stage that I must focus on_ the new stimulation, so it's in this moment that I need to focus. It is precisely this cycle that, like they call it and like they represented it through the cycle of self-renovation. But then the Law, or the so-called Law of Roux, Arndt-Schulz, says that if the functional load...and I say if the performance is not repeated the exaltation phase diminishes and disappears progressively. _Therefore, the importance of_ continuity even in the biggest discontinuity. This _pattern of intermittence which guarantees_ the existence not only in the alternation in the Morphocycle in a group of training units but also in the training units themselves is absolutely indispensable. That is why I said earlier on that the Law of Roux, Arndt-Schulz refers to the value of the functional load, _to the value of the performance_ that triggers all the other processes that we mentioned earlier, but _all these processes must be linked to what we are looking for_.

They say this may be expressed in the following way: an excessively extreme excitation destroys the cellular functions, and it is extreme not only due to the, let's say, intensity of the load but also by not respecting the time required for reconstitution. So, they say, great excitation, great in the _optimal sense_ are the ones that improve and allow us to overcome. The great is the _maximum relative intensity_ so, with _maximum concentration,_ they must be _playing,_ and this is only maximum when I am _fresh, I_ cannot find a better word than this. So, all the normal ones are of no interest, and the poor ones diminish. These _concepts_ of extreme, great, normal and poor, these are _categories of the axiological framework,_ and therefore _judgements of value_ that I must identify concerning the way of playing that I choose. So, if they are categories they are judgements of value. And they can be extreme, great, and in this case the great ones, that is why I talk about maximum relative intensity, _are exerted over the scales of the_ hypothetic Specificity, and therefore the maximised Specificity, either it is global, intermediate, individual or through the exaltation that Specificity to contribute towards a qualitative improvement of the emerging Specificity. _This should find support on_ individualised repercussions, the Self-Eco-Hetero.

So, what is this? It is what I refer to when, regarding Tactical Periodization, I talk about the relationship between two dynamics, _the dynamic of the effort and the dynamic of performance._ Effort must be performance, it must characterise the performance, so that the effort is specific, within boundaries, convenient. And it is this _dominance of the performance dynamic_ that leads me to _the dynamic of adaptability, but what? There needs to be another dynamic here, the dynamic of recovery,_ because otherwise...there can be a lot of good will, but there is no recovery. That is why when Friday is used as it usually is, with a lot of goodwill – Hell has loads of that! And not only with long-term repercussions in the cells, because they have already been getting injured with the reaction of the organism, and many injuries are due to that and people cannot see it. Look, if you are familiar with or linked to the Principle of Horizontal Alternation in specificity, you are necessarily connected to the Principle of Propensities. Because it is with contents related to the way of playing, that I believe we can favour the appearance of contexts in which the relationship promotes a certain type of emergences, but it is also essentially marked out by the Principle of Complex Progression. This _recovery is achieved in connection_ *with the pattern of effort! So, to finish, we could say: performances, or as they say, functional loads, if they are repeated next to each other, it won't work. In such a way that the new efforts, if this happens, will be achieved before the processes of restoration allow the achievement of the initial and higher level, of a level that is better than the one we began with.*

What is the conclusion when this happens? The outcome is that if I do not respect the Morphocycle (and that is why in the beginning I said that every-thing lies on the understanding of the Morphocycle), exhaustion will occur, the guys will say they are tired.

That is why it's very important that we recognise that we are colonised by a traditional way of thinking, by a traditional way of feeling, by a traditional way of reflecting, a traditional way of training, and these are cultural reinforcers[72] that lead several people to think and feel in the same way. So, the convention has its foundations in the concept of the athlete, it's about running more, run-ning faster, running longer, and jumping higher, and even individually. The so-called universal biological principles can be all and nothing. The so-called rational principles of the game have no collective characteristics, the principle of penetration, where is the collective sense in that? Containment, what does that shit have to do with the pressing zone? And all that influences us con-sciously, and even worse subconsciously.

When this happens (alienating the freshness) I make an effort and go, but I go at the expense of other fuel that is not the one I should be interested in. Therefore, this system of reinforcers that any culture possesses, and the western has those that I was, in fact, saying were essential, and all that is not necessarily to throw in the bin, that's why I mentioned the example of the text. I grabbed it 40 years after to give them, and none knew about it, it was Chinese! I said: "look, this is all wrong and all right. It is all right if I use the glasses of Tactical Periodization, of systems theory, or the glasses of the sec-ond cybernetics, or the glasses of fractal geometry, etc., etc., etc....This is all right!" You only need to reconvert it.

We can say that it is fundamental to recognise that in a certain culture there is a system of reinforcers, and the individuals have preferential behaviours depending on those. They have preferential thought processes depending on those, they have preferential habits, preferential subconsciousness. Therefore, there are common reinforcers within a great number of people, and the so-called universal biological principles, overload, specificity, reversibility, adap-tation, but these are notions or categories that...there is polysemy in here. It is all almost correct, without being correct. Even though the concept of load bothers me because for me the donkeys are the ones that have to deal with loads, right?! And football should be a pleasure...that is why it is difficult for people to imagine that if training three times a week is a pleasure, but under these conditions..." you don't have to train more", and in fact mostly due to the existing conventional reinforcers.

---

72 On the topic of cultural reinforcers: "We cannot run our kind of life, in the physical and social environ-ments that have become the human habitat, without reflective, conscious deliberation. But it is also the case that the products of conscious deliberation are significantly limited by a large array of nonconscious biases, some biologically set, some culturally acquired, and that the nonconscious control of action is also an issue to contend with". (Damasio, 2010, p.335)

But we know that certain stimulating or stimulatory conditional circumstances that are continuously brought to life, under the same conditions or under similar conditions, are 'stimuli' that are received by perceptual-sensorial mechanisms and by energetic mechanisms and by adaptation mechanisms, that with time, if the relationship between effort and recovery is protected, will lead to an adaptability. I don't know but many times, the understanding of people is low with regards to this, and that is why it is difficult to recognise... because what characterises the nature of playing, of competition...what is it? It's the multiple interactions. And more or less, more or less complex, this has to be always the dominant context, and I have to know that the causality linked to this is non-linear. I need to take this into account to propose, as I need to take this into account to think, that is why many times the quantification or the evaluation of what is happening can be done with probabilities, I need several times to notice a tendency or some tendencies, a regularity and all that.

I get back to the ATP because I have given out a text very recently to some of the staff at FC Porto and not only. And I would say that this is something that is out of the domain for 90% of the people, if not more, including those working in academia around the World. But there is a lot of evidence to back it up, even though it has been seeking acceptance for decades. It is about the effects of ATP, it being something else other than the supplier of energy and this something else is very important and especially for what we are interested in, the cooperative or coordinative synchronism within a whole that is the team that we have. But with regards to what I was mentioning in the Morphocycle, with regards to the importance of the Morphocycle, with regards to the importance of training and getting tired, recovering in order to get tired again and being able to get tired without getting to that point, meaning, to improvement, and so there is the cumulative and adverse effect.

So, the effects of ATP in the blood vessels, for example, that text that I gave referred key aspects, regarding the ATP's dual functionality. And it said that in the moment of contraction, in the moment of contraction of the vessels, the cells...so, it's a "stress", it's a tension that is exerted by the need to do something. The contraction occurs in the vessels, so who comes to assist us or the muscles so that they can work is the sympathetic nervous system. The cells of the sympathetic nervous system, at this moment, release ATP together with a neurotransmitter[73], so the ATP is also a neurotransmitter, something that will lead some people to say: "here we go, this guy is again inventing something", they cannot even be bothered to go and do some research. So, it gathers, together with the ATP, a neurotransmitter that is noradrenaline. The ATP connects to the receptors of the muscular cells that shape the walls of the vessels, causing a rapid contraction so that the blood can flow, etc.

But then, not only is this like this...this logic can be impeded if we are stressed or whatever. But if we know it is this way, and if we know that this is how the effort we aim for looks like it's about contracting and relaxing (in the blood vessels, dilating), so we can also help, getting the organism used to do

---

73 Neurotransmitters: biochemical messengers that allow the communication among neurons. Its typology is diverse, with more than 50 different types. Usually they act as an excitatory stimulus of a neighbouring neuron or as an inhibitor supressing the activation of the electrical impulse that travels from the cellular body through the axon (extension of the neurons that transports the impulses to the other neurons).

this. And if we <u>do not allow the tissues to get injured,</u> we are doing even bet-ter. <u>Dilation </u>is the responsibility of epithelial cells[74], that under tension being under tension due to what one aims to achieve, release ATP as well. So, the ATP connects to certain p2y receptors, in the nearby epithelial cells and the blood vessel, or the arteries, relax due to that, and also due, it seems, to the nitric oxide[75], I think you say it like that.

For us, this is fundamental, very important because this has to do with what?

With the changes in the bloodstream, which is what must happen when we are working, and it must be smooth, it must be fluid as well. When these changes occur, there is a permanence tension, and that needs to be more and less, it's like the contraction, and then it has to do with the sodium and with the calcium[76]. Here when they produce that tension, in the epithelial cells, which coat therefore the walls of the vessels, they release ATP. When the ATP is released, it will activate the receptors in the nearby epithelial cells, so there are specific receptors to which the ATP is directed, and if it is ADP or AMP there will be others, and this is not irrelevant. When this happens, the ATP travels to the receptors of the respective cells and releases the nitric oxide that will allow the vessels to relax. If anything is impeding the fluidity of the process, then the system will break down. This happens when there is overtraining.

---

74 Epithelial cells: groups of cells that form a tissue called epithelium in a juxtaposed way. Its main func-tions are the coating of the external surfaces of the body, organs and internal cavities. In this interview, Professor Frade is referring to the epithelial cells that coat the walls of the blood vessels. The perfect union between the epithelial cells makes these cells efficient barriers against the penetration of invasive agents and the loss of bodily fluids. Nonetheless, they are selectively permeable to allow, for example, the necessary exchanges between the bloodstream and the cells of various tissues.

75 Nitric oxide: also known as nitrogen monoxide and azote monoxide, it is represented by the chemical formula NO1. It is a soluble gas, highly lipophilic, synthesised by the endothelial cells, macrophages, and a certain group of neurons in the brain. It is important for intra and extra-cellular signalling, and acts by inducing guanylyl cyclase, which produces cyclic guanosine monophosphate (cGMP), which among other effects, leads to the relaxation of the smooth muscle, provoking, as biological actions, the dilation of the vessels and bronchi.

76 Muscular contraction: for the muscle to contract, it needs a stimulus that comes from an impulse propagated through the motor nerve. When that impulse gets to the nerve endings, these produce a substance – acetylcholine (ACh) that acts as a facilitator in the transmission of that electrical impulse. This neurotransmitter connects to the receptors in the fibre membrane (sarcolemma) and, if the quantity of ACh is sufficient, an electric charge is created, and propagated throughout the whole fibre (action po-tential). This impulse is transmitted through the t-tubules and the sarcoplasmic reticulum to the interior of the cell. The arrival of the impulse leads to the release of the calcium stored (Ca2+) by the reticulum, which is directed to the interior of the cell. At rest, tropomyosin (one of the proteins that make the actin filaments) prevents the connection of the myosin heads to the actin, impeding consequently the possi-bility of contraction due to an absence of contact points. With the entrance of Ca2+, it connects to the troponin (one of the proteins that make the actin filaments), provoking the removal of the tropomyosin and allowing therefore the myosin heads to interact with the actin, starting the process of muscular con-traction. This mechanism, multiplied by thousands of myosin-actin connections, promotes the shorten-ing of the muscle and consequence production of mechanical work. The relaxation occurs when the Ca2+ is again pumped into the reticulum and the tropomyosin acts once again, preventing the contraction (Soares, 2005). The reference to sodium (Na) in this interview is due to this chemical element playing a role in the gradient differences that can be verified at a cellular level and also due to its relationship with the calcium gradients that are involved with the contractile mechanism.

There is a functional oscillation in many teams, but that is why there should be a lot of reflection on Barcelona's way of training...see, in the traditional... people will say the following: "No, we need to stay away from an adaptability that is acting, and we need to recharge 'batteries' and whatever...". And then they don't understand why these oscillations happen, the loss of Specificity, which goes beyond the possible anomaly!

When this is not accomplished as it should be, and just like in training, for example, moving again to the Morphocycle, what happens is the possibility of damage to the cells, <u>and that is why I talk about 'paranecrose'</u>. This is when we feel pain and then inclusively take anti-inflammatory medication for that. And we know that nowadays there are some cases of sudden death caused by excessive use of anti-inflammatory medication.

So, when the cells are damaged, they spill ATP, they release ATP, ATP that is broken, broken down into ADP, the ADP connects to specific receptors, the p2y, but in the platelets. When this happens, in the organism there is the formation of clots that try to close the wound, to fight it...What does this lead to? The contraction and relaxation, if not accomplished through certain ways, can lead to the coagulation. Because most of the times, people that are coaching end up killing the guys! It is another significant advantage of Tactical Periodization. So, the blood coagulation happens, the ATP gets out of the cells in an injury and is broken down into ADP and then is reconnected, or links to the platelet receptors, these respond. And they respond to create a blood clot that starts circulating. This is disturbing either in the epithelial cells and in the muscular cells, therefore not only with a loss...imagine that there is not really a big problem, but there is a problem of intervention of something that is anomalous with regards to the Specificity, it's like you having something in between your teeth, it doesn't come out and you cannot chew properly, so you end up biting your tongue, etc., etc. But when this happens it may end up originating, for the reconstitution of the cells in the context, the cell pro- liferation that regards the reconstitution of what is damaged, and therefore the cells multiply, and the result may be, in a longer-term perspective or even medium, the re-narrowing or the narrowing down of the artery, something called stenosis.

This particularity of the metabolic functioning, circulatory of the ATP itself and now having in mind...I believe it is only respected by Tactical Periodiza- tion, even before I had understood these things, what ends up being amusing.

So, from that text that I gave, it is inclusively much more complex and much more detailed and mentions the ATP connections as signalling, or as signals that transmit messages to the exterior of the cell and that interferes positive or negatively for example, with the brain, in the brain, with learning, with memory, with the movement articulation. And curiously they say that when there is excessive signalling, of signals present, therefore once again there is the Specificity here protecting this, it may have a correlation with brain cases, for example with epilepsy or even some psychological issues. Inclusively with most sensorial organs, with the heart, etc., etc., etc. Curiously, <u>the immune system</u> reacts and naturally, reacts 'a la longue', <u>reacts in accordance</u> to the need of having to react regularly in a certain way, I don't know, I will spec- ulate, but probably the sudden deaths may also be related to that in some extent. Because <u>the immune system, when</u> the ATP is requested, is released by the injured tissues, leading the immune cells to cause inflammation, which is a response that can even cause pain, once again here you can see the parabiose and the 'paranecrose'. The excessive and prolonged inflammation may damage the tissue, and examples referred here in the text like rheumatoid arthritis, etc., etc., etc. _The transmission of signals by the ATP also helps or can help the immune cells to kill the cells infected by anomalies, bacteria and others._ But see if on the one hand, _if there is a condition, if there is a kind of inversion and_ if this happens he has to intervene, but the inflammatory condition is not, or the damage of tissues does not occur, and _the action of the immune system is advantageous, and it is indeed an important aspect._

I would tell you the following just to end, I would end as I started, it is the lack of understanding of the Morphocycle.

<u>Why did I name it Morphocycle?</u>

Why does it consider the recovery and the performance effort?

Why, and how is the sporting shape considered having the collective and the individual in mind?

Why must recovery be contemplated in a certain way?

What does the colour symbology mean?

So, I imagine that the emergence is the way how I want to play football, it emerges from realities in presence, so I recall two primary colours like blue and yellow that, when mixed, become green. Green is the emergence, it's the organisation. So if you imagine the fuel, and not only the fuel, and in this case the particular way of functioning of the muscular groups either in speed or under tension, which characterise the nucleus of regular performance, and how these indicators, or these aspects, when they occur just like that, _they demand the expression of bioenergetics and of a dominant relational pattern,_ conditional, among the various types of muscular fibres. This is the guarantee, when I happen to paint the blue with the blue – always -, the yellow with the yellow – always -, in the individual, without this becoming an anomaly with regards to the recovery, because it exists on Wednesday (Wednesday is the most fragmented day), on Friday...because you know, for example, the 100m world-record holder, he runs a 100m race, breaks the World record, rests for 30 minutes, and then he is ready to try and break it again. So, I don't interfere with the recovery, and at the same time I activate, catalyse a reality that I know that exists and that focusing on the individual will not disturb the recovery. Maybe it will even help me speed it up, and when it happens regularly, this blue and this yellow do a better job getting the green. _And this must be constant._ In the green of the week I am concerned with the Macro Principles and Sub-Principles, fundamentally with the macro, making the intermittence present there as well, and every time I reduce the activity I must not impoverish it, and this non-impoverishment contains all dimensions, the temporality of execution, the dynamic or the dynamism of the dynamic to bring to life.

And that is why I give you the example of a while ago, the guy, alright, proposes a 'small-sided activity. He does X minutes and is not concerned that the guy is intervening, he intervenes 20 times in a certain space, when in that space he would intervene 2 or 3 times in a real match? _It is obvious that the repercussions_ in metabolic terms, as a consequence for the _adaptability_ are not the same. So, if throughout the time I don't have that in consideration, I will be tying, I will be placing a straitjacket. That won't happen if the Morphocycle is respected, but the Morphocycle does not arise from a vacuum. That is why I say that there are two levels: a more conceptual, more theoretical level, which belongs to the sphere of values, and that has to do with the way how I want to play. This is the way how I want to play, and I will I give birth to that? And the way how I will give birth to that is, when training, always training the same way?! Maybe yes, but what?! I contemplate all levels of complexity that this has?! Maybe not, then I will have to reduce this. And how can I reduce it without impoverishment? Well, but this is a whole with individuals! And how can I avoid losing the best of those individuals?! Then it is through...therefore, already on the praxiological or operative side or operational or phenomeno-logical, or methodological! How do I have to do this? Through the existence of the contemplation of the Specific in this weekly framework, repeating this way, and therefore systematic repetition but the systematic repetition is that of the Morphocycle! I think that's enough!

Is it enough? No, it's not enough!

Not only, but the more-or-less high performance does not occur 'in vitro'! The quality of good football relies on a collective way of playing, with the lat-ter being achieved through competition, precisely the superior performance. A reality that contains as well, a club, directors, members, players, coaches, and the opponents, which can also be characterised in the same way! And the media, what are they in this problematic? So much 'sand' for such a 'big truck'! You don't need much more than common sense to understand that it is unavoidable to recognise the presence of a fundamental pre-condition that is part of the competition! Which? The conflict. Recognising it necessarily, also essential in structuring the psychologic of what is Human, relative to the per-sonality of individuals.

It is not possible to alienate the dominance of the presence of conflict in a latent context mixture and/or expressed in the development of the eventual context of trainability, and above all, of competition. So, the selfishness, the egocentrism, and even the egotism, or the tendential simulation of the indi-viduals in this competitive phenomenology, this is not fiction! And when this happens, it collides with what should be the consistency, the robustness, the cohesion, the fluidity, the empathy, or the mutual attraction, in the existence of a collective, with objectives to be reached as for such? This emotional pil-low, meaning the sentimentality, affectivity, empathy, synergy, all necessary, they become like the reason for the emergence of a feeling of confidence in the group even before its existence!

So, it is not a phenomenological framing 'in vitro'. The conflictive inherent to the eventual does not allow the one leading, the coach, to pretend that it is not present. In the village where I was born people used to say: "you must have them in their place!". The leadership style is another thing. Mourinho has one. Andre Villas-Boas has other. Guardiola, a different one. See for example how Mascherano (he was not bought as if he were a random player!) has been integrated!

Regarding these issues of affectivity, since long-time psychoanalysis has alerted that everyone, in different degrees, clearly ignores, or better, we are not conscious of many aspects related to what we feel, and therefore the way we see ourselves is never equal to how the others see us. To be at the TOP as a coach it is absolutely indispensable not to trick ourselves, otherwise, we will still be in the movie, but watching it upside down!

Therefore, even though a while ago I said it is not enough, it is good if I highlight that in the end, it is very handy not being mistaken with regards to what Tactical Periodization should be, what it is as a methodology! But then there is the fearful coach, the shitty coach, etc., etc., and then the one that can lead! And the latter does not do it...because if he did it like the Dalai Lama or Obama, or like Mother Teresa used to do...surely, he won't get there! And the same will occur, if as a coach he thinks like if the future to 'achieve', with regards to the way of playing that he wants to achieve, has no present. The future can only be 'pre-seen', it cannot be predicted, meaning that it can be prepared through periodization!

Therefore, all the mistakes produced in the operationalisation of Tactical Periodization are linked to a single mistake: the lack of understanding of what Tactical Periodization is. This can be observed over two levels: a conceptual – theoretical – level; and, resulting from the multiple deficiencies regarding it, a second, methodological level. In summary, it could be argued that the mistakes result from the lack of understanding of the Pattern-Morphocycle.

These mistakes become clearer when we work in a High-Performance context. The incoherence and inconsistency are then visible, regarding some essential things in Tactical Periodization, like the management of the colours or the management of doses from match to match and from training to training.

It is crucial for the understanding of Tactical Periodization that one admits (like the majority of coaches do) that a team, after a performance with maximum demand (a match with maximum demand), needs four days to be able to undergo another effort of maximum demand (either a match or a training session) without experiencing lower levels of performance. This means that the specific bio-energetic support, linked to all the others, which allows for the expression of the functionality of the team without a loss of quality, will only be ready to be activated again in its maximum capacity, four days after a match with maximum demand.

That is why in the Pattern Morphocycle with a match every Sunday, the most demanding training session is half-way through the week, on a Thursday. Since the previous match – Sunday – until the most demanding session – Thursday – we will have four days of recovery while having three days left until the next match – Sunday. We know that a training session with maximum demand will have less demand than a maximum demand match. Therefore, we will need fewer days to recover the specific bio-energetic support and all the rest which is always connected. The conditions to promote during this session with maximum demand – Thursday – should be very similar to those that the team reveals to work as a team during a match. Therefore, this training with maximum demand will focus fundamentally on the whole, on a more Macro level.

Now, we know the whole is only guaranteed as whole if the elements that compose it as such do not lose maximal possibilities of expression when it is expressed. So, in those other two acquisitive days – Wednesday and Friday – there is a need for individual improvement, to focus and evolve a more Micro level. If this recovery that must occur between efforts of maximum demand is so essential, the correct recovery will not be less essential, as this is another typology of recovery that should exist between repetitions and exercises. That is why we always must pay extreme importance not only to ensure that the exercising times are adequate but also that the recovery times are appropriate to (between exercises and inclusively in the same exercise). This is something often overlooked, especially in High Performance, revealing incoherence and inconsistency influenced by the conventional logic.

As if I have said the management of the doses is so essential in the operationalisation of Tactical Periodization, we must admit the importance of the existence of dominance on the different days of the

Morphocycle, allowing for the recovery between efforts of maximum demand, together with the respect for exercising and break times (recovery) on each of these days.

If we admit the 4-day 'rule' we can understand that a Pattern Morphocycle with a match every Sunday will look like this: effort of maximum demand on Sunday, recovery on Monday, Tuesday, and Wednesday (although Wednesday contains acquisition), training on Thursday, recovery on Friday (with acquisition too) and Saturday (with activation), and effort of maximum demand on Sunday. It is crucial, therefore, that we recognise the possibility of the existence of a 'single training day', Thursday, in which there should be no loss of the adaptability Matrix, just like during the other days.

If it is so, why do we say that there are three acquisitive days in the Morphocycle? Because it is possible to perform acquisitive training without a loss of recovery. We should guarantee that the acquisition falls on the individual, and that the possible individual growth supported in an indicator (eccentric contractions or maximum speed of contraction) but directed by Actions or Inter-Actions of our way of playing – therefore, a collective goal – is performed based on a metabolic pattern that is similar to our more global playing Matrix, a metabolic web with dominance of the anaerobic alactic metabolism in our case, as we understand that this is the metabolism that is more expressed in those ways of playing with high quality.

Only by having the guarantee that this occurs uninterruptedly every week can we not only maintain the same bio-energetic profile, but also, be in good conditions to improve it, or at least, not make it worse.

This is something that would not happen if there is no respect for breaks, which could end up risking adaptability and even potentially changing it. The lack of respect for the break times means that the effort does not guarantee the dominance of the desired metabolism, and therefore, there is no respect for the metabolic pattern – a canvas among the metabolisms – which is desired as a support for our way of playing. This effort may end up under the dominance of the anaerobic lactic metabolism. If this happens repeatedly, there could be changes in the adaptability that must be the consequence of the presence of the same metabolic pattern every day, something that is only guaranteed with a perfect understanding of the Morphocycle.

Therefore, the adaptability to a certain way of playing and to the bio-energetic support that it demands can be changed if the exercising times and the breaks are not adequate and the days of the Morphocycle are not respected. After an effort - the adequate one – we should allow enough recovery time so that when resuming the effort, the players are fresh, being able to express it with the desired metabolic pattern once again. In our case, it means with the dominance of the anaerobic alactic metabolism (without a loss of the relationship with the other metabolisms, in a specific association of our way of playing). If the break times do not allow enough recovery, being too short, we will restart the exercise with the dominance of the anaerobic lactic mechanism, something that in continuity would alter the desired adaptability. We would no longer be training Specifically.

So, it is fundamental for Tactical Periodization to train always in Specificity. As we know, the energy is provided by the ATP, which can be involved in different metabolic processes. Without the presence of ATP, with its rupture, its synthesis, or re-synthesis, there is no energy. Now, if this ATP is involved in a metabolic process 'A' with the dominance of the anaerobic alactic mechanism or if it is involved in a process 'B' with the dominance of the anaerobic lactic mechanism, the phenomenology won't be the same. There will be a change in the participation of the ATP receptors and of those enzymes involved. This alteration will also apply to the information transmitted by the ATP to the other cells and to the exterior.

It is essential that the exercising times are appropriate and require a significant stimulation, including the need for fatigue in the cells. Also, the break times must be sufficiently prolonged so that the organism can restart the activity with the desired pattern. In our case, with the dominance of the anaerobic alactic mechanism, allow for the self-renovation that, as Vitor Frade suggests, leads to self-generation. If these time-frames are not respected, we may induce what Frade designates as a state of 'paranecrosis', provoking organic lesion, lesion of the tissues, to which the body will react by developing changes in the way it relates to the ATP, which may bring undesirable consequences.

The relevance of Specificity, of the way of playing that I seek, is undeniable and I can get to it through a trainability that I operationalise, and that is complex. It must take the circumstances into account. If it is complex we must treat it with complex tools – Tactical Periodization – considering the causality with the importance it deserves. So, the acquisitive cannot be any acquisitive. Conditions that require bringing them to fatigue, to the limit (concerning the whole or quasi-whole or to the individual) and allowing them time to recover until being once again ready to restart the activity.

When we invest in one activity, football in our case, we influence the organs, the systems, the functions, we affect the individual. In football, we affect the individual in the co-relationship and co-difficulty, as he acts with other players and against another team. What Tactical Periodization seeks is that this is done considering the capturing sensitivity of the individuals concerning the circumstances. We must have concerns regarding the first timing of expression of the body parts involved, in the co-contractibility that must occur so that the moment is fluid, and in how this happens with the need for adjusting the circumstances to the environment. Many times, this can be decodable in advance. The experiencing and familiarisation with a context can promote this anticipation. But anticipating what? The choices. And this will be easier if there was somatisation, which is related to the second time.

All this is achieved through a Process of trainability that, as I have explained before, is able to accomplish the effect of delayed performance that we look for. It requires a certain 'engagement' between the metabolisms. An 'engagement' that interests me and that, if I know it in advance, can be actioned during this Process. Therefore, we produce a stimulation that conduces to a decreased functionality – which provokes a metabolic acceleration – that leads the involved things to disassemble, then reassembling, self-renovate, reappearing improved.

This self-renovation occurs very rapidly. However, the time it takes to develop will not be the same depending on the dominance of the metabolisms involved. Once again, it is undeniable the importance of Specificity during the whole Process, together with Recovery, which is performed through the activation of this metabolic web, while diminished in time and with much intermittence, with very large breaks. What the other logic says is the opposite: although you get tired due to a 'complex whole' acting on the aerobic metabolism, you recover.

If we 'direct' the Process towards one metabolic pattern or another, with dominance of one metabolism or with a certain relationship between this one and the others, we can say that this constant self-renovation is deliberate. It is fundamental then, to know how I must deliberate and to do this it's essential that we know what the Tactical Dimension is for Tactical Periodization. It only exists a priori as a theoretical, conceptual configuration that I seek. And exists, *a posteriori*, as an emergence, the way of playing that I execute. It is the somatisation of certain Principles and Sub-Principles that enable a certain identity, which I regularly express at a Macro level.

Therefore, the foundation of Tactical Periodization is training to learn a way of playing, doing so under certain circumstances and with determined bio-energetic support. This learning process can occur by reception – with the primacy of the frontal cortex, in rationality – and, as Tactical Periodization proposes, by discovery – with the primacy of the brainstem, and the presence of emotion when we act, independently of the sentimentality or understanding of the Principles that may occur after, etc.

To learn and somatise this way of playing we produce an expenditure of energetic substances that need to self-renovate – through recovery, the adequate break – to restart this learning and this somatisation with the desired conditions.

We know that oxygen is a capital element, among others, for the re-synthesis and reconstitution of phosphocreatine and ATP that are used during the effort. The organism consumes it the most avidly during the alactic effort. This reconstitution, when performed under optimal conditions, achieves an increase of everything involved, there is a kind of super-compensation. Everything here is related to the Specific acquisitive and not to just any acquisitive. The organism improves. But if the performance is not repeated, this stage – the so-called exaltation phase – diminishes and disappears progressively. That is why continuity is so important, even if in discontinuity. It is necessary that this pattern of intermittence occurs, as it guarantees the alternation during the Morphocycle in a group of units and during the training units themselves.

Now, if we provoke an excessively extreme excitation – perhaps due to the intensity of performance or due to not respecting its time of reconstitution – what we get is the destruction of cellular functions. So, what we want is to provoke great excitations, because they are the ones bringing improvements. These great excitations are reflected in Maximum Relative Intensities, with maximum focus. They relate to the Specificity of our way of playing and can only be achieved if we are fresh. If the efforts, or the performances, are repeated in a very short time frame, without allowing the processes of restoration which lead to improvements to take place, we end up jeopardising the desired acquisition, our acquisition. Because what happens is the extenuation, and consequently, an Adaptability that we don't desire.

We should start realising that we are colonised by common logic, by cultural reinforcers that influence us consciously, and worse, subconsciously.

So, when facing the question: "Professor, today many people are trying to train using Tactical Periodization, there are some people more identified with it than others, but in your opinion, which are the most common mistakes in the operationalisation of Tactical Periodization?", we can say that all these mistakes arise from the lack of understanding of the Morphocycle and also by a lack of knowledge of what Tactical Periodization is.

It is clear that the more or less high performance does not occur 'in vitro' and that the training methodology designated as Tactical Periodization is not foreign to it. Naturally, there are other fundamental things to consider. The decoding of the context, of everything that surrounds the club in which you work, the clubs which you will play against, the press, etc. And it is necessary to recognise the presence of a fundamental premise: conflict. Therefore, it is not about a phenomenological framework 'in vitro'. The coach cannot be blind to the conflictive that is inherent to the eventual, and that is why leadership is so important. What kind of leadership? There are many types.

We must realise that to get to the way of playing we desire, that we aspire to achieve in the future, we must execute a Process that occurs in the present and for which we are responsible.

> Vitor Frade's PhD project: this precious docu-
ment shows his long-time concern with a paradigm
that differs from the mainstream. Although the project was written in 1990, he had created Tactical
Periodization earlier.

> TACTICAL PERIODIZATION'S BIG BANG

Xavier Tamarit

> Foreword

....

Rui Faria

Football Manager

"To operationalise! Going deep into the roots of methodological knowledge."

"Despite the process lasting for months, a new starting point arrives in the search for objectives. Ten days of commitments with their National Teams and 90% of the players return to the club. Spanish, Portuguese, German, Argentinean, Brazilian, Turkish and French. Ten days of 'separation', ten days of 'experiences' throughout the different corners of the World. New challenges and the complexity of emotions that reproduce themselves in a globalised feeling of returning to each other's cultural origins. New ideas, new concepts, different cultures and game philosophies other than different methodological habits!

The different experiences of those past days have led the players into different feelings and levels of shape. These are now a very particular concern to all those directing the process and anticipating the needs of both the individual and the team while looking at their team's/club next match. They are all again players on the same team. All of them! With more or less game time, with more or less flying hours, with more or less individual or collective frustrations. It is mandatory to reflect carefully on the moment's singularity. A coach is a person submitted to priorities! There is not much time; there is less time than desired to practice, less time than desired to recover, to remember, replicate or simply rehearsing the conceptual bonds that characterise the team. It is urgent to rapidly replace different game perspectives proposed by the different National team managers with the club's ideas, the club's coach. It is urgent to select exercises that fit the current situation, the 'intentionalised interactions', the concepts. It is urgent to invent a determined moment coherently because that is what the moment requires. It is urgent to find the SPECIFIC exercise, ephemeral-strategical as a momentary emergence. It is urgent to direct the temporal impact of the 'intentionalised interactions' in the application of the concepts and through this allow the effective manifestation of the 'intentionalised interactions', taking into account the upcoming match. It is urgent not separating, not dividing, not castrating. It is urgent to promote the variability of the context and the constant search for adjustment within those mentioned interactions. It is urgent to practice without having time (for the quality of the 'intentionalised interactions'), and it is also urgent to have time to explain and understand (due to the complexity of the 'intentionalised interactions'). It is urgent to direct the set of emotional states bearing in mind the needs of the team. It is urgent...it is urgent...and it is urgent to reflect on what the process is asking for in a perspective of creativity and intelligence, of operationalisation and reflection, of knowledge and (re)cognition while 'observing' and 'seeing'. Seeking conceptual support in the methodological essence is urgent. It is urgent not to lose oneself in the road one wants to follow. It is urgent to consider the multiple differentiating moments, which even though demanding differentiated approach themselves, share the same common matrix behind the doing. It is urgent to accept that in this particular context the variability of the process during a whole season is effectively complex. The competitive density and the permanent influences and disturbances to the group's performance stability are as unpredictable as the game itself. It is urgent to understand the diminution of that unpredictability of the game through the 'collective knowledge' of the team as well as the diminution of the unpredictability of the process through a 'wholeness' that is the knowledge associated to the coach's imagination. It is urgent!

The theme and the relevance of this book have allowed me to do an exercise of reflection/description about the experiences related to the practical reality that develops on the pitch and that constant 'novelties' that this leads us to. The objective is to provide meaning to the importance that it holds in the daily regulation of the process, in every training session - the reasons and shapes through which this is (un)consciously organised. Through a description of options and decisions associated to training in a specific moment, treating them as starting points (principles) of the promotion of a methodo(logical) occurrence of a determined moment of training the competition!

In the same way that the reflections gathered by the author through his interviews are an interesting contribution towards making this book an essential tool for the lovers of high performance, clarifying the concept of Tactical Periodization – the primary goal of this book – is as necessary as urgent! There are many doubts regarding the concept, and there are many (uncertain) certainties regarding how to operate under the concept. There are no two equal coaches; no two brains are thinking the operationalisation of a process in the same way or deciding identically in an emergency. Nonetheless, some guidelines allow the coach to have criteria assisting him/her making sense of the journey ahead. Moreover, those can be the ones of Tactical Periodization here brought to a level of excellence by Professor Vítor Frade.

In my perspective, the objective has been achieved. The author also successfully managed to decompose the complexity of the concept/method in emerging questions that meet the needs of all those directing training and competitive processes. He explains and validates the foundations of a knowledge that cannot generate doubts to those in contact with it. Nonetheless, you either believe, or you do not – there is no intermediate position!

Rui Faria

> Introduction

When I finished writing my previous book, I promised myself it would be the last one. As you come to read these words, you will have realised that I lied to myself. Several inter-related circumstances have contributed to this fate: among them, the success of my first book among the readers and those close to me provided an incentive to create what you have today in front of you...together with what I consider having been the misinterpretation of Tactical Periodization.

I was invited to speak at conferences, masters, and clinics, many of which where others spoke about Tactical Periodization. I read articles, blogs and internet forums, as well as books that referenced it. I talked to many people who told me that they understood and applied it in their practice. After all this, I was almost convinced that I was the one who knew nothing about Tactical Periodization. Nearly every person added something or took something out. Others misinterpreted it or interpreted it at their convenience. There were some who put effort into understanding it, who was on the right track. However, most people were promoting or learning something called Tactical Periodization that had nothing to do with the one created by Professor Vítor Frade, the one he had himself explained to me, and that step-by-step I could understand.

There were people that after reading just a couple of books already understood it fully (?) and would even improve it, adding their elements. Others would discard it without providing any justification, and some who had vaguely heard of Tactical Periodization would devalue it by saying that they had been already doing it centuries ago without, in reality, knowing anything about it! Tactical Periodization has been criticised for some things: because it did not consider the individual, because it did not pay attention to the physical side, because it was only theoretical, because it was extremist! Even because it openly refused certain things that others do and, in the end, did them covertly!

In summary, this is why I felt a great needed to write once again about this topic. I felt the obligation, due to the existence of a 'navel-string' between myself and this interINDEpendence, to write a book that could alert people for this misinterpretation that is being widely publicised, while simultaneously trying to help those who want to learn about it.

There would not be, and there will never be, a better way to understand it than through the words of its creator and through the words of those surrounding him and applying his methodology to their current practice. In my opinion, the excellent contributions from Mauricio Pellegrino and Rui Faria, who wrote the forewords to this book, increase its quality.

For all those that ignore the true Tactical Periodization, for all those that know of a distorted version and for those who know something about it: Vítor Frade clarifies!

libro
futbol
.com
AL GOL DE
LLEGA LEYENDO

141

1

> The birth of a new Logic

"The oppressive leadership of the Church was finally challenged by Renaissance scientists who came on the scene like a breath of fresh air. With a liberating and more humane, sane view of knowledge, scientists promised to keep an open mind and apply an unbiased eye regarding truths".

"However, over time, after science had solidified its position as civilisation's "official" truth provider, practitioners of that paradigm also began to profess and defend its truths as absolute and infallible oppressively. Subsequently, in the modern world, the term 'scientific' is synonymous with true".

(Bruce H.Lipton and Steve Bhaerman, Spontaneous Evolution, p.92)

Xavier, I do not know how to explain it in objective terms. I think it was not a single moment, and even if it was, I could not recall it (...)

Vítor Frade (1)[77]

Vítor Manuel da Costa Frade was born in Vila Franca da Beira, district of Coimbra (Portugal) on 29 September 1944. He is the creator of the training methodology known as Tactical Periodization, transgressive of a logic that has been accepted as absolute truth by most existing training theories and methodologies, and potentially by all sports. This 'new' methodology was created almost 30 years ago, but it became more known internationally after the successes of Portuguese manager José Mourinho. Together with his staff, he managed to bring Tactical Periodization to excellence on a practical level.

Tactical Periodization is a process who evolution can be confounded with the history of Professor Vitor Frade, who was a lecturer for 33 years in the Faculty of Sports at the University of Porto (Portugal). He was also an assistant manager with different professional teams from the Portuguese League, such as Boavista FC (for six seasons, although he was also a caretaker manager during some short periods), Rio Ave FC (two periods of three seasons each), and FC Felgueiras (one season). Furthermore, Frade spent more than 20 years at FC Porto (working with the First Team from 1993 to 1997 and between 1999 and 2000). He won national titles (three Primeira Liga trophies, four Portuguese Cups and four Portuguese Super Cups) and took part in international competitions (arriving at the semi-finals of both Champions League and Cup Winners Cup).

His methodology, therefore, is not something that arose from an «a-ha!» moment. It is neither something extracted from other area and transferred to this mass phenomenon called Football.

(...) I had a particular sensitivity for what we called the body, for what was the relationship between the body and some activities, and what that relationship should be. So, as a student, I was already susceptible to some domains, such as psychomotricity, for example. Remember, we were in the 1970s. In Portugal, there is a reference, a pioneer, regarding questioning the dualism that existed in Physical Education between body and spirit, and that reference is Professor Nélson Mendes[78]. I was fortunate to have him as a lecturer, and he had a significant impact on my views of the mainstream and on a potential refusal of that mainstream. (...) I had been a professional football player[79] and had to take a break so that I could go to University. There, I also had to choose another sport beyond football, and I picked volleyball. There, I also met people that thought volleyball differently, like Professor Puga[80], the father of FC

77 Vítor Frade: interviewed by Xavier Tamarit in 2010.

78 Professor Nélson Mendes: Professor in the Faculty of Human Kinetics (FMH) at the Technical University of Lisbon (UTL). He was once the director of the Portuguese National Institute for Physical Education (INEF).

79 As a professional football player, Vítor Frade played for FC Porto U-19s, FC Tirsense, FC Lixa, Boavista FC and UD Vilafranquense.

80 Professor Puga: Professor in the Faculty of Human Kinetics (FMH) at the Technical University of Lisbon (UTL). Volleyball coach. Portuguese National Champions for several times and former Portuguese

Porto's First Team doctor, Dr Nélson Puga[81]. He saw the game very differently: you had to be intelligent, to think the game. (...)

Then there is my childhood that was spent mostly on the street, in a very traditional area of Porto, the Sé[82]. We were in the 1950s, walking barefoot was something usual, as was having to run away from the police because we were not allowed to play football on the street. It happened to me several times. I was arrested twice for playing football. As a player, I had certain characteristics; I was more inclined to reflect on the game, it was something fundamental to me, even though I recognised the need to be technically able but depending on the existing circumstances. So, there is a history that you cannot put aside regarding sensitivity. However, as I said previously, with regards to training, I was just like the other students. I tried to learn what I was supposed to, even if in some cases I saw great fragility in some ideas. So, my development regarding training, as a student, was fundamentally conditioned by the Eastern Block, especially the Soviet Union, with names such as Matveiev[83]. I absorbed all that knowledge because I needed to, with a certain level of disagreement, which I did not express very openly at the time. (...)

However, during my degree, I went abroad several times: conferences, seminars, and other events. I believed that life more complex than we were taught, and training was not different, even if at the time it was not my central concern. I had broader concerns, although in 1969 I ended up doing a Football course, in Sète, France[84].

Moreover, at the end of my bachelor's degree, I decided to write my dissertation the other way around; you had to start from the end. I wrote all of it the opposite way. Moreover, I did so with the intention of provoking my assessors from the moment they would receive the dissertation. It aimed to make them feel uncomfortable because it drifted from the conventional and to read it they would have to get different aspects of the brain and body to work. That structure was indeed support for the content. So, as a student, I was weird, because I thought things thoroughly, I kept searching...and the differences regarding information and with regards to key authors were significant. Because I have always been interested in other areas since very early, such as Psychoanalysis, Anthropology, Psychology, and I was fortunate to have some lecturers...probably if I had others, I would not have been like this, or maybe I would have anyway, who knows? However, fundamentally I had that one, Nelson Mendes, and[85] Vítor da Fonseca, who were different from other people, and that highlighted the importance of knowing the nervous system and the

---

National Team coach. He played a key role in Vítor Frade's appointment as North of Portugal U-19 coach and also Portuguese National Team U-19 coach at the 1979 European Volleyball Championship.

81 Dr. Nélson Puga: Expert in Sports Medicine and First Team doctor at FC Porto. He also played professionally with FC Porto's volleyball team.

82 é, Porto: A neighbourhood with medieval roots, located in Porto's old city; also known as Porto's Cathedral neighbourhood.

83 Lev Pavlovich Matveiev: Born in 1924. Graduate at the Physical Culture Institute in 1950. Awarded a doctorate in Training Methodology, which he also taught at Moscow's Physical Education Institute. Wrote several documents about theory and methodology of training and physical education.

84 Sète: French village located in the district of Montpellier.

85 Vítor da Fonseca: Former Full Professor at the Faculty of Human Kinetics (FMH), Technical University of Lisbon (UTL).

brain to understand those things. As I had interests related with Cybernetics, mostly through studying [86]Laborit

In the beginning and after that, because since he was a doctor, both the nervous systems and the brain deserved his attention when looking at the problems of Cybernetics. So, all that conditioned me shaped me, maybe even formatted me. However, none of it was my central concern about training, to the game or football. Because curiously I was initially a volleyball coach, before moving to football.

(...) One day, in an experiment in Professor Vítor da Fonseca's class, he suggests unusually performing a usual task, so I decided to write my signature with the left hand (I usually write with the right one). My name is Vítor, and in my identity card, in my birth record, you can read 'Victor' with a 'c'. Since I was 17, more or less, and I cannot explain why, maybe because no-one calls me Victor – they call me Vítor -, why should I keep the 'c'? So since then, I made the 'c' disappear from my signature. On my identity card, my name has a 'c', but it is absent from my signature.

And as you know, my signature is a bit twisted, well, not twisted but inclined to the left. When Professor Fonseca suggests that we do this task, I had stopped writing Victor with a 'c' for maybe 10 or 12 years, but when I was signing with my left hand...oh! I call the professor: 'Vítor, come here, see!'. I had written my name with a 'c' when writing it with the left hand! I can also recall another episode when I was more or less five years old. I lived in a very traditional area of Oporto where [87]Sao Joao was celebrated.

Also, it was usual to dance on the street. I dance very well, but I don't know who taught me how to dance, except my mum's memories. My dad had bought a cellar. He had had one previously in [88]Boavista, but only for a short period. Then he bought this one. And people would ask my dad: 'how does your son dance so well? Who taught him? Where did he learn it?' And my mum would tell me that it had been a man who sold the lottery, who was a customer of the cellar (of that first one that my dad had bought in Boavista). He would put my feet on top of his and then he would dance. But had no recollection of that! I remember being 9 or 10, in primary school, and while facing a complicated problem that no-one in the class could solve, getting it right intuitively. And the teacher was astonished and asked me 'but how do you know it?'. 'I don't know, but the answer is x'. This is not to illustrate that I was brilliant or that I am made of a different material, not at all. But I was always curious, and I really liked to think about things. And I remember asking myself: how can I know it if I don't know how to do it?

---

86 Henri Laborit: Born in 1914 in Hanoi, Indochina – 1995, Paris. Studied medicine. Worked as a surgeon in the War Navy but quickly started looking at the biology of behaviour, philosophy and sociology. Invited professor of bio-psycho-pharmacology at the University of Quebec. Director of the journal 'Agressologie'. Among his most known works are 'The man and the city' and 'Introduction to the biology of behaviour'.

87 Sao Joao's (Saint John's) celebrations: very important popular festivities in the city of Oporto. On the night of the 24th June, people eat barbecued sardines and watch fireworks near the river Douro. The celebrations end by sunrise, near the beach area.

88 Boavista: One of the modern neighbourhoods of Oporto. Very commercial and touristic area, where the famous Casa da Música and Boavista roundabout can be found.

Tactical Periodization is born from a number of personal events that go back to Vitor Frade's childhood and last until today: as a kid playing on the streets of the city where he was raised, Oporto; as a professional volleyball (he played one season for Uniao Academica de Avintes in the Premier Division) and football player. It also emerges from Frade's pathway as a student of different degrees (Engineering, Physical Education, Philosophy, Medicine) and as a lecturer in different areas (Theory and Methodology of Training, football specialisation). Finally, it benefits from his experience as a coach that starts first in volleyball (one of the first three Portuguese National Team coaches taking part in the Junior European Championships, being responsible for the North region) and then in football; as a person recognised both in professional football and in academia. A mixture of lived and learning experiences, inspired by several thinkers but also self-taught, linking theory and practice. An assemblage of knowledge from football, the game, and culture from other areas, because as Professor Frade says: 'those who only know about football, know nothing about football'. All of this added to his passion for this sport.

Already as a student, he thought differently, which led him to propose doing his assignments from different modules altogether. Not all his lecturers understood or accepted it. Therefore, he wrote a final dissertation that aimed to show a path and a vision that were different from the so-called 'correct' ones (which persists nowadays). He wrote his work manually, from the bottom to the top, from right to left, with some intentional spelling mistakes and other strategies that would allow him to demonstrate this reasoning when facing the panel of assessors. In the end, that became the object of this and many other books.

When I finish my degree, I come back to Oporto. Then, after 1974, the so-called Institutes of Physical Education – that are now faculties of Sport – open and I am invited to join because I had graduated with a very high grade and people talked about it. So, the people that were responsible for starting the faculty invite me, but they ask me with the objective of coordinating an area that was starting then: Foundational Physical Education. And I accepted it because the offer had something concrete and very relevant: I had to invite 10 other colleagues of mine. I would be the one choosing the lecturers that would be responsible for teaching the subject, and that was what got me excited. So, it happened: I came to coordinate, teach classes and also to be the overall responsible for Foundational Physical Education and get it working. So, I invite those 10 people, and we start putting a programme together. The schedule included Theory and Methodology of Training that would only begin, I believe, in the second year. And due to the initial agreements, that led to the creation of the faculty, there was a protocol with the Faculty of Medicine that led students that had passed from the first to the second year of the Medicine degree to transfer straight to the second year of the Physical Education degree without doing the first one! I don't remember the details, but that was the first group that took Theory and Methodology of Sports Training without having the first year of the course. This because they saw their modules of Medical Anatomy, Physiology and others recognised. And those students turn up to Theory and Methodology of Training and to other classes of the second year. So, the Installing Committee decides to ask me to drop Foundational Physical Education, leaving all my colleagues there. I stay as responsible for Theory and Methodology of Training. I confess that at that moment I was not too keen, but after they insisted and after I reflected on the circumstances and on the module, I decided to accept it. And that is when I become concerned with systematisation. Everything I knew and also what I didn't know was a result of my role as a student and due to my curiosity regarding some subjects, but I had never systematised them nor coached (...).

And that is when I start. And when I begin systematising to lecture, to build the module outline, that is when I find myself disagreeing with several things. I could be right, or it could be merely the result of my ignorance. But with time, and with an increased understanding of the area...and with being on the field coaching (!) I started to confirm my ideas. I left volleyball and moved to football. I went to the Premier League, to Boavista FC, where I stayed for 6 years. I had the responsibility of helping the team increasing their possibilities of winning and taking part in European competitions. Volleyball is an exceptional sport, even though it is called a team sport, it even has a border which you cannot cross even with a passport. But when I started coaching football, I started also contextualising my problems and my doubts. In my first couple of years in Boavista FC, on the Premier League, the circumstances were a great 'help' with regards to my certainties (...).

Theory and Methodology of Training was general, it was for everything. But when I started being on the pitch, I started telling myself 'no, this can't be! Especially not for football'. So, I started having a lot of questions. Already with my bachelor's dissertation, I put things upside down, I did not agree with the mainstream direction. Moreover, there was no football specialisation here...I decided to do another degree, Philosophy, at the same time that I lectured my classes and then the Installing Committee asked me to teach Sport Psychology in addition to Theory and Methodology of Training. I accepted it. I was building the programme and the possibility of starting the football specialisation arose. There was a terrific group that year, with many people interested in and connected to football. So, it made no sense that there were other specialisations and no football. The students came to me and asked me to teach them Football Methodology. I told the students that I could not do it because I had already committed to lecturing Theory and Methodology of Training and Sport Psychology.

Furthermore, I was finishing Philosophy at the same time. We were at the end of the 1970s, beginning of the 1980s, and I had no interest nor time. So, I try to solve that problem by referring to [89]Artur Jorge. As Artur Jorge had worked with [90]Pedroto and I got along really well with him... I had been an under-18 with Artur Jorge in FC Porto – and with Pedroto. I explained him the problem. At the time you only needed a bachelor's degree to lecture, and he had a degree in German Philology. I thought it could be interesting for him and he ended up accepting it. Pedroto also allowed (at the time Artur was going to be Pedroto's assistant), and things move forward, but just before the start Artur Jorge says no. He said he had changed his mind. And because everything was already set up, if it ended up not going ahead due to a lack

---

89 Artur Jorge: One of the greatest Portuguese football players and coaches. He played with teams like Academica de Coimbra, SL Benfica, CF Os Belenenses and also with the Portuguese National Team. He graduated in German Philology at the University of Lisbon in 1975. He studied Football Training Methodology in Leipzig, Germany. He coached FC Porto, Academica de Coimbra, SL Benfica, Racing Paris, Vitesse, CD Tenerife, CSKA Moscow, Portuguese National Team, Swiss National Team, Cameroon National Team, Al-Nasr, US Creteil, PSG. His biggest achievement was winning the 1987 European Cup with FC Porto, beating Bayern Munich in the final (2-1).

90 Jose Maria Carvalho Pedroto: Portuguese football player and coach. Played with teams like Leixoes SC, Lusitano VRSA, CF Os Belenenses, and FC Porto. Represented the Portuguese National Team for 17 times. As a coach he worked with Academica de Coimbra, Leixoes SC, Varzim SC, FC Porto, Boavista FC, Vitoria SC and the Portuguese National Team.

of lecturer, there was a serious possibility of taking another 10 years until we were given another chance to get the specialisation going. So, the students insisted with me, day and night, even going to my house: 'you must do it!'. So, I ended up saying yes, explaining the situation to the Installing Committee. I stayed as responsible for the Football specialisation.

I had already been lecturing Theory and Methodology of Training for a few years and told the students that I did not really agree with many things, but it was supposed to be like that. I tried to explain to them my reasoning, and when I start taking the football specialisation, I start systematising what I then called Tactical Periodization, so what is more specific. I did not have to work anymore with a curriculum that included all activities. I only had to work with a single one – football – in which I decided to focus exclusively. I was even working on the field. That is how I start systematising (...).

So, since then, not only due to an increasing belief, not just due to a growing systematisation, but mostly due to a need (mine and institutional), I had to create a conceptual and methodological framework. A framework that was different, transgressive in comparison to all other views. So, I don't know...it did not arise from a single 'a-ha' moment, not even remotely. It stemmed from a whole history, whose crucial event may be when I took the Football specialisation and had to systematise the programme. Even if before, when I was working on the field, I was already being considered by others as a heretic, because I did many things differently from the norm. (...)

So, when Vítor Frade took the Theory and Methodology of Training module first, and then, more importantly, the Football specialisation, he started systematising his thoughts and his understanding of training, creating a new training methodology with different Methodological Principles in comparison to those of other methodologies. It was a different vision, a different horizon within the football world at least. And that is how Tactical Periodization was created.

As we can see, unlike most think, its creation does not emerge merely from theoretical thoughts imported from other areas (as is the case with other trendy systemic methodologies). Instead, it is firstly shaped and only then starts to see itself mirrored in other areas of knowledge. But always having the game at its heart.

(...) Maybe it is worth to remind that I attended classes in different degrees. The first course I went to was Engineering, even though I never completed a single module there because I was playing football. I suppose I went there only to see some beautiful girls. I always carried a piece of paper to take some notes, but I never did anything! Then I went to military service and when I returned I asked myself 'will I continue in Engineering?'. I could not imagine myself doing anything related to Engineering. At the moment, people talked a lot about having a job at EFACEC as a guarantee for the future. But what I really wanted was physical education, sporting activity. The problem is that the course only existed in Lisbon. So, I had to sell my car – I had an MGB convertible as any 'good' football player – to go there. Not everyone does that, already with a certain age, at around 27. I did four years of military service, I did not go overseas, I did not go to the colonies, but I did four years of military service. The degree was outstanding, with exciting modules like Anthropology for example. The lecturers were interested in the brain, in the nervous system, all that. And then there was my passion for football, my obsession with football. And my obsession for being with the best. I got to know and was strongly influenced by Henri Laborit, whose work helped me immensely in systematising

things, in being sure that that was the path I had to follow. But I got to know Laborit due to my concerns and merely by chance (...).

(...) sometimes, even in my existentialist thoughts, I would tell myself: 'this cannot be like this'. I could not agree, but I would tell myself: 'maybe you are the problem, maybe it's your problem'. I would reflect and would end up thinking it could not be like that. I used analogies. I reflected as any normal person, as a student, as a player and then as a coach. But as a coach, you have different obligations, and you must systematise – also as a lecturer! And of course, my passion and my interest in football, and my understanding of the sport made me realise that football went way beyond football, that is was an activity that was being built by people and therefore was directed in a balanced way – or not – by the coach. So, my passion made me drop the conventional, made me feel the need to drop it, because I became more knowledgeable (or at least less ignorant) in other areas: Psychology, Anthropology, Cybernetics, Systems Theory, Fractal Geometry, etc...so that I could explain and validate. So, I can say that I left what I knew better and moved towards what I knew worse so that I could extract something beneficial for what I knew better. That is what led me to attend more than one degree. I went to Philosophy, not because...when I finished the degree, they invited me to stay as a lecturer, and I told them 'no, I came here because of training, and because of the problems of Epistemology, the problems of science and others'. And then I went to Medicine for the same reason, so that I could reap the rewards even regarding time. Because I always kept lecturing and being on the field, I thought 'if I have good lecturers, then I will end up gaining valuable time!'. I went to Medicine because of the nervous system and the brain. Then I heard about Chaos Theory, the concept of fractals, Systems Theory and Cybernetics. I was always concerned with applicability to training and to the game because these are sciences that are concerned with an identifying reality, a whole constituted by elements that interact. This contrasts with what has been the history of the theory of those so-called sports sciences, that are more focused on the individual, with the atomistic. And due to my attempt to systematise something that could stand by itself, something that could relate to my interest – football – and that is how Tactical Periodization started! (...)

It had to find support necessarily in areas that, at that moment, were completely unknown to the majority of people and that nowadays are not foreign at all. In reality, they make great contributions. What I always tried to avoid, was that it was mentioned in an empty way, without the presence of football contents, identifiers of its validity and of the methodology. But in the end what many people did was exactly that: dynamic systems here and there, talking about it without actually talking! But it does not work that way, I need to mention the Principles, I need to mention the Game. I need to know about football so that I can then use that knowledge conveniently. And more and more I need to be able to justify it with an appropriate language, adapted for football so that I can establish a logic – or more logics – that relates to all those realities. As you know, I have a library at home with more than 25,000 books, and a great part of those books relate to those subjects. That was very important for me. But I think I was 'pushed' there by my awareness of things, by the unavoidable empirical side of things, and the possibility of realisation and reflection, and the intelligence placed on those things. It is only possible to do that more profoundly from the moment that you depart from a mere concern with what is and should be the activity – in this case, football – but also with what is the person (...).

(...) establishing an analogy. I believe you have read that book [91]'Proust was a neuroscientist'. It is a book written by a neuroscientist who proposes to demonstrate in which way many times Art precedes Science, using some examples, like [92]Proust, that regarding looking at memory was a 'neuroscientist'. If he 'came' here today, he would be satisfied to know that, according to neuroscience, he was thinking appropriately. I also feel a certain pleasure in reading things that I have written in the 1970s or at the beginning of the 1980s, which at the time were very controversial, and that nowadays are confirmed by some advanced scientific writings. It seems I was not that wrong, and it even seems I was right! But that was a different paradigm from the one that was – and still is! - institutionalised. So, that was not the dominant paradigm, and you know that even here at the Faculty (Oporto) is still dominant.

This new horizon discovered by Professor Vítor Frade was so different that he decided, through its own name, to create a more significant impact on people. Its designation tries to use words known by most people to demonstrate a new understanding of those same words: *"Periodization in the sense that there is the need for some time to create the type of game that you aim for. Tactical because the game is about decision-making and therefore tactical, but those decisions, individual or collective, may be different depending on the desired behavioural patterns (interactions. Therefore, that decision must not be abstract, but instead built within the desired behavioural matrix (inter-relational or intentional) meaning that the decisions should be contextualised and specific to the team"[93].*

Jorge Maciel[94] (1) explains that *"the designation Tactical Periodization is justified because it is effectively a periodization. There is a need to establish chronological points (although not stationary) that allow for the acquisition and the emergence of a certain Collective Intentionality, a way of playing, a certain Tactic throughout the season".*

According to Vítor Frade (2)[95], *"the designation Tactical Periodization is slightly aggressive, provoking, precisely to show there is a periodization. And when we mention this concept, it should be understood what I mean, using a certain timeframe to make a certain order emerge. But if it is Tactical Periodization,*

91 'Proust was a neuroscientist': A unique portrait of eight fundamental modern artists by Jonah Lehrer. Proust predicted in a way the foundations of modern neuroscience with regards to memory. These are some suggestions made by Jonah Lehrer in his book 'Proust was a neuroscientist': "Every time we recall something, the memory's neuronal structure undergoes a delicate transformation, a process called reconsolidation (...). Memory is modified in the absence of the original stimulus, focusing less on what we can remember and more in ourselves. While we have memories to recall, their borders are constantly being modified to fit better with what we know now". "Every memory is inseparable from the moment that is recalled. (...) The state one finds herself in distorts the sense of past". "The memory of past events is not necessarily the memory of how things happened".

92 Marcel Proust (Paris, 1871, 1922): French writer, author of several titles like 'A la recherche du temps perdu'.

93 Guilherme Oliveira: Foreword of the book 'Que es la Periodizacion Tactica? Vivenciar el 'juego' para condicionar el Juego'. Xavier Tamarit, MC Sports, 2007.

94 'Pelas entranhas do nucleo duro do processo'. Unpublished article, 2010.

95 Vitor Frade (2): interviewed by Fabio Moura. Dissertation: 'O Periodo Preparatorio como espaco privilegiado para a plantacao do nosso jogar, de forma a podermos cultiva-lo e enraiza-lo...dentro da logica da Periodizacao Tactica', 2010.

libro
futbol
.com
AL GOL DE
LLEGA LEYENDO

151

that time is spent trying to emphasise the Tactical side, but even here it is provoking in the sense that its conceptualisation refers to a Tactical that is not the one commonly referred, related to a merely organisational and intentional aspect of playing. It also relates to the acculturation of principles in a team's playing dynamic. And if in fact, this way of playing has quality, it takes time to be constructed. That drifts away from all the logic of conventional periodization".

And it is so, that for many years, and still, nowadays, it has deserved strong criticism. To the point of being put aside by the rest of the football society. A society that was unable to understand this thinker, that could not believe that the world was not exactly like they had been told. A culture that keeps itself apart from the (il)logical, even when facing the 'threatening' results it continues to achieve.

Even the designation that I give it initially, precisely that of Tactical Periodization, is provocative. Because I knew that straight away people would say "but periodization is something else and it is not tactical...!". That is precisely the intention, that something different emerges, because in general terms, all the other times it is used, all the other periodization is used with a focus on the physical, with a focus on those so-called conditional capacities, or energy sources, it all gravitates around that. So, mine was, in reality, a transgressive logic. 'Tactical Periodization' involved two terms that were well-known to people and that people saw differently! So, "what the hell does this guy mean with this?!". Complementing the terminology to elucidate them better, designating or referring to it in a different way, but not necessarily, because I believe that even within one year of training the periods are different depending on the specificity of the circumstances and I have to anticipate this, and I have to find a logic that provides sustainability to that need. And the concept of 'Tactic' is a central concept for me in the Game of football. It is the Organization, and Intentionalised organisation, a 'dynamism of dynamics', which therefore has a broader – 'macro' level, which is what emergences from the collective references, encapsulating the totality of sectors and the relationships between sectors, and in this case the inter and the intrasectoral, etc. Then a 'micro' level, which in my perspective will be more diverse, diversified, or unfinishable, depending on the quality of the first level, the 'macro'! But that is an Organisation, a dynamic built from different sub-dynamics that I have to feed regularly, respecting a causality that has...that is so vital in its bottom-up logic as it is in its top-down logic. Consequently, the micro interferes in the macro and the macro interferes with the micro. It has to do with the ability to sustain this constant sense of balance. Because there is some terminology that we take from Cybernetics, some references that sometimes we follow and that make sense, but the vocabulary itself, from my perspective, sometimes is not adjustable! (...)

Threatening results that imply that each day Tactical Periodization is mentioned more frequently and in more places. The problem is that understanding it is not simple, and most people are not able to move away from the conventional ideas, which leads to a deformation of the interpretation of Tactical Periodization that makes it lose its meaning. It makes it different while staying within the boundaries of the same conventional logic when in reality, it can only be revealed within an entirely different Logic.

You know, I usually say that the most apparent symptom of ignorance is insolence. I also assume that Tactical Periodization, for those who do not mention it, represents many different things. And this depends on the ability of each person. Because even when following the other logic, more or less conventional, not all coaches are the same, there are good and bad ones, so not everyone that identifies with Tactical Periodization is…. the problem is in the people.

I can guarantee you that the problem is not in Tactical Periodization, it is in the people. (…)

This book aims, therefore, to clearly show, using different realities (people that work in different contexts 'in the field'), the foundations and the way of operationalising this methodology. It aims to show the differences between that 'Tactical Periodization' that many talks about, many that claim to understand a methodology that is outside of their logic, to whom its real Logic does not matter. Unable to understand it, they deform it, add to it, move away from it and make it 'invisible' to the eyes of those that may be really interested in understanding it. I intend to transform this 'secret' into empirical evidence.

2

> A Logic that allows for Specificity, both macro, micro, and meso of course.

"*Pioneers thinking outside the box are now precipitating upheavals at the leading edge of science, and their new thoughts are radically rewriting the way we see life. With the revolution underway, the old guard, defending the institution of old science, has dug in to defend its territory.*"

(Bruce Lipton & Steve Bhaerman, 'Spontaneous Evolution', 2009, p.93)

For Tactical Periodization, that does not exist. It does not exist because...
proprioception by itself, and it inclusively has its own exercises, the day of
proprioception and whatever, that does not exist for Tactical Periodization!
Because proprioception results from what I have to do! It is a result of what I
have to do, feeling it. It has nothing to do with what they say. Now, because
there is an activity I have to safeguard the continuity of the body, by cali-
brating it. Every day I do abdominal work, but not any. I have selected the
abdominal exercises because some are harmful! There is no 'abs-day', I do
them every them. But maybe I do them more during the breaks of Wednes-
day's training unit, even because there are more breaks that on Thursday for
example. I do extensibility every day, stretching every day, during the breaks
and in the beginning, but that is not to compensate for anything. When the
players finish the training, they have to go eat, and at night they have to go
to bed. If they don't sleep, then they will be tired the next day. And if it were
raining, I would have to consider that as well. And if for some reason, I don't
know...there were fungi on the grass and I could not use the grass, then we
would use the sports hall. But if the sports hall were slippery, then we would
still have to do something. If the next day the players feel a curtailment of the
posterior muscles, obviously I will have to do more extensibility on that day,
but I do not call it 'the day' of anything! (...)

That is why I say that Tactical Periodization is a 'tailor-made suit', and only
those who know can make a tailor-made suit. The rest does a pret-a-porter
suit, it is already made. The compensations are already prepared, the strength
is already prepared (...). Tactical Periodization has nothing to do with it, nor
does it care about it. It actually refuses it because it is not useful. However,
Tactical Periodization cares about the individual accomplishing her tasks and
needs to help the individual in a way that the development of her body is not
anomalous to the body itself and to the individual. The player may have one
leg shorter than the other so I can tell her "get some insoles". But with the
insoles, the player even gets worse! Does this have to do with the intelligence
of Tactical Periodization? Tactical Periodization is concerned with the whole
and knows that a little detail can...that is why I keep repeating that the Game
Model is everything, and I am only operationalising it well if I have as much as
possible inside the head of that which conditions me in the concern of doing
things. But I am always worried about the way of playing and with having the
players fresh to play. And that, just by itself, is already beyond the 'recipe',
which does not provide the real end result.

Vitor Frade (1)

Since a few years ago until this date, several complementary or compensatory exercises have become trendy within the training methodologies that follow the conventional logic (conventional methodologies, integrated and 'systemic'): injury prevention, proprioceptive, re-balance, which are performed analytically and in a decontextualised manner usually. These are general exercises for every kind of player and every way of playing, and even further, these are general exercises for all types of sport. Football players, basketball players, runners, tennis players...all doing the same kind of tasks when the demands of their sports are entirely different, starting with the surface in which they play. Entirely different players, teams that have different styles of play...they all do the same exercises.

In the Logic of Tactical Periodization, this does not exist. In Tactical Periodization, just like in life, everything results from the adaptability to a certain environment, to a Specificity. That is why Tactical

Periodization is a tailor-made suit, depending on the context and on the circumstances. This is in opposition to the conventional logic, where there is an annual plan that details everything that we will do physically, tactically, and inclusively at a complementary level throughout the season. And every player does the same. There is an understanding of the Process as something linear and with no interferences, like a ready-to-wear (pret-a-porter) suit, when it is in fact NON-linear.

"Perhaps the most important message offered by both quantum physics and field experiments is that everything is related. Our Universe is not hierarchical and linear; it's relational and fractal" (Lipton & Bhaerman, 2009, p.125).

For us, proprioception is the result of what must be accomplished regarding playing, and the feelings that come with it. Therefore, this and other 'details' of the context are not something complementary. Instead, they are part of the Specificity, and we consider it accordingly. For us, it is fundamental to think **"all the needs of the game and all the needs of the individual, along with the whole Process and in concomitance"** Vitor Frade (1).

To achieve it, we try to ensure that the player **"performs her role, and while performing her roles, the kind of development that the body achieved is not anomalous to the body itself or to the individual"**. Vitor Frade (1)

We try to ensure that the players are fresh for the next match, so proprioception is present in each exercise, we do abdominal work, stretching…before, during, and after, every day, or almost every day. This is not complementary or compensatory of anything! It is a need that arises from experiencing a Process in Specificity. It is, therefore, a tailor-made suit and not a ready-made suit like in the conventional logic, with the compensatory exercises, proprioception, strength…all prepared even before starting the season, written in books or prepared without considering when, for who, where…ignoring, therefore, the context and the circumstances.

2.1. The importance, and the consequent danger, of the 'cappuccino' strategy in the Process.

When Mourinho arrived at Chelsea players also asked him "so, are we not going to do this and that?". And he would say: "I am the one who won titles, not you". It is different if I arrive there having won nothing before. If you get to a club without having won anything, you need to use the 'cappuccino' strategy, taking baby steps. That is a matter of intelligence, it is strategic thinking if you wish to call it that way. (…).

When I discuss the Methodological Principles and the Game Principles, there is something we need to add – a Meta-Principle, the Principle of Divine Proportion. Divine – from God – and Proportion, because some have it and others don't. It is a kind of praxiological sensitivity! (…)

Then, wherever you end up going, it is likely that you will be contradicted. And you will have to 'give in' after considering the context. Otherwise you are not intelligent. It is vital, because you may be thinking that the individ-

ual understands it, but he might have wanted to do it that way, it is just his body that has not understood it yet. He is in a different wavelength and that is counterproductive. You need to have, as much as possible, that opposing information, and that is why Mourinho says that the Model is everything. With the Model being everything, if you consider that not even Jesus Christ can detect everything at the same time, it is important to recognise that things take time to develop. Consequently, this contextualisation is necessary! Therefore, those who are identified with this area...if everything were favourable, it would perhaps work at 80%. This way, maybe working only at 40 or 50%. And that is one of the richnesss of Tactical Periodization. That is why I say that it is a tailor-made suit and not one pret-a-porter. It is a theorem-in-action. You need to understand well the conceptual foundations, and then you need to be able to enhance its applicability, but in that enhancement, you need to consider the extraordinary relevance of decoding the context, and the context contains people. And the exterior side of people does not always reflect what people area. It is normal that it is like that because people, usually, do not even know themselves that well, and many times they need to disguise to defend themselves. So, that is the richness of Tactical Periodization. (...)

The 'cappuccino' is just like that: you drink the coffee and the milk, and perhaps it looks dark. You don't see the coffee, but it is there! Sometimes, considering the circumstances, I need to disguise the coffee with the milk because I know that the players say that if they drink coffee, they won't feel well. The session is over, and there we go: "guys, ten laps around the pitch". And the guys will be happy because they can say they ran. But it does not really matter. I tell them they do it and get their legs a bit loose, and they can say they did their running (...).

That is the 'cappuccino', a need that I have to find strategies. I did it especially in the beginning (...). What the player has in her head as the game is what the game means to her, and she might have 'anything' in her head. When I refer to the head I mean everything, including the toenails, it's the whole body, even the subconscious. Now, a lot of it is contrary to what I want, but I cannot go straight from 8 to 80, I need to have that in mind. That is the pedagogical or strategic side of the term.

Vitor Frade (1)

The 'cappuccino' strategy consists in 'hiding' what we want our players to do — the coffee — in what our players feel that they 'need' to do because of cultural or subconscious reasons — the milk. This means training in accordance to our Logic and giving them 'small doses' of what their whole body feels that it needs to be well to play football, of what they learned since they were little, those cultural reinforcements.

The use of the 'cappuccino' strategy will depend on the context and on the circumstances, on the culture that your players may have...For example, if these are players that got to their current level training the 'physical' side analytically, or if they got there using other methods; it depends on who you are if you have a lot of prestige due to great achievements; or who you will be coaching with. This means that it is not the same to arrive at a club where there was a more 'analytical' coach that won many matches, or where the previous coach had a different vision and also won.

Therefore, we must analyse the context and the circumstances that we face. We need to find out what our players believe in, especially subconsciously – what they 'need' to feel well, and then apply our Logic – because we think that it is the best way to achieve our objectives – giving them a bit of what they believe they 'need' and that will allow them to feel confident and serene. We must do this until they feel the need. But this must be done without losing sight of our Logic, and that implies being very well identified with it.

This strategy consists, in a way, in 'disguising' our Logic, in implementing it without changing 100% of what was being done previously. Operationalising in accordance with our Logic without overlooking certain conscious, and more importantly, subconscious 'needs' of our players that arise for cultural reasons. This until we manage to open the 'door' of their beliefs and make them realise that they can achieve 'success' by following paths that are often not so well recognised – Tactical Periodization.

In this strategic thinking, it is fundamental, as I have mentioned earlier, to decode the context, to understand what the people we are working with have in their minds. Just like our interviewee Vitor Frade, when I refer to the head, I include the whole body, from the top of the head down to the toenails. Each and every of the 50 trillion cells that result in the Human Being. *"Each of which is biologically and functionally equivalent to a miniature human"* (Lipton & Sherman, 2009, p.27).

Therefore, it is fundamental that our players feel well, so we need to find strategies that allow us to give them what they still 'need', while still following our Logic.

It is crucial not to go against our Logic because without it there is no Tactical Periodization. The objective is to reduce this 'need' until it entirely disappears. And this strategy shall be used not only in a methodological perspective but also regarding the conceptualisation of the game.

Referring to the importance of our beliefs, Bruce H. Lipton suggests that *"brain cells translate the mind's perceptions (beliefs) of the world into complementary and unique chemical profiles that, when secreted into the blood, control the fate of the body's 50 trillion cells"* (2015). And let's not be mistaken, our beliefs are imposed or at least influenced by the society we are part of. *"Beyond our individual subconscious programming, societies also hold several collective – and invisible – beliefs"*.

Guilherme Oliveira (1)[96] gives us an example of how, perhaps, he would prepare a team that was used to practice in a more analytical way. *"In those situations I must first identify it, then I need to 'trick'[97] them: at the beginning of the session I do some of these analytical drills, and they think – "well, we also do this, so there is no problem, because we are well, we have this".* And these are parts that have no meaning at all with regards to the rest of the session. And if you end up winning…from the moment, they start trusting me I can stop 'tricking' them. Many times, I use these strategies".

Mara Vieira (1)[98] tells us her experience and explains that she *"had the need to 'trick' her players due to the culture of the club. For example: at the end of each session they did some running from one side to the other. Or half-way through the session, whi-*

---

96 Interviewed by Xavier Tamarit in 2010.

97 To 'trick' does not mean here lying to the player. It relates to the coach's ability to decode the context well and recognise the player's 'needs' due to cultural reasons. Then the coach can cater for these 'needs', as long as it does not interfere with our Logic, and always with the objective of reducing this 'need' until it vanishes.

98 Interviewed by Xavier Tamarit in 2010.

le they were resting, I would tell them to run some laps around the pitch. Initially, I had to do this to gain the players' trust. Then, with the development of the process, they stopped asking about the 'physical' side".

Vitor Frade (2) also talks about this topic, providing the following example: ***"you arrive at a place, and people have habits. Even if you explain why they should work differently, not only do people have their ingrained habits, but they may also not have the ability to understand things like you understand in a way that they can believe in it immediately. Initially, if the players do not like the so-called conventional work, and you get them to 'only train with the ball', they will like it. But if then they lose, they will question everything after".***

As we can see, it is not easy to arrive in a new place with a certain culture, in this case, influenced by a paradigm, and change the way of training instantly. It must be understood that Tactical Periodization is a methodology that is very different from the others – transgressive and revolutionary – and in some occasions, we will need to use the 'cappuccino' strategy, and do it progressively until we can finally serve only the coffee. Notwithstanding, the process's Matrix must always be the same. The Logic of the Morphocycle must remain unchanged.

For Vitor Frade (2), ***"sometimes it is imperative that we go from 100% to just 80% of applicability so that we can progress better. Because at a conscious level they may even like it, because they think they won't also have to run as much, etc. But perhaps their bodies are not used to it. It's just like an addiction, and they are not exactly used to what they will do, because they are used to something else. So, there is no harm in giving them 'cappuccino', in giving them what they are used to in a way that does not count for anything. Inclusively in the surroundings...look, if you are training in a place where no-one to a way of practising that does not involve anything 'physical', then you just get them to do some laps around the pitch. That does not interfere with your work, and they can say they did some running. So that is the metaphor of the 'cappuccino'.***

We can observe that it is crucial to understand that the subconscious must accept our way of training, and therefore the latter must be implemented gradually. Even if one insists on making it conscious with the development of the Process, that will be the aim.

Vitor Frade refers that ***"these habits that we talk about, or inclusively vices and superstitions, occur mostly at the subconscious level, they are not conscious. And when you are not available subconsciously, it is complicated because sometimes we might say that we do something without truly doing anything. Tactical Periodization can be applied 100% and can also be applied at 70 or 80% if there is an impossibility, or if there is a deficit in the quality of people available. Even if there is maximum interest from two coaches in learning and applying it, the simple fact that our Playing Idea is not exactly the same will make the applicability of Tactical Periodization something relatively different".***

As all our interviewees mentioned, it has to do with respecting the cultural needs, the beliefs of the subconscious – and why not say, also the conscious! – of those things, that players 'need' to be able to feel well to play football. This does not have to be always done, it will depend on the context, on the circumstances, and on our ability and sensitivity to decode it.

That is why it becomes imperative that in the Youth sector a process of conceptual and methodological 'acculturation' is developed, with the players entering the logic of the club, and in this case, being embedded in the Logic of Tactical Periodization.

However, even if the 'cappuccino' strategy is critical to help those who know the Logic, it becomes also dangerous to those who are not well identified with the latter. The 'cappuccino' strategy must be used very carefully by the coach because if he does not understand Tactical Periodization well, he might be the one being 'tricked'. Being far away from the Logic of this methodology can be very dangerous with regards to the team's performance, and Tactical Periodization might end up receiving the blame, even if indeed it was never present.

Moreover, the 'cappuccino' strategy is a good (?) excuse for those that claim to do 'Tactical Periodization' without believing in it...just to look fashionable!

2.1.1. So, is the physical aspect not important in Tactical Periodization?

(...) Tactical Periodization says that the Tactical is an emergence, that it is an Organisation, that it is not physical, not psychological, not technical, but without all these, it does not exist (...)

It does not have the physical concerns that many people say should be 'the' physical concerns. That is why I say that there is a paradigm that is dominant, the paradigm of the 'athlete': jumping higher, running longer and faster. But that has nothing to do with playing. Playing is something different – I also have to run, but I have to do it sometimes at speed (...).

Vitor Frade (1)

Within Tactical Periodization, the Physical Dimension is not essential: it is crucial! But, which physical? Understood from which logic?

As it has been shown throughout this book, Tactical Periodization is based on the Specificity of a way of playing that is allowed by its Methodological Principles. A way of playing that is composed by the Physical Dimension, the Technical Dimension, the Psychological dimension, and the Tactical Dimension. Sometimes, there is also the Strategical Dimension. This methodology is based in Principles that allow all dimensions to work together during the training session, as in the Game they are inseparable. However, due to the Logic of the Process that intends to achieve a certain way of playing, the Tactical Dimension – or Tactical-Strategical in certain moments – is the Dimension that orientates the Process. That is why the Tactical Dimension is designated as a Supra-Dimension, and that is also why the other dimensions emerge with it. They are specific to the Specificity of the way of playing.

According to Carlos Carvalhal (1)[99], *"we don't say that the physical is unimportant because it is in fact very important. What we say is that our exercises and our daily, weekly, monthly, quarterly, and annual objectives gravitate towards the improvement of the team's abilities That is our biggest and primary concern. Of course, it is connected to the idea of organisation and to the conceptualisation of the game is the psychological side, is the physical side, the technical side, but it is that idea of organisation that directs everything that we want to do since the beginning of the preparation".*

For Vitor Pereira (1)[100] *"the tactical is what defines the training, what defines the behaviour (intentionalised interaction). On that day I want to train transition – offensive and defensive, our loss of possession and our reaction to the loss of possession...but just because my main goal is to do that I do not drop my concerns with physiology".*

Through the words of our interviewees, we can show that it is the Tactical Supra-Dimension, or Tactical-Strategical at times, that directs the whole Process. But because of that, it does not mean that no attention is paid to the physiological, bioenergetic, bio-motor, biochemical, neuronal...This attention, within the Tactical Periodization framework, is specific to the effort/performance required by our way of playing.

Carlos Carvalhal (1) highlights that *"this perspective that we refer to does not talk about improving physical targets, it focuses primarily on the idea of having the team playing in the way that we want because that is the key idea. And then arises the question: so, is the physical not important? It is, but it is important to support our Playing Idea. It ends up being important but derives from our Playing Idea and from those Principles we designate. In the end, being physically fit means, for us, being able to sustain the demands of the game generated by our Playing Idea".*

Therefore, in Tactical Periodization we talk about an objective Physical Dimension and not something abstract. What is being physically fit? It depends on the sport that we want to practice! The needs of a swimmer have nothing to do with the requirements of a sprinter, of a rugby or a futsal player. And even within the same sport, football, for example, each team will require different adaptations. And what about each way of playing inside the team's global way of applying? The Specificity will allow us to work both individually and collectively.

Saying that Tactical Periodization has no concerns with the physical side means not understanding what Tactical Periodization. Otherwise, why mention the Principle of Horizontal Alternation in specificity, for example? In this methodology, contemplating the Physical Dimension is essential, and it is made clear by the Morphocycle. We will look more in detail at this issue in the chapter titled 'The abyssal zone of Tactical Periodization'.

What is correct to say is that Tactical Periodization's concerns with the physical have nothing to do with the 'physical' interests of those following the conventional logic.

Moreover, for Jorge Maciel (1), *"the contemplation of the physical dimension, not any but that referring to a given way of playing, is fundamental to enhance the quality of the process. Only by not compromising the manifestation of a certain expres-*

---

99 Interviewed by Xavier Tamarit in 2010.

100 Interviewed by Xavier Tamarit in 2010

sivity or collective gesture (with individual particularities) is it possible to see an Intentionality emerging. Playing is expressed with the whole Body, and because of that, it is important to acquire and process a certain Intentionality. Without the latter, the motor response would perhaps not be coherent or would not emerge in the adequate timings. This is only possible through the appropriate operationalisation of the Pattern Morphocycle".

libro
futbol
.com
AL GOL SE
LLEGA LEYENDO

163

"

Xavier, when they say that...let them say whatever they want, I don't care! But what they are
talking about is not Tactical Periodization! Tactical
Periodization does not need what they say it is
missing. Now, if they want to do Tactical Periodization, then they must report it as it is. If they don't,
then they can keep doing what they are doing, and
I won't be bothered at all, especially now that I
am 66 years old, and retiring from the Faculty. My
concerns with Football have to do with the reflection about Football and the Body. Nothing else.

Therefore, I have no patience because this is not
rhetoric. This is not something that you just preach,
this is about practice. And the role model, at this
moment, is Mourinho (...)

But Tactical Periodization is also that, it requires
that I am aware of what a kid is. In FC Porto, since
2006, since I got there, kids started practising one
less time a week. (...) Practice is a crime because
it is an energetic expenditure for the kids and they
also need energy to grow. If they lack it, they won't
develop. (...) So, the kid needs energy to grow,
so I need to be careful regarding the demands of
energetic consumption so that the kids are not prevented from developing, that they don't stay small.
That is my view, even if the tendency is the opposite! I am talking about practice, and street football
is not 'practice'! (...)

Have you seen the kid that is going to play the
piano, running first around the piano, doing pull-
ups or push-ups?! No. The kids get there – if they
are two, they say 'you play here, and I play there';
if they are eleven, they say 'six here and five there'.
That is what they do, football with a ball! This can
lead to the gestation of a sublime triad more football, more kid, more development'.

My Game Idea is a football with a lot of positional play, they work fundamentally in triangles, the intermediate sector is very relevant. So, in the intermediate sector, the characteristics of the players must be distinct in the regular context of what happens, articulating the back and forward sectors. (...) We want that even for the kids, for the 6-year old kids. In FC Porto they play 4v4 or 6v6, and the rules that they impose, are used with the objective that certain things emerge

2.2. Proprioception: a relationship of our body with our own body and our way of playing.

"In larger organisms, for example, only a small percentage of cells are concerned with reading and responding to environmental stimuli. That is the role of groups of specialised cells that form the tissues and organs of the nervous system. The function of the nervous system is to perceive the environment and coordinate the behaviour of all the other cells in the vast cellular community" (Lipton, 2015)

In Tactical Periodization, proprioception is fundamental. In fact, we can say that this methodology maximises it.

A small number of cells that can 'see' what is happening outside warns those in command that we are in the environment so that it can decide (without asking us) how to react. In an environment that repeatedly occurs the organism will adapt with the intention of improving its performance. Proprioception works as part of this adaptation process. What sense does it make to train it in a decontextualised manner? A kid that plays football on the street will develop a proprioceptive adaptation that is different from another kid that plays basketball in that same street, for example.

Therefore, we are discussing a concrete Proprioception of a certain way of playing, which is, therefore, Specific. This is something corroborated by the words of Guilherme Oliveira (1) when he suggests that *"the way we work maximises the Specific proprioception". The interviewee reports that "proprioception is being trained through Specific exercises. We work it a lot. And through the way, we train when doing Tactical Periodization, that proprioception is almost maximised".*

So, in Tactical Periodization, as we always practice in Specificity, everything happens in a Specific manner. This is why in this methodology there are no proprioception drills apart from our way of playing because as we have already said at the beginning of the chapter, Proprioception must be specific to the sport and specific to the way of playing. It is about adapting the organism to its surroundings so that it becomes more efficient within the environment it is developing in. Each sport has specific needs and requirements. So does each player and so does each way of playing. The same exercise cannot be used for all sports, mainly because football, because of being played with the feet, is an apparently Anti-Natural Phenomenon[101]: the same drill cannot be used to improve every way of playing because they have nothing to do with each other. And the same drill cannot be used for all players because each has a certain body and a certain relationship with that body. Depending on that way of playing and depending on her position, the relationship between playing and the body will necessarily be different.

---

101 Football as an apparently Anti-Natural phenomenon: This sport requires a higher participation of the lower limbs, especially of the feet (and therefore its designation of foot-ball). In evolutional terms these have had a secondary role in comparison to the hands, due to structural, functional, and mostly cultural issues that create a very different significance in their cerebral representativeness. Consequently, it can be considered an apparently Anti-Natural phenomenon, even if as Jorge Maciel suggests in his book ('Nao deixes matar o bom futebol e quem o joga: pelo futebol adentro nao e perda de tempo', Chiado Ed., 2011), the adverb apparently must be stressed.

Marisa Gomes (1)[102] explains that, in her interpretation, proprioception in football is *"a game capacity, an ability to play, even if I am standing still, but in a way that there can be an intervention in the context"*.

For our interviewee, Proprioception is also Specific, and therefore, individual, considering that individuality within our Logic, which is collective at the same time. It is inevitably linked to the context and in a continuous dependence of the circumstances. So, it must be directed by the Tactical Supra-Dimension and in certain contexts by the Tactical-Strategical.

Marisa Gomes claims that proprioception is achieved *"through playing the game"*. We must somatise this way of playing so that the Whole organism is able to recognise it as its own. And this somatisation is individual but simultaneously sectoral, intersectoral, etc. Marisa concludes that proprioception is *"the somatisation of the adjustment with the other with the decisions made, in all the pitch, and involving every event that occurs (...), the speaking, the involvement (...), but the proprioception discussed in the books has nothing to do with it"*.

Everything is so decontextualised due to the conventional understanding that it ends up being abstract and 'sold' to us through general and non-specific exercises, with an illusion of improvement. For example, they tell us that running on a staircase improves the coordination of the individual. Yes, it does, it improves the coordination, but relates only to running on a staircase. And nothing else. Coordination for playing football has nothing to do with the coordination for other sports and even less with the running technique on a staircase. Or was Maradona not coordinated? I really doubt he has done any running technique drills throughout his development. What he did was spending the whole day with a ball, going down his house's stairs with the ball, playing all day, barefoot...and that allowed him to gain an exceptional sensitivity in his feet and his Whole body. That must have resulted in much higher representativeness of his feet in the brain in comparison to those who only use them and believe they are a uniquely motor organ and not a fundamentally sensitive organ. That is why someone that is born without hands can play guitar or piano with their feet as well or even better than anyone could do with the hands.

As we see, Proprioception, and everything else, within the Logic of Tactical Periodization, has to do with the Specificity of the Process, and his trained through playing, because the latter is intimately related with emotions, with feelings...

According to Carlos Carvalhal (1), *"proprioception here ends up being developed inside what we plan regarding exercises, not in a particular way (...), it is considered in the context, it doesn't have to be performed in the gym in a decontextualised way"*.

In line with our discussion, Mara Vieira (1) proposes that *"that 'specific' proprioception can and should be developed, in my perspective, in the training session. You can only activate specific mechano-receptors or proprioceptors in the context of the game"*.

This Proprioception that implies the ability to interact with the environment in an efficient way can occur, therefore, in the training session, in a more macro or in a more micro level, more collectively or individually, but always respecting the Specificity of our way of playing.

Proprioception, according to Tactical Periodization, is developed Specifically when the Specificity of our way of playing is trained, not through exclusive or isolated 'proprioceptive' exercises, as it happens with other methodologies that see it as something abstract, where the environment does not matter much.

---

102 Interviewed by Xavier Tamarit in 2010.

2.3. Tightening 'nuts and bolts': Abdominals, Flexibility and Mobility; much-needed Sub-Specificities to avoid muscular chain atrophy.

"The problem, therefore, is not at all the insufficiency of our posterior musculature, but its excessive strength. We mustn't, therefore, 'strengthen' the back muscles, which are already contractured, nor help them to better supper the vertebrae. On the contrary. It's necessary to stretch the posterior muscles so that they'll release their hold on the vertebrae that are kept in a concave arch" (Bertherat & Bernstein, 1989, p.75)

(...) I did a lot of mobility work at the beginning of all training days, between exercises. A lot of mobility of the whole body, interfering with the dorsal-lumbar mobility, in positions of tension and extension for the dorsal-lumbar region. And extensibility for the dorsal-lumbar region, especially for the forwards, and even more for the centre-backs. I also did abdominal work every day, always the same (...)

You have five muscles there (adductors), and each muscle has endless motor units that in consequence work with different stimuli. This diversity, the degrees of freedom in the relationship between these muscles is endless as well. You won't find anything to work them except for letting them do what they need to! Can you invent any machine or something for Messi's adductors to do? (...) What you need to put is...and having that in mind: ah! Careful, you need to have a great mobility of the pelvis and always through, in each session, allowing great extensibility to the adductors, and being cautious with the very common shortening, and the potentiation of the anomalous iliac psoas, that due to its insertion, because it is located in one of the lumbar vertebrae and...(12th thoracic). So, it causes atrophy of the mobility of the pelvis, the leg...So you need to drop several abdominal exercises that are not convenient, that make it work, that put the iliac psoas under tension...that you don't want that, you need to suppress that!

Vitor Frade (1)

There is no better prevention that getting the muscle used to the unpredictability and spontaneity that the Game provides, together with the Specificity of a way of playing that respects the diversity of the Game. The muscles must be given great degrees of freedom. I cannot understand how using a machine you can achieve the so-called 'injury-prevention' as it is called in the conventional logic. I think that all you can do is to narrow the degrees of freedom of your movements, potentiating certain muscles that end up removing amplitude and mobility to others of the same muscular chain. You end up strengthening neuronal connections that are not those required by playing, silencing the proprioceptive capacity...through decontextualised experiences, that have nothing to do with the ones that the player will face on the field of play. That 'injury-prevention', just like 'proprioception', is the same or very similar independently of the player's morphotype, her position, chosen way of playing...it's completely abstract! It is even, many times, the same for different sports. That is a fragmented understanding of the body. As Therese Bertherat suggests, "the dissociation not only of the limps but of all the parts of the body is very common and considered normal. We don't know how the parts of our body behave about each other, nor do we know how they're organised or what their functions and real possibilities are" (1989, p.38). Bruce Lipton (1) argues that "living organisms must receive and interpret environmental signals to stay alive. In fact, survival is directly related to the speed and efficiency of signal transfer". The author goes further to explain that "while the organisms interact with the environments, their perceptions activate epigenetic mechanisms that improve gene expression to increase the survival chances".

Every day more, in the conventional logic, exercises for the strengthening of the adductors are performed, as well as for the dorsal-lumbar region...before, during or after the training session. This means that we are requesting that a muscle that is highly demanded during the Game, that needs to rest...to do extra work so that we can strengthen it. But? Yes, that is its problem!

Only for those considering the muscle as a 'blind' organ can this logic be valid. The same logic that then talks about 'proprioception'. A logic that has nothing to do with the Logic of Tactical Periodization, that considers the muscle as a sensitive organ, which is therefore in constant adaptation to increase its efficiency with regards to the environment it is exposed to, according to what it experiences.

With regards to the 'injury-prevention' exercises, according to Mara Vieira (1) we only get nearer to what is real by *"playing; through playing and doing exercises that allow for contact with the ball (…). A handball player who plays football often ends up injured or feeling muscular pain. And he has an excellent physical preparation, and in his sport, there are also frequent changes of direction and all that. So, the sensitivity that we have is related to what we regularly do"*.

This kind of exercises (which belong to a conventional logic) performed, as it's claimed, to prevent injuries and also to correct potential imbalances, may create themselves an imbalance in the body, just the opposite of what we aimed to do. This is because our body learned with time to manage our shortcomings, so there may not be many benefits in the end.

Mara Vieira (1) gives us an example that can relate to what we are trying to explain: *"Amalia Rodrigues...do you know who she was? She was a 'fado' singer, the best ever in Portugal. She had separated teeth, and some people say that she started singing worse when she put a device to help to join the teeth together. It seems that the sound was coming out differently. This is an excellent example to explain that when something interferes with our morphology, it may end up making it less functional"*.

As we see, all this is a little more complex than the conventional logic tells us.

Indeed, there are critical areas that we must pay attention to. The adductors zone is an over-worked area in football, and therefore, a region that must be protected. It must get a lot of extensibility and mobility so that it does not shorten. This area and other muscles like the iliac psoas and all the posterior muscular chain (the posterior musculature, due to our evolution and to our current standing posture, is over-developed and acts all the time. Francoise Mezieres discovered that all the posterior musculature, from the head down to the tip of the toes, including the neck, back, glutes, legs and plantar areas, are a single muscular chain and, in consequence, act in connection. This over-development in comparison to the anterior musculature provokes its shortening, and this is not only due to *"the effort to keep our balance that shortens our posterior muscles, but all movements of medium or broad amplitude executed by the arms and legs"* (Bertherat & Bernstein, 1989, p.75). Moreover, attention must be paid to the abdominal exercises because these will be crucial. These exercises will also have to be performed in a certain way, as we will discuss later.

As Carlos Carvalhal (1) tells us, *"the adductors are a very over-loaded area, a vital area, especially in football. Therefore, it is prone to imbalances, and reach the balance that we wish this is a fundamental area, the pubic area, and it needs a lot of attention regarding stretching"*.

Marisa Gomes (!) explains us in an unambiguous manner how we should protect our players from pubic problems: *"you need to work very well the abdominal area, you must stretch it, and you must also, above all, 'compensate' a lot of the work you do. See, in the long term there will be consequences for the adductors, in those little muscles that are told to contract so many times, and that ends up becoming rigid and swollen frequently due to the great pressure that the other, bigger muscles, exert to close. In football, quadriceps and posterior muscles grow very strong, so there must be compensation to promote agility of the muscular chains because the muscles must be SENSITIVE. When that does not happen, the abdominal muscles disturb the agility of the legs. In the end, the abdominals are like puppets: they coordinate and allow for the great agility of the lower limbs. When the abdominals are super-developed and very rigid, they will impede a fresh, fluid rotation. (...)"*

The abdominal work, or more precisely, the correct abdominal work, is fundamental for the well-being of our players.

Nonetheless, it must have some characteristics and a structure that meets our Logic. In this way, we must make sure that despite their strengthening, they do not become rigid and closed, because as Marisa Gomes says, this would harm our agility. They must be, just like the others, sensitive muscles.

To achieve this, the abdominal work is performed every day or almost every day, between exercises, in a way that allows for much recovery between sets, preventing therefore hypertrophy. They must be followed by stretches that also prevent, or at least mitigate their shortening.

As our interviewee tells us, *"the abdominal cannot become a rigid structure because you lose agility regarding rotation and in fundamental movements with regards to the relationship with the ball and with the game itself. It also interferes with your predisposition for the game, when asking for the ball, in standing. I would always use movements that would allow for that reinforcement, but with an amplitude of movements and opposing stretches, to minimise the effects of that rigidity that is achieved with the increasing of contraction. I would therefore to a lot of recovery so that hypertrophy would not happen, let's put it that way. In the end, I would be promoting a specific reinforcement.*

For Vitor Pereira (1), the objective is not to promote abdominal hypertrophy, *"the objective is essentially toning"*.

Carlos Carvalhal (1) reveals that *"we don't promote hypertrophy, we normally work what we believe is the necessary abdominal work, toning. We never exaggerate. We do this work daily, and that is why we consider it toning. We don't do it in a way that increases the abdominal wall significantly, we are just interested in maintaining and strengthening the abdominal wall"*.

We must also make sure that while we exercise these muscles, we do not request the 'assistance' of the iliac psoas — activating it or even potentiating it even more — because this is something that frequently happens in many types of exercises for the abdominals. That is the contrary of what we are looking for. We should also try to avoid the activation of the posterior muscular chain. Guilherme Oliveira (1) tells us that this kind of exercise *"has some characteristics that promote a specific work of the abdominal area without over-working other structures that are often overloaded when abdominal work is performed incorrectly".*

Abdominal work, for example, will be performed every day, or almost every day, in between exercises, in a way that promotes high recovery between sets and a low number of repetitions. In the days with more extended recovery periods, the quantity can be higher. These exercises must be accompanied by stretches that minimise the shortening. It is very important that during the abdominal exercises, the iliac psoas does not interfere directly, because this is a much-requested muscle that has the tendency to shorten. To do this, one must avoid fixating the legs, which must be loose with the knees positioned at a 90-degree angle relative to the body. Every abdominal exercise that requires the legs to stretch, with the knees going over a 90-degree angle, will be promoting the contraction of the iliac psoas. Over-demanding the posterior musculature must also be avoided. Therefore, the back must be well supported, and the head well relaxed, to prevent the hyperactivity of the neck muscles.

The abdominal musculature is formed by the rectus abdominis, the external oblique, the internal oblique and the transversus. When we perform any abdominals exercise, they all get involved. This means that while there can be more emphasis in the fibres of a certain area in a given task, all areas will be activated to a varying degree (Vitor Frade (3)[103]).

With regards to the isometric abdominal exercises that are so trendy nowadays, Marisa Gomes (1) explains why, in her perspective and following the Logic of Tactical Periodization, these should be avoided, at least as a pattern: *"isometric is a kind of exercise that allows improving your ability to contract, while static, right? But when you are playing what you need is to have a predisposition, in the sense of them being agile. If in a structure like the abdominal or dorsal you have very strong and rigid muscles, then the agility is lost. And this becomes even worse if this happens at the level of the insertions. A weightlifter that has highly developed abdominal muscles looks like he is low because there is a strength of contraction and if you performed the abdominals with movement, without having the legs locked, you would strengthen while also promoting the agility of the membrane. Your pelvis is adjusting, you promote a certain zone, but the chain is not locked, is not fixed. The isometric work, just like the weight work, results in strengthening, but it's a narrow strengthening. And all that we do in football must be aimed at opening the muscular chains, not narrowing them. Opening muscular chains: the sensitivity of the muscles, of the nerves, of the tendons and in this case of the abdominals, implies mobile structures, with a low number of repetitions, followed by extensibility".*

The abdominal work must, therefore, go beyond toning, it has to allow them to become agile.

Everything that we are referring to done every day or almost every day, and that is part of the Specificity of the Process, is designated by Vitor Frade as "tightening nuts and bolts". It refers to fine-tuning the Organism after it is put out of tune between matches and training sessions.

---

103 As cited by Jorge Maciel in 'Pelas entranhas do nucleo duro do processo'. Unpublished article, 2010.

For Vitor Frade (3), *"the work results in the potential loss of range, in the hypertrophy of some things, and I need to know that. But that is not any kind of compensation, it is something that goes side-by-side with recovery, it's about tightening 'nuts and bolts'. So, in the same way, that Formula-1 cars, at the end of each race, are out of tune and then get tuned again, the Organism is the same. But that is part of specificity. What I need to know is: of which specificity? Of what I want to be accomplished regarding playing, how the body reacts, and that is why there is no specific day for flexibility, or as they say of medium strength or abdominals, etc. That is done every day because it is indispensable, this is the necessary specificity related to the required specificity, it has nothing to do with that other logic of compensation that some people refer to".*

So, this tightening of 'nuts and bolts' is done specifically about the Specificity that is requested from players. As this plays a role in the overarching Specificity and being constantly linked to it, it cannot be understood as something complementary, but as something essential. There will be more influence in some days and less in others, with a stronger emphasis on the recovery days (and not only in the so-called day of recovery) as we will see later in the chapter dedicated to the Morphocycle.

Vitor Frade (2) says that *"what needs to be clear is that, with regards to Tactical Periodization, there are certain days that we consider acquisitive, acquisitive of a way of playing, and there is an alternation in that acquisitive to avoid mere repetition, and it has methodological principles that promote that. And inclusively in the sessions, in the breaks between different moments, it must be considered that some muscular groups were requested. For example, on a Wednesday, I was performing a series of exercises having in mind the objectives of the game, but because it is a Wednesday, it is fundamental that these exercises are designed in a way that increases the tension at a muscular level, through the presence of eccentric contractions. This is part of the specificity, and it implies that you consider the adductors (remember, they are not three, but five!), that you stretch them appropriately. You need to stretch them in a certain way, you need to find different positions to avoid losing amplitude, and to avoid unnecessary hypertrophy. Also, you must recognise that you must provide the pelvis with mobility so that there are no losses. With regards to the abdominals, you must know that some exercises are harmful, you need to know which you can do, which are appropriate for football. The iliac psoas structural and functional problematic must constantly be in your mind".*

As we can observe, in no moment I referred to exercising the dorsal-lumbar region. It is already an over-developed region, which is consequently shortened, so working it further would be counter-productive. What we need to do is pay particular attention to it, not allowing its excessive involvement when abdominal work is performed nor during stretching. If, as it has been shown, all posterior muscles are connected forming a single muscular chain, I must ensure that I will not be shortening some while stretching others. For example, I need to consider that perhaps while performing a calf stretch I may be, simultaneously, contracting the neck muscles. And what can we say about the consequences on that muscular chain of performing exercises with weights or in resistance machines? I don't think it is that important. Or is it?

2.4. Weight training: blindfolding the muscles.

I just need to give you the example of Mourinho. Mourinho's teams are usually said to be very athletic. So, if they are, they are due to training the 'athletic' without training the athletic. That is because Tactical Periodization does what you are referring to (...).

(...) I used to say that no-one in the World would do more strength training than players, because they would do it every week, just without using machines. It was a 'strength'...I mean, a muscular sensitivity, sensitivity in the acquisition and execution of a way of playing, relative to the own evolution of the player and to the growth of my team, having in mind everyone's roles. Now, that is not an easy thing. (...)

Why did Del Neri[104] leave just after arriving at FC Porto? Mourinho had been here, he had won everything, they had been European Champions, there were the same players and they...here it is, the Game Model is everything... they opposed...they refused...and that is why Del Neri did not even start the League. They even took the stones out of the ramps, with so many repetitions they were doing! The players would discuss between themselves: "so, we won everything without ever needing to do this, we never went to the gym, only worked with the ball which is what we enjoy, and we were better than everyone, and we won. And now we will have to do these things?!". Obviously, they were unhappy until there was no way back and the chairman had to dismiss the coach.

And didn't he have prestige? Didn't he have a CV? Didn't he achieve things? But perhaps, having in mind a question you asked me, maybe he should have arrived here and thought: 'what is the culture like here? Wait, perhaps here with these players...maybe I am the one that is mistaken, maybe I won't go against the players'...do you understand?

It has nothing to do with the gym. I would take my players to the gym 'many' times, you know for what? I would bring them there, bare feet...once I even brought the players bare feet, and because the wood was so hard they even got some blisters, but they were not upset. I would bring different balls with different sizes for them to play. So that..and there it is, a player that did not know how to do somersaults would do somersaults...playing there, dancing, bringing to the limit the proprioception through playing! Making their body, more and more, belong to them! So that then they could be more fluid, more agile, and pleasantly achieving that (...).

So, it is not about the gym. I can go to the gym and do some football-tennis or a 1v1, or playing against the wall and all that...

You just have to know what the mechanoreceptors are, what is proprioception. You have to understand that the muscle, due to the neuromuscular spindle but not only because of that, is fundamentally an organ that must be

---

104 Luigi Del Neri: Italian football player and coach. As a player he represented clubs like Udinese Calcio and UC Sampdoria, among others. As a coach, the worked with Chievo Verona, AS Roma, UC Sampdoria, Juventus FC. Del Neri arrived at FC Porto after Mourinho left to Chelsea in 2004, but he did not make it into the official season, having been dismissed before the beginning of the League.

receptive to the small changes of its surroundings that we cannot predict. A lot of those details are unexpected and need to be internalised so that a response can emerge. I mean that there is an adjustment period for the muscular co-contractibility and another timing that adjusts it to the circumstances when performing the effort of facing them. The machines, no matter how sophisticated they are, remove precisely that! Furthermore, the machines are individual not for the relationship with the others, it is an individual fitness, not a playing fitness, so it doesn't make sense.

Now, it is not easy to keep creating exercises systematically. That is why I don't tolerate that some talk about the 'tension day'...because it is fundamental that on Wednesdays you select exercises depending on the existing needs, but knowing that those you are using imply a significant increase in tension. But they are aimed at playing better! And if this is done with regularity, through the accentuation of the emergence of significant tension in some muscular chains, together with dynamic correspondence, certainly the muscle will work in full potential (...).

Vitor Frade (1)

"The relationship between all parts of our body changes in accordance to the different activities we perform and the different postures we assume."

Moshe Feldenkrais[105]

Within Tactical Periodization, 'strength' — understood as the conventional strength training that uses machines or additional weights — is not part of the Process. As we have shown earlier, due to the 'cappuccino' strategy or also due to medical issues, it is possible that certain players work with resistance machines in an optional manner. This may be because the medical departments demands it for players that have suffered certain injuries, or because players have been 'accultured' since very young ages in a certain logic and have the 'need'. This should be controlled by the staff, that will try its best to reduce this kind of work out and try to end it gradually. Except in the case of players that have undergone surgery and that 'clinically' need it (?), 'strength' training for the upper body will only be allowed for those that 'need' it and ask for it voluntarily.

Resistance machines promote narrow exercises that predispose the muscle for a reality that has nothing to do with the reality it will face on the field of play. These are exercises that 'blindfold' the muscle, the 'trick' it, predetermining the muscle to do something decontextualised. It is like learning how to drive a train that runs on a railway, in an 'automatic' manner, and *"then having to drive a bus 'in a situation of a high volume of traffic' — the rules are there, but the driving requirements on those different paths are highly variable"*, Jorge Maciel (1). We have to decide when to turn, where to turn and how to do it, using our own hands.

This 'strength training' leads the muscle, with its blindfold, to a cliff, prepared to contract as it learned, in an automatic or guided manner, with no spontaneity or variability, with a single way of contraction.

---

105 Moshe Feldenkrais, 'La sabiduria del cuerpo', Editorial Sirio, 2015.

Exercise to potentiate the quadriceps using a resistance machine: the same type of contraction, repeatedly, isolated from the muscular chains with which it interacts when facing the different stimuli of the game, practically, always the same neuronal connections intervening, 12 repetitions, 3 sets, twice a week. The muscle gets used to a reality that it won't face out of there. A reality that demands from the quadriceps diversity in its contraction, different fibres now, different fibres then, neuronal connections that are not those that we have repeatedly trained in the machine until the creation, due to the lived experience, or in this case re-lived ad infinitum, of a sturdiness in certain connection identically, that may lead the muscle — fatigued — to lapse when facing situations that demand other connections… increasing the probability of an injury! As Vitor Frade stated at the start of this section, the *"organ that must be receptive to the small changes of its surroundings that we cannot predict. A lot of those details are unexpected and need to be internalised so that a response can emerge. I mean that there is an adjustment period for the muscular co-contractibility and another timing that adjusts it to the circumstances when performing the effort of facing them. The machines, no matter how sophisticated they are, remove precisely that! (…)"*

According to Carlos Carvalhal (1), *"the gym is not part of my work. I have never included the gym in my planning. Some players have that need. There are two types of players that in my opinion have that need. One type has pathological needs due to a previous injury or because he has undergone an ACL surgery and needs to tone the vastus medialis, or players that have some atrophies and that is not my job — that is the job of the medical department or of the physiotherapists. They are the ones usually doing that work, so it is not even my task, even if I need to oversee it. Then there are those players that due to their culture, to their history, have an absolute need, because they have done that work for some many years, they need to do it sometimes. They can do it, we control it, but our goal is to try and eliminate that work as much as possible. So, we have the intention of reducing that kind of work to zero (…), to reduce that kind of work until we can tell the players that it is not crucial, that it is not important for playing, that it is not important for us. But clearly the cultural side is very important, and we have to understand that some players feel that need due to their habits, having done it for many years. Without it, they don't feel well and what we want is that players feel good to play".*

As the interviewee witnesses, although this kind of 'work' is not part of his Process, it is important to consider the players' culture and, therefore, allow controlled access to these exercises for those who 'need' them. Ensuring, however, that it is the least harmful possible for our Logic and aiming at reducing them gradually. As it can be seen here, the 'cappuccino' strategy is present again, even if at an individual level.

Vitor Pereira (1) also discusses this topic, revealing that while he does not bring his players to the gym *"the Brazilian and African players usually enjoy this kind of work very much, especially for the upper body. No problem, you want to do it? You can do it. But you need to do it in those days which will cause less harm to our training Process. People are working the upper body the whole year, normally those working the lower body are those who had injuries and that have been advised (?) to do it. They do a maintenance programme the whole year. But I never bring them to the gym".*

Even though players can follow their gym programmes, we intend to gradually make them understand that they do not need it and convince them to reduce it as much as possible. According to Mara Vieira

(1), *"telling a 30-year old player to stop doing gym work after he has been doing it since he was 15 or 16 might not be advisable. Initially, he must be explained why he should reduce or stop doing it. Because if he does not trust, he may end up attributing a potential bad performance on the match to the training and that will make him feel bad. I believe we need to be very careful with that"*. Once again, the interviewee refers to the importance of decoding the context in which we find ourselves.

Therefore, as Guilherme Oliveira (1) suggests, *"there are certain moments in which we, in my perspective, should 'allow' the players to do what they enjoy so that they feel well. If they feel well, then it is much easier for us to achieve all the rest"*.

The interviewee gives us a couple of clear examples that synthesise the importance of the culture of those players you coach. *"When it was the other way, when players would spend 2 or 3 years with me, they would see what they could achieve and would see that it was achieved through this methodology, and then when they went to work with a coach that used a different methodology, they did not enjoy it. Why? Because they came to play football with a certain quality, to be champions as we were, and they did not need to run in the woods, they did not need to go to the gym and do strength training, they did not need several things. That is what happened in FC Porto when Mourinho was here. First, they won the UEFA cup, then the Champions League, they won the Portuguese League two years in a row using this methodology. And then other coaches arrived with a different methodology, and the players thought: "what are we doing here? We were European champions practising only on the field, and now this guy brings us to the ramps and to the gym? We don't need that for anything!". That is normal because they developed, that team was developed with that methodology. Therefore, it is also completely normal that if we go somewhere where players have achieved many things and have the habit of doing a certain type of things..."*. In another example, Guilherme Oliveira (1) discusses his work with the Portuguese National Team: *"I have players like Ricardo Carvalho, who was coached by Mourinho for several years, winning titles with a certain type of work. He does not demand that type of work, he does not do that type of work. The strength training that he does is due to several injuries he had in the past, it is a training directed to a certain type of injuries, that helps with specific problems that arose from the surgeries he had. He only does that because he says it makes him feel better, he makes him feel more confident. He does some work in the gym because of that kind of situation. He does nothing else"*.

As we can see, in Tactical Periodization, 'strength training' is not part of the Process. However, some players can be allowed to perform it, due to the circumstances highlighted previously. For our Logic, it is not only necessary but also counterproductive, because of what I mentioned earlier regarding 'blindfolding' the muscle, but also because in football, in its dynamic, no muscle is exercised in isolation. It always interacts with a certain muscular chain, in a way that when it works and evolves, it does so together with all the muscular chain, something that does not happen when the work is done in isolation in the resistance machine. Moreover, this kind of 'automatic' exercise using machines, or on the 'railway' goes against Proprioception, without requesting information from the exterior, as the context is always identical.

UNIVERSIDADE DO PORTO

FACULDADE DE CIENCIAS DO DESPORTO E DE EDUCAÇÃO FISICA

Projecto para a prestação de provas de doutoramento

A INTERACÇÃO, INVARIANTE ESTRUTURAL DA ESTRUTURA DO RENDIMENTO DO
FUTEBOL, COMO OBJECTO DE CONHECIMENTO CIENTIFICO - UMA PROPOSTA DE
EXPLICITAÇÃO DE CAUSALIDADE -

Porto, 4 de Dezembro de 1990

Autor: Vitor Manuel da Costa Frade

Orientador   Prof. Dr. António Teixeira Marques

Co-Orientador Prof.Dr.Adalberto Dias de Carvalho

Título: A INTERACÇÃO, INVARIANTE ESTRUTURAL DA ESTRUTURA DO RENDIMENTO DO FUTEBOL, COMO OBJECTO DE CONHECIMENTO CIENTÍFICO - UMA PROPOSTA DE EXPLICITAÇÃO DE CAUSALIDADE.

[anotação manuscrita: → conceptual]

Preocupações de que partimos:
. A inexistência duma matriz teórica ajustada a esta actividade desportiva específica.
. A desadequação empírica da singularidade irredutível, do que elevamos a objecto de conhecimento científico, ao corpo de conhecimentos disponível, supostamente válido.

[margem esquerda manuscrita: inteireza irredutível]

Objectivo(s): *[manuscrito: + MODELAÇÃO]*
. Construir um objecto particular de conhecimento, "A INTERACÇÃO" - demarcando assim, um "suposto" campo científico, que é o do modelo teórico do futebol -.
. Outra inteligibilidade do objecto de conhecimento científico e sua aplicabilidade pragmática.
. A unificação numa só teoria da acção integrada das variáveis fundamentais - das quais as acções do jogo são função -, como cientificação muito específica globalmente rendível.
. A modelação "projectiva" (ou teleológica) do processo de treino. *[manuscrito: → Operacionaliz. específica]*

[margem esquerda manuscrita: ?MO OBJECTO ?? obscuro o ?U horizonte -empírico]

Hipótese inicial: A explicitação de causalidade (fenomenológica e representacional) para o problema fundamental, ou seja, de como os jogadores agindo - na estrutura do rendimento - são levados a interagir com os conteúdos da actividade proposta. Portanto, do processo, e não da acção dos jogadores sobre os conteúdos nem dos conteúdos sobre os jogadores.

[manuscrito: emergente   modelo]
[manuscrito: → de construção contínua e processual onde o sujeito tem 1 papel activo   JOGO!]

Hipóteses adicionais:
. A DIMENSIONALIDADE NÃO-INTEIRA do objecto-empírico específico - como o único objecto que resta globalmente invariante, durante toda a evolução deste sistema dinâmico específico -. *[manuscrito: → complexo de evolução ? linear!..]*
. O "ISOLAR" da INTERACÇÃO, dimensionalidade multifraccional onde se origina toda a variedade e complexidade dum processo.
. A NÃO-SEPARABILIDADE DAS VARIÁVEIS e o maior poder de predição da teoria.
. A dimensionalidade fraccional, uma MEDIDA COMPARATIVA para o conteúdo testável. Modelação de situações controladas, para IMPUTAÇÃO "CAUSAL".
. Médias estatísticas, O CÁLCULO para capturar a dimensionalidade multifraccional dos padrões da interacção, inerente à estrutura da acção, no processo de treino como interpretação objectiva e realista da probabilidade -.

[margem esquerda manuscrita: PADRÕES {TODO NAS partes E partes E estão no TODO   ?CEDA..   VERSUS..]

Metodologia:
. Método de abordagem: Hipotético-dedutivo *[manuscrito: → Dimensão da partes ? são identificá na ??? do Todo. A densif. e probabilit]*
. Método de procedimento: Descritivo, comparativo e explicativo. *[manuscrito: E mede NA qualif face   Espec do objec]*
. Técnicas de recolha e de registo observacionais:
    . Documentação indirecta - Pesquisa bibliográfica, em jornais e vídeo.
    . Documentação directa - Observação directa intensiva (participante e pesquisa de terreno).
. Instrumentos de pesquisa: Vídeo; ditafone; "diário de campo".

[manuscrito: SEM descurar o Horizonte Empírico ONDE o fenómeno decorre e se constrói]

Porque não podemos "naturalizar" a modelização, no Futebol de rendimento superior. O nível de descrição "morfogenético" enquanto "fio de Ariane", ou condição de explicitação.

Vítor Manuel da Costa Frade
Faculdade de Ciências do Desporto e de Educação Física (U. do Porto)
Gabinete de Futebol

- Rendimento superior. Aferição dum processo, um problema empírico.

- Um nível de descrição da dimensionalidade fraccionária, medida comparativa para um conteúdo testável.

- Dinâmica das cargas versus modelização dum "algoritmo de construção" ou de projecto.
        - Dimensão algorítmica da "interacção estratégica de informação assimétrica".
        - Rendimento, um estado de adaptação pronto a usar? Naturalização do objecto ou a essência de coisa nenhuma.

PROJECTO DE DOUTORAMENTO

Para a Tese que me proponho realizar, no âmbito da Teoria e metodologia de treino e do ensino do Futebol, prevejo um tempo para a sua realização, de 3 anos, assim distribuidos:

1 - Recolha de material e modelação   - 8 a 12 meses
2 - Redacção   - 18 a 24 meses
3 - Dactilografia, provas, revisão e defesa da tese - 6 a 8 meses

Mudei o nível de percepção do OBJECTO e, nesse mesmo acto, Mudei o OBJECTO. [...] Mudar o nível de percepção multiplica os OBJECTOS, como uma espécie de espelho diabólico.

Roland Barthes in Conversa (com Stephen Heath)

O CONHECIMENTO necessário é o de OBSERVAR O QUÊ.

Edgar Allan Poe in The Murders in the Rue Morgue

"Tudo o que é factual É JÁ TEÓRICO", dizia Goethe [...] Nada existe senão como OBJECTO de um ver que a TEORIA é, um speculum da racionalidade que investe os discursos do saber, mesmo quando eles se iludem em denegá-la.

Destacamos um conjunto de autores, nos quais é permanente, nos seus mais recentes trabalhos, o apelo à necessidade do desenvolvimento de UMA TEORIA GERAL DOS JOGOS DESPORTIVOS: (Cei 1990; Tschiene 1988; Schnabel 1988; Schmidt 1986; Zanon 1983; Pitera, Minocchi 1987; Singer 1984; Meinel 1984; Achmerov ed al. 1982; Gulinelli, Morino 1983; Konzag 1983; Manno, Camilli 1982; Neumeier, Ritzdorf 1984; Piéron 1982; Rieder 1983, 1984; Teodoresco 1983; Talaga 1984).

Curiosamente, uma individualidade de prestígio mundial no seio da ciência,

.../.

como é KARL POPPER, promove a objecto das suas mais recentes reflexões, também, quase pode dizer-se, o mesmo problema, ou seja, o questionar de UMA TEORIA DOS JOGOS MAIS GERAL.

Leccionamos há doze anos nesta Faculdade, as áreas da Teoria e Metodologia do treino para a alta perfomance. Dez destes, foram simultâneamente vivenciados no "terreno", enfrentando as "exigências" dos factores condicionantes do elevado rendimento, fundamentalmente dum jogo desportivo colectivo, o futebol. Deparamos com diversos momentos de INSATISFAÇÃO PRÁTICA, resultantes do aparecimento de "factos estranhos" no quotidiano do treino e da competição. A DESADEQUAÇÃO EMPÍRICA destes à TEORIA DO TREINO STANDARD, motivou-nos para a problematização deste conhecimento de base. Como consequência — na tentativa de resolução dos problemas — formulamos e testámos HIPÓTESES no "laboratório" do treino e da competição.

As nossas INQUIETAÇÕES ACADÉMICAS em relação à necessidade de ALTERNATIVAS TEÓRICAS, têm por isso origem em problemas práticos, saídos do conflito entre factos e teorias tidas como verdadeiras, e continuam-se, ao questionar a consistência teórica da ordem científica hegemónica do treino, na necessidade para nós, de reflectir sobre O EIXO PARADIGMÁTICO SUBJACENTE a esta.

A nossa opinião, confirma, a dos autores referidos acima, ou seja, A INEXISTÊNCIA DUMA MATRIZ TEÓRICA AUTÓNOMA PARA OS JOGOS DESPORTIVOS COLECTIVOS. Obviamente, também para o futebol. E como chegar aos fundamentos dum conhecimento "sem fundamento"?

A Teoria e metodologia do treino do futebol é redutível, por exemplo, à fisiologia do esforço ?

O primeiro problema a enfrentar, refere-se À NATUREZA DO OBJECTO EMPÍRICO deste jogo desportivo colectivo, e o segundo, À MANEIRA ADEQUADA DE ESTUDÁ-LA. Ambas são questões epistemológicas. A primeira pertence aos fundamentos deste jogo desportivo. A segunda pertence aos principais métodos de investigação. Estas questões supomo-las de significativa importância já que, qualquer resposta à segunda — metodológica — depende em parte, da resposta que se dê à primeira — teórica —.

O futebol, apesar de frequentemente encarado como "realidade-inferior", disciplina de importância menor, desprezada, pouco vocacionada a despertar pessoas para uma carreira académica — como especialidade e investigação consequente —, é no entanto, um objecto de estudo complexo, na medida em que uma multiplicidade de factos e de acontecimentos, se dão a ver ao mesmo tempo. Enquanto prática social, o futebol tem uma história, inclusivamente, uma geografia. Daí, não se tome por único o que é plural, e por plural o que é único. O futebol pré-existe à ideia que dele se tem. O problema está em saber, se as ideias que dele se tem, se lhe ajustam.

A relevância da "fenomenologia do futebol" é tal (pelo menos por enquanto), em todos os aspectos da vida contemporânea, que o estudo científico de qualquer das facetas deste fenómeno, me parece justificado.

Uma das dimensões, relaciona-se, com A IMPORTÂNCIA DOS FACTORES CONDICIONANTES DA ELEVADA PERFOMANCE. É aqui que se concentra a preocupação fundamental desta tese. É nela que se FIXA O CONTEXTO DE SENTIDO, que atribui o valor explicativo concreto ao objecto de conhecimento científico considerado, possibilitando, seleccionar a posteriori o tipo de questionamento científico para o objecto em causa, e conferindo, um direccionamento a uma possível análise hermenêutica da produção de sentido.

A explicitação do OBJECTO DE ESTUDO, vai fazer-se na continuação do "isolar", daquilo que na NATUREZA DO JOGO DE FUTEBOL, é CONSTANTE e FUNDAMENTAL, ou seja, o único objecto que resta globalmente invariante, durante toda a evolução deste sistema dinâmico específico.

A questão do seu VERDADEIRO OBJECTO, da sua DELIMITAÇÃO, da sua ESPECIFICIDADE e dos seus FUNDAMENTOS, questiona-se assim, de acordo com a respectiva LOCALIZAÇÃO DE SENTIDO. O estatuto problemático destas investigações coloca contudo, questões epistemológicas e metodológicas, de uma especial acuidade e actualidade como: repensar certas fronteiras disciplinares "empíricas" e "científicas"; questionar uma certa confusão no emprego da expressão ciências do desporto — ciências que são essencialmente ciências do individual —; reflectir outra inteligibilidade do conhecimento científico nesta área e sua aplicabilidade pragmática; problematizar uma Teoria e metodologia do treino do futebol METAMATVEIEVIANA, que não ignore Matveiv mas que o transcenda...

Os problemas da ciência do treino e do ensino do futebol, são PROBLEMAS àcerca de SISTEMAS DINÂMICOS.

└ DE NATUREZA COMPLEXA
(DE EVOLUÇÃO LINEAR)

..../.

O trabalho que nos propomos realizar, inicia-se com a existência de UM PRO-
BLEMA FUNDAMENTAL, que é a consequência lógica, da insatisfação prática e concomitan-
tes inquietações académicas, e que podemos "isolar"na seguinte QUESTÃO-CHAVE: O VER-
DADEIRO PROBLEMA ESTÁ EM SABER, COMO OS JOGADORES AGINDO — na estrutura do rendimento—
SÃO LEVADOS A INTERAGIR COM OS CONTEÚDOS DA ACTIVIDADE PROPOSTA.
     É um tipo de problema, em relação ao qual existe já, um excesso de dados em-
píricos. O que falta, é um modelo teórico. Assim sendo, a pergunta que esta questão-cha
ve nos coloca é TEÓRICA — não abstracta —, mas CONCRETA. Não é portanto, a partir de
qualquer generalidade abstracta que o processo de investigação se inicia, mas a partir
da realidade, que transformada em OBJECTOS TEÓRICOS, torna possível com base nestes,
FORMULAR HIPÓTESES que ultrapassam sem dúvida, o campo do estritamente observável. Hipóteses que devem submeter-se no entanto, às CONDIÇÕES DE REFUTABILIDADE.
     Aceitando como "forças" básicas do jogo, as QUATRO VARIÁVEIS FUNDAMENTAIS con-
vencionais, formulamos a seguinte HIPÓTESE: A UNIFICAÇÃO NUMA SÓ TEORIA, DA ACÇÃO INTE-
GRADA DESSAS QUATRO COMPONENTES FUNDAMENTAIS. Ao reconhecermos também, "no-centro-da-
-questão-chave" um sistema dinâmico, representacional da NATUREZA COMPLEXA DO PRÓPRIO
JOGO, a delimitação do objecto de estudo fazêmo-la a partir daqui, isolando, como "coisa" concreta, A DIMENSIONALIDADE NÃO-INTEIRA DO OBJECTO-EMPÍRICO ESPECÍFICO — A INTE-
RACÇÃO COMO INVARIANTE ESTRUTURAL—. Estrutura primordial cuja natureza não são "natu-
rezas", mas sistemas de relações, que originam bloqueios teóricos, obstáculos epistemológicos e metodológicos, cujo cordão umbilical se entrelaça no status quo do cientismo dominante desta área. Sentimos que o seu efeito se exerce particularmente no universo da LINGUAGEM-OBJECTO, que funciona, em parte pelo menos, como MODELO SÓCIO-COGNITIVO
Os dados não são portanto, dados brutos, já que os factos não se reduzem às suas dimensões externas, observáveis e quantificáveis.
     A Hipótese da unificação numa só teoria, da acção integrada das quatro variá-
veis, constitui-se como guia que nos conduz a novos resultados observacionais, ou seja,
como uma teoria ou um modo específico de conceptualizar a realidade. A DELIMITAÇÃO DO
OBJECTO-EMPÍRICO ESPECÍFICO torna-se então, num instrumento de grande alcance operacional e conceptual, já que, qualquer tentativa de UNIFICAÇÃO TEÓRICA, como autonomia disciplinar que se persegue, deve ser compatível com os fundamentos deste jogo desportivo.
Quer isto dizer, que A TEORIA deve ser VÁLIDA tanto à escala MACROSCOPIA (do Jogo) como
ao nível da dimensão "MICROSCÓPICA", ou NÃO-INTEIRA da INVARIANTE-ESTRUTURAL (Adequação empírica). A ADEQUABILIDADE DA TEORIA SUBENTENDE ESTE PROCESSO, E A PERIODIZAÇÃO TEÓRICA".
     O significado das consequências metodológicas da tese integrativa, deriva da
COESÃO DO SEU CONTEÚDO — REFERENCIAL TEÓRICO DO PROCESSO — que é satisfeita pela dimensionalidade não inteira, da padronização dos conteúdos da invariante estrutural, ou
seja, como tendência do "todo" se formar em cada uma das suas "partes". Portanto, para
que uma dimensão fraccional seja "futebol", terá que satisfazer condições tais como,
"a parte" ser semelhante ao "todo". A hipótese de solução do problema é de inegável importância prática, já que procura, "leis" cada vez mais abrangentes e profundas, que
expliquem o "mecanismo interno" do fenómeno, e englobem um grande número de casos.
     Como parece acontecer frequentemente na HISTÓRIA DAS CIÊNCIAS, determinados
objectos ou fenómenos não parecem ser tomados em consideração, senão a partir do momen-
to em que um conceito, muitas vezes simples, permite analisá-los. Sucede que, para nós,
a área do treino está cheia de ILUSÕES VERBAIS, metafóricas; não são objectos reais. O
saber do treino vive uma crise de INDIFERENCIAÇÃO GENERALIZADA, ou seja, DEU-SE O FIM DA
DIFERENÇA ENTRE OS "REAIS". Em relação ao futebol, a Teoria do treino de base parece-nos
até, uma espécie "essência de coisa nenhuma".
     A importância do que na natureza do jogo de futebol é constante e fundamental,
consiste assim, na possibilidade de se "isolar" essa invariante estrutural — um exemplo
imediato de "lei" simples —, dimensionalidade multifraccional onde se originam toda a variedade e complexidade dum processo. O objectivo essencial do estudo dos sistemas dinâmicos é PREDIZER a sua EVOLUÇÃO. Aspiração central também da metodologia do treino, e

..../.

que levanta necessàriamente problemas no que se refere por exemplo às "condições inici-
ais" e à "quantificação". Em relação a esta última curiosamente refere Tschiene 1985,
"NÃO É POSSÍVEL CONSIDERAR-SE ... UMA VEZ COMO SER CONDICIONAL E UMA OUTRA COMO SER
TÉCNICO, SUBMETENDO-O A MEDIÇÕES SECTORIAIS EM RELAÇÃO ORA A UM ASPECTO ORA AO OUTRO".
No futebol português o "saber-do-treino" não tem pròpriamente história. Mais,
a "história do treino" em Portugal é para nós uma história demasiado recente. A formação
de treinadores em Portugal está a ser baseada em documentos escritos que postulam conceitos errados, que adulteram o significado das palavras e desse modo o sentido das
coisas. A consistência da identidade conceptual do seu discurso, deve constituir-se
numa questão central, que os teóricos do treino e do ensino do futebol não podem alienar, procurando concomitantemente, evitar que quaisquer discursos se regidifiquem em
linguagens-objecto, que sacrificam, a efectiva complexidade dos problemas e apenas con-
tribuem para a histerização "tecnocrática" de múltiplos matizes.
No sentido de subtrair o estudo do objecto de conhecimento científico considerado, do monopólio da fragmentaridade dominante, uma dificuldade metodológica, situa-se
— ao "isolar" o objecto-segundo conceptual — no questionar da problemática ciências do
desporto/ciência do treino e disciplinas científicas tradicionais.
Alguns indicadores da "patologia" em questão, fora dum referencial hermenêutic
tendem para fetiches, ou seja, tabus sobre os quais é quase proibido interrogar-se. Ao
indivíduo como entidade biológica complexa, por exemplo, caracteriza-o uma extraordiná-
ria capacidade, A ADAPTAÇÃO ÀS SITUAÇÕES. Este "poder de autoadequação" está largamente
estudado, quer em função da filogénese (selecção natural), quer em função da capacidade
de espontânea modificação do organismo humano, após estimulação de acordo com um tempo
determinado (Teoria do treino). Na "prática desportiva", é frequente e completo o despre-
zo pelo presente conceito. O resultado desta inconsciência teórica tem como consequência, que o termo preparação se conecte com a ideia, de uma acção voltada para a "CONS-
TRUÇÃO" de qualquer coisa. (um pronto a usar...)
Treinar-se deve pelo contrário, significar, colocar em acto uma fantástica
capacidade de que o nosso organismo dispõe: A ADAPTABILIDADE-ADAPTAÇÃO. A preparação
deve então ser entendida, como reflexo da necessidade do organismo se modificar, em
função de determinada INTENÇÃO ou PROPÓSITO.
NÃO SE TRATA DE UMA CONSTRUÇÃO (o construtivismo dos cartesianos é a negação
do processo adaptativo.
Pode dizer-se que numa óptica biológica, a resposta dita física do treino, é
uma espécie de mecanismo de autodefesa, que o organismo "põe-em-acto" para conservar
a própria homeostasia (equilíbrio funcional). Corresponde, num certo sentido, a uma
adaptação preventiva do organismo, que se AUTOMODIFICA para estar mais capaz, em grau,
num próximo futuro, de neutralizar por exemplo, os efeitos nocivos, duma fadiga muscular. Logo, treinar-se significa, informar o(s) próprio(s) corpo(s), da futura tarefa
que este deverá enfrentar. (Ginásio)
PADRÃO
Nesta óptica, a metodologia do treino corresponde, à linguagem empregue neste
processo de autocomunicação, em que o verbo de acordo com este paralelismo, é o estímu-
lo dito físico. Treinar consiste no informar o(s) próprio(s) organismo(s), que deverá
reorganizar-se, no sentido de enfrentar novas situações.
Muito embora comecem a surgir certas condições favoráveis, para o futuro estudo do futebol em Portugal, julgamos necessário que isso aconteça, respeitando-se
alguns princípios que nos parecem essenciais, se queremos perspectivá-lo ajustadamente,
nomeadamente por parte de quem ensina e investiga no "interior" do futebol. Princípios
que têm de ultrapassar lacunas e deturpações nas ideias comuns sobre a prática interdisciplinar. Logo, princípios que têm de estipular a impossibilidade de um jogo desportivo, como disciplina desportiva específica, permanecer fechada sobre si mas, e im-
portantíssimo parece-nos, a inoperatividade de uma abertura, quando esta se constrói
à margem da natureza peculiar, metodologias e limites do campo de onde se parte, para
outras áreas do saber. Assim o parece referir Boaventura Sousa Santos quando diz: "Co-
nhecer o que conhece pior através do que conhece melhor".
Supomos também necessário, assumir, que é importante ultrapassar a habitual
desvalorização do conhecimento do senso comum "dos-do-terreno", quando se hierarquiza
ao nível do domínio científico sobre futebol. Convirá ainda, pensamos, não identificar
o pretenso alto nível da hierarquia com a fidelidade do saber académico, e o outro com
"empirismos", se estamos empenhados nas questões do conhecimento do futebol. O "pensar"
não me parece que seja, atributo de alguma classe particular ...

..

Pergunto-me por exemplo, quantos não serão os "dados" existentes àcerca da pergunta seguinte: Quais são, os elementos estruturais de todo o jogo de futebol ? A estrutura da acção não é mecânica no entanto, o saber compartimentado do "nosso" futebol segregou já demasiadas previsões especializadas. Deve continuar o "futebol", a deixar-se cegar pelo erudito reducionismo ? Para nós a formulação de MODELOS DE INTELIGIBILIDADE afastados DA FRAGMENTARIDADE DOMINANTE, e ajustados à natureza complexa do objecto-empírico, parece-nos de premente necessidade.

A INTERACÇÃO, como realidade condicional requer que categorias de inteligibilidade ?

BERTALANFFY (1977,56) dá a seguinte noção de SISTEMA: "COMPLEXOS DE ELEMENTOS EM INTERACÇÃO". Ora, a relação causa a efeito (de acordo com o nosso propósito), situa-se dentro de uma totalidade dinâmica autoteleologizada. A originalidade deste Modelo, reside no facto de possibilitar uma VISÃO TOTALIZANTE, dinâmica, INTEGRADORA DO TEMPO e que engloba simultâneamente a RELAÇÃO e a EVOLUÇÃO. FAZENDO NOSSOS OS QUESTIONAMENTOS DE AVENTURA S. SANTOS Um conjunto de interrogações se nos coloca: Quais as características do nexo causal deste sistema dinâmico peculiar ? É pensável uma reflexão crítica sobre o problema representacional dessa causalidade ? E em relação às dificuldades que nos coloca o problema metodológico: Quais os critérios de causalidade ? Como reconhecer um nexo causal ou testar uma hipótese causal ? E os problemas sobre o nexo entre "o que aparece" e "o que é", ou seja, o fenomenológico e o representacional ? E numa situação em que a causalidade circular é a regra, constitui um problema empírico destrinçar a causa do efeito, no que frequentemente são interacções e "interpolações" (o desejo de verificar cientificamente uma hipótese formulada empiricamente) ? → PARA UM QUADRO COMPETITIVO

Uma investigação cuidada sobre o fenómeno da "INTERACÇÃO" exige um estudo "desta-em-si" (ou seja, do processo) e não da acção dos jogadores sobre os conteúdos nem dos conteúdos sobre os jogadores. Estudo — da constituição básica da estrutura do rendimento — a partir do qual, através dum esforço marcadamente teórico, se pretende LIBERTAR "O JOGO" (e o treino) dum DETERMINISMO MECANICISTA, dum CONSTRUTIVISMO CARTESIANO, duma FASCINAÇÃO POSITIVISTA e dum FISIOLOGISMO ENERGICISTA mutilantes, tentando demonstrar, a necessidade de utilizar no conhecimento do futebol, INSTRUMENTOS CONCEPTUAIS e METODOLÓGICOS, adaptados ao questionamento da "INTERACÇÃO" NA SUA ESPECIFICIDADE multifraccional. C/SINGULARIDADE IRREDUTÍVEL

As dificuldades normalmente enfrentadas, ao pensar "objectivamente" num sistema dinâmico, esta realidade condicional que se revela em função de níveis de organização diversos — realizando-se o processo como problema, como fenómeno sistémico e como aprendizagem de novas sequências de acção do colectivo, ("quantificáveis" em termos das distribuições de probabilidades, no que se refere a permanências, desenvolvimento e evolução), — resultam, fundamentalmente, da AUSÊNCIA DE MATRIZ TEÓRICA AUTÓNOMA, neste jogo desportivo colectivo.

Foi nosso propósito salientar que não se trata do apelo a qualquer "ficção" teórica. Já que pode desejar-se teòricamente, mas se esse quadro de referência não constitui parte da experiência efectiva (conteúdo empírico), não nos parece que deva ser considerado. Supomos "intolerável" até, colocar numa estrutura teórica, uma característica, que não tem uma característica correspondente no nosso sistema de referência.

Os teóricos do treino consideram normalmente, QUATRO VARIÁVEIS FUNDAMENTAIS, como que constituindo as quatro "forças" básicas do jogo, ou seja, a táctica, a psicológica, a técnica e a física. Sentimos a necessidade de hipotetizar, o UNIFICAR NUMA SÓ TEORIA A ACÇÃO INTEGRADA dessas quatro componentes. O "instrumento" fundamental da investigação, terá que ser o amplo e completo horizonte empírico, singular ao jogo de futebol, PROBLEMATIZANDO-O, na relação com o UNIVERSO TEÓRICO-EXPERIMENTAL dominante.

A consolidação das ideias àcerca dos CONSTITUINTES FUNDAMENTAIS (e implícitos na invariante estrutural) DO JOGO de futebol, e a hipotética unificação das quatro variáveis numa teoria comum é, conjectura, o problema fundamental da Teoria e metodologia do treino e do ensino do futebol. A compreensão da estrutura "microscópica" do jogo de futebol é uma das chaves para a sistematização do universo teórico e metodológico deste jogo desportivo colectivo, que no entanto, mais do que uma "teoria dos alvos", será fundamentalmente a "arte das trajectórias",* ou seja, como "construção sistemàticamente inacabada".*

Para nós, há muito mais "real" no jogo do que aquele que podemos ver, espreitando por quaisquer dos instrumentos privilegiados pelo "universo teórico-experimental" dominante. Apesar de tudo "mensurável"!

* Expressões tomadas de Malho, Levi A. - Filosofia e Teoria dos Jogos, 17/18.

.../.

Conseguir estabelecer uma explicitação, clara, objectivada e unificada da acção das quatro variáveis ao nível da DIMENSIONALIDADE das "INTERACÇÕES" é de inegável IMPORTÂNCIA PRAGMÁTICA.

O significado de CONSTRUIR UM OBJECTO PARTICULAR DE CONHECIMENTO, A "INTERACÇÃO" —demarcando assim, um "suposto" campo científico que é o da Teoria do jogo de futebol— parece-me elevado. Fazendo-o, a partir de procedimentos que obrigam A UMA MAIOR INTIMIDADE COM O OBJECTO EMPÍRICO, e de acordo com uma grelha conceptual de base, sistémica. Há no entanto, ao realizá-lo, que pensar a partir de um quadro teórico, que já não é "o seu".

Os novos modelos de racionalidade "pós-moderna", não são particularmente propícios a qualquer projecto epistemológico "energizante", quantitativo, disjuntivo, tradicional. É o que sentimos. O "futebol" necessitará de olhar e ver - para "crer" -, que também "atravessa" a chamada pós modernidade. Como não existe sequer uma "ciência do jogo único", daí, a descrença que habita todas as metodologias e discursos, cujo propósito seja argumentar contra o edifício teórico que vigora, e "sustenta" um afunilamento epistemológico, dominador.

Um programa de pesquisa que visa a construção do OBJECTO DA TEORIA DO JOGO DE FUTEBOL, segundo uma grelha conceptual de base, sistémica, implica antes que tudo, ENCONTRAR A ESPECIFICIDADE DESSE OBJECTO: um objecto-primeiro empírico, um objecto-segundo conceptual, isto é, uma determinada problemática mais ou menos "académica", em torno da qual se construiu um sistema de conceitos. Todo o trabalho teórico consiste pois, em isolar o conceito, "representacional", da invariância estrutural do jogo de futebol, e na abertura interdisciplinar a partir deste, poder construir um objecto-terceiro científico, verdadeiramente específico deste desporto de situação, e por isso pragmático.

Fundando uma "ciência do futebol", a partir de um objecto específico que se origina num 1º corte epistemológico do objecto empírico, "senso comum-futebolístico", e num 2º corte epistemológico do objecto conceptual, cientificado (o "resto" dos empréstimos das chamadas ciências do desporto e da teoria do treino ...).

Assim, ao procurar a explicitação, a objectivação desse objecto, a partir do próprio material de que é feito o jogo, não apresenta o perigo de desembocar num empirismo rasteiro, que pretenda poder distinguir num jogo, supostas qualidades intrínsecas que por si, o definem como científico. Ora, uma epistemologia chamada de pós moderna obriga-nos a ENCONTRAR A OBJECTIVIDADE ESPECÍFICA (é aqui que reside o segundo passo do "acto epistemológico") deste produto HUMANO, que é o JOGO de futebol, na prática específica que ele implica.

Portanto, o terceiro passo da construção do objecto da teoria do JOGO de futebol não pode alienar a historicidade específica desse "objecto", reconhecendo nisso, que a Teoria do treino standard sempre se tem constituído como uma resistência, que é inerente ao seu objecto, próprio.

Moles A. A. em "Les Sciences de L'imprécis", tendo como baliza a actualidade do problema que levanta, o modo como se propõe tratá-lo e o que espera concluir, diz ser necessário construir, para o efeito, uma epistemologia, uma metrologia e uma metodologia. Aquilo que, na busca dos fundamentos dum conhecimento "sem fundamento", também aspiramos concluir:

1 - Uma Epistemologia: estabelecer as regras que dão acesso à verdade (e não, certeza.), ou seja, a reconceptualização das condições epistemológicas do conhecimento científico deste jogo desportivo colectivo, já que a alteração do regime conceptual do treino resultará no questionar do status quo metodológico do futebol, e este tem em "stock" a informação que circula na rede de que ele é um elemento.

2 - Uma Metodologia: conhecimento dos procedimentos que possibilitem agir sobre a especificidade do próprio objecto.

3 - Uma Metrologia: ciências e técnicas de medida, das distribuições de probabilidades da "interacção", como dimensão não inteira do objecto-empírico específico, cuja mensuração se realiza no âmbito da correspondente explicitação de causalidade estatística.

../.

DESENVOLVIMENTO DA PROPOSTA DE TESE

1. Introdução
   - Justificação da escolha e actualidade do tema.

2. Um Jogo desportivo colectivo singular, o futebol, no contexto da hegemónica "ordem científica" do treino.
   - O enclausuramento teórico deste J.D.C.-um saber sem objecto-.
   - A objectividade da Teoria do treino standard não é senão debilidade.
   - A falência dos pilares epistemológicos dos modelos explicativos que vêm subjazendo ao desenvolvimento do "saber do treino" deste J.D.C.
   - Questionamento do eixo paradigmático, subjacente à Teoria do treino standard. Pretensões centrais do paradigma dominante.
   - A concepção sistémica uma ponte para um novo paradigma.
   - Os problemas da ciência do treino e do ensino do futebol, são problemas àcerca de sistemas dinâmicos não lineares.

3. Teoria específica ou modelo teórico e Teoria geral dos jogos desportivos colectivos.
   - O carácter "pré-paradigmático" do saber dos J.D.C.
   - As condições sistémicas do elevado rendimento, no futebol, concretizam processos de optimização não lineares.
   - Problematizar o enclausuramento teórico do status quo, do cientismo dominante nesta área.
   - Os fundamentos dum conhecimento "sem fundamento" e a necessidade de subtrair o estudo do objecto de conhecimento científico, do monopólio da fragmentaridade dominante: um compromisso paradigmático.

4. O saber comum "futebolístico" e problematização científica.
   - Hipótese básica: O objecto de pesquisa, uma "coisa" concreta.
   - Isolar um objecto-primeiro empírico. O contexto de sentido da dimensão não inteira deste objecto problemático-invariante estrutural- é fixado pelo jogo concreto
   - variáveis das quais as acções do jogo são função: a táctica, a psicológica (componente cognitiva e sócio-psicológica), técnica e física.
   - A natureza específica deste objecto-empírico problemático: a invariante estrutural enquanto realidade "causal", uma desordem ordenada com virtualidades sistémicas.
   - A dimensão fraccional da interacção: um modelo de representação da própria estrutura do rendimento, ou seja, dos elementos (as variáveis) de uma estrutura primordial invariante e universal.
   - Problematização da linguagem-objecto e da produção de sentido: conteúdos dos enunciados ou "adequação (da palavra) à coisa".
   - Enunciados de base: "qualidades físicas, fontes energéticas, periodização e estruturas orgânica, locomotora, perceptivo-cinética ...".
   - A matriz sócio-cultural de base: o contexto do elevado rendimento do futebol em Portugal.

5. Estratégias metodológicas e selecção de indicadores e observáveis.
   - A função heurística da elaboração metodológica-sistémica: condições de percepção, categorias de inteligibilidade e operatividade cognitiva.
   - Descrição, avaliação crítica e interrogações de registos directos em "diário de campo", registos em vídeo, pesquisa bibliográfica e em jornais.

6. O questionamento do objecto-segundo, conceptual: uma problemática interdisciplinar.
   - "Isolar" a invariante estrutural do seu contexto, problematizando a sua relação com os "objectos científicos" diversos, no quadro geral das ciências.
   - A dimensionalidade fraccional — da invariante estrutural — um instrumento de grande alcance operacional e conceptual.

..../.

7. A construção do objecto-terceiro, científico e sua objectividade específica: Uma outra inteligibilidade do objecto de conhecimento científico e sua aplicabilidade pragmática, *ISTO É PRAXIOLÓGICA. "MATERIALIZAÇÃO TÁCTICA" NA REESTRUTURAÇÃO EPISTEMOLÓGICA.*
   - A autonomia disciplinar da unificação teórica (fenomenológica e representacional): conceitos teóricos ou proposições.
   - Hipótese fundamental: Teoria integrativa (unificação numa só teoria, da acção integrada das quatro variáveis fundamentais) e um maior nível informativo.
   - A não-separabilidade das variáveis e o poder de predição da teoria: consistência conceptual e adequação empírica.
   - A "inteireza inquebrantável do jogo" e a "dimensionalidade não inteira da invariante estrutural": a relação "parte-todo" pode conceptualizar-se.
   - Unificação, redução e integração: Teoria integrativa e níveis de organização da interacção.
   - Níveis de organização: um princípio de "conexão das partes" — a dicotomia da "condição-de-parte" e da "condição-de-todo" ou a preeminência do jogo na dimensão fraccional da interacção—.
   - Consequências metodológicas da tese integrativa: a estrutura da acção não é mecânica; o agir como apriori da pragmática; a pragmática como crítica real da teoria; pragmática teórica e pragmática real. *A IMPORTÂNCIA DA DIMENSIONALIZAÇÃO PRAXIOLÓGICA.*

8. Hipótese integrativa — uma matriz teórica dum real unificado — e condições de refutabilidade ou conhecimento conjectural objectivamente testável.
   - Teoria científica e redução a um tamanho confirmável.
   - A dimensionalidade fraccional do objecto, uma medida comparativa para o conteúdo testável — a unidade de medida para exprimir o fenómeno —.
   - Uma realidade condicional mensurável e reproduzível em termos de distribuições de probabilidades — a ordem (padrões observáveis) subjacente a um processo de interacção —.
   - Formulação de hipóteses e modelação de situações, controladas, para imputação "causal".
   - Operacionalização da não-separabilidade das variáveis — dimensionalidade não inteira dos padrões da invariante estrutural — e causalidade estatística.
   - Médias estatísticas, o cálculo para capturar a dimensionalidade multifraccional dos padrões da interacção, inerente à estrutura da acção, no processo de treino.

9. Leitura, interpretação e discussão dos dados. *ESPECIFICIDADE!*

10. Conclusões.
    - A função da "INTERACÇÃO" não é apenas mais uma, mas sim a função das outras funções e o que possibilita que possamos entender — Teórica e pragmaticamente — o Jogo e o Treino com sabedoria integrada, *LOGO PRAXIOLOGICAMENTE.*
    - A importância da EXPLICITAÇÃO DE CAUSALIDADE dum processo, na construção do OBJECTO verdadeiramente específico — e por isso pragmático —, da Teoria do Jogo de Futebol.
    - O cálculo das distribuições de probabilidade da "unidade de medida," em função da explicitação de uma nova causalidade estatística.
    - Uma "Sistemática" ou processo de padronização dos níveis de organização da dimensão não inteira da "interacção" visando a racionalização dos seus conteúdos e formas, ou seja, a íntima coesão das formas e dos conteúdos, como referencial teórico do processo — condições iniciais, o cálculo e o imprevisto —.
    - A corroboração determina o conteúdo de verdade da Teoria — ao resistir a testes (experiências cruciais) que visam refutá-la —.

> "Agora, inventar arte e maneira:/De juntar
> o acaso e a certeza,/Leve nisso, ou não
> leve, a vida inteira",
>
> o escritor José Saramago

Porto, 4 de DEZEMBRO de 1990

Vitor Manuel da Costa Frade
(Ass. Conv. da Faculdade de Ciências do Desporto e de Educação Física - Porto)

TACTICAL PERIODIZATION
VS
NOITAZIDOIREP LACITCAT

VITOR FRADE CLARIFIES

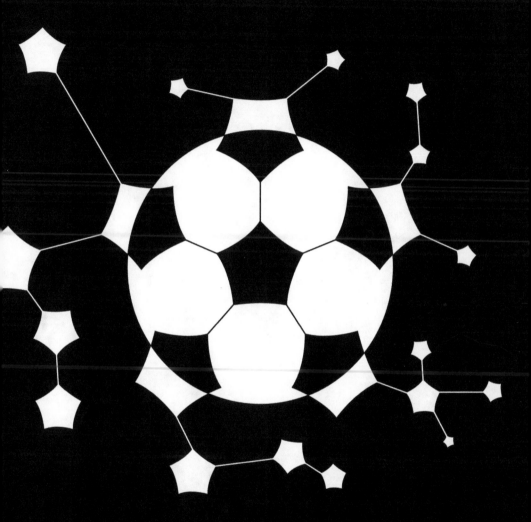

XAVIER TAMARIT

Foreword: Rui Faria

Translation: Francisco Fardilha

Vitor Frade (6)[1] explains that using machines will change *"the relationship of the body with the body, meaning that...there are two types of timing. The coordinative timing of the muscles between themselves, which is the co-contractibility – therefore, there will be chains which will start fighting, which will start disturbing each other. Because it is coordination that leads it to oppose the flow that suggests and requests the spontaneity of the football game. Also, there is another type of timing that is related to the muscular adjustment of the regular systematic alteration that is demanded by the environment. By using the machine, you will interfere with that, you will be tricking the nervous system. You will be obstructing the different possibilities of expression that the body could have when playing football. If it was done during the development phase, it could even block growth, for example, of the bones and other structures. It would bring hypertrophy to an area that is muscular when we know that the tendons do not develop in the same way...because it is not natural!"*

The interviewee finishes by saying that *"someone that knows a little bit about motor learning, about motor coordination, about the timing of muscular expression and muscular coordination, etc., will end up saying that that way of thinking is mutilating. But even here in the faculty, some lecturers say that the muscle is blind! They are the blind ones, because the muscle is, clearly, much more a sensitive organ rather than a power generator. And maybe, while they claim that the muscle is blind, they suggest that proprioception is important. Basically, they have no clue of what they are saying. Because proprioception is precisely what makes the muscle fundamentally a sensitive organ. Several mechano-receptors adapt to capture, let's put it this way, the evolution of the body over time and space. Good football, in whatever position, presents a diversity of agility and mobility that..."*.

There are many reasons why using resistance machines or doing strength training decontextualised from football are kept away from Tactical Periodization, both in High Performance and Youth Development.

According to Nuno Amieiro (1)[2], *"I (the player) have a history, in this case, a 'motor history', that, in part, is shared with my species and that, in another part, is personal, derived from my experiences. If I think about 'growing' or trying to gain something regarding my body that I don't have, I will be interfering with that history, that is my heritage. With that, I will be probably jeopardising much of that 'coordinative heritage' that the environment I have been exposed to for years led me to acquire against the 'hominid nature'"*.

We have a 'coordinative heritage' that arises from who we are and from our experiences, and that makes us who we are, in this case in football terms. By changing our morphotype, we risk distorting that heritage and losing certain abilities that have made us the player that we are.

So, although at times, due to the previously mentioned 'cappuccino' strategy, the use of resistance machines is allowed, it does not make part of our Logic. Guilherme Oliveira explains that he does it "bearing in mind the circumstances, the context. But this is not Tactical Periodization, Tactical Periodization

---

1 **Interviewed by Nuno Amieiro in 2009 in 'A Conversa com Vitor Frade', Blog 'Falemos de Futebol'.**

2 **In his blog 'Falemos de Futebol'**

does not need this kind of work to achieve what it intends regarding player quality and playing quality". So, it is "simply a matter of sensitivity that we need to have with the players".

With that in mind, in Tactical Periodization *"strength training is performed in accordance to the individual evolution of the player, having in mind the growth of my team and the roles of each one" Vitor Frade (6).*

Moreover, the demands that regularly that individual faces make him progressively more resistant and abler, and we should not want to go beyond that, because when trying to gain some things we will have to lose others. What is essential is that the player can 'resist' and to have 'strength'...but it is important that one understands that what I mean with this has nothing to do with the mainstream understanding".

For our Logic, having 'strength' means *"having the ability to start, stop, start again but on the other direction...".* So, this strength is not the conventional one.

2.5. The re-adaptation of injured players: getting to play through receiving small playing doses

You will always have problems. You may have issues with the medical department. Because even within the clinical logic, not everyone thinks the same. Physiotherapy is not, all the same, there are different conceptualisations. Then.... but it is easy to solve the problem! I used to say: "no problem, you do whatever you need to recover him, and you will only send me the player back when you have no need to work with him. From that moment, I am the one working with him". And then he will do whatever I think is more convenient for him to adapt. (...) Now, here we have to consider the Complex Progression! What is the logic of the conventional? He is missing resistance, so he trains a lot, and then the next day he comes back fatigued and then gets injured again. No, what he needs to do is just a little. So, if the players that are training usually do not train a lot, why should the player that is returning from an injury do it? But that is the logic: first resistance, then whatever...what I want him to do is that he starts being 'resistant' so that he can do what he needs to do. And in the beginning, he needs to do just a little, so that he can feel fresh! He needs to recover so that the next day he can do something else. I often used the wine jar metaphor: if I want to drink 5 litres of wine and I never drank wine before, I first need to drink a small glass. And after that small glass maybe I will be tipsy, blushing...and the next day I drink a little more than one glass, and so on. Training is the same. So, I increase the volume but the volume of something objective, not of something abstract. It is not an abstract complementarity, not at all.

Vitor Frade (1)

When a player is just returning from an injury that led him to the medical department, it is evident that its recovery will be directed by the latter. There, they may use resistance machines or not, depending on what they determine. They (doctors, physiotherapists, etc.) are the ones responsible for recovering the player in clinical terms. But in functional terms, the re-adaptation of the player will depend, or should depend, on the logic that is being followed throughout the process – in our case the Logic of Tactical Periodization and considering the Methodological Principle of Complex Progression, in a particular way for certain player.

In the Logic of Tactical Periodization, the re-adaptation of a player that returns from injury is done Specifically and according to the Methodological Principles, seeking a re-adaptation to a certain way of playing.

When Guilherme Oliveira (1) receives a player that was injured and has just been cleared by the medical department, he performs the 'same' practice as his colleagues. *"Naturally, the player that was away for a while, when he restarts training, cannot do what the others do regarding the length of the exercise, but he will do the same exercise. If he is well, he will do the same exercise, but while the others do three sets of five minutes perhaps he will do two sets of five minutes".* For Oliveira, the re-adaptation *performed through a conventional logic, where improvement is achieved through running and decontextualised conventional exercises "is not appropriate for football, for basketball, for rugby nor for handball. Why? Because the demands from handball are very different from those of running, and the same with basketball and football. So, to play football, you must train football, to play basketball you must train basketball…".*

As we see, the discussion is about getting back to playing through small playing doses. Involving the player, as soon as possible, in the Specificity and individualisation. In our Logic, a player that returns from injury, and therefore, from being inactive – in football terms at least – must have higher recovery times and lower exercising times, in opposition to what the 'other' logic does – a kind of 'pre-season- with the intention of getting the player 'physically fit' to get back to playing as soon as possible. But, how can he work with a higher volume in comparison to his colleagues, wasn't he physically unwell? So, how can he be training more than the rest? That is the conventional logic, that demands higher volumes of effort after inactivity – just like in 'pre-season – instead of improving gradually.

2.6. The warm-up in Tactical Periodization.

I make this joke very often: I never heard of a thief that was caught stealing and that had to warm-up before running away from the police! Now, what happens is that if you did not warm-up systematically, you could accumulate micro-traumatisms that, with time, make the organism more prone to injury. That is why it should be done. But, on the other hand, for you to get into a more demanding effort, more dynamic than the previous one, there are a series of mechanisms that must adapt. There is even a discussion about the 'steady state', the capillaries have to open and all that. Besides, if you are in great shape in your football team, and just for fun, this week you are playing handball or basketball, the next day everything is aching! So, you need to adapt, you need to go from low to high, but from the low-high to the high-high, and the low-high is the 'less football' (...).

Vitor Frade (1)

The warm-up is fundamental in Tactical Periodization just like in the other training methodologies. But it does not seek only the adaptation of the organism to a superior effort. It is also based on the adaptation to a Specificity to all levels required by our way of playing. It means that if on a certain day we want to promote one or more Principles or Sub-Principles during the session, which will require, due to the horizontal alternation, an increase of tension or speed of muscular contraction...the warm-up must focus on the adaptation of the organism to that same effort/performance. Furthermore, if the circumstances allow, we should already start promoting actions that are related to those Principles, Sub-Principles, or Sub-Sub-Principles of the Game we want to train.

The warm-up will serve, among other things, to require on a Wednesday, following the Pattern Morphocycle will a match every Sunday for example, a significant increase of the tension of the muscular contraction, because on that day that will be dominant. Our interest would be promoting this increase while using exercises that can already support the interactions that we wish to see in that session, at least partially. But, as we have mentioned earlier, that will depend on the circumstances. Here, we can fit, for example, the 'cappuccino strategy', using the warm-up to do some drills with sprints, skipping, etc. and satisfy some of our players' cultural 'needs'. Even if I have already warned for the potential dangers of that strategy in a previous chapter.

As Guilherme Oliveira (1) explains, the warm-up will depend *"on the practice. It will depend on what we want to do"*.

If we are preparing a warm-up, for example, on the day of the Sub-Principles and Sub-Sub-Principles, with augmented tension of the muscular contraction, we should promote since the beginning actions – 'micro' concerns of our way of playing – that require a great number of eccentric contractions like braking, starting, jumping, change of direction, etc. Therefore, even if we have to consider the 'cappuccino' strategy, at least in part of the warm-up, the exercises that we pick should consider the type of effort/performance (and not only with regards to the contractions) that we want to promote.

The warm-up before matches must also follow the same Logic. They should be an introduction to the way of playing we want to achieve during that game, at both tactical, technical, physical, psychological and sometimes strategic levels. So, they must be Specific.

Carlos Carvalhal (1) tells us that the pre-match warm-up *"is usually very Specific and directed to the match. We can even try to experience some of the things that we want to do during the match (...)"*.

libro
futbol
.com
AL GOL SE
LLEGA LEYENDO

193

3

> Other Sub-Logics that surpass the logic

"Even though these myths have been undermined by new science, they leave behind institutions and structures that were designed to support and propagate scientific materialism's paradigmatic wisdom"

(Lipton & Bhaerman, 2015, p.163)

Index

3.1. "Individualised Training" vs a Maximised and Specific individualisation

Look, there is nothing more individualised than Tactical Periodization because they always practice in accordance with their positions and to their roles. And when operationalising it, you need to pay attention to the global and to the individual at the same time. And it's its detection, against certain things...for example that player has mobility problems, he deals badly with the body, he cannot even perform a tumble, which is important. He needs to go through it. And it is that attention that will lead him to improve. So, there is nothing more individualising. But this is a contextualised individualisation, not something abstract! Because a while ago you were talking about compensation and complementarity, those are abstract things. And I need to take all the needs of the game and all the needs of the individual into account, but along the whole Process and concurrently. That is why I say Tactical Periodization is a tailor-made suit, but those are not complementarities of anything, those are things more connected to the micro level or to a more individual level while taking into account the team's functionality. In the end, the team is fulfilled by individuals. The team will operate better if the individuals operate better, but only if the individuals are committed to collective references. That is the growth Process and, since the beginning, one must understand it and try to make it happen.

Vítor Frade (1)

Individualised training is conceptualised in different manners by the conventional logic and by the Logic of Tactical Periodization.

Within Tactical Periodization, individualised training is taken to its maximum potential. What does this mean? It means that by operating exclusively in Specificity, each player will be training Specifically inside the Specificity of the team, at all levels. So, each player will be training, on each moment, what she really needs to accomplish her role in the team's game, both at micro and macro levels. Tactically, on a plane of effort/performance, technically, psychologically, or at times strategically, Specifically. Therefore, this is an objective and contextualised individualisation, which pays attention not only to the global but also to the individual in parallel.

This methodology, in opposition to what most think, and as we have been showing throughout the whole book, is not exclusively based on the global. Everything is essential. And we know that the Whole is made of parts, and that, consequently, the intervention occurs at both the Whole and the parts. This is something that I already referred to in my first book[3]. As Guilherme Oliveira (1) reports, *"for Tactical Periodization, the global is important. But the individual is important too. Often, people only look at the global, they overlook the individual. And we need to consider both. The interaction of the individual will make the global. And if the indivi-*

---

3 'What is Tactical Periodization?', Xavier Tamarit, Bennion Kearny, 2015.

dual is not well, it will affect the global profoundly. And many times, because the global is so strong, it manages to disguise the weaknesses of the individual. But we need to have the ability to see the global and the individual because otherwise we only get a partial view of things".

The interviewee clarifies that *"many times people think that Tactical Periodization is exclusively global. Nonetheless, although Tactical Periodization is global, it also considers the individual, the interaction between the individual and the global, and the interactions between the different individuals".*

Now, it is about improving at an individual level (intervention in the parts), but within a collective matrix, that is formed by the Macro Principles of our way of playing. As Vítor Frade (1) states, **"(...) Football is a collective sport. Being collective, the priority has to be the collective matrix, that represents the rules of a certain society".**

So, we shall not forget that Football is a sport constructed by individuals (players), but these individuals are part of a certain society (team), which works in accordance to certain rules (collective Game Idea). That is why Professor Vítor Frade (1) designates football as an Anthropo-Social-Total Phenomenon. As he explains: **"precisely due to the interference on the individual as an evolution, not only functional but also 'structural', it impacts the 'anthropo'. It is not exclusively social in the synchronic sense! Therefore, I call it an em-bodiment, an em-<u>body</u>-ment, having in mind being part of a group, being in a community, co-existing! There is a deliberate intention, that is why that idea of deterministic chaos makes sense, because there is a deliberate intention to make it happen, firstly from the coaches and then from the players, together with the coaches, to head in that direction".**

Players need to understand this: they will improve with the help of the collective, but at the same time, they will improve the collective with their individuality. Guilherme Oliveira (1) says that this is something achievable with Tactical Periodization, because *"one of the fundamental characteristics of this training methodology is that everyone knows what they need to do in any moment, in both collective and individual terms. So, it is easy that we know if you are respecting the team or not, and it is easy for the players as well. So, there is almost a relationship between the players and the team that...there is a relationship, a commune of interactions, of information exchange among us, in a way that each one is respectful and giving".*

He provides an example to illustrate his perspective better: *"consider Messi for example. He is in your team – you cannot be too rigid with Messi, so that he can fully express his ability, but you cannot also be too open, allowing him to do whatever he feels like. That team must provide Messi with the conditions to maximise his individual capacity and characteristics, his key strengths, right? The team must give that to Messi. But with what he does, he also needs to give a contribution to the team. And that is something that I can see now, in contrast with what happened when Rijkaard was there. These are different things, Messi is different. Of course, he is now more mature, older, but is way of playing is totally different. He is now essentially a team player, with an amazing individual ability. But he does things that respect that team's way of playing. So, in his own way of playing, there is a permanent interaction between himself and the team. This did not happen before. And we need to understand this. So, it is about giving freedom to the player, but the player needs to understand that his freedom must be framed under the team's Great Principles (Macro Principles). And that respect for the players, for the individuality, from the players towards the team – that is fundamental! Through training, we should make them understand that".*

As we can see, we are discussing creativity at the service of a way of playing. We are talking about the creation of a 'non-mechanical mechanism', something that I have also mentioned in my first book.

The individualisation of training in the conventional logic is something completely different, and most times, is framed at the physical level. The physical parameters determine the (decontextualized) training each player should do. For us, it is something totally different, as shown by the expression of our Logic.

To end this section, here is another quote by Vítor Frade (1), on the individualisation of training: *"when I am worried with the details of a player that plays as a winger, I am also concerned with the player that plays as a centre-back, but in a different manner, because he is on a different space and uses different combinations (...)".*

3.2. Creativity: that essential aspect of life that allows us to avoid being mechanical and that depends on the coach's intervention

Creativity must happen in life. When I talked about contexts...that is why I talked about contexts and not about behaviours! If Tactical Periodization prioritises the Game, if it promotes confrontation...confrontation always involves unpredictability. Teams are not only positively distinguished when they show a great ability to be diverse. The quality of play always brings the need of solving situations in a creative manner. So, depending on the experiences in those contexts that each one 'draws', without using the eraser. The creativity that a player must reveal as a centre-back is different from the one that a forward must reveal. But it is indispensable that within those contexts the originality emerges. And who has the responsibility to make it happen? The players! But only if they are brought up and trained having to think, having to decide, having to feel, the decision-making must belong to them. The decision-making in accordance to a general objective, to a previous intention, that they recognise. But they must act considering the circumstances. They may solve the problem better or worse depending on the habits they have created and on their decision-making ability, on their

"

Now, I can tell you that I had players that initially had some kind of whim, but after working with me for two or three years...they put it behind. But I did not force them, they put it behind gradually. Acquisitive changes require time. So, if that is done since youth development, it becomes much easier.

I was amused by Jose Guilherme Oliveira when he was coaching the u-17s and the u-19s. He would tell me: 'Professor, I never spend less than three hours imagining a training session'. And now, with the Portuguese National Team, he says: 'I never spend less than four or five hours'. It seems like a paradox. (...) The more you understand the 'totality' of things, all those things start having an impact on you.

I say that every chef has a specialisation. But how can some be better than others? That's because manufacturing has something concrete, different, original. And that has to do with the dose. Oh, it does! You just need to use too much of a certain ingredient and it will taste very different. That is non-linear causality.

There is nothing with more common sense than Tactical Periodization, especially because it pays attention to the here and now in the management of the process.

"

ability to choose...so it is essential to promote this. But, just like Jorge Valdano used to say: "there is not creativity without order. But, what is our *understanding of 'order'? Order is that organisation that brings us together, it is that leads six or seven players, within the same team, to think the same thing at the same time! That is affinity with the Principles. But the Principle, as the word implies, is an orienting matrix that promotes a logic that leads to the emergence of certain things. But in the end, it's about the decision, the intention-in-action, and to solve that there is no equation! It will be as easy to achieve as the existing quality and the quality is supported by habit creation. So, quality has to do with that. What distinguishes us from other species is that...we got here and got to be who we are because of...creativity! In opposition to what is commonly said, it is the self-generation that allows us to overcome difficulties, at an individual level. What happens because of that, considering groups...today there is a discussion on the intelligence of masses, or on the intelligence of swarms and anthills. But even there, there is an essential need for creativity! I normally use a metaphor: in a newspaper they have a theme, but they are the ones doing the writing, and the writing will be related to the context and with the capacity in that precise moment. But it's theirs! And many times, it's across time, in the continuity of the exceptional causality that improvements arise, coordination improvements, improvements in the team's organisation. An essential condition for people to exist is having creativity!*

Vitor Frade (1)

Creativity is a fundamental aspect of the human species. And it is also essential in the game of football, because the sport has a lot of unpredictability, although the unpredictability it requires should be determined by a predictability – the way of playing. That is why our way of playing should not dismiss this creativity, on the contrary, it should promote it, if it respects the collective matrix that leads to Organisation. This means it should always respect the Principles and Sub-Principles (of our way of playing), allowing for a disorder created within the order. If the intended way of playing must promote creativity, then its emergence should be allowed in training sessions, something that is essential in our Logic, which arises in consonance with the Methodological Principles of Tactical Periodization.

For Jose Tavares (1)[4] *"if the order was only order it would not work. Now, why do our players feel free to create? Because they feel supported by the organisation". It is through the organisation, not any but ours, that creativity emerges, that it can be specific and not abstract, supported by the Principles and Sub-Principles of our way of playing. The principles we are able to express regularly. So, "our team creates new things because the team provides conditions for the creation of something new".*

When we refer to creativity we are not only referring to the creativity of players that operate in the attacking sector, but also to those who play in defense, including the goalkeeper. Moreover, we are not only referring to the moment in which we have possession of the ball. We must also look at when we don't have it, otherwise, we are only seeing one part of the Game. Therefore, we refer to a creativity in decision-making, to an originality in the solutions found by the player, while always having in mind the Previous Intention – Principles and Sub-Principles – and considering the circumstances.

---

4 Interviewed by Xavier Tamarit in 2010.

To this refers Jose Tavares (1), when inquired about creativity he replies that *"we usually only look at attacking midfielders, wingers, forwards, and so on...can't the defender be creative? He also creates, but he does it differently, we need to create situations that allow them to create as well"*. Tavares adds that *"creativity is no longer present when you jeopardise the organisation of your team, then you are not being creative, you are being simply irresponsible, and they must understand that"*.

So, creativity must be expressed in connection to the intended way of playing, respecting certain Principles and Sub-Principles that operate as a **"orienting matrix that promotes a logic of emergence of certain things"**.

This creativity must be promoted in training. The exercises should allow for creativity, it should be experienced in training and should emerge within a determined logic of the game that ends up supporting it. For that to happen, we should respect Tactical Periodization's Methodological Principles. The exercises should not be close-ended, they should allow for unpredictability. Learning should happen through discovery and not through mere delivery. Moreover, by making our way of playing something sub-conscious, it will free the conscious to look deeper at the detail, to offer original solutions. So, as we explained in section 2.2.2., 'a tailor-made suit', it is the conscious mind that has a great capacity of creativity. Therefore, this creativity ends up becoming Specific to our way of playing, instead of being an abstract creativity. It is something new and original, but supported by a determined way of playing, and it is something that makes sense for us, and not for others.

Tactical Periodization creates 'non-mechanical mechanisms', through the promotion of creativity and by experiencing it in training. It is supported by the Game, it is supported by playing, by the confrontation, and by the intervention of the coach; consequently, there is no room for robots in the team.

As Carlos Carvalhal (1) says: *"if the team responds mechanically and only has the solutions that you give them, obviously that will be the reflection of what you are providing them in training"*.

For Jose Tavares (1), close-ended contexts deny the emergence of creativity. Therefore, when this happens, *"it is no longer a game. It is a limited game, it is a forced game, the player is not free, our player is a robot, he only does what the coach demands"*. If we consider the game as unpredictable and that our players, supported by an organisation, should have the ability to solve unpredictable situations, *"shouldn't we give them that freedom? I cannot consider the absence of unpredictability, it is part of the game and must be part of training sessions. It is not an open-ended exercise, it is an exercise in which they must create, they must play. What? What we are looking for, they need to accomplish what we are looking for. How? In many ways, it is not a static general principle"*.

That is why Vitor Frade defends that one must give birth to the context, not to behaviours.

Getting our team to be creative will highly depend on the coach's intervention in training. Not only on his interactions during exercises (in the creation of emotions and feelings), but also in the way he manipulates and presents these exercises. On the type of exercises promoted. It is essential to understand this.

For Carlos Carvalhal (1), *"an exercise, no matter which, without feedback and without an orientation, ends up being a merely general exercise"*. The interviewee considers that *"the feedback you provide to the players makes up its richness"*.

According to Vítor Pereira, *"the quality of the exercise will depend on how needed the intervention of the coach is"*. It should allow for learning through discovery. But the interviewee also highlights the important of intervening by adding: *"obviously the intervention makes the difference (...)"*.

The more the quality, the more the creativity. The clearer the Previous Intention and the ability to put it into practice, the higher the playing aesthetic. Aesthetic that is intimately linked to efficiency, both primary aspects in football. Their balance is essential for the emergence of our desired way of playing and should be understood as an unbreakable wholeness.

3.3. The Game as an unbreakable wholeness: training our way of playing without having to constantly express the whole way of playing

I usually say, and usually people misinterpret it, that the Game is an unbreakable wholeness. Why? Because the Game is only Game if it has something uncontrollable, and it is Game if I need to defend, to attack, to go from one moment to the other. But it doesn't stop working that way if we are not 11v11. I can be performing a passing drill without losing the unbreakable wholeness. It is about the lack of absolute control of the situation, in that sense...So, I can be very concerned with the evolution of something related to my desired way of playing, so I needed to focus on that. But, one thing is that I consider that while removing the contextual timings he is still evolving. No, I can introduce the timings inclusively in a situation with low complexity!

Vítor Frade (1)

Training must always be oriented by a Tactical Supra-Dimension, but it does not have to encapsulate the whole desired way of playing in each drill. For example, one day it may be more directed to the micro level, a part of that way of playing — intersectoral, sectoral, individually — without having to move away from Tactical Periodization.

Not all moments need to emerge in every exercise, only those we need to improve our way of playing. Let's imagine that we want to work on shooting with some of our players — do those exercises include all moments? There is no need for that. However, if they are proposed according to the Logic they will not break up with the Game's unbreakable wholeness.

Why? First the players need to understand that part within the Whole, they must contextualise it in our desired way of playing — according to the Specificity Supra-Principle, an exercise will only be Specific if the players understand the objectives and aims of the exercises in the whole — and for that it is essential to include the Previous Intention of that way of playing. Secondly, our exercises will not be close-ended, they will contain the unpredictability of the Game.

So, not matter the exercise, more micro or more macro, with or without all moments, something that needs to exist always is that intrinsic unpredictability that the Game contains, in such a way that it doesn't break away from its 'unbreakable wholeness'. It is mandatory that there is no absolute control of the situation, meaning that the uncontrollable condition of the Game should emerge.

As it is shown here, the 'unbreakable wholeness' occurs equally on an 11v11 and on a part of that way of playing like a passing or shooting drill, at a macro or micro level in all their senses. Therefore, for Tactical Periodization, in opposition to what most think and as I have been trying to show throughout this book, the Micro level is also a fundamental part of the Process (an intervention on the whole but also on the parts).

3.4. The Strategic Dimension: a dimension that will always abide to the Tactical Supra-Dimension.

You are only a good musician if first you understand the song so that after you can improvise. You don't improvise without first knowing the song. In what concerns Tactical Periodization, hierarchisation is constructed through a matrix that identified the Game Idea. Therefore, until you solidify that intentionalised organisation in a way that all players are comfortable with it, and that also contains a certain spontaneity when happening, it makes no sense at all that you emphasise this or that detail. Even less if that detail relates to an opponent. That is why it makes no sense that people talk about Youth development saying that they plan each match, depending on the opponents. That is silly. That should only be done in the elite adult teams, and only when they already have an identity. Only then should they be concerned with targeting the opponent's weaknesses, without a loss of spontaneity or organisation and without losing the opportunity to implement their own dynamic, the one the team is comfortable with.

Vitor Frade (1)

Many people associate strategy with set-pieces. Strategy, however, in our interpretation, refers to the focus of our way of playing on the opponent's weakness – or their least strong points – or on their strengths, with the intention of overcoming the latter with our own. That does not mean changing our way of playing. Instead, the aim is to trim it in certain marginal aspects for that match, without ever compromising its Matrix.

For Jose Tavares (1), *"the coach – and I am referring to those in high performance – has to prepare the team for everything. The team needs to recognise in advance the contexts it will play in, the challenges it will face. Anticipating what will happen, the coach must provide his team with the conditions to respond well with regularity to those contexts".*

So, after analysing the next opponent and recognising its identity (the regularities they present on each match), the coach should predict which type of match his team will face, being also aware that there is always unpredictability. He shall then prepare it in the best way possible, through the hierarchisation of Principles and Sub-Principles of play, and by trimming some marginal aspects, without ever compromising the key aspects of the team's way of playing. The intention is to minimise the virtues of the opponent while exacerbating its weaknesses. For example, there may be a benefit in pressing some opponents high on the pitch to avoid them playing from the back comfortably, while for other opponents it may be better to explore their 'back'. This does not imply dismissing our usual way of defending, so these are just slight modifications and do not interfere with the Matrix. If we face an opponent that will wait for us on the half-way line, with the intention of creating space in our 'back' to attack quickly after recovering possession, then in our hierarchisation we should prioritise the attack-defense transition, keeping balance, defending counter-attacks, etc.

This Strategic Plan depends always on our opponent and must be considered very carefully, especially if our players are still trying to learn our way of playing and are struggling to make it emerge regularly with a certain spontaneity. In the end, the Strategic Plan may end up interfering with that identity.

Mara Vieira (1) clarifies that through the Strategic Dimension *"you will not change your way of playing (...) you will just pay attention to some good and bad regularities of your next opponent".*

First, we must achieve an identity through the acquisition of the Principles and Sub-Principles of our way of playing. Only then, and only if it is advisable and necessary, shall we enter the Strategical Dimension, meaning that we start being oriented by the Tactical-Strategic dimension, changing some marginal aspects of our way of playing to benefit from the opponent's weaknesses while improving our protection against its strengths.

Carlos Carvalhal (1) exemplifies mentioning that *"throughout the week we picture the match and its strategic side. Why? Because the dynamic for a certain match can change depending on what we are looking for, and we must not lose our identity nor our Principles. But there are things that can be adapted, bearing in mind the information we gathered and counting on some unpredictability that may exist".*

Having in mind the Strategic Dimension does not imply changing the way of playing. As Mara Vieira (1) says, *"strategically you may lower your defensive reference, but the principles remain the same".* So, you may not defend so high on the pitch, and adopt a more intermediate positioning, conditioned by the opponent's characteristics. But you won't change your way of defending.

This Strategical Dimension may appear in all acquisitive days of the Pattern Morphocycle, and as a reminder in the activation day, and not only one or two days before the match. As I have mentioned earlier, it must respect the Methodological Principles of Tactical Periodization, meaning that we should create contexts that allow for the emergence of the desired Principles and Sub-Principles in a regular, systematic way. We should monitor the complexity of the exercises depending on the Morphocycle's training day and considering the Horizontal Alternation in specificity. Naturally, the experiences should always be Specific.

Therefore, their <u>operationalisation</u> must occur in the acquisitive days, without being a concern during the recovery days. In an Exceptional 'Morphocycle' this dimension will have to appear more theoretically and not in such an acquisitive manner, because recovery must be the priority.

With regards to **Youth Development,** as Vítor Frade mentioned, and especially in the lower age groups, this Strategic Dimension should not be considered.

> Vítor Frade clarifies

Note from the translator: this chapter contains the full version of Xavier Tamarit's interview with Professor Vitor Frade. On the Spanish version of this book, Professor Frade's words were transcribed verbatim (in Portuguese) as the Tamarit considered that "its integral translation could lead to potential misinterpretation". However, given the many misinterpretations of Tactical Periodization to date, inclusively due to a lack of English translation of trustworthy sources, we have accepted that risk, taking the responsibility of assisting English-speakers on a journey through Professor Frade's brilliant mind. Not rarely does Professor Frade use neologisms, metaphors, and analogies that may confuse those familiar the conventional logic, and unfamiliar with – the real - Tactical Periodization. The following pages consubstantiate a genuine attempt to bring some clarity to its essence.

Xavier Tamarit (XT): How, when and why did you realise that the existing training methodologies, many of which still present contemporarily, were not heading in the right direction in your opinion?

Vitor Frade (VF): Xavier, I am unable to give you an objective or precise answer, also because it was not an 'a-ha' moment, and if it was I could not recall it. I would maybe have to...when I was doing my degree in Physical Education, as a student, I had already had a module on Sport Training.; So, I already had a certain sensitivity regarding the body, and what its relationship was – or should be – with the activities. As a student, I was already susceptible to a certain group of areas, like psychomotricity. These were the 1970s. In Portugal, fundamentally, there is a pioneer in the refusal of the body-mind duality in Physical Education, that is Professor Nelson Mendes. I was fortunate to be his student, and that provoked in me a sensitivity regarding what was institutionalised and of a potential rejection of what was standardised. But regarding training, more objectively, when I did my degree in Lisbon, there was no specialisation in football for example.

I had been a professional football player. I had even stopped my career to do my degree, but I was obliged to choose a different option, and I chose volleyball. I also met people that thought volleyball differently, like Professor Puga, the father of FC Porto's first-team doctor, Dr Nelson Puga. He thought the game in a completely different way, it required intelligence, thinking the game. I also had a history as a professional player that allowed me to contact different coaches. Jose Maria Pedroto was my coach in FC Porto's under-19s. He was different from all the others. I met many coaches who made us climb staircases carrying rocks in our hands. So, that was all mixed. Then, my own childhood, spent mainly on the stress, in a very traditional area of Oporto, the neighbourhood of Se. We were in the 1950s, and it was usual to walk around barefoot. It was customary to run away from the police because playing football on the street was forbidden. That happened to me several times, and I was arrested on two occasions for playing football. As a football player, I had certain characteristics which related more to thinking the game, I gave a lot of relevance to that, and I recognised the importance of being technically able, but always considering the circumstances...so all that is a history that cannot be put aside regarding sensitivity. But as I was saying earlier with regards to training, I was just like the other students. I tried to learn what I had to, even though in some cases the contents seemed too fragile to me.

So, what I learned regarding training as a student was fundamentally conditioned by the Eastern European countries, especially by the Soviet Union – Matveiev and all that. There was a need for absorption in relative terms and also of disagreement to a certain extent, but not in a very open manner. Things change with regards to reflection because around 1971-72, in the third year of my degree, I propose to conduct a study based precisely on complexity, Dynamic Systems, Cybernetics, strongly influenced by the work of Henri Laborit. I did it because I wanted it to be the same assignment for all modules, to provoke a joint exam. That was a strange thing at the time, so 9 out of the 13 or 14 lecturers accepted and 4 did not. Among those who refused it was Manuel Sergio for example. So, at the time I already had some receptivity for those ideas.

During my degree, I went abroad several times for conferences, seminars, and other developmental events, because I suspected that things were more complex than the way they were often presented, and training should not be different. However, training was not my main concern at the time, even though in 1969 I had already completed a football-specific course in Sete, France. So, when I finish my degree and complete my final dissertation, I present it the other way around, starting from the end. I do things the opposite way precisely with the intention of provoking a discomfort in the assessment panel, upon receiving the document. They would have to move away from the conventional, get some aspects of the brain and the body to work to solve that situation. And that was the motivation behind the content. So, maybe I was a weird specimen as a student because I would think deeply about the issues, I would search... and there were big, or at least relevant differences, regarding key authors. Also, I was always very interested in different areas, since very early, areas like psychoanalysis, anthropology, psychology, and during my degree, because fortunately, I had some lecturers - probably if I had others I would not be so interested...or maybe I would, I don't know! But I had fundamentally that one, Nelson Mendes, and Vítor da Fonseca, who were very different lecturers from the others, who at the time were already highlighting the importance – or necessity – of knowing the nervous system and the brain to understand those things. As I already had interests related to Cybernetics, primarily through the work of Laborit in the beginning...in the beginning and after that, but I mean in the beginning because as he was also a doctor, the nervous system, and the brain, were some of his concerns when thinking about Cybernetics.

So, all that conditions me. It shapes me, and perhaps even formats me. But nothing emerges as a central concern regarding training, the game, or even football. Inclusively, I was a volleyball coach before being a football coach. I coached the Portuguese National U-19 team that took part in the 1979 European Championships. I was one of the three coaches, responsible for the North region. There was another responsible for the South and then the National manager, and the three of us, together, were responsible for the team. I even played in the Portuguese volleyball Premier League for one year, because I had left football and it was much easier to keep active playing volleyball than continuing to be a professional football player because the latter was very limiting concerning my Physical Education degree.

When I finish my degree, I come to Oporto. Then, in 1974, the National Institutes of Physical Education (ISEF) open. Those were the precursors of today's faculties. And I was invited to be part of the staff because as a student I had achieved a very high final grade, and you know, people talk about it. So those responsible for the Installation Committee invite me, but they wanted me to coordinate an area that was by then just starting: Foundational Physical Education. I accepted because the offer had a very relevant singularity: it allowed me to invite 10, I believe, 10 colleagues of mine, that I could choose to come and be responsible for teaching that area, and that got me excited! So that was what happened, I came here to coordinate, lecture and also be responsible for Foundational Physical Education. I invite those 10 – or more, I can't recall precisely – and then we start getting the programme together. But in the meanwhile, our schedule included Training Theory and Methodology, that would only be taught to second-year students. And due to the existing installation agreements, there was a protocol with the Faculty of Medicine that resulted in us receiving the exceeding number of students that had passed from the first to the second year, here in the Physical Education course, without them having done our first year! So, they are transferred here, because they choose to, I don't really remember the particular circumstances, but I know they were a group, and they were my first Training Theory and Methodology class, without having completed the first year of our course, because they had already been taught Medical Anatomy, Physiology and all that. And those guys show up in Training Theory and Methodology and in other modules, I think that was the second year. So, the Installation Committee decides to invite me to be responsible for Training Theory and Methodology and leave Foundational Physical Education to my colleagues. At the time, I confess that I was not very keen, but then due to their insistence and due to my reflection on the module and on the circumstances, I ended up accepting it.

And that is when my systematisation concerns start. So, what I knew and what I didn't know was a result of my role as a student and my confrontation with those subjects. But I had never systematised it, and I had not coached, because we were in 1977/78 if I am not mistaken, because I think I came here in 1977 and I only started coaching volleyball in 1979, so I did not have...I had only been a player! And that is when I start...when I start systematising to lecture so that I could do the module outline, that I find myself disagreeing with several things. It could be, I could be right, or that could just be the result of my insufficiency. But with time, understanding the area better, understanding the issues better...and I also went to the field to coach! So I leave volleyball and move to football, and I go straight to the Premier League, to Boavista FC, where I spent 6 years and with responsibilities of preparing the team to win and to play in European competitions. So, not so much with volleyball because it is a rather special activity, even though it is designated as a team sport there is even a border that you cannot cross – not even with a passport! But when I start training football, I start to contextualise my problems and my doubts.

In my first two years in Boavista, in the Premier League, the circumstances where really 'helpful' regarding my beliefs. In the first year, the manager that was obsessed with training quantity leaves with three months left until the end of the season. I am promoted to first-team manager, I reduce the training time to a third, only with 'playing' until the end of the season and we stay in the Premier League. The next year, arrives a new manager, Mario Wilson, former manager of Benfica and the Portuguese National Team, allowing me to continue lecturing in the Faculty. Boavista signs a player from Desportivo de Beja named Agatao, who said it was amazing to train like this, that he had never felt so good. He was even called to the National Team. In previous years, he was always complaining of general pain, getting frequently injured. Comparing the so-called pre-season...what a difference! Boavista finished the first turn of the League in 2nd place, only one point behind Benfica, and ahead of FC Porto. In the first six matches of the second turn, Boavista did not win a single match, losing and drawing, moving down to the middle of the table. Mario Wilson left with 11 matches remaining. Joao Alves ('the Black Gloves man'), who was also a player, is the new leader of the team. Agatao, who was the main supporter of this type of training, that had a big effect on him, blamed the situation on us not having done the 'pre-season' differently, and the consequences were now visible! But Alves takes the team and tells me that I needed to control everything and leave it as it was because he was only going to decide the line-up and the team talks. So, we kept doing exactly what we had been doing, and in the end, we won the 11 matches left and even went to the UEFA Cup! I was 'lucky' here with the circumstances, but the evidence that there was no issue as they were trying to claim, is that we kept doing the same and won those 11 matches!

While it is general...because Training Theory and Methodology was broad, it was for everything, but when I start working on the field, I start telling myself 'no, it is not possible', 'it can't be like this, at least for football'. So, I start having a lot of questions. Already in my dissertation I had put things are another way around, I disagreed, and that was the line. Moreover, there was no football specialisation here...in the meanwhile, I signed up for the Philosophy degree alongside my lectures. And then the Installation Committee decides to invite me (and after pressures me) to lecture Sport Psychology together with Training Theory of Methodology. I accepted, and while I was making up the programme the possibility of starting a football specialisation arises. It was a fascinating course that year, with a lot of students that were either interested in or connected to football. It made no sense to have other specialisations and no football! So, they came to me asking me to take over that specialisation. I refuse because I was already busy with Training Theory and Methodology, Sport Psychology, which I find interesting, and I am also trying to finish Philosophy. These were the late 1970s, beginning of the 1980s, and I am not interested and have no time. So, I try to solve their problem by bringing in Artur Jorge. Because Artur Jorge had worked with Pedroto and I got along really well with Pedroto – I had been an under-19 in FC Porto with Artur Jorge and got along very well with Pedroto...I explained Artur Jorge the problem because at the time to lecture you only needed to have a bachelor's degree, and he had a degree in German Philology. It could even be interesting for him. He ends up accepting it, he says yes, and Pedroto agrees as well (he was going to be Pedroto's assistant). So, things move forward, but suddenly, when we were almost getting started, he says he thought twice and cannot do it. We were already well into it, so if the specialisation could not start due to the lack of a lecturer, perhaps it would not open in the next 6 years. So, the students put a lot of pressure on me, day and night, even going to my house – "you have to...".

I ended up giving in. I explained the problem to the Installation Committee and became responsible for the Football module. I had already been lecturing Training Theory and Methodology for several years and had already told the students that I disagreed with many things, but that was how it was, but...I tried to support my views, and when I start teaching the football specialisation, systematising, let's put it this way, Tactical Periodization, so what is more specific. I did not have to include many activities anymore, only one and the one that I had chosen as my definitive choice. I was even on the field working. So, I start making things systematic. And that increases more significantly when I start working on the field, facing certain things and thinking 'no, this can't be!'. And I start doing. I taught Training Theory and Methodology for 13 years until Professor Marques arrived from Leipzig, Germany, with a doctoral degree. This is because at the time we were grouping into subject areas and I wanted to stay only in football. I said I only wanted to be in football. So, since then, not only due to an increasing belief, but also due to an increasing sys-

tematisation, and especially due to an increasing need, from my point of view and from an institutional point of view needing to face a conceptual-method-ological framework that was clearly different, transgressive with regards to all other methodologies.

Therefore, I can't tell you, I did not wake up one day, and that was it, it was nothing like that. It has to do with a history where perhaps the most critical moment was when I took over the football specialisation and had to systematise a programme for the specialty. Even if before that I was already working on the field and was already heretic in the eyes of the conventional logic because I operated differently. That is more or less the history, and it already has at least 30 years.

XT: So, you do not get your ideas from systemic theories, neuroscience…only later do your ideas meet these areas?

VF: No, I don't think so. I do not want to seem petulant, but it is anterior to my sensitivity. Since a few years, people have been asking me that question frequently. Who? People that come here from Japan, Argentina, others coming from Spain or Brazil, etc. They ask me: how did it happen? And myself, due to my inability to answer precisely, started looking back at my existence, my history, and remembering things that happened to me.

I recall that…I used to give an example quite often…in the beginning, I was very interested in Psychomotricity and one occasion, in an experiment suggested by Professor Vítor da Fonseca in one of his classes, there is a task in which we are required to perform a usual task unusually. I decided to write my signature with the left hand, as I usually wrote with the right one. My name is Vítor, and in my birth certificate, my name appears with a 'c', Victor. But since I was 17, more or less, and I cannot also explain to you why there must be some reason beyond this one, that I don't know, maybe because no-one calls me Victor, everyone calls me Vítor, then why the hell should I have the 'c' there?! So I made the 'c' disappear from my signature. In my current identity card, there is no 'c', only in my birth certificate but my signature has no 'c'.

And as you know, my signature is all crooked, well not crooked, but inclined to the left. Then he suggests what I mentioned, and I had not written Vítor with a 'c' for at least 10 or 12 years. And when I am signing my name with the right hand, in the end, …what?! I call the professor, "Vítor, come here, come see this!". I had signed with the 'c' using my left hand!

I remember for example when I had more or less five years…I used to live in a very typical zone of Oporto, where the Saint John festivities were celebrated, and people used to dance on the street. And I dance very well. I don't know who taught me except for my mum's reports. My dad had bought a cellar, but he had had another one for a short period in Boavista, and only after did he buy this one. And people would ask my dad 'how can your son dance so well? Who taught him? Where did he learn?'. And my mum would tell me that he was a man, who sold the lottery and was a client of my dad's cellar – that first one my dad had bought in Boavista – and he would put me on top of his feet and dance. I would be on top of his feet dancing, but I had no memory of that at all!

I recall that with 9 or 10 years, in primary school, while facing a problem that the whole class could not solve, I got it right 'intuitively' and the teacher was surprised – 'but how do you know it?'. I don't, but the answer is x! This is not to say that I am made of a different material, but I have always been curious, and I liked to think about things. I asked myself, how can I know it if I don't know how to do it?!

I also remember that when some research was done for a 'dance' subject, about Folk dance, around the country, in the folk group of Santa Marta, there were doubts about the side upon which the pairs start moving to. When asked, firstly the director calls the first dancer, who would open the dance, and he also does not know, until he ends up saying "just play the music". And they start dancing. And we could finally get our answer!!!

Even as a player (I am 1m70 tall) I left the under-19s and went to the Championship and the possibility of being released or replaced by an older or bigger player was always present! I had to fight against that...

Maybe it is worth to remind that I attended classes in different degrees. The first course I went to was Engineering, even though I never completed a single module there because I was playing football. I suppose I went there only to see some beautiful girls. I always carried a piece of paper to take some notes, but I never did anything! Then I went to military service, and when I returned I asked myself 'will I continue in Engineering?'. I could not imagine myself doing anything related to Engineering. At the time, people talked a lot about having a job at EFACEC as a guarantee for the future. But what I really wanted was physical education, sporting activity, the problem is that the course only existed in Lisbon. So, I had to sell my car – I had an MGB convertible as any 'good' football player – to go there. Not everyone does that, already with a certain age, at around 27. I did four years of military service, I did not go overseas, I did not go to the colonies, but I did four years of military service. The degree was excellent, with exciting modules like Anthropology for example. The lecturers were interested in the brain, in the nervous system, all that. And then there was my passion for football, my obsession with football. And my obsession for being with the best.

But I believe that...I got to know and was strongly influenced by Henri Laborit, whose work helped me immensely in systematising things, in being sure that that was the path I had to follow. But I got to know Laborit due to my concerns and merely by chance. I was a member of a political party for a while. Well, I cannot even say I was a member, I used to travel a lot with a guy that was linked to the party and that later becomes very important in the Socialist Party. It was the 'MES' (The Socialist Left Movement), and as a good friend of a Full Professor from what is today the Faculty of Economy, Jose Manuel, who was a member, we would do some things together. And one of those days I attend a seminar or something like that, I can't recall it precisely, but it had to do with urban planning, I went with him and some other guys, and there were a lot of books in the exhibition. And there was a book that caught my attention: it was 'The Man and the City' by Henri Laborit, and when I read the subtitle I noticed that it said something like "The Biology of the Nervous System" and that made me curious. So, I opened it and when I saw that it also included Cybernetics, wow! I got really into it, but I did not even know the author. That I read all his books and he was, in fact, an author that influenced me very strongly.

But I don't think it was because...sometimes, even in my existentialist thoughts, I would tell myself: "this cannot be like this". I could not agree, but

I would tell myself: "maybe you are the problem, maybe it's your problem". I would reflect and would end up thinking it could not be like that. I used analogies. I reflected as any normal person, as a student, as a player and then as a coach. But as a coach, you have different obligations, and you must systematise – also as a lecturer! And of course, my passion and my interest in football, and my understanding of the sport made me realise that football went way beyond football, that is was an activity that was being built by people and therefore was directed in a balanced way – or not – by the coach. So, my passion made me drop the conventional, made me feel the need to drop it, because I became more knowledgeable (or at least less ignorant) in other areas: Psychology, Anthropology, Cybernetics, Systems Theory, Fractal Geometry, etc...so that I could explain and validate. So, I can say that I left what I knew better and moved towards what I knew worse so that I could extract something beneficial for what I knew better. That is what led me to attend more than one degree. I went to Philosophy, not because...when I finished the degree, they invited me to stay as a lecturer, and I told them "no, I came here because of training, and because of the problems of Epistemology, the problems of science and others". And then I went to Medicine for the same reason, so that I could reap the rewards even regarding time. Because I always kept lecturing and being on the field, I thought "if I have good lecturers, then I will end up gaining valuable time!". I went to Medicine because of the nervous system and the brain. Then I heard about Chaos Theory, the concept of fractals, Systems Theory and Cybernetics. I was always concerned with applicability to training and to the game because these are sciences that are concerned with an identifying reality, a whole constituted by elements that interact. This contrasts with what has been the history of the theory of those so-called sports sciences, that are more focused on the individual, with the atomistic. And due to my attempt to systematise something that could stand by itself, something that could relate to my interest – football – and that is how Tactical Periodization started!

Even the designation that I give it initially, precisely that of Tactical Periodization, is provocative. Because I knew that straight away people would say "but periodization is something else and it is not tactical...!". That is precisely the intention, that something different emerges, because in general terms, all the other times it is used, all the other periodization is used with a focus on the physical, with a focus on those so-called conditional capacities, or energy sources, it all gravitates around that. So, mine was, in reality, a transgressive logic. 'Tactical Periodization' involved two terms that were well-known to people and that people saw differently! So, "what the hell does this guy mean with this?!". Complementing the terminology to elucidate them better, designating or referring to it in a different way, but not necessarily, because I believe that even within one year of training the periods are different depending on the specificity of the circumstances and I must anticipate this, and I have to find a logic that provides sustainability to that need. And the concept of 'Tactic' is a central concept for me in the Game of football. It is the Organization, and Intentionalised organisation, a 'dynamism of dynamics', which therefore has a broader – 'macro' level, which is what emergences from the collective references, encapsulating the totality of sectors and the relationships between sectors, and in this case the inter and the intrasectoral, etc. Then a 'micro' level, which in my perspective will be more diverse, diversified, or unfinishable, depending on the quality of the first level, the 'macro'! But that is an Organisation, a dynamic built from different sub-dynamics that I must feed constantly, respecting a causality that has...that is so important in its bottom-up logic as it is in its top-down logic.

Consequently, the micro interferes in the macro and the macro interferes with the micro. It has to do with the ability to sustain this constant sense of balance. Because there is some terminology that we take from Cybernetics, some references that sometimes we follow and that make sense, but the terminology itself, from my perspective, sometimes is not adjustable! For example, from Prigogine, in Thermodynamics he postulates, and it is important, the "distance from balance", but I think that we should take the risk and there sometimes I am not far from the balance, I am far from the ideal balance, or far from a certain equilibrium, but I cannot be out of it! This sense of distance makes it look like it is no longer balance, but no, it is a balance that is more likely to break, but by not negatively revealing itself, being even an ideal occasion for me to potentially evolve and take benefits out of it. All those areas influence me enormously and many years ago; so I came to lecture the Training Theory and Methodology module for the first time in 1977, I placed a foundational task in the module that mentioned the need to consider the complexity of human movement, let's put it this way, and especially the human movement in a coordinative action with the others or coordinated to oppose another coordinated action. It had to find support necessarily in areas that, in that moment, were utterly unknown to most people and that nowadays are not foreign at all. In reality, they make great contributions. What I always tried to avoid, was that it was mentioned in an empty way, without the presence of football contents, identifiers of its validity and of the methodology. But in the end what many people did was exactly that: dynamic systems here and there, talking about it without actually talking! But it does not work that way, I need to mention the Principles, I need to mention the Game. I need to know about football so that I can then use that knowledge conveniently. And more and more I need to be able to justify it with an appropriate language, adapted for football so that I can establish a logic – or more logics – that relates to all those realities.

As you know, I have a library at home with more than 25,000 books, and a great part of those books relate to those subjects. That was very important for me. But I think I was 'pushed' there by my awareness of things, by the unavoidable empirical side of things, and the possibility of realisation and reflection, and the intelligence placed on those things. It is only possible to do that more profoundly from the moment that you depart from a mere concern with what is and should be the activity – in this case, football – but also with what is the person, and in that sense, there are people who are not very informed academically, and have no sensitivity for those issues! That does not allow them to become experts in such area, no matter how much they open their throats, no matter if it is Christmas or Carnival season! It is fundamental that the knowledge about people increases and matches what they are today. And if we know that Neurosciences, for example, are recent and how they are important – they have proven it -, so it is indispensable that...establishing an analogy: I believe you have read that book 'Proust was a neuroscientist'. It is a book written by a neuroscientist who proposes to demonstrate in which way many times Art precedes Science, using some examples, like Proust, that regarding looking at memory was a 'neuroscientist'. If he 'came' here today, he would be satisfied to know that, according to neuroscience, he was thinking appropriately. I also feel a certain pleasure in reading things that I have written in the 1970s or at the beginning of the 1980s, which at the time were very controversial, and that nowadays are confirmed by some advanced scientific writings. It seems I was not that wrong, and it even seems I was right! But that was a different paradigm from the one that was – and still is! - Institu-

tionalised. So, that was not the dominant paradigm, and you know that even here at the Faculty (Oporto) is still dominant.

XT: Many people, when they talk about Tactical Periodization, consider it 'extremist'. What do you think about that?

VF: You know, I usually say that the most evident symptom of ignorance is insolence. I also say that Tactical Periodization, for those who do not mention it, represents many different things. And this depends on the ability of each person. Because even when following the other logic, more or less conventional, not all coaches are the same, there are good and bad ones, so not everyone that identifies with Tactical Periodization is.... the problem is in the people. I will use a metaphor: imagine that I give you a banana to eat. You have never eaten a banana, and I tell you it's a fruit. Probably, you will eat the peel and throw the 'pit' away, but after I tell you it works the other way around you will even tell me it actually tastes good. It even seems that the green banana has some kind of anti-inflammatory properties that the ripe one has not. If you don't know this, you are also not taking full advantage of the fruit. With Tactical Periodization it's the same. Tactical Periodization also has its formal side. Let's build a house: who is there? Who was there? And then the other left for holiday and is not there anymore, and then I found out there was an ideal place to build a well. The formal house versus the real house! Sociology is not only one, is it? There is even Micro-sociology, then, is it not related to Economy? Is it not related to Anthropology? Is it not related to Psychology? And each of these areas has many contradicting streams.

Myself, since more than 30 years, have been dealing with this and even nowadays I find myself 'inventing', adjusting things, and I think I am not that stupid, so that guy that looked at this and said what you mentioned, it's like the guy that looks at the banana and says 'ok, this is a fruit', and eats the peel and throws the inside away, saying that it is really hard to eat. So, I know that exists because sometimes I even laugh...You have the example of some people that are 100% with Tactical Periodization, for example, Professor Guilherme, you know how much I like him and cherish him and even admire him. But Professor Guilherme's understanding of Tactical Periodization was different when he started working only with u-19s and u-17s and when he moved to the professional game. He was then one saying then "wow, actually it works!!!". And it really does. Popper used to say that the crucial tests are the crucial tests. Marisa for example is an unusual case, but she never worked with adults and, for example, the dynamic of efforts was never a problem for her. So, when she was working on her dissertation with Professor Jose Guilherme, she led him to look at the Principle of Horizontal Alternation in a way that was not fully correct. Perhaps today she would have done it differently, but if she had managed an adult team, maybe she would have faced some 'conflict' because she has been in an area where that isn't a problem. That is why I keep saying that the evaluation of Tactical Periodization should be done at the top-level. But then there is the reality of younger players, which is also specific. I need to know what a child is and all that!

So, some people can deal with it, and others don't. I can assure you that the problem is not one of Tactical Periodization, the problem is in people! I have no patience to put up with...and as you know recently there were people here from Japan, but they are the ones that have to come here, I don't go anywhere, I am happy to talk to you because you are a special case, and if it is someone that, like the other day, someone that came from Argentina to talk to me, I think it is about decency, I need to speak to him. But I have no more patience, I am tired of having to explain. See, the other day there was a colleague of yours who said that recently, in Spain, he had seen a professor from this faculty presenting Mourinho's book, trying to make it look like those were his students, and that was his faculty. See how much people try to take advantage, but then when they are here, it is the opposite. But haven't other lecturers in other subjects done the same? So, will I be worried about that? No, I have plenty of other stuff to do. But I know it happens.

And will I be worried about the guy that does not even coach a cricket saying that this is radical? You know the history of that video that I was asked to give a positive comment to, a video of a former manager of the Portuguese Premier League and all that. He says more or less the same, he is just a fool. When a guy says something like that and then comes to ask me for something, nothing surprises me anymore!

Look, I even brought this! It's an article from Stockholm, from the Scandinavian University, even with the contribution of Bangsbo on its second part, that concluded.... this was published, if I am not mistaken, now in May 2010 in the Journal of Sports Medicine, so just recently, and they say that the continuous practice of football, in non-professional setups, improves some aspects of the organism, like the bones, in terms of strength, bone mineralisation, at all levels without having that as an objective, and 'that' is what Tactical Periodization achieves, having it as a concern! It is through the game, and that is what Tactical Periodization does. It is a scientific article, these are scientists saying it. Furthermore, even with regards to osteoporosis, which is a bone degeneration, football fights it much better, regarding bones, in comparison to running which is usually advocated as a conventional solution.

Now, look at this, I even find it funny, and I make jokes about it quite often – when people ask me if I don't get upset "because that guy said something that you allegedly said, and, in the end, you did not say it?!". I also frequently say "Our Father, who is in heaven, Holy is Your Name" and I did not invent it. So, who cares? This here is something that I have said, and that inclusively when Mourinho went to Israel some years ago said "look, I am going to use a sentence from my friend Vitor Frade" and then he writes that in an article – a pianist, in order to improve, does not run around the piano to improve resistance – and I find it funny because this guy, Han Berger, who is Dutch and is responsible for football development in Australia, says that Mourinho is..."his sentences are cool, nothing conventional in his training, that is great football, and Australia will move forward and whatever".

This other article is about Genetics, the genetic differentiation without losing the matrix that is given by multiplication, it is a need; therefore, this is another logic for Genetics that leads us to a discussion about Epigenetics and Eco-Genetics. If we grab this here, recent Neuroscience says that children, so, the conventional way...I would even risk comparison with the way football is operating nowadays! Have you heard what Carlos Queiroz said? "I brought my game plan to tire the other team out". This is not a game! The game is always beyond any plan, and I am only correctly in the game if I can be in it, and that is what allows me to assimilate after, as a complement, the strategic plan. Concerning kids, when kids are born they are like sponges and depending on the regular confrontation with some reality they start 'narrowing down' and gaining a certain rhythm, just like the stem cells! That is what a recent book – 'The Philosophical Baby' (Alison Gopnik) defends with regards to the brain.

So, what does Cruyff tell us? "If in football you must run a lot, it is because you are poor".

All these things deserve my attention, and it is all an amount of information from different areas that may even negatively oppose football, especially if I am not tuned with this logic. The logic of Tactical Periodization. Those guys that normally say that they know nothing because for them everything in football has already been invented, it is something that allows them to speak with an open chest. And Mourinho already said when presenting his book, to the four guys that showed up, "you take this into account, most guys that are training at a national level, they will read this 50 times and will still not assimilate the essential". I usually joke, but perhaps it makes sense when God distributed intelligence, some guys were on the queue, others were in the end, but some were not even there. So, no, no...! You see how much people were available, in this case, Mourinho and Rui Faria, even for scientific works, to say "no, we do this and that" and even then, people "don't believe"! Some people do not want them at an institutional level, and then will take advantage of them behind their back! And does this only happen in Sport?! Of course not. Look at politics, it's the same! Why should I be concerned? I am 66 years old, as you know I am here, but I haven't been exiled. Every year I sign a contract with the University, if they did not want me, I would leave. So, if up to this moment I was not worried about it, now even less, I am minutes away from retiring.

But the truth is that I had mentioned that I would only leave here at the age of 70, and for different reasons, I have no patience to put up with some stuff, and I will leave four years earlier than I had initially planned. So perhaps it's right, I have no patience to put up with certain things. I cannot lose my mind, I don't care! That is especially...and more and more! It is interesting to see someone coming from Argentine, who says that only two or three years ago got to know about it and go interested in it to the extent of travelling here and scheduling an appointment with me, trying to see me and talking to me.

And as you know, I try my best to speak to people, even if that means changing my schedule to talk to them informally. And I realise that the main problems or one of the main issues of Tactical Periodization for people, is understanding the Methodological Principles. People run away from them like a cat from hot ashes, and usually, I try to ascertain their degree of identification by asking them about...! And normally I am surprised with the degree of familiarity of some people that come here, much better than half of the students that spend many years with me here.

So, either they are stupid or the degree of interest they have...but, in the end, they are not pushed to this specialisation, they come here because they want. And as you know, I award degrees from 20 (maximum grade) down to fail, and these are people that go to the classes after choosing this area.

So, I cannot be concerned with that, I have plenty to do, and above all, I want to, as I told you last time, that my concerns at this moment are reflecting, but reading also other areas, and even in the literary dimension, because there are things that I consider art and that are unmissable. They are an exceptional gain, and therefore I have several things that I am already looking at and writing about because what concerns me is finding some 'entertainment' while I am around and, how will Football be in 20 years? If it will be something! And at all levels, as a social phenomenon, a cultural phenomenon, economic, because it is increasingly a business, but above all, I am interested in the Game and training phenomena. But those do not exist without the others! Football has to worry about training and with the game because it is, in fact, an activity that makes the world stop when certain events occur.

You know that I am leaving, I am still here now, but my retirement has arrived, and you know that I could have asked for it two years ago. I am also here because Professor Jose Guilherme went to the World Cup! I have to look after the modules and get the grades out, so until the end of July, I am here. Then I will leave, I will stay in FC Porto, which is more than enough, and then I will keep myself busy, maybe writing and thinking about some things, and very little worried about those people who I don't really care about. I ignore them, I have no concern about them. But, it pleases me that more and more people are interested in Tactical Periodization. I recognise that there are people with a different capacity to think about it. For example, I can point you an example that you may also identify – Jorge Maciel, who is an unusual guy, I call him an 'Einstein'. And that is maybe why, and maybe because he is so busy, he is interested in everything, and because he is not really on the field yet, the identification...?! Even though he writes about it! I have recently put out another volume of texts, and once again I toasted to him by writing two texts, one of them about the Horizontal Alternation Principle, which is the core of everything for most people. But he needs...being in Dragon Force does not solve his problem of understanding...perhaps now things will change when he goes to Belenenses. Even though it is a Championship team, it will bring him extraordinary gains, because there is the need to do things at a different level, and the level matters! And we know that when, for some reason, something happens very quickly, normally that leads to sharp turns because we have certain anchors that make many things impossible...And at this level, it is a protection. Then, wherever you end up going, it is likely that you will be contradicted. And you will have to 'give in' after considering the context. Otherwise, you are not intelligent. It is essential, because you may be thinking that the individual understands it, but he might have wanted to do it that way, it is just his body that has not understood it yet. He is in a different wave length, and that is counterproductive. You need to have, as much as possible, that opposing information, and that is why Mourinho says that the Model is everything. With the Model being everything, if you consider that not even Jesus Christ can detect everything at the same time, it is important to recognise that things take time to develop.

Consequently, this contextualisation is necessary! Therefore, those who are identified with this area...if everything were favourable, it would perhaps work at 80%. This way, maybe working only at 40 or 50%. And that is one of the richness of Tactical Periodization. That is why I say that it is a tailor-made suit and not one pret-a-porter. It is a theorem-in-action. You need to understand the conceptual foundations thoroughly, and then you need to be able to enhance its applicability, but in that enhancement, you need to consider the extraordinary relevance of decoding the context, and the context contains people. And the exterior side of people does not always reflect what people area. It is normal that it is like that because people, usually, do not even know themselves that well, and many times they need to disguise to defend themselves.

So, that is the richness of Tactical Periodization, and that is what makes me highlight...even now, the guy Jorge is going to working with, Mourinho's former assistant, who in a recent interview revealed that "Mourinho works in football 14 hours a day!". So, people should ask themselves, "so, the guy wins everything, achieves the impossible, and cannot prepare a training session in 30 minutes?!". It's the opposite! Because more and more he pays attention to what is relevant, and so do I because you can only reach the Top if you are systematically concerned with objectivity, with efficiency, with efficacy. Bearing in mind what football is, I need to be permanently disturbed, I need to be concerned, I need to be permanently concerned with the aesthetics of the game. And the aesthetics are the finest thing regarding allowing objectivity to be objectivity. If I exaggerate regarding the loss of aesthetics, I will lose there, if I exaggerate in the improvement of aesthetics I will lose there, and that is not for anyone. Because many times, at a Top level, the simple fact of diminishing the aesthetic range, let's put it this way, will lead to less fatigue, because it is less complex, and people cannot understand that! Now, Mourinho can, and that is why he is who he is, and others are not. I don't know if I told you this, but maybe I didn't...Rui Faria told me: "oh Professor, what does that matter?! The Italians work the opposite way, they don't see and don't want to see, they don't care about anything, this is everything...". Will he now turn to them and say, come and see how you prepare a training session?! No, he wants to win and all that...

So, will I be worried about some fool that, if I talk to him, cannot understand that 3 and 2 can also be 32? No, that does not really annoy me, what bothers me are those guys who for some reason get close to me and then keep biting me behind my back. Oh, when I get them, and I don't do it that much anymore, because my physique is no longer the same, but you know that even with a couple of slaps some issues can be solved. It does not really bother me and even...Look, for example, you know who Rita Santoalha is, she is another Marisa, well not another Marisa, because in training she is not like Marisa, but she is brilliant, she is special. At a time when training is not that needed yet, at 7 years, and at 6 and 8, she is great and is also a great girl. You know that a potential affirmation strategy for Dragon Force in opposition to development regards the coaches! Recently, Aspire Academy came to play against the Dragon Force under-13s, and they almost did not play, they were just watching them playing...It is a big loss if Rita leaves. Marisa's invitation? I asked her, and she said, "what do you think?". Don't look back, for me it's the same, and I am still very pleased because I know that she may lose some things but will get others. Just because she will be working with Marisa, and Marisa being with her...it's already a great achievement. That really pleases me, that really makes me satisfied!

The rest doesn't matter. You know that I don't even go to the office, I only go there to get my mail. I went there to give the interview to the Japanese, other than that...that's not relevant. Because people never seek that when they come to see me. So, a guy that talks about something he doesn't know about is either stupid or insolent, and I have no pity for people like that. Because today, generally, it is no longer possible to say you do not know Tactical Periodization, because of the books, and several other things. Now, that does not end Tactical Periodization! Like, for example, Jose Guilherme interpreted when I mentioned "lived hierarchisation", he initially misinterpreted it, "it is the A or B alternative principle", no! It's nothing like that. That is how we build that hierarchy, how are we going to start? First by the macro, articulating defence with the attack or the attack with the defence, it's that, hierarchisation is that, and then depending on the week "what is not working so well?". Hierarchisation is not that, because if it were only that, we would be thinking about football as a Game with mandatory pathways, with a single level, with a single dimension, and it is nothing like that. That is why from a certain point I made a distinction: "no, the game is one thing, playing is another" because you bring your way of playing to confront the other way of playing and that Game arises from that. You do not have absolute control of the Game, but if your way of playing is better than the other, normally you overcome it.

And therefore...it is much more pleasing, for example, having Carvalhal coming here with Freitas Lobo and asking for my writings, and asking for my suggestions because they want to write a book...I would have referred you if you were here, it would make things international. Because they want to make a book, a dialogue between them, discussing themes, but they wanted a moderator. The book belongs to the two but with the collaboration of a moderator, a guy that could, depending on what they discuss, point out other topics, and I suggested Jorge. And that is what pleases me, the rest should not make anyone lose their time.

XT: You mention that Tactical Periodization is a tailor-made suit and that in depends on the context, on the people that are part of the Process...but, are there certain things that must be present so that we can say that it is Tactical Periodization what is being performed?

VF: Sure, that that is why I systematically talk about two levels and always highlighting the indispensability of the Methodological Principles! Because it can only be Tactical Periodization if you have an idea for playing and if you make it systematic. And the operationalisation is something very complex, the possibility of you being concerned with the sectoral, intersectoral, intrasectoral and even individual improvements. Imagine this, you are not able to do a tumble, and I get you to do tumbles, and you say: "that is not Tactical Periodization!". It is, because the diversity side of it, you are improving something that then when you perform a bicycle kick or some other kind of kick, leads you to an improvement! So, the training is finished, and it is boiling outside, you drink what is that not Tactical Periodization? Is it no longer Tactical Periodization because you drank water? But some players did not drink water, are you going to force them to drink? All those things are part of diversity.

What Tactical Periodization is, depends on what you are doing as a pattern. If it directs the Process for everyone while simultaneously allowing each one to improve individually so that they can interfere with the Process. And for it to work that way you need to have a way of playing, a systematised way, and so this diversity is as good as the idea and depends on it being achievable through experiencing the Methodological Principles. That is why I ask, what means playing well? People should worry about that! And after that sometimes you can achieve it, sometimes being more concerned with some things that make that idea, sometimes with others, but the sense of direction must be present, with a specific hierarchy, and the loss of that sense of direction can only be avoided if they have a previous idea about the collective matrix, if it is in their minds already, and then the same thing occurs regarding the tumble for example! It is not a punishment. And then the whole Process, considering one or considering ten, twenty, thirty-five, it always abides by the logic of the Methodological Principles. Otherwise it is not Tactical Periodization!

Now, the guy performed a tumble, those are complementary exercises. Not really complementary, they are complementary but with a small case. Like drinking water. What directs the Process is a matrix, an idea of playing and operationalising, because Specificity is only guaranteed...it is not guaranteed by the macro level, it is guaranteed by the intervention you are able to have in all the details, in the sense that they contribute to the whole, because otherwise, it is not Specificity. Because if you do not realise that Joaquim is different from Manuel, and this is different from that...So, Specificity is also there, if the parts improve, the whole improves. Now, how to improve?! That needs to be done through the logic of Methodological Principles, it is not easy, no-one should think it is easy. I was amused by Jose Guilherme Oliveira when he was coaching the u-17s and the u-19s. He would tell me: 'Professor, I never spend less than three hours imagining a training session'. And now, with the Portuguese National Team, he says: 'I never spend less than four or five hours'. It seems like a paradox. Oh yes, it is! The more you understand the 'totality' of things, all those things start having an impact on you. If you don't know and you want to understand something you don't know, usually it's a fuck up! And that is what these guys want, they want to regulate something, problems, that they know nothing about. And you only need to want to know more about what the game is!

You see the pundits discussing on the television, and they speak as if the game (or better, playing) is only one. The first concern they should have: "does this guy want his team to play how I am saying he should play?!". And after that, they say "no, I would put this one and that one1". Even to play chess, I first need to buy the pieces and the board. But don't they train?! So, they talk without knowing, but I am not worried about that anymore, they are fools. But I am not the only one saying this, the guys that study the so-called sciences of Humanity, say that only 10% of people are intelligent. Even if I consider that an exaggeration, if it weren't more or less like that, things would be better, and it is shit at the moment! And see, how long have the Ten Commandments been around? How long have they been written? And what kind of (dis)Humanity do we have?

XT: Can you explain Tactical Periodization's Methodological Principles?

VF: Sure, it's easy.

The Principle of Propensities is a term coined by Popper that I use, that I got from Popper because the propensities have to do with the <u>context</u> being more prone to X than to Y, because normally people say, "I want you to do this or that". No! I want him to do depending on a certain context. So, I need to give birth to a context, not to the behaviours, and that confuses people badly. One if the Principle of Propensities, I must articulate depending on how I play, defending in a certain way to attack in a certain way, for example, I am concerned with the defensive transition, and with the attacking transition.

Transition, and that is another confusion, have you seen what people say transition is? It is when...already in attacking already, if you are fast or not, no, no, that is a way of attacking. The transition is passing from one moment to the other, so I say the moment is one thing and the instant is another. So, what helps me deal with those instants to take better advantage of the moments is the understanding of the game and the ability to anticipate, that is psychological! A transition is that it's switching from a mental configuration to another and if maximally qualitative, it is collective, that's what it is, and depending on this or that it is performed faster or slower.

So, I need to create conditions for that to be organised more preferentially so that there is a certain familiarity with a certain logic. I create a context that leads towards that happening, and that can result in....I don't know, the guy is distracted, "look, the guy is distracted", so I need to intervene individually with him either because he misunderstood it or because he is thinking about something else, alienating the timing, so it's a context! The behaviour I can't predict, and it is not even beneficial for you to know what is going to happen. It needs to be adjustable to...that is why I find it absolutely shocking what my friend Carlos Queiroz – with all the respect – said on the television, that is game plan was to tire the Spanish team out so that he could put the speed up. That is not football, for me, it is something that may look like it, but it is not football! Maybe that is why against Sweden, here at the Dragao, when Portugal was dominating and getting near the Swedish box, penetrating with the ball, with triangulations, and Tiago had the key role in that, he took Tiago out! A minute earlier he took Hugo Almeida out, who was creating danger and he took him out...now, everything that is happening, because Cristiano told Queiroz "no, Carlos, like that we are going to lose". This planning is the robotisation, it's the freeze-drying, the stretching, the ignorance of what an activity is, of what people are, independently of how much information you may possess about "things"! That is why I say that Anatomy, Physiology, Anthropology, Sociology, etc., all of them are very important for the degree, but in isolation, they have zero importance for the football specialisation! Or am I capable of knowing, through isolating the object of study, in this case playing, of knowing of much each area contributes? Even doing that, it would be complicated. How many Psychologies exist nowadays? For example, nowadays Developmental Psychology is no longer a stage-like Psychology, I must know that and use that or this reality, and that can only be achieved by someone that is keen on considering it, but above all, that person must know a lot about Football. And that is not easy. So, the Principle of Propensities is that, the eventual context. We are here. What is the context? We are both talking, but there is no damage, there is no shooting because there is no-one else here, so propensities exist for this, not to promote further deviation. This is the context, the propensity for...

Then there is the Principle of Complex Progression, because the Complex Progression relates, on the one hand, with the growth of the way of playing, with the weekly distribution, with who I am going to play, with this guy that entered the team...it is complex because progression is not linear and involves several things! It has to do with these principles that were "solidified" but now fail to appear with regularity for 3 or 4 times....and therefore we have... that is why it is complex! That is why I say: the fundamental is the pattern of connections between all of this.

And then we have the 'heaviest' Methodological Principle, the Principle of Horizontal Alternation in Specificity...even more at the top level, because...I defend that it is absurd to train what is trained and how much it is trained...if we see Germany playing, only if we are contaminated by what I referred earlier can we say that they run a lot? No, they stop, exchange the ball, and the same with Spain. Portugal ran more than Spain! So, I need to train less than usual, my pattern is 90 minutes, more than that is unnecessary! But playing every Sunday, it is a waste if I don't use more than one day for training, but I can only do that if I have the guarantee that I am training in accordance to my way *of playing, but not always working on the same contents of my way of playing! That is what alternation is about. And that is only guaranteed if I can, relative to a certain objective that is non-discussable, ensure that I am trimming here, and trimming there, but always trimming the same object!*

So, what did I imagine, if the effort arises from having to contract muscles, having to move them, three indicators characterise the way muscular contractions are expressed. And it is also different the way in which the extension of its expression or of its fatigue.... then we must work on calibration there. It is about bringing to the extreme or maximising, let's put it this way, one indicator on one day, the other on another day, and so forth. Having the guarantee.... but that is why I feel outraged when people talk about training the tension, it's nothing like that. It is not the day of tension, it's not about doing something with tension, and that's it! Because that leads people to become concerned about tension, so they do something that involves tension, and that's it done. No! It's the day of details, of "small" principles, small things, the micro-levels and all that...in attack or in defence, but with the guarantee that there is a significant number of eccentric contractions, so, there is an increase in tension, but in details of the bigger picture of playing! I need to be concerned with providing variability to my sessions, inventing and going through those game situations, that are what I care about regarding my desired way of playing. So, I have two things, I need to invent that, and I need to know that there is increased tension. It is not the day of tension. Otherwise I would just put some shit out, doing some leg skipping, and it is nothing like that, it's precisely the opposite! And the next day, let's say it's more about the Macro-principles, there are other references, space... but not necessarily using the full pitch, but it makes more sense that the training is not so intermittent. But if I manage to include some intermittence in the non-intermittence even better. This means, that if I am able to do four or five 10-minute times instead of 2 times 20 minutes or 3 times 15 minutes, that's even better! Because there are breaks and that is what ensures the logic. But where I am again radical, because look, I say that we need to train much less than people usually train, because most teams are training, playing, relatively fatigued, and I think that you can train to be fresh, because intelligence is not always evolving, it is already great if it is great, it always deals well with the reality(ies), and Football must be that! The idea of equalling load is the one placed by the other logic. I say that in recovery.... great, they rest or they do nothing, but it doesn't make sense! So, I have 3 days and they will be 3 days off? Then, they will go there and do 'nothing'! Or even better, they will keep doing 'nothing' due to the length of breaks that I need to provide. But I need to act over (in energetic terms) the bioenergetic 'wool-ball' that is involved there and that supports the adaptability, and it is tired. So, it's only about playing 3v3 and shooting for example and they stopped, and then they play again but for a very short time only! Because, what will make him rest 'is not' that, it's about resting from there, the different breaks! So, he goes there and trains, but trains without training, keeping the stimulation of the essential, but without getting tired, but I can only do that if I rest properly...people seem to have a tendency not to rest, and they keep saying that "having 7 breaks is the same as having 3!", or 3v3 is the same as 6v3, but 3v3 and 6v6 are not the same things. The ideal is, in reality, going there to train 'without training'! If you put it this way: "I have a match with maximum demand, and my team can only play another maximum demand match in four days", then why you think about it from Sunday to Wednesday and don't think the same from Thursday to Sunday?! It's the same! Or almost the same, because the demanding match and demanding training are different.

And regarding that, I have no doubts that only Tactical Periodization, well-understood Tactical Periodization, solves the issue. Now, the difference I have in comparison to other people is that for 13 years I lectured Training Theory and Methodology, meaning that I am at ease with Physiology, Biochemistry, etc. But because people don't understand...like that example I gave you of the banana, the ripe one is the sweetest, so you will eat the ripe one if you don't know the benefits of the green banana! And the Physiology bit also counts, and it is really complicated and so is Biochemistry, etc.

So, the core Methodological Principles are these, then if we want to talk about Specificity it is a 'categorical imperative'...these three, for the methodological core, these three are enough.

XT: When you mention the Principle of Complex Progression, are you always referring to going from the lowest to the highest complexity?

VF: Yes, that's obvious. But even that is not linear. Imagine that you are going to coach a new team, you have all the interest that it identifies with your general ideas, macro, how you want them to play. And understand if this is more or less complex than training a transition or something else...That is why I say that hierarchisation must be...and on the first session, look, you don't know what you will find, but they must know since the beginning how you want them to play in general terms. So, the hierarchisation starts from the macro level, from the object, from the acquisition of the contours of your way of playing. It's Gestalt, do you understand?!

XT: This Principle of Complex Progression, does it also have to do with the Morphocycle, does it also consider tactical fatigue?

VF: Yes, and that is why I call it complex. Because for some reason, even an unexpected one, you cannot do, or you think it's better that you don't do what you did the week before. I give an extra rest day for some reason, I don't know, maybe you had two players sent off, and the team had to work harder...That's why it is complex, non-linear, it goes back and forth, and that means that all aspects, all circumstances enter your domain, and it is in that sense that I keep highlighting what Mourinho says, that the Model is everything.

The Model is everything because...what is the Model?! It is the picture, or maybe the echography that you take of reality so that you can model, it is in this modelling that the approximation between the model and what you are looking for happens. But if you neglect relevant aspects, you are modelling badly. That is why the Model is everything, what ends up being a completely different logic from that one that leads people to say that the model is 4-3-3 or something like that. Look, if a guy...a context, when it is experienced, leads to some postures, attitudes, behaviours, many of them resulting from a habit that might even be sub-conscious, we might not be aware of it, so it is very complex. What I want is an affinity of emotions, a kinship of affection, conceptual sympathy, of a playing idea, and that is achieved through a context, but it cannot be an empty context, like "it's 11v11 and this and that!". No! No! These are fractioned contexts concerning a hierarchisation of what I conceive, which is not mandatory, it depends on my deviations, on my circumstances, on my intelligence, that's it. But it needs to be like this, without losing meaning.

That is why I emphasise the Articulation of Meaning. This is complex. You cannot go like that. You cannot have a pre-made road map. No. That is why I say that the 'here and now' is extremely important, and then alright, organisational levels like Marisa does in the book about Ze Guilherme...otherwise you are alienating!

Imagine a great poet, who was writing to his whole family and suddenly had a cramp on his finger. Even though it is something localised, I cannot write the poem that is in my mind. So, I can have tired legs and then what? I think the game, fantastic, but then what? I can't play! So, that so-called more physical side is important and is considered by the Horizontal Alternation in Specificity. That is the side the allows me to be fresh to play. And people pass by Training Theory and Methodology, which is a key module, they memorise that and end up knowing nothing. Then because they have less time to spend in the specialisation, it's only about "Game Model" here, drills over there, Biochemistry and all that...What is that? Maybe it's shit.... And just a few are interested in what is essential, the others don't even notice it. And I talk about Marisa because she is an exceptional case, abnormal, positively, and she has herself alienated the Principle in a given moment!

XT: So, people that say that Tactical Periodization has no physiological concerns are mistaken?

VF: I think they are stupid, I think they are stupid, and if someone tells me that I will say he is stupid! Because Tactical Periodization says that Tactics are an emergence, an Organisation, which is not physical nor psychological, nor technical but that does not exist without all these so he will be stupid! He will be stupid and insolent! It does not have the physical concerns that most say should be 'the' physical concerns. That is why I say that there is a paradigm that is dominant, the paradigm of the 'athlete': jumping higher, running longer and faster. But that has nothing to do with playing. Playing is something different – I also have to run, but I have to do it sometimes at speed...If Usain Bolt goes for a race with Messi, maybe Messi will start faster, but then when Messi gets to the middle Bolt is already there. Cristiano is fast, but does his speed have anything to do with Messi's?!

Then, we could go to the aesthetic side of the Game, in its collective and individual dimensions! So, this is related to what I am highlighting, with efficiency and efficacy but then...this is important, and it is pointless not to consider it, because I think that training and playing to win, and that is why I say that I am constantly focused on efficacy and efficiency, but also continuously concerned and even disturbed by the aesthetic problem! I watch again that Brazil of 1980, 1982 and even of the 1970s, and I love watching that. But is that transferrable to our time? Regarding attack, yes, but now I have to worry about the balance within the team, something they didn't worry about back then if I want to win. So, I am interested in the aesthetics! That is why I say that the next revolution must be structural. I already told you my thesis that I am more and more convinced, there will be a 'second-goalkeeper- revolution, that is about having three guys exclusively focused on a more Specific situation, just like it happens with the 'goalkeeper'. Now, think about the consequences of that for complexity! But, are those individuals not good players? They must be if I have three guys like Pique. It is ideal, not three hammers. And without losing aesthetic sense! Because aesthetics are very relevant with regards to the attack when looking at defence maybe the global side, the formal side may be rich, but the individual cannot, otherwise...in the attack, it can be the opposite! Playing with this possibility in attack and at the same time providing defensive guarantees...even because most goals are scored due to significant defensive imbalances.

Why did Chile get everyone excited and then was kicked out? Because they get out of balance, they have no game criteria, with Mexico, it was the same thing...those are teams that...That is why Mourinho says...look at how stupid it is, hearing people saying that Mourinho's team is defensive! So, the guy wins leagues, has the team that scores the most and the team the concedes the least! How can it be defensive? And they win! People do not know what being an attacking team means. Attacking means scoring systematically and not necessarily scoring seven goals. Portugal beat Korea by 7 goals and was kicked out. They did not score on the other matches. This is a problem of ignorance, I cannot hold myself back, it is a problem of ignorance, in this case of what Football is, objectively. And Mourinho does not have this problem.

Mourinho gave a genius interview, I put the second part there, he gave this interview right after arriving in Spain, predicting how it would be. And people don't know, sometimes they take that chit-chat on board that look pretty and are socially well-accepted, but that are also empty, they mean nothing! And I do not remember, because I read an interview by Manuel Sergio to Marca, if I am not mistaken, because it has some 'pretty' things like "we need to remain united, we all need to pull together", that is nice! The Ten Commandments and this is something I use to joke about, they have been written for a long time, and the world is how it is. For example, the 9th Commandment says that you shall not covet your neighbour's wife, and what did priests say? Not this neighbour's wife, the other one! And the reality does not end with language, in the terminology that we use. Many times, as a mass phenomenon, the language that is used in Football is a language that comes from a different reality to decode something that is a little more complex; it is simple, but the simple is not basic. Otherwise we keep the unreality of reality. The simple is maybe the maximisation of transcendency. That is why I love watching Spain play. I think that nonetheless, Spain is a hybrid, I think there is there...I think they could even play better with the players that they have because there is something there that...

So, the Methodological Principles are...and notice that for a long time, 90% of the people that talked about Tactical Periodization, did not even mention the Methodological Principles which is the point I highlight the most with students, because everyone has an idea for playing, for playing in a certain way, then making it more or less systematic, but how do you build that? I say that every chef has a specialisation. But how can some be better than others? That's because manufacturing has something concrete, different, original. And that has to do with the dose. Oh, it does! You just need to use too much of a certain ingredient, and it will taste very different. That is non-linear causality. You know, that was already the theme of my doctoral thesis, the non-linear causality in the casual structure of high performance.

XT: When you arrive at a new team, what do you do first? Is there an a priori evaluation?

VF: Exactly, but usually when you say evaluation what does that mean? You will run some tests.... Do you know what Mourinho said when he now arrived at Real Madrid? He was asked about...and he replied, "no, I am the one asking the questions now, because I need to know some things, I am the one that needs to know things". When Mourinho arrived at Chelsea players also asked him "so, are we not going to do this and that?". And he would say:

"I am the one who won titles, not you". It is different if I arrive there having won nothing before. If you get to a club without having won anything, you need to use the 'cappuccino' strategy, taking baby steps. That is a matter of intelligence, it is strategic thinking if you wish to call it that way. We usually say that if I am facing an ox to feed him, I am not going to grab the ox by the neck to make him get to the food. Instead, I need to get the food to the ox.

Many times, I give an example that happened to me when I was doing my degree in Lisbon. I was on the 3rd year, and I had a room-mate who was a 2nd year student and a Trotsky supporter. He had applied for a grant from Cuba, and that seemed an endless process. It only arrived when the year has already half-way, and he was in trouble, having to teach a few hours here and there, even in a tough institution for deprived kids, and he was asking me to help him. I tried to tell him I was busy as well, but because I wanted to be nice, I went and replaced him for six months. And the first time I went there, I had not met the students, I was introduced to the headmaster, and there I was. The kids entered the sports hall, and I would call them, and they would not answer. They were on the ropes, playing around, and I was telling them to check page 1, page 17..." What am I going to do with these guys? If the headmaster comes here...". Maybe they hadn't done anything with my room-mate as well! That was the context at the time. "What am I going to do??!". And I did exactly what they were doing, I jumped on the ropes, and then they stopped and started paying attention, thinking "this teacher is mad!". And since then I was able to act.

Then, when I discuss the Methodological Principles and the Game Principles, there is something we need to add – a Meta-Principle, the Principle of Divine Proportion. Divine – from God – and Proportion, because some have it and others don't. It is a kind of praxiological sensitivity! Everything has to do with the scientific method, which resembles at times like something that is always right!!! You cannot walk, but you have a method, and there you go. Of course not, it's nothing like that!

XT: What do you need to consider when you must create a Game Model when you get started with a new team?

VF: There are two different things: one is the Game Idea, and the other is the Game Model. It might seem a paradox, something weird, but first comes the Game Idea and only after the Game Model. The Model is also submissive to the circumstances. The Model is everything because it is the Game Idea plus the circumstances, and the circumstances can relativise what I would do in different circumstances, but regarding the pattern, it's the same! I want to play more or less like that. Now, if I was managing Barcelona and now come to a fourth division team, it's different, I want them to pass the first touch, and they cannot do it even with a gun on their hand. The ball is not afraid! People must have enough intelligence. I mean at the top level. Do you think there were many differences between Chelsea and Inter? No, there were not. There is more depending on each match, depending on the circumstances. Even in FC Porto, but FC Porto had no Zanetti nor other players like him, and I need to take that into account.

Now, the Game Idea is something, the creation of the Idea has to do with the circumstances, and that is the Game Model, that also implies the existential dynamic of the Methodological Principles. And the Model is everything, even sometimes something unknown to me, something that 'promotes' mod-

elling, because if I didn't take it into account, I blew it! Now, in general terms, the way a guy understands the game, it does not make sense that he doesn't look for the same things, but he needs to adapt that to the circumstances.

I even defend, and I used to teach that in my lectures, my Game Idea is a football with a lot of positional play, they work fundamentally in triangles, the intermediate sector is very relevant. So, in the intermediate sector, the characteristics of the players must be distinct in the regular context of what happens, articulating the back and forward sectors. (...) We want that even for the kids, for the 6-year old kids. In FC Porto they play 4v4 or 6v6, and the rules that they have, are used with the objective that certain things emerge. That is why I say that it makes all sense to fight for good football, for playing well. What is playing well? Maybe for me, it is something, and for others, it's something different. No, but for me, it is like this, even if we are talking about kids...look that promotes passing, Barcelona, Germany or Spain, they may lose, but they have more ball possession for a certain type of ball circulation in comparison to other teams, and that needs to be something constant in my way of playing.

Now, it's evident that if I get to a place where they only like breaking out, penetrating, obviously I don't want them to go from 8 to 888, and maybe I will even say "I need a player like this, and another like that for..." ...and that is art! It's art because this is a problem...Marisa talks a lot about that issue of interactions, adjustments and readjustments, and therefore this is inter-intentionalised! That is why it works better if you have a previous idea, a Previous Intention, which is the Game Conceptualisation, the Game Idea, and that should be showcased already in the beginning, so that the people that you will work with can already familiarise themselves with it. Some may say "but this is not how it should be!". But those are the setbacks that you will have to deal with and overcome with time.

XT: Some people tend to say that Tactical Periodization is a good methodology only for good teams. Do you agree?

VF: I am sure that is false. Whoever says that is a fool.

XT: So, do you believe that a team with little quality can be good?

VF: At this moment, where you can see it more clearly is in all FC Porto's youth teams, up to 14 years old, and then even more at Dragon Force, because kids go there just like they go to swimming classes or to gymnastics classes, they have 3 classes. That is why I told you, the under-13s, the under-13s that have been there for 2 years, so they arrived with 11 years and these were kids that had never played football before, they played 9 tournaments, lost the first one and won the other 8. So, those who say those things know nothing. Look, either you admit that the Process to play football occurs by learning Football, and if it is by learning Football, only Tactical Periodization does that. It does that without any other concern, since the beginning, because Tactical Periodization has a methodology to support that. It has a Principle that helps all that. In the youth sector, the Principle of Horizontal Alternation in Specificity is the least applicable regarding physical effort. They even 'train' only 3 times, there is not even the need to have that concern. And there is another problem, a problem that is a true cancer, which is people wanting the kids to practice a lot! When a kid is growing, he needs a lot of energy to grow, and if I am tiring him out, I am provoking problems in his growth. But that is Tactical Periodization, it's about being sensible regarding what is a kid. There is the

story of the green banana, knowing that the green banana.... If I don't know, I eat the ripe banana and get some diarrhoea or whatever, or I eat the peel and throw the content away!

XT: So, you are saying that kids should not practice a lot?

VF: No! Normally, for example in FC Porto (grassroots) since 2006, when I got there, kids start practising one less time per week. And I would say that in most age groups, up to under-16, three or four times a week were enough, and then five, even if with 'homework' and without stopping to play in school...and on the street. But the tendency was that sometimes it was even twice a day, morning and afternoon and five days a week. Well, especially if it is 'training'! Training is a crime because it is an energetic expenditure for the kids and they also need to have that energy to grow. If is taken from them, they will not have what they need to grow. That expenditure is much lower if in Football they make the ball move and do not run as much themselves. If Football is an intelligence phenomenon as Cruyff said, it should not involve too much effort, maybe being intelligent does not involve as much effort if this is done in intervals. That is what I mean! So, the kid needs the energy to grow, so I need to be careful regarding energy expenditure because I don't want to prevent their growth, to make them small. It is in that sense, but the tendency is the opposite. The logic of being an athlete is training twice or three times a day, sometimes even four, look at the gymnastics people, and other areas, they do this or at least they used to. That is all related to the athlete para-digm, jumping higher, running longer, running faster...I shoot that shit, that is not necessary for Football!! And look at how they speak – "my athletes", I think that is a crime. They are my players; a player is something else. Messi and Maradona were coming out of a match, and Messi is really 'tall'! Mara-dona would almost hit the others' testicles! Great players like Maradona and Messi...'athletes'?! Yesterday, at Constituicao, did you see that game they were playing? There was Rui Barros, who played with Juventus and was even smaller than Maradona...!

XT: I asked that question because one of the fundamental aspects of learning in street football is the number of hours of practice...

VF: Yes, that is true, but they stop when they feel like, and when they re-start they play as they feel like. I am talking about training and street football is not 'training'. That is why the richness of street football is that guys do that for themselves, not for the adults. But can't the adult add value?! Sure, but what, every adult? No. Those who know, and the great number of adults that got closer, that killed it! I went to see some street football tournaments spon-sored by Oporto City Council, but that is not street football, it is just football on the street because the only thing missing there is the ambulance. Other-wise, it's just like in adult football, because they distort everything. That is not essential. If you don't know what you are doing, don't touch it, and that's already not bad.

XT: In Tactical Periodization there is the first week of adaptation...

VF: No, it's not like that. Xavier, you start, and you don't know how they will turn up, they can even say that they have done some activity every day, but can they measure well? Do they know what it was? So, as a precaution, and for other reasons...if it is the same team, or if it is a new team, it makes all sense for you to identify the players, the group...that is why sometimes it makes sense to go somewhere else for them to know each other better and all that. And that makes all sense in the methodology...and that is why the players should warm up, but if they don't, they won't die. I make this joke very often: I never heard of a thief that was caught stealing and that had to warm-up before running away from the police! Now, what happens is that if you did not warm-up systematically, you could accumulate micro-traumatisms that, with time, make the organism more prone to injury. That is why it should be done. But, on the other hand, for you to get into a more demanding effort, more dynamic that the previous one, there are a series of mechanisms that must adapt. There is even a discussion about the 'steady state', the capillaries have to open and all that.

Besides, if you are in great shape in your football team, and just for fun, this week you are playing handball or basketball, the next day everything is aching! So, you need to adapt, you need to go from low to high, but from the low-high to the high-high, and the low-high is the 'less football'. But it's only because of that, so, in the beginning, for example, if the guys are used to a different logic, we can even do some light running so that they think they ran. With Fernando Santos, and unfortunately, I never got the newspaper where that came, "Fernando Santos, in the previous season, had pushed the players hard and now with Vítor Frade, they have made an agreement...' – I don't know there the journalist discovered that – 'and now 70% of training will be different'. We went to Spa, in Belgium, and I was responsible for organising all training sessions. I did not know him, even if I knew he was different. But I did not even know what his Game Idea was, I had a general idea and that he used to push the players hard! After we went there he said "Professor, let's maybe practice twice a day to keep the schedule busy?". And I said "no, we will even practice three times!". And I would do that so that I could reduce the other two sessions. So, those three, what were they? In the morning we would go running, 1 minute on, 30 seconds off, or some stretching or abdominals, then the same with 2 minutes up to 6 or the other way around, and we would leave with me saying "no-one gets ahead of me!". And then normally, between the trees, there was some gorse, so I used to tell them that they were training the eyes in their feet! It is a matter of general adaptation to effort. And if in that time I say "Look, we will look to play like this and that...!".

But that is about common sense, that is Tactical Periodization. Tactical Periodization requests the best possible common sense. You may have 2 days in which you are not worried, or just a week, for the players to spend in a more diversified activity. Normally they return from being sedentary, and you do several different things, some fun stuff, that is all positive...and, they can identify with the formal aspect, with the way they are going to play, as you want, as you will coach. I am a strong believer in creating straight away a great resemblance with the Morphocycle we will face! I don't have a match? I can create one, that may even be...it will be in a smaller space, or three-quarters of the pitch...rest, Tuesday, Wednesday, Thursday, Friday training and then Saturday and Sunday, to create in the organism the adaptability to the configuration of the Morphocycle. We are an animal of habit, an organism in habituation, so we should create an identification with the Morphocycle since the beginning.

XT: Right from the first week?

VF: Yes, and if not from the first week, at least from the second. But why do I speak like this? Because when I was in FC Porto, I never had a month to train, to prepare the team, only 20 something days maximum, I could not be 'wasting' time. And many times, I had players, six or seven, that were returning from their National teams, from the World or European Championships and when they arrived I had already spent two weeks with the others, so there were only a few days left before the start of the league. And you know who played? Those coming back from the National Teams, and they would come back doing what the others were doing, but in smaller quantity, in lower dose, because they were coming back from holiday! Now, if a guy returns fat, then there are other concerns, but the medical department will point it out immediately.

XT: Is it essential to understand the Game Idea that we want to implement right from the beginning?

VF: Yes, the earliest and the deepest the better. Because one thing is understanding the game, the other is Intelligence in the Game. But I defend that the understanding is not something like it is done in schools, it is wisdom for the player and therefore...don't tell me that Eusebio did not understand the game. He might not be able to express it, that's another story, but he would understand it, could someone play like him not understanding it? Something else is being a coach, taking advantage of that, but that is also another matter, do you understand? So, I need to lead the players to understand the game, to understanding the way of playing, that is why I say that Tactical Periodization associates the 'knowing how', which is something that you can even learn by yourself, with 'knowing about knowing how', in coexistence, since the beginning. It has to do with getting the players to identify, since the beginning, the Game Principles that I want, which in the end is my Game Idea. And that since the beginning, and even with the kids. Now, obviously there needs to be a 'lower' degree of complexity for the kids, it must be different. I need to understand that a kid 'doesn't have' capacity for abstraction, I need to find metaphors to use with the kids, I have to...but that's a different story, you have to know a lot about people, and that younger people are different from older people and so on...

I often use two concepts, one is the understanding of the game, and even more appropriately, the understanding of the way of playing, because that is the one I am looking for, but the general understanding of the game is also culture e it is already something important. And many times, the general knowledge of the game that they have can be an obstacle for the understanding of the way of playing that I seek. That is something...there are journalists that know a lot about the game, but know knowing about training, nor about playing. So, another thing is the Intelligence in the Game, intelligence in that game, and it is only expressed, it only emerges – or not – when you play. But I think that the better that player understands our game, the better he will be. That is why I should care, as soon as possible, about the identification of the players that I will work with, with the way of playing that I am looking for. That is why I say that Tactical Periodization, since the beginning, is simultaneously a 'knowing about knowing how'. It is about the players identifying the Game Principles that I want, what in the end is my Game Idea. And that since the beginning, even with the kids. I see the kids, with 6 years, already asking Mara, because of...sometimes..." no but my dad said...". And these are 6-year-old kids. "But he said that we". "That is...". That is why I believe that these texts are increasingly relevant because in opposition to what was "thought", that kids were maybe slow or mentally retarded, no they are not! Those are different things!

XT: When we perform a drill, should the players understand it in the global perspective of our way of playing?

VF: It is convenient. I used to say that drills have potential information, so if it is possible to impose a certain dynamic on the drill, the information will be converted into ability, meaning that allows for the assimilation of certain things. And one of the requirements to make it happen, is that who performs the drill is identified with what we are looking for, and what we look for in training is not always, and most of the times it is not the whole game, it is just a part of the game. So, it makes sense that they know to which part that part belongs to, and they will only know it if in the meanwhile they know that we are concerned with an intersectoral problem for example and that that is related to... They are not mentally retarded, clearly there are some more intelligent than others but...Now, understanding does not lead them to do better, but it certainly helps, it helps because many of our behaviours, against what many things, they belong to the sub-conscious sphere. But due to what? Due to habits! So, if they are used to a different logic, it is fundamental that it is dismantled. But depending on what? On the assimilation of the logic that we look for, and when it becomes a habit, then it becomes spontaneous. The habit is an intention acquired in action, let's put it that way. It is through action that you get there. Every neuro-scientifically or neurobiologically it is not the same thing, I even say that only the intentional action is educational. So, the birth of the action as a previous intention, being a conscious realisation of what it is, when it doesn't...but the relationship after that, and even the subsequent feedback is different regarding the intervention of different elements of the brain and nervous system, depending on the existence – or not – of a previous intention!

XT: When you say that we don't always train the whole game, but just a part of it; does that mean that we should not train all the moments of the game at the same time or should we train them always together?

VF: No. What I usually say, and usually people misinterpret it, that the Game is an unbreakable wholeness. Why? Because the Game is only Game if it has something uncontrollable, and it is Game if I need to defend, to attack, to go from one moment to the other. But it doesn't stop working that way if we are not 11v11. I can be performing a passing drill without losing the unbreakable wholeness. It is about the lack of absolute control of the situation, in that sense...So, I can be very concerned with the evolution of something related to my desired way of playing, so I needed to focus on that. But, one thing is that I consider that while removing the contextual timings he is still evolving. No, I can introduce the timings inclusively in a situation with low complexity!

XT: So, not all the Principles must emerge together...

VF: No, and that is not advisable, even if I am playing more formally! That is why I mention Principles, Sub-Principles and even Sub-Sub Principles. The Sub-Sub are the ones I control the least because of these 'result' from the occurrence of the Principles and Sub-Principles. Due to what? To the setbacks and singularities of the players, on what is being played, etc. But if they occur very frequently, perhaps they are converted into regularity, and that can even be inconvenient, right? For example, I have this guy who is a right-back and closes spaces well, but he is not closing it, and he is creating a relationship with the centre-backs and the guys up front, that maybe I don't find conve-

nient...this is a Sub-Sub and I need to pay attention to this because if one is not, shit breaks! It involves 2 or 3 guys, and the player must know it is because of that, that is why it is important to have the Articulation of Meaning. He must know it's because of that, and he needs to have that explained to him, sometimes even with video or pictures. Because many times you are speaking and thinking that he is picturing something, and he is not. Using images can make it easier.

XT: So, images are very important in this first stage of understanding?

VF: And in all others as well. Look, if we run a test now, there are 20 people here, and you go to the first one and whisper him a secret and ask him to pass it on to the other and so forth. When it gets to the last one, ...you have said nothing like that, so if I want precision, objectivity...it is in that sense that I talk about an object, an object of study. And our object of training is the way of playing. Why object? Because for me, in scientific terms, it can be objective. I have to make it objective in its key aspects, in its fundamental areas that when in interaction, interact and produce an infinity of those things, and those things, when they happen, can be beneficial or not. And that is very hard, do you know why? Because especially at a top level, I can only have these concerns in three days and that's why because if they are tired and I want that dynamic to be relevant, focused if I want it to go beyond the apparent redundancy, not because the guys are tired. That is why it's not the day of tension, it's the day of Sub and Sub-Sub principles. I need to be worried about that, I need to be concerned about what is happening. And that means a lot of work because otherwise, I could just put there some obstacles, some skipping runs, brake here and there, and that's it. That is the day of tension, but that is not what we want!

XT: Why is the training structure in Tactical Periodization called 'Morphocycle'?

VF: Because it is a cycle that resembles the next cycle, depending on what? On the shape of dynamism that causes repercussions! Because what you want to happen is for certain geometrical configurations to emerge but depending on the way that you want players to interact. That is a shape, Morpho because of that, a morphology, the logic of dynamics. So, it has nothing to do with the micro level, which is even less micro if you play midweek...but it doesn't lose the essential shape, because you need to guarantee the uninterrupted, constant presence of the pattern. And the pattern is related to the Idea, with the Idea in its...you can have an idea of a map and you put there the cities and all that. What about the holes? But that is an idea! And that is why it makes sense to speak about fractals. Otherwise, it doesn't! You fractionate, but without losing the configuration.

XT: Are there any differences in the Morphocycle when you have one or more than one match per week?

VF: Yes, but it is still a Morphocycle. It is a Morphocycle that is expressed in a diversified way because you have two matches in one week, that's it. But you cannot think about the drills differently; they must be identifying, they have to be identified with your intended way of playing, and the same with resting. It has to do with the shape, with the Morphology. Morphology is, in fact, the science of Dynamics, let's put it that way. How do you identify the teams? By certain patterns, and these patterns have a shape, and it is the dynamic that provides it with...you can to create that dynamic in training, then you must do it through those shapes. So, the exercises you invent may be less complex, they may resemble the micro dimension, but they need to contain the way in which you want to play, they have to have that dynamic correspondence. Therefore, that is what directs the adaptation, the same shapes, and in those shapes are involved all elements required to create them – the physical, technical, tactical... more or less complex, depending on the different days, and that is why Tactical Periodization talks about Complex Progression. The fact that you are giving more priority with issues that are more 'micro' in one week does not mean that you are not respecting the Complex Progression as you should. Because causality is a spiral, if you prefer, it is non-linear.

XT: Many people, when they talk about Tactical Periodization, refer to the 'strength day', the 'resistance day', the 'speed day'. Is this what Tactical Periodization is referring to?

VF: Let's divide it into parts. People are saying that, but those people do not have a clue about Tactical Periodization, because it does not care about it. And I am the 'only one' who know about Tactical Periodization as Tactical Periodization!!! And those who want to talk about Tactical Periodization must talk about it as I do. Otherwise they can talk about something else. People who talk like that are maybe thinking of working, and maybe putting it on Wednesday and putting resistance on Thursday and then at certain times, hurdles on a Wednesday, do some runs on Thursday or increase the time playing with the ball...that is not Tactical Periodization because Tactical Periodization does not care about any of that! Tactical Periodization is concerned with getting the players, on a Wednesday, to develop game objectives, Sub-Principles that are related to the details that I am looking for in my way of playing, more at an individual level or in combinations of two, or whatever. When these occur on a Wednesday, because there are some that do not require increased tension, those I move them to Friday. So, the team is powerful, the guys are powerful and resistant, but they are so in a different way. Because when I am concerned with the details of some guy that plays as a winger, I am also concerned with the one that plays as a centre-back, but in a different way, because one is in a certain space, and the other occupies a different one and uses different combinations from the other, even with increasing tension. What strength? He is being capable of playing with contraction and relaxation in the way that I seek, proactive and spontaneously.

There are several preconceived ideas about what strength, speed, and others are and I like to make fun of that. I really love good cycling, especially in the mountains. I love watching Contador and Schleck leaving everyone behind when they go up, even those with a more athletic morpho-type. Why do they leave the rest behind? Do they use a lift? And with that more or less 'weak' musculature, even looking like that shirt is riding by itself. Do they not have the strength? Then how the hell did they climb it? If they don't need muscular hypertrophy is because it is related to something else! That has nothing to do with strength because in conventional terms strength is nothing like that. Now, do they get stronger? Yes, maybe they do. If that is what strength is about, no-one does more strength training than me. And that implies several other things, protecting the 'finetuning' of the organism. That is why, in the sphere of recovery, I have daily concerns with tightening 'nuts and bolts'. The same way the guy that is under the sun will have to drink, the guy that also does certain things will need to stretch the body so that it doesn't shorten. Because if I do this here to my limit, and you only need to do a single contraction, it will be shorter straight away. So, I need to know and take that into account, but none of this is complementary. Complementary in the sense of complementarity that they talk about! This is part of Specificity. I care about tightening 'nuts and bolts' Specifically, depending on the Specificity of consequences.

Ah, this is not easy! It is not easy, you need to know a lot! But it has nothing to do with that. I already told you, it's like someone punches me in the testicles when someone talks about "the tension day, the resistance day, and the speed day"! Because it's nothing like that. Perhaps I also have some responsibility regarding that, and why? When I did, and I think I only did it back then...I had never worked with Fernando Santos, and he made me responsible for preparing the training sessions, and he wanted me to capture the logic embedded in all that, so I would tell him: "look, here is the kind of strength-session, here is the kind of resistance-session". And because I gave that, as you know I don't hide anything, I give it all, I gave that to the students and maybe because it was easier, they...! But Jose Guilherme is also responsible for that to some extent, because sometimes, also trying to make things easier...'it's the tension day...'. It's not the tension day!!! Is there no tension on the other days?! Yes, there is, but it's not maximal. But there is tension. On Friday it's a day of tension if I do some bursts...when you do a burst, initially there is high tension, but because of what I am interested in after that is the speed of contraction, then it's not. People don't have a clue about these things!

XT: The compensatory that you mention that other methodologies use (proprioception, injury prevention, etc.), does it also exist within Tactical Periodization?

VF: For Tactical Periodization, that does not exist. It does not exist because...proprioception by itself, and it inclusively has its own exercises, the day of proprioception and whatever, that does not exist for Tactical Periodization! Because proprioception results from what I have to do! It is a result of what I have to do, feeling it. It has nothing to do with what they say. Now, because there is an activity I have to safeguard the continuity of the body, by calibrating it. Every day I do abdominal work, but not any. I have selected the abdominal exercises because some are harmful! There is no 'abs-day', I do them every them. But maybe I do them more during the breaks of Wednesday's training unit, even because there are more breaks that on Thursday for example. I do extensibility every day, stretching every day, during the breaks and in the beginning, but that is not to compensate for anything. When the players finish the training, they have to go eat, and at night they have to go to bed. If they don't sleep, then they will be tired the next day. And if it were raining, I would have to consider that as well. And if for some reason, I don't know...there were fungi on the grass and I could not use the grass, then we would use the sports hall. But if the sports hall were slippery, then we would still have to do something. If the next day the players feel a curtailment of the posterior muscles, obviously I will have to do more extensibility on that day, but I do not call it 'the day' of anything! I had National Team players, I would do some shit with them, tell them to stretch, and they would stretch what they did not need to. This is a ritual!

That is why I say that Tactical Periodization is a 'tailor-made suit', and only those who know can make a tailor-made suit. The rest does a pret-a-porter suit, it is already made. The compensations are already prepared, the strength is already prepared (...). Tactical Periodization has nothing to do with it, nor does it care about it. It actually refuses it because it is not useful. However, Tactical Periodization cares about the individual accomplishing her tasks and needs to help the individual in a way that the development of her body is not anomalous to the body itself and to the individual. The player may have one leg shorter than the other so I can tell her "get some insoles". But with the insoles, the player even gets worse! Does this have to do with the intelligence of Tactical Periodization? Tactical Periodization is concerned with the whole and knows that a little detail can...that is why I keep repeating that the Game Model is everything, and I am only operationalising it well if I have as much as possible inside the head of that which conditions me in the concern of doing things. But I am always worried about the way of playing and with having the players fresh to play. And that, just by itself, is already beyond the 'recipe', which does not provide the objective end-product. I told you already, it's like the other guy that interprets the 9th Commandment in a certain way...and if some guy takes that, it says there 'Wednesday – tactical-strategical purposes', I am concerned with who I am going to play against, but I am concerned since the first day of the week already, when I am still recovering, because that is recovery but, nonetheless, I will identify myself with it, with what it will be. Because otherwise, it is not a Process, it is a mixture, a juxtaposition of different shit, just fulfilling a random group of things. No, I need to incorporate that gradually, again, there's the Complex Progression, so that it becomes part of the whole, so that after it flows nicely and does not overshadow the essential, like in the logic of the plan. To hell with the plan! The plan is part of the strategy and what I need is to play, the quality I have playing is what allows me to adapt, with regards to complements, strategically, more like this or more like that. Because otherwise the thing changes and I have no plan because I had only planned for that. When you bring great plans to the Game, you won't be paying attention to those the Game will have to offer you!

XT: Some people also say that as a methodology Tactical Periodization is missing on some strength training...

VF: I am not worried about those guys. Those guys, I tell you once again... They have no neurons, they have 'neurotics'!

XT: Do you think that with Tactical Periodization you are able to achieve the minimum strength levels to compete? Do you think players should go to the gym to work on strength?

VF: No, I am sure they should not. Look, I could answer you with my own case and give you examples of players I have worked with, even though I cannot say I was applying Tactical Periodization 100%, but because I worked many years at the top level, the circumstances implied that rest increased, that recovery increased...and it would often become clear that some players, like Domingos Paciencia, who was very 'skinny'... and then there would be some big guys and Domingos would shoot better and with more power. But I don't even want to go down that road... I just need to give you the example of Mourinho. Mourinho's teams are usually said to be very athletic. So, if they are, they are due to training the 'athletic' without training the athletic. That is because Tactical Periodization does what you are referring to.

I used to say in the beginning, because now I have no more patience...I have the patience for you here because if it were another guy, I would have already told him to go fuck himself, and I wouldn't be here at this time with a match on, because I have other stuff to do! But I used to say that no-one in the World would do more strength training than players, because they would do it every week, just without using machines. It was a 'strength'...I mean, a *muscular sensitivity, sensitivity in the acquisition and execution of a way of playing, relative to the individual evolution of the player and to the growth of my team, having in mind everyone's roles. Now, that is not an easy thing. There are many people, or at least some people adhering to Tactical Periodization, and they are different among themselves, some are better than others because this is complex.*

Now, I usually give this example: if we need to demolish the hospital back there, they will grab those machines, the hammer guys, some guys with picks, others with explosives and all that, and some end up in the hospital because they got hurt. They were supposed to be X and ended up being Y...Tactical Periodization is the implosion! You come here and boom, it's done! So, if I think it is like that it does not need others. The only thing it needs is to refuse in full what the others...Tactical Periodization only needs one thing, intelligent people...but this does not mean we should respect the others, because they have results. Generally, that is it. Now, because they don't know, they are not capable of understanding Tactical Periodization. First of all, the players love it!

Why did Del Neri leave just after arriving at FC Porto? Mourinho had been here, he had won everything, they had been European Champions, there were the same players and they...here it is, the Game Model is everything... they opposed...they refused...and that is why Del Neri did not even start the League. They even took the stones out of the ramps, with so many repetitions they were doing! The players would discuss between themselves: "so, we won everything without ever needing to do this, we never went to the gym, only worked with the ball which is what we enjoy, and we were better than everyone, and we won. And now we will have to do these things?!". Apparently, they were unhappy until there was no way back and the chairman had to dismiss the coach. And didn't he have prestige? Didn't he have a CV? Didn't he achieve things? But perhaps, having in mind a question you asked me, maybe he should have arrived here and thought: 'what is the culture like here? Wait, perhaps here with these players...maybe I am the one that is mistaken, maybe I won't go against the players'...do you understand?

XT: So, is the gym not important in this methodology?

VF: It has nothing to do with the gym. I would take my players to the gym 'many' times, you know for what? I would bring them there, bare feet...once I even brought the players bare feet, and because the wood was so hard they even got some blisters, but they were not upset. I would bring different balls with different sizes for them to play. So that...and there it is, a player that did not know how to do somersaults would do somersaults...playing there, dancing, bringing to the limit the proprioception through playing! Making their body, more and more, belong to them! So that then they could be more fluid, more agile, and pleasantly achieving that. But what is that on Wednesday, is that on Thursday? No, it is on the recovery days, or it is a 'complement' of some other day. It is not the gym! One season, even more than one, when I was in Rio Ave, for example, manager Carlos Brito would say "Professor, in these 8 days just pretend we are doing nothing, so that we can be together and all that!". "But I must train, Carlos...here there is no pitch, we can go to Vila do Conde, but it's still quite a few kilometres, so leave it". So, we would train on the beach! But with a ball. I would find an area, we would check when would be the low-tide, and off we went, but with the ball. And we would also go to the woods, and we would have games there. It is not about the gym. I can go to the gym and do some football-tennis or a 1v1, or playing against the wall and all that...

XT: I was talking about machines...

VF: Machines never!

XT: But, you don't use them because you don't think they are not important for Football in the eyes of this methodology or because they may even be counterproductive?

VF: That's it! But that any non-ignorant will get! You just have to know what the mechanoreceptors are, what is proprioception. You have to understand that the muscle, due to the neuromuscular spindle but not only because of that, is fundamentally an organ that must be receptive to the small changes of its surroundings that we cannot predict. A lot of those details are unexpected and need to be internalised so that a response can emerge. I mean that there is an adjustment period for the muscular co-contractibility and another timing that adjusts it to the circumstances when performing the effort of facing them. The machines, no matter how sophisticated they are, remove precisely that! Furthermore, the machines are individual not for the relationship with the others, it is an individual fitness, not a playing fitness, so it doesn't make sense.

Now, it is not easy to keep creating exercises systematically. That is why I don't tolerate that some talk about the 'tension day'...because it is fundamental that on Wednesdays you select exercises depending on the existing needs but knowing that those you are using imply a significant increase in tension. But they are aimed at playing better! And if this is done with regularity, through the accentuation of the emergence of significant tension in some muscular chains, together with dynamic correspondence, certainly the muscle will work in full potential. Imagine you have two Formula 1 cars, they depart from here and they are exactly the same, they have to brake before the wall otherwise they will hit it, and there is always one guy that wins concerning other. And who wins? It's the one who has better brakes, who manages to wait longer and brakes later. It is through a logic of functioning...and more, notice that...if people reflected maybe they would get many answers regarding what is happening in the World Cup! Look at the African teams, except for Ghana they are all huge guys, really impressive guys, proper 'beasts'! Resistance machines are everywhere, and those guys impress us...should we buy them? But, altogether, they are just like a 'herd of elephants'! Look how hard it is for them, they cannot be anyone. Now, look at the South American teams, they are all skinny, small guys, and that sometimes miss the collective support, but at least...look at the European teams, all formatted excepted for Germany, Spain...this, just by itself should deserve...! I mean, the richness, the variety of Italian football, the variety of French football, the variety of English football...it all fits in just two pages. You can't do that with Argentina, you need a textbook and all that.

People should reflect on these things! I think it was real luck to find Mourinho because Ronaldo is regressing! I am not the only one seeing that, I am just surprised that more people don't! Many times, he approaches the ball without coordination, because he is only using power. And already Newton used to say that a body in movement tends to stay in movement, especially regarding linear speed of motion.

Another thing is...Messi, because it includes braking and having to come back, etc., and that is why I call it 'the speed of speeds'. And Cristiano lacks that, however, he keeps doing the same things by himself with the ball, but in the game, he does not do those things. What is different from Messi. Maybe Messi doesn't waste time in the gym.

XT: The so-called Day of Recovery is probably the least understood day by many people because those of us who have written about Tactical Periodization have not expressed it appropriately. Could you explain it better, please?

VF: Recovery does not occur in one single day. A few moments ago, I told you that after a game with maximal demand we know that you need 4 days to be ready to face an identical situation, so it's a space of 4 days at least. Even in those days in which I am training before a match, how do I consider recovery? Even on a Wednesday, maybe, that is why I have so many breaks! But it is essential that the recovery is made by not going there, not training, because if it is a recovery, getting out of the environment works as a mental recovery, it is very important and very necessary, indispensable! But then when I go back to training, still needing to recover, I can recover in many ways, even dancing I can recover! I can, yes, I can, why not? I have there 10 guys that played, doing some light movements, but making sure that at least that will alert them for the strategic aspects relative to the opponent we will play next, or to our own team, is that a waste of time? But that is not how the recovery, especially the biochemical, will work! Because the 'specific' bio-chemistry needs to be activated, and especially if I am feeling slow, I don't activate it! The activated is, in fact...I can only guarantee it if I am doing an 'objective' 3v3, only like that I can know that the three, in the minute they are there, are back and forth, there's a shot, and it stops! Am I making myself clear? So, they can spend three days recovering, doing 'nothing'. But maybe they can go there 'doing nothing either', doing something else that can benefit recovery even further! How? Through the solicitation of the same bioenergetic things, but within a very short timeframe. I don't know if I am making myself clear?! Diversifying the organisational scales of our way of playing throughout the week. Because I need the same singular bioenergetic support, which is what supports my performance. And only through what? Through an action that represents a fractal of that, and it is only a fractal if it is, in fact, a tiny fraction, with a very short duration. If you are standing for one hour, you will feel tired, because those depth muscles, the posture muscles, will be activated. Even those guys that used to do continuous running stopped doing it and took up the bicycle, for example, and that's not too bad, it's better than continuous running. Because if you want to activate the circulation, that can do it and it won't put too much pressure on the body. Now, with that strength training shit, those guys with big chests, they will be running around for 90 minutes 'carrying' 90kg on their backs! That is why you don't see any marathon runner with the body type of a sprinter, and these guys want to play for 90 minutes with bodies that are increasingly looking like those of sprinters. This is being stupid, this is being stupid!

XT: But even if it is better, the bicycle is also not part of Tactical Periodization...

VF: No, that is part of their logic! Within their logic, it ends not being too bad. Just like integrated is better than the conventional. But that has nothing to do with Tactical Periodization, nothing to do with it! We are talking about what is not important, the importance of Tactical Periodization relates to its ability to install a logic of adaptation. And in recovery, I must act on what is responsible for the same logic of adaptation! But if you are fatigued, I will not overload you. I will wake you up! That is what guarantees the maintenance, and because when I do that, to protect rest, I will only need to repeat it a little later. If I do it 5 or 6 times, I will have fulfilled 1 hour or 45 minutes, and I was doing something very easy for 4 or 5 times, and it promotes the two sides of the coin: Adaptability and Recovery.

XT: This day, the first training day after the match, will it be different depending on how many days we have until the next match?

VF: Yes, obviously. The difference has to do with the degree because the logic stays the same. Now, when you have a match on Saturday and another on Wednesday, everything is very tight. You have 4 days to rest, but you will want to do something, then you will do something following the logic of recovery that can simultaneously rest and revive! So, it needs to be just a little! But if you do this straight after the match, maybe it's a mistake. But you have Wednesday, Thursday, Friday, and Saturday, so you only have Thursday and Friday, when should you do it?! Not on Thursday, maybe Friday, but Friday is just before Saturday, which is the match day! That's the same thing when you are going to play a match, and during the warm-up, you do some speed sets and repetitions, and they don't get tired because of that. A guy that competes on a 100m race breaks the World record, rests for 30 minutes, and then he is ready for another race. A guy that runs a marathon is only fully prepared for another a couple of months after. So, following this logic, what you need to do is...no-one, even fatigued, is incapable of performing a maximal run? That's it, to achieve the effect that I am looking for! But when he does it, he appeals to what is responsible for the existence of...the Adaptability's nature. And my thesis is, this request for the intervention of that 'inside' the total recovery, will not destroy the recovery and will even speed it up, while keeping it safe as it was accomplished over the same thing, making it present! And it will only be like that if it is an apparent situation of play. That is why I recommend a maximum of 3v3, in a small-sided space, so that during the minute or 1m30 that they spend there provides them with the possibility of having acquired the same pattern of demand of the match while in movement! For example, I used to do that, 3v3, so I had several teams in which they would come on and would never do less than 5 recovery blocks! Sometimes it was not possible so I would tell them to stretch and do abdominal work, guaranteeing the separation between 'demands'. Then it's about art, it's art playing with this, a hymn to sensitivity!

XT: When there are more days, there is the possibility of performing this recovery in a more fun way and thinking less about the next match?

VF: The problem is not if it is fun. You can do those 3v3 in a fun way, you just need to say "whoever loses has to pay a juice to the others, or piggyback them, or will have to get all the balls..." it must always have that fun side, involving emotions. Because one thing that makes me sad is watching some matches, especially youth matches, and I remember that I have seen happier people in some funerals, and that should not happen in football. Valdano usually says "if the face is not smiling, how can the feet laugh?". You need to feel pleasure and joy when you are playing. The fact that they are recovering should always have a fun aspect involved. Usually, the first thing I would do was 'automatizing' the guys, saying "look, today is Wednesday, but it's like if it was Tuesday, or today is Thursday, but it's like Friday". And depending on that they would know, and they would end up saying "Professor, today is Wednesday, but it's Tuesday, or today is Tuesday, but it's in fact Wednesday...". All that is related to the Articulation of Meaning, with an understanding of the Process, with the complexity of the Process, and they are not stupid. Now, it depends on how you make it happen! Mourinho's players understand it, but he doesn't talk to them in a sophisticated way, like an academic, he has to find analogies that...and with the kids even more.

XT: Is creativity something that should always be present in Tactical Periodization?

VF: Creativity must happen in life. When I talked about contexts...that is why I talked about contexts and not about behaviours! If Tactical Periodization prioritises the Game if it promotes confrontation...confrontation always involves unpredictability. Teams are not only positively distinguished when they show a great ability to be diverse. The quality of play always brings the need of solving situations in a creative manner. So, depending on the experiences in those contexts that each one 'draws', without using the eraser. The creativity that a player must reveal as a centre-back is different from the one that a forward must reveal. But it is indispensable that within those contexts the originality emerges. And who has the responsibility to make it happen? The players! But only if they are brought up and trained to have to think, having to decide, having to feel, the decision-making must belong to them. The decision-making in accordance with a general objective, to a previous intention, that they recognise. But they must act considering the circumstances. They may solve the problem better or worse depending on the habits they have created and on their decision-making ability, on their ability to choose... so it is essential to promote this. But, just like Jorge Valdano used to say: "there is not creativity without order".

But, what is our understanding of 'order'? The order is that organisation that brings us together, it is that leads six or seven players, within the same team, to think the same thing at the same time! That is an affinity with the Principles. But the Principle, as the word implies, is an orienting matrix that promotes a logic that leads to the emergence of certain things. But in the end, it's about the decision, the intention-in-action, and to solve that there is no equation! It will be as easy to achieve as the existing quality, and the quality is supported by habit creation. So, quality has to do with that. What distinguishes us from other species is that...we got here and got to be who we are because of...creativity! In opposition to what is commonly said, it is the self-generation that allows us to overcome difficulties, at an individual level. What happens because of that, considering groups...today there is a discussion on the intelligence of masses, or on the intelligence of swarms and anthills. But even there, there is an essential need for creativity! I normally use a metaphor: in a newspaper, they have a theme, but they are the ones doing the writing, and the writing will be related to the context and with the capacity in that precise moment. But it's theirs! And many times, it's across time, in the continuity of the exceptional causality that improvements arise, coordination improvements, improvements in the team's organisation. An essential condition for people to exist is to have creativity!

XT: A wrongful understanding of this may end up creating teams that are very 'mechanical' (through close-ended 'tactics')?

VF: Look, people say...grabbing what you have just mentioned, it can bring you the opposite way! You can say, I want creative kids, so I won't interfere, and they will have no contextual orientation and end up being a hallucinated team! You see a frenetic team, all connected to the defibrillator, a team with plenty of 'generosity' but imbalanced, completely imbalanced, losing identity. The other side of what you referred to...I usually say Mourinho's teams are organised, so they are tactically evolved, but, is Barcelona also not evolved? Now, which type of organisation do they have? That is why I said at the beginning that I am obsessed with efficacy because you can only win at the top level if you have efficacy if you win, but the efficacy is the result of efficiency, and that is why I said I am permanently anxious and disturbed by aesthetics. So, efficiency is related to the aesthetic, but you must weigh both things! Those who do not think like that, end up creating robots, but I have nothing to do with that! I do what I can, so it doesn't happen. Now, those who wonder "is it Tactical Periodization that..."? That is a problem of people, not a problem of Tactical Periodization. I am sorry, but Tactical Periodization is the only that solves things maximally! Now, not everyone is able to solve them independently of identifying with it, because it has great demands and not everyone knows how to work with it. Even Mourinho or someone else that felt identified with it, today they deal with Tactical Periodization better than in the beginning, and back then they already identified with it.

XT: Earlier on we talked about the first week of adaptation. Is the Pattern Morphocycle introduced from the second week?

VF: The initial adaptation does not mean that you are working outside the Morphocycle. You are...it's just like watching a match at a normal speed and then watch it in slow motion! You are only...Tactical Periodization must contemplate the circumstances, so, if you know that people just returned from doing nothing, from holiday, progression has to do with that. It's a matter of common sense, but that can be perfectly framed under the Morphocycle. Why is it the Morphocycle? How do you identify it? Why do you say "look, that team is Barcelona, and that one is...whatever team"? You say it due to the geometric expression of teams, due to the identification of patterns. So, they play like that, the drills that you need to use to create must resemble the suggested geometrical expression, and then there are the possible dynamics which lead to the adaptation of teams, there is the construction of an adaptation of individuals and teams. For example, good teams, when the match is progressing through the right side, for example, you can see them improving like this or like that, and you can look at the adjustments. They are not thinking, I need to go here or there, they adjust depending on the habituation, and that is identifiable straight away... so, what happens is not only relative to the guys near the ball. It's not just those who show the team is organised, but you can see it also in the guys that are far from the ball, how they move and adjust. Have you seen this recent match between Brazil and Holland, where was the organisation?

When things became harder, that was total anarchy on both sides. The 'de-rationalisation' of Holland's game when they were on top is the evidence that they are not intelligent, that they are unable to think, the way they continued to play was not appropriate for the favourable situations they were facing. And that has nothing to do with...this has to do with...! Tactical Periodization is not that, it's precisely the opposite, it wants people to become conscious and then em__body__ that regarding habituation. This is where a clear mind and intelligence always exist. So, I speak about Auto-Hetero or Auto-Hetero-Eco-Generation! But you can only do this properly if the individual has subjective autonomy. He coordinates as well as he is conscious and has the need to collaborate and cooperate, this is the appeal. Football is a team sport, so if it has a team, first you need to respect certain collective matrixes, that in the end are the rules of a certain society or something like that!

XT: In so-called conventional methodologies there is 'individualised training'. What is your opinion about it? Do you think it is truly individualised?

VF: I don't think so. Look, there is nothing more individualised than Tactical Periodization because they always practice by their positions and to their roles. And when operationalising it, you need to pay attention to the global and to the individual at the same time. And it's its detection, against certain things...for example, that player has mobility problems, he deals badly with the body, he cannot even perform a tumble, which is important. He needs to go through it. And it is that attention that will lead him to improve. So, there is nothing more individualising. But this is a contextualised individualisation, not something abstract! Because a while ago you were talking about compensation and complementarity, those are abstract things. And I need to take all the needs of the game and all the needs of the individual into account, but along the whole Process and concurrently. That is why I say Tactical Periodization is a tailor-made suit, but those are not complementarities of anything, those are things more connected to the micro level or to a more individual level while taking into account the team's functionality. In the end, the team is fulfilled by individuals. The team will operate better if the individuals operate better, but only if the individuals are committed to collective references. That is the growth Process and, since the beginning, one must understand it and try to make it happen.

XT: Do you say football is an "Anthropo-Social-Total Phenomenon" because a team is formed by individuals?

VF: Precisely due to the interference on the individual as an evolution, not only functional but also 'structural', it impacts the 'anthropo'. It is not exclusively social in the synchronic sense! Therefore, I call it an embodiment, by it, is an em-__body__-ment, having in mind being part of a group, being in a community, co-existing! There is a deliberate intention, that is why that idea of deterministic chaos makes sense because there is a deliberate intention to make it happen, firstly from the coaches and then from the players, together with the coaches, to head in that direction.

XT: The use of energetic aid, the blindfolding of feet without the existence of injuries.... isn't it possible that this is going against the body?

VF: Look, I could even go beyond that, but those are just my thoughts. When I started as a football coach, I did everything I could to avoid that in the pre-season players were given multivitamins or got massages, or something like that! You cannot imagine how long it took to reach an agreement. Because what I am seeking is the adaptation of the organism so I cannot be giving it aid. During the season is different, due to the impossibility of controlling everything. Because if you have a match three days after the previous one and the other team has had four resting days, there are some players that you will need to use more than others, so some levels of overtraining or tiredness or fatigue may emerge – or not – but there you need to think about the possibility of providing massages, vitamin supplements, etc., etc...! But not initially.

I even think further, for example, I have been thinking a lot about several of these things, for example, when a player has a sprain and the blood vessels 'leak', is it really advisable to use ice? Because the inflammatory reaction is a defensive reaction from the body. Now, if it goes past certain limits I need to stop it with a tourniquet or whatever, but initially, I don't think so, I don't think so to defend the body. So, that idea of taping the feet or similar, these are cultural issues, which are (un)necessary and so you have it...the Game Model is everything, it is everything that the players have in their minds. If a player comes to me and...I had a player who asked me to perform the warm-up by himself, and I said, "but what is warming up by yourself?". For him, the idea of warm-up was different. He had been the top scorer, a Brazilian guy. The guy wanted...we told him "you cannot do it by yourself, you need to do it with the others, but in the 30 minutes before that, you can do whatever you want!". He wanted to be in the changing room by himself, he would do stretches, he would pray with his underlined Bible. What is the problem? Even regarding other things, imagine...No, it's not only...There are others who pray and am I going to tell them "don't pray because it's not good for you"?! But that is unrelated, that is part of the endless details of reality, and one or other may not even be so aligned with the configuration of those details related to the pattern, but that is no inconvenience at all. Now, I can tell you that I had players that initially had some kind of whim, but after working with me for two or three years...they put it behind. But I did not force them, they put it behind gradually. Acquisitive changes require time. So, if that is done since youth development, it becomes much easier. But that does not mean you will stop having a great problem to deal with – parents! 'Everyone knows about football!'. And the parents are always chatting. Now, what I know is that kids are not mentally retarded, the parents are sometimes! And the kids tend to become like that due to the influence of parents. So, this is a complicated game to play, it's a difficult game, it's not easy, but thankfully the reality keeps showing that...

I insist a lot in Mourinho, I highlight Mourinho because those who doubt Tactical Periodization's capacity are either stupid or have a bad intention. I am not saying that there are no other ways that lead you to victory, but what I know is that you win by constructing the game! I have already told that I am not really enthusiastic about Mourinho's way of playing, I enjoy much more like a spectator to watch Barcelona, Spain, Germany. I really disliked Brazil, so what I was saying...if Germany or Spain don't win, I hope that Argentina does, but Argentina regarding organisation does not fulfil me. But what I know is that any of these ways of playing can be built better by using Tactical Periodization and the evidence is in Mourinho, who beyond his genius is able to develop his own which is then expressed in the way of playing that is even athletic. With players of a certain age, and being able to compete in all cups and league, and winning in all of them by playing only football!!!

XT: When you talk about the use of ice, are you also referring to recovery via cryotherapy?

VF: This is not easy, for example, the use of cryotherapy, and that is useful especially when discussing recovery, but I am talking about an injury with a leak from the blood vessels because the inflammation is not allowed! Because the inflammation is a positive reaction...and what do you want...? I am convinced that today many people's immunological deficiencies are due to the antibiotics and others...! For example, those sudden deaths that have been occurring with extraordinary frequency, today there are even scientific studies that point that it may be due to the excessive use of anti-inflammatories. And because there is an increasing competitive density, then sudden deaths...it's not me telling it, these are scientific studies, so the reasoning is the same! I talk about this, my son has two degrees, one in Psychology and the other in Physiotherapy and I talk about this with him, and he is not totally stupid. Now, quite often there are time issues, it needs to be fast, and there are some shortcuts used, and sometimes there are some things done...for example, a few years ago pubalgia would be treated with surgery because they thought that was the fastest solution, not recognising that some players, faster, more explosive, would never recover properly because of the area which they would usually cut. So, what I can tell you is that Tactical Periodization is complete, it's plentiful if the individual is able...let's say, if he is minimally intelligent.

XT: Could you explain what you mean with the 'cappuccino'?

VF: The 'cappuccino' is just like that: you drink the coffee and the milk and perhaps it looks dark. You don't see the coffee, but it is there! Sometimes, considering the circumstances, I need to disguise the coffee with the milk because I know that the players say that if they drink coffee, they won't feel well. The session is over, and there we go: "guys, ten laps around the pitch". And the guys will be happy because they can say they ran. But it does not really matter. I tell them they do it and get their legs a bit loose, and they can say they did their running. Or those I used to do with Fernando Santos, running for 1 minute and stopping for 30 seconds, running for 2 minutes, stopping for another 30 seconds, until getting to six minutes, but that...If I go to the bus, and the bus is suddenly leaving, I run after the bus and does that have anything to do with...do you understand? That is the 'cappuccino', a need that I have to find strategies. I did it especially in the beginning, then I would do like Mourinho when he got to Chelsea, 'I am the one that knows, I am the one who has won already here'. What the player has in her head as the game is what the game means to her, and she might have 'anything' in her head.

When I refer to the head I mean everything, including the toenails, it's the whole body, even the subconscious. Now, a lot of it is contrary to what I want, but I cannot go straight from 8 to 80, I need to have that in mind. As I told you earlier, if I am facing an ox to feed him, I am not going to grab the ox by the neck to make him get to the food, and instead, I need to get the food to the ox. I am not going to push him; otherwise he does not allow me to feed him. That is the pedagogical or strategic side of the term. One thing is if I arrive at a team, the players have certain technical limitations, and I want them to play the first touch, only if I am dumb! Even to play 3 or 4 touches, it's already a struggle! And where does this come in? In the articulation of the Principle of Propensities with the Principle of Complex Progression, I need to decode the reality. That is why I say, once again, that the Game Model is everything, but it is everything, including what I am yet to detect, that exists and interferes with the rest!

XT: That 'cappuccino' can also be served at the beginning of the season when for different reasons you need to do double sessions?

VF: Yes. It is not necessary, it is required depending on the circumstances! I will give you an example, Carlos Brito told me "Professor, we need to find one day every week in which we train twice. You know how it is; otherwise they come, the chairman and all that...!". So, I told him: "no problem, we do that in the recovery day. In the morning we do some runs and all that, and then in the afternoon some foot-volleyball and that is it. Now, I would explain it to the players, they would know it themselves if it would be Monday or Tuesday when they had to do it. That is awareness, it is about common sense. There is nothing with more common sense than Tactical Periodization, especially because it pays attention to the here and now systematically, in the management of the process.

XT: Can you also split one session into two, respecting the Sub-Dynamic that you want to work on?

VF: Yes. Even because one thing is doing two sessions, in the example I gave you previously it was related to recovery. But it is different if I, I can even, I can even...And many times it is even advisable in certain circumstances, on a Wednesday for example, if instead of one, but these are not two training units, it is one but divided, you have a bigger break let's put it that way. In conventional terms, you have two sets, a set that you perform in the morning, then the break, the food, and then the second set. And instead of 1h30 or 2 hours, because in the morning the session can sometimes last 2 hours due to the breaks, because it is necessary, especially earlier in the season, to give very long breaks, and then you do one hour and then another hour in the afternoon. You can, but that is why I told you a while ago, some coaches would say "See, we could do three trainings session and...", and I would reply "We can even do 5!". Maybe by doing 5, I treat them better than others doing just three, it depends on what I do in those 5!

XT: We can say that it is also a way of respecting Maximum Relative Intensity…

VF: Yes, because what is essential is that...you can only have the guys in maximum relative intensity, doing things fresh, if they are indeed fresh! While you don't understand that you don't understand Tactical Periodization!

XT: Exactly the opposite of conventional methodology…

VF: Exactly. There are those who train fatigued so that...because there it is, they think that training fatigued they will make better use of energy, improve lactic acid and tolerate lactic acid in circulation and more. I don't defend any of that, I defend precisely the opposite. What I really look for is a certain 'date' that then allows for a 'marriage', and an ever-lasting 'marriage' with all energetic sources, depending on the fundamental response type. And then recovery is also about that if I am tired due to a mixture of the relationship between 3 or 4 energetic sources, or the one that we want, and then I act on one, and I recover everything?! Don't play with me, I am not that stupid. I need to recover, but not only one of them. But how, if they are tired? This is where the problem lies. I recover totally by requesting one? Don't trick me, come on!

XT: You don't believe in physical tests?

VF: No. Since many years I have been saying that any kind of test is only convenient and necessary for those who don't need them! Because I must evaluate, and I might find convenient for some reason, even to motivate...but if I am with certain players that I have known for quite a while and knowing that that is the logic, will I motivate them through something that is not...? Do you understand? I ran another kind of tests, linked to reality. No, I don't... that is all bullshit. For me, that is all bullshit.

XT: And the heart-rate monitors, don't they matter?

VF: No. I don't care about any of that. Tests are like bikinis, they show many things but hide the essential. Within the modules that I have lectured, there was one called 'Evaluating in physical education', that I taught for four years, more or less the time that Professor Jorge Bento was in Germany doing his PhD.

XT: How can you promote the re-adaptation of a player that returns from injury?

VF: You will always have problems. You may have problems with the medical department. Because even within the clinical logic, not everyone thinks the same. Physiotherapy is not, all the same, there are different conceptualisations. Then.... but it is easy to solve the problem! I used to say: "no problem, you do whatever you need to recover him, and you will only send me the player back when you have no need to work with him. From that moment, I am the one working with him". And then he will do whatever I think is more convenient for him to adapt. For example, with Jorge Costa, when he came to me, he arrived with a recommendation to run and whatever, "but how can it be? You say that he is! No, but is he? And then if he is clinically recovered, you are the ones giving orders? So, he is not recovered, send him back when you think he is!". And when he returned, I talked to him: "Jorge, you are a centre-back, so do you remember the preparatory period, do you remember what you did, you trained and took part in some games, those you guys did, to be specific regarding your centre-back position?". And he replies: "Professor, I had a knee ligament injury, I cannot" "Of course you cannot, and you won't touch the ball. What you will do, you will stand behind Aloisio (another centre-back), and you will mirror everything that he does". As you may understand, this looks like a kids' thing, but because they are not stupid, and then they see that that is the ideal, they hyper-motivate themselves. Now, here we must consider the Complex Progression! What is the logic of the conventional? He is missing resistance, so he trains a lot, and then the next day he comes back fatigued and then gets injured again. No, what he needs to do is just a little. So, if the players that are training normally do not train a lot, why should the player that is returning from an injury do it? But that is the logic: first resistance, then whatever...what I want him to do is that he starts being 'resistant' so that he can do what he needs to do. And in the beginning, he needs to do just a little, so that he can feel fresh! He needs to recover so that the next day he can do something else. I often used the wine jar metaphor: if I want to drink 5 litres of wine and I never drank wine before, I first need to drink a small glass. And after that small glass maybe I will be tipsy, blushing... and the next day I drink a little more than one glass, and so on. Training is the same. So, I increase the volume but the volume of something objective, not of something abstract. It is not an abstract complementarity, not at all.

XT: Within recovery should we consider certain players that due to their age or characteristics may need more time to recover?

VF: That is a false problem. You also need to be careful because, due to being young, you should not exaggerate because he also gets tired. Now, his will, because he is young, he wants to do it and so on... But he also gets tired! And that is why it is essential to set rules if I know that four days are needed for everyone to be capable, even if I am not coaching 50-year-old people! Now, perhaps two, three or even four would be fine after just three days, especially on the first third of the league, but I am interested in those four days *because the team is the whole! And then the response of the individual when he starts training gives us some indications if he is, because if he is playing football, and where he wants, and either he is dead, or he is tired. Or if I talk to him and he is holding his breath, then he is tired. I have never used heart-rate monitors, in 28 consecutive years on the field, I have never used a stop-clock. And I have always been well paid, 'won' leagues, I was in Champions League, 'won' cups...so...!*

XT: Nowadays, people are working on the potentiation of the adductors, through analytical exercises, to avoid injuries to those muscles. What do you think about that?

VF: It's foolish, it's foolish! You have five muscles there (adductors), and each muscle has endless motor units that in consequence work with different stimuli. This diversity, the degrees of freedom in the relationship between these muscles is endless as well. You won't find anything to work them except for letting them do what they need to! Can you invent any machine or something for Messi's adductors to do? Then don't be foolish! What you need to put is...and having that in mind: ah! Careful, you need to have a great mobility of the pelvis and always through, in each session, allowing great extensibility to the adductors, and being cautious with the very common shortening, and the potentiation of the anomalous iliac psoas, that due to its insertion, because it is in one of the lumbar vertebrae and... (12th thoracic). So, it causes atrophy of the mobility of the pelvis, the leg...So you need to drop several abdominal exercises that are not convenient, that make it work, that put the iliac psoas under tension...that you don't want that, you need to suppress that! And that is why I give those abdominal exercises that you see in the class notes, just half-a-dozen of them, and then a dozen that you should not do because they are dangerous...!

XT: What about the abdominals? Some time ago I read in an interview that Cristiano Ronaldo did 3,000 every day...

VF: Sure. I am sure he does! And more and more, Cristiano is playing worse! I think no-one doubts that! (XT's note: this interview was done in 2010, it refers to the season 2009/2010, when Cristiano Ronaldo was playing under Manuel Pellegrino. It does not apply to this date, with Jose Mourinho as a manager).

XT: So, how should abdominal and dorsal muscles be prepared?

VF: I already told you that every day, in every training day I would do a lot of mobility in the beginning, between exercises, a lot of mobility of the whole body, with interference on the dorsal-lumbar mobility, in positions of tension and extension for the dorsal-lumbar muscles. And extensibility for the dorsal-lumbar muscles, especially for the strikers and even more for the centre-backs. Abdominals, always the same, every day for everybody. And that is why I told you that FC Porto should hold a Guinness record, because in FC Porto, with Bobby Robson as a manager, we played 72 matches in one season (official and non-official), 55 consecutive matches without being defeated. 'Culturally', Robson did not like to make substitutions, so we used 13 players, won the league, were kicked out of the Champions League in the semi-finals, by Barcelona, won the Super Cup and the Portuguese Cup, using just 13 players, practising once a day. So how? We had no injuries because otherwise, we could not have used only 13 players, and Robson's way of playing, everyone knew it as high-pace or whatever. This was even on the notes down there!

So, I...I...it's just because it's you and because of your objectives, because I have no patience for this anymore, I have no patience. This is not just something that I say, there is evidence, and more...wait for Mourinho once again! Look, you...even in dissertations, the one written by Carlos Campos takes pride in mentioning that...So, if people are not interested that's fine, just don't annoy me. Each one can do the session they want, publish whatever you want! I was a lecturer here for 33 years, and I always said my contracts only lasted one year! If you want to talk about the conventional I can talk about it, at least at the same level as them, I lectured Training Theory and Methodology for 13 years, that is a long time, only a dumb guy does not learn, having to teach for 13 years. So, I have no patience, I have no patience, because this is not rhetoric, it's not loose language, it's not about someone preaching, there are examples! And the critical example at the moment is Mourinho, now that <u>they are in Madrid,</u> although the access to the training centre is difficult because to get there you need to drive for a few miles after passing the entrance. He has already imposed some rules there. The Italian that put that centre there, he wants it to be fully shut, why not? And they also asked him: so, how is it? So, what about strength training? So, nothing? What they do, because it is so different, it is normal that they doubt. Because it was always like that, it was always said that it should be like that. I have no doubts that it is like that.

Now, Xavier, when they say that...let them say whatever they want, I don't care! But what they are talking about is not Tactical Periodization! Tactical Periodization does not need what they say it is missing. Now, if they want to do Tactical Periodization, then they must say it as it is. If they don't, then they can keep doing what they are doing, and I won't be bothered at all, especially now that I am 66 years old, and retiring from the Faculty. My concerns with Football have to do with the reflection about Football and the Body. Nothing else.

XT: Many say that to achieve high levels of performance at the top of the Game, there should be a multi-disciplinary path throughout the developmental stages. What do you think?

VF: I think that those are some slogans that are socially appealing and that in some cases ended up being converted into theories, but...Look, did Zidane have any kind of multi-disciplinary development?! Did Pele have any kind of multi-disciplinary development? Did Messi have any kind of multi-disciplinary development?! Go to hell with those jokes! And there is no other sport, no other sport that is so multi-disciplinary like Football. Now, I should not be obsessed to have a 6-year-old, even if he is showing that he can be very good at the back, I should not be putting him there all the time. I will give you a concrete example. Tiago has an under-11 team that has a kid that is entirely out of this world, his name is Estrela. He is 10, plays 7-a-side and likes to play on the wings, but Porto's way of playing in these ages is not about running with the ball, the ball gets to the wings, and you play, but many times there are also 1v1 and nothing else, no compensations, no covering, so you need to take advantage. And that kid did that better than anyone. But Tiago had several kids to play in those areas and did not have a guy who could play as a pivot. And everything led him to believe that if he played as a pivot, he would fix the team's problem. That kid has extraordinary intelligence, he can see everything one year before the others, and so Tiago did that. And at some point Tiago had a conversation with me, he suggested that and I said, well, I agree he can play well there but...Tiago had the sensitivity to recognise that my opinion was not wrong, bringing him to the wing at times because despite him being a genius there, it was essential that he kept facing the contextual singularity of the wings...in a logic of intentional acquisition! Freitas Lobo even wrote an article in 'A Bola' just because of the kid, he went to watch him!

Now, the context that emerges when he is on the wing it is not the same that emerges over there, and if he has some characteristics when he is on the side, if he is permanently in that other area, he will miss the opportunity to showcase his full ability. So, a dominance here, but at times also playing on the wing! But what is fundamental, right from the start, few kids will go far, where we say "well, he can play anywhere", that is a lie! Now, the difficulty is for me to realise where he can play better. And then, that idea of multi-functionality, it has to do with the type of football that I am looking for. That fit within the collective, I always have the kid that play there, sometimes he is in another area of the pitch, performing more than one role. He changed his position, he changed his role.

Now, it is evident that in 7-a-side the complexity is lower in comparison to 11-a-side. And in youth development, there is less complexity, but that has to do with my understanding of what is Tactical Periodization 'a la longue'! I already told you that in those ages and up to 14 or 15 maybe, the Principle of Horizontal Alternation is not entirely accomplished, it is not managed with the same rigour, but it should be taken into account, even because of growth and normal development, trying not to request excessive energy when performing, energy that is clearly needed for growth. So, only that Principle of Horizontal Alternation is not performed like at later stages, the others are executed exactly the same. It is about contextualising the situations, therefore including the Principle of Propensities and the Complex Progression too, maybe it is even more complex then because you are working with kids undergoing a growth process. Knowing what we know these days, and that is why I showed you that text and mentioned 'The Philosophical Baby', which is now published in Portuguese, that talks about the baby's brain, and those are all texts that I have put there, that is why when a child is born it can be bilingual or trilingual straight away, and only after that it becomes more difficult, but in the beginning she can do anything. So, she has multiple abilities by herself, but from a certain moment she starts showing what she can do better, what she can't do, and what she can regularly do well, that is talent. I need to know, I need to pay attention, it's like Valdano says 'talent can be expressed in a million ways!"

XT: So, in your opinion, Football should be started at early ages...

VF: Exactly. Have you seen the kid that is going to play the piano, running first around the piano, doing pull-ups or push-ups?! No. The kids get there – if they are two, they say 'you play here, and I play there'; if they are eleven, they say 'six here and five there'. That is what they do, football with a ball! This can lead to the gestation of a sublime triad more football, more kid, more development'.

XT: So, since those early ages, should they already focus in a certain kind of football?

VF: In street football, they use the models that they have in their 'imagination', they mimic the older players, their surroundings. That is extraordinary, that is much better than most academies do, where there are adults that know nothing, that only create damage, that only format them. But, the possibility of the adult intervening with quality in the sense of improving the player, there it makes sense. And there, he should promote a certain type of football, and that is what FC Porto does. A football where passing is the most important component. Because it is through passing that the collective is expressed. Then, in complementarity, then yes the training with character and whatever, so there are conditions that make it more likely for passes to emerge, players positioned in a certain way, experiencing more than one structure so that when they grow up it is almost indifferent if they go here or there, because they are by then more or less comfortable anyway. What did Xavi say after the match against Portugal? "For us it was easy, they gave us the ball, and if we are comfortable with the ball, that's great!". And that is why the Ajax kids, a few years ago, would turn up on the first team at 16 or 17 without any problem. Why should they, if they have been playing like that since the age of 8, why shouldn't they play? That is something that has been distorted, and much!

XT: Professor, many people today try to start training under the framework of Tactical Periodization; some people have more identification with it than others, but in your opinion, what are the main mistakes that are happening when they try to operationalise Tactical Periodization?

VF: It may look like I am going to give you an empty answer, but it is the understanding of what Tactical Periodization is. Because sometimes, due to the level of demands, to the existing reality, there may seem to exist an affinity with Tactical Periodization, but once the situation is more compatible or more corresponding with maximal demand, then a certain incoherence emerges. Because either you understand the way it started, and that implies that you study, that you identify yourself, but deeply, with what exists, with what is conventional. Or if that does not happen, then we are also possessed by much of that conventional, when we try to operationalise the process, or even when we try to identify it. So, there needs to be...because that...and sometimes it's even worse...! It is about what is essential regarding the conventional, but because there is a lower level of understanding or because it implies too much work and there is no capacity to identify that, that side is a very important gap, especially the metabolic processes, what we call bioenergetics[5].

So, I said that, in the first place, we need to understand the phenomenon as something complex and if it is complex we need to act upon it, reflecting upon it, acting upon it without never forgetting that complexity, it needs to be complex in a higher or lower degree. When I planned to do a PhD that was already the topic of my research, the problem of causality[6]. And many

---

5 Bioenergetics: one of Physiology's main themes, especially dedicated to the study of the various chemical processes that make cellular life possible from an energetic point of view. It seeks, among many other things, to explain the main chemical processes that occur in the cell and to analyse its physiological implications, mainly with regards to the way how those processes are framed in the global concept of homeostasis. The understand of what 'energy' means and how the organism can acquire, convert, store and use it, is key for understanding the organic functioning in both performance sports and recreational and leisure activities. The study of bioenergetics allows for the understanding of how the capacity to perform work (exercise) depends on the successive conversion of one in other energetic elements.

6 Causality: the relationship between a certain event, usually designated as cause, and a second event designated as effect. In a linear conceptualisation, the latter is a consequence of the former. We can distinguish two types of causality: linear and non-linear. Gleick (1998, pp.23-24) clarifies that "linear relationships can be captured with a straight line on a graph. (...) Linear equations are solvable, which makes them suitable for textbooks. Linear systems have an important modular virtue: you can take them apart

times, the lack of understanding of these things, and the rush to think they are experts in the area, leads them to...now, because this is the context, one that does not have maximum demand, it is not so obvious, and it is so that people's conceptualisation of learning is one of reception, instead of one of discovery. So, because this is not a framework of maximum demand, the problem of tiredness, for example, cannot be put the same way. Also, the problem of continuity of the same adaptability record cannot be set the same way, etc., etc., etc.... So, you need to face this reality, recognising it as non-linear, and all thought should have that foundation, non-linear.

And I see very often vertigo, for people that seem to be more or less identified, certain vertigo in building a catalogue of reality, and that has nothing to do with non-linear causality. On the contrary, it is a certain type of vertigo with linear causality. To answer your question, I used to think, until a short time ago, that a certain inability to deal with Tactical Periodization within the limits of possible was the result of – even though I continue to think that it is essential – the non-familiarisation of people with High Performance[7]. Because there is a very unique constraint there, where you either can deal with it, or you don't and end up drifting, right? It is indispensable to "play" on the borders of things. Those conditions, or those circumstances, if they don't exist, the degree of possibilities ends up changing, and it may look like we are better or worse and not as we really area. But as I was saying, until some time ago, I thought it was the result of that. I still do, and that's why I imagine that without the possibility of being at that level, it would be challenging for people, in what is related to dosing, which is an essential aspect, to detect and be conscious of the extreme sensitivity of these things to make it work. So, there are some key aspects, that may not be so easily understandable, but I have realised that in cases like Marisa, for example, who is not working at a top level, or recently Jorge, who understand it without needing this guarantee.

So, I go back to my initial question, to my initial answer, which is, in fact, the non-understanding of what is – or aimed to be – Tactical Periodization. This is situated in two levels, right? The first, the conceptual level, therefore theoretical and then, because of many insufficiencies at that level, the methodological level[8]. To be more objective, I could say that with a higher or lower

---

and put them together again – the pieces add up. Nonlinear systems generally cannot be solved and cannot be added together. (...) Nonlinearity means that the act of playing the game has a way of changing the rules. (...) That twisted changeability makes nonlinearity hard to calculate, but it also creates rich kinds of behaviour that never occur in linear systems". We can say that causality of determination of a phenomenon is the specific way in which events are related and emerge and that is why learning or trying to decode the general characteristics of causality of a phenomenon means understanding the relationships that are established and the amplification that may result from those relationships. This is what allows for an understanding of the global intelligibility of a system, even if, in the case of non-linear causality, as is the case of football, such intelligibility should stay away from the 'vertigo' of categorisation, because its details are not decodable. That is why Professor Vitor Frade claims that "there is no equation for the detail".

7 High Performance: the highest level of performance one can achieve. This is the performance level where the top teams and top football players operate. A high level of demand, high level of aspiration and high competitive density are its main characteristics.

8 Conceptual and Methodological levels: these two levels are the great pillars, or matrixes, around which the whole process should develop, and they necessarily require a convenient Articulation of Meaning, so that what emerges from the process makes indeed sense, the sense we want to give to the

degree of confusion, with a higher or lower level of understanding, I think we can say that in the end, the mistakes result from the lack of understanding of the Morphocycle. Because you either understand why the Morphocycle was created and what it aims to be, or you don't, even partially mistakes can always happen. So, we have in first place to agree, understand, feel, and because of that I sometimes imagine 'but if people are not at the top level, they cannot feel that". But that's not true, it is possible to feel it without having been there because people have a head to think. And if you ask a question to a hundred guys who have been at the top level, and are at the top level as coaches, independently of their answer being impossible to justify, if it proves within the current framework of science, it is empirical evidence. So, all of them, or 90 something percent of them, will say that after a maximum demand effort, a match with maximum demand, that team who had to perform that effort, will only be ready again to perform at the same level, without boiling, without seeing its usual functional flow disturbed, four days after. So, this is the key, this is the key for everything else. Either people recognise the validity of this claim, or they will not fully understand the essence of the Morphocycle, and consequently, the essence of Tactical Periodization. So, if this is true, if this is true, imagining that the competitive framework has, as a pattern, one match every week, that is why I say, Morphocycle as a Morphocycle is that period or that cycle that is identifiable by the presence of two matches separated by one week. All other conditions are exceptional, and that exceptionality can be more or less regular, but if they become a rule, we then need to change some fundamental things.

So, the Morphocycle is definable by the presence of one match on a Sunday and another on the other Sunday, for example. So, if I know, and I am convinced that, and I have no doubts that only after four days I will be able to perform an effort like that, then just after four days I will be able to demand a level of effort that requires maximum availability regarding the team's effort. So, there is very little time left to train, even if I say that a maximum demand in a match is different from a maximum demand in training, but even like that certainly I won't say that I need less than three days...if it is absolutely indispensable an effort of maximum demand. Because without tiredness there is no training, without fatigue there is no training, without fatigue, there is no improvement, and with fatigue, there is an absolute need for recovery so that you can be ready, and with a certain time to allow for that to happen[9].

Process. The Conceptual level also demands, at its internal level, an Articulation of Meaning so that the fluidity can be coherent and the way of playing represents a truly unbreakable wholeness. That is the level related to the Game Idea and includes the Game Principles that construct it in its different scales (Great – Macro; Sub – Meso; Sub-Sub – Micro). The Methodological level is what allows for the operationalisation of the Conceptual level, is what brings it to life, it is composed by Tactical Periodization's Methodological Principles. It also requires an Articulation of Meaning, since the process dynamic implies the dynamic interaction between the different Methodological Principles.

9 Fatigue is also a need for Tactical Periodization, it is even one of its central aspects. It appears to be indeed one of the very few common points this methodology has with the others. However, this is just an illusion because there are highly significant differences, especially in what represents the stimulus that ignites performance, a qualitative and not quantitative stimulus, and not less relevant in the recognition of the need to recover from those constant performances and consequent states of fatigue, what does not happen with conventional methodologies, where the logic favours a quantitative emphasis and its objective is to perpetuate fatigue with the objective of allowing the organism a higher capacity of response under conditions of continuous and accentuated fatigue. On the contrary, in Tactical Periodization, inducing fatigue has to do with the possibility of aspiring to states of structural, functional and

So, as I mentioned, having as a reference a Morphocycle of this kind, everything is played in this Morphocycle, so only half-way through it, I am able to perform an effort of the same type, half-way which is on a Thursday. Then I still have Friday, Saturday, and Sunday, only three days. Therefore, I say that if on Thursday we have the training of maximum demand, even if it is mandatory to have a maximum demand, it will be below, it will be below maximum demand in comparison to a match, also because there are only three days left for the next match. So, I know that this effort of maximum demand of my team, when in play, is characterised by a dynamic of the team that expresses a functionality. But to make it happen, it is supported by certain bio-*energetic adaptability, so only after four days, I can be sure that this bio-energetic support is ready to be activated again. Even if this is training and not a match, the conditions that need to be promoted will be analogous to those that as a team, the team reveals to work. Therefore, it's this logic that allows for continuity, and that is why I say that <u>systematic repetition</u> is the weekly expression of the respective Morphocycle*[10]. But then, this type of work, let's put it this way, of trainability, focuses principally on the whole, but the whole is guaranteed as a whole if the elements that are part of it as a whole do not lose maximum possibilities of expression in the whole, when the expression of the whole is required! But because training, thought this way, is concerned with the whole, the probability of not everyone being stimulated in the same way is a reality.*

So, how can I prevent that?! That is why I operationalise the Morphocycle bearing in mind that "if he played here, he needs four days to rest, he will train there". This time that separates both matches should be a time of recovery. How can I, while protecting recovery, ensure that the individuals, as players, are not losing possibilities? I should ensure that I provide them with stimulation that leads them to evolve even under these conditions, do I make myself clear or not? So, because the whole is made of parts, I need to ensure, or guarantee, that also the parts do not regress, and only working on the parts

---

organisational re-organisation successively higher (even if not linearly), which are only possible if the recovery from those efforts is completed. The adaptability that emerges from there arises from a process that represents some kind of biological resilience and does not aim for a higher response capacity in a situation of heightened fatigue, but instead a higher quality of performance through a better management of fatigue, safeguarding its perpetuation.

10 Weekly expression of the Morphocycle and systematic repetition: that is the reason why the Pattern Morphocycle is the nucleus, the core of the process, a methodological matrix that assumes itself as an invariance through its continuous repetition throughout time, in terms of logic, and not necessarily in terms of content. It is this methodological regularity that allows for stabilisation without crystallisation – hopefully - of the team's way of playing.

I can be sure of that[11]. So, imagining that the bio-energetic algorithm[12] may be, and so the colours...the symbolism of the colours, can be considered as having the need present, due to the specificity of the performance, of the eccentric contractions and also the need of muscular groups or muscular chains that are more involved, directly involved, required for the collective functionality, expressing themselves at the maximum speed of contraction. I thought that working on each of these aspects in those days that, if using a formal framework, would belong to the recovery period...by doing that without losing that recovery...working individually could contribute to the improvement and guarantee the individual development of the players.

So, this is a logic that must be respected without interruption, and that requires awarding significant importance not only to the duration of exercises as you mentioned earlier but also, and essentially, to the resting times between each exercise. And at this level of the Morphocycle, there can be many incoherencies, the dosing is something that I notice is often overlooked. Here it is, why? Because they are too influenced by the conventional, notice, you only need to practice once a week! In the eye of the conventional that is almost a crime, almost a crime. But when you are facing a framework of maximum demand, these conditions pose by themselves a need for this kind of attention and care. When it does not happen, of course, if you have sensitivity and intelligence you will have to admit "but, then..."...and that is why that it makes a lot of sense to highlight the importance of periods that emerge with two matches a week (with one match in the middle of the week), but even further, to highlight that the possibility of being in good conditions (without training) when that happens is something viable! Even if you have no control over the midweek match, so that is out of your control. But that does not happen when you have a normal Morphocycle. So, the biggest, let's say, confusion, lies here, and then it has to do with many other things, the lack of knowledge of the reality, also in what refers to...

For example, I gave away a few days ago, in a meeting I had with other coaches, a short text that must be around 40 years old. A key text for my

---

11 Hologrammatic principle: one of the foundational principles of complex thinking, allowing us to understand what Professor Frade refers to when he discusses the issue of reciprocal implications between the parts and the whole. Morin (2003, pp.108-109) clarifies that "in a physical hologram, the smallest point of the hologram's image contains the almost entirety of the information of the represented object. It is not only the part that is in the whole, the whole is also in the part. The hologrammatic principle is present in the biologic and sociologic worlds. The idea of hologram overcomes, not only the reductionism, which only considers the parts, but also the holism, which only sees the whole". He adds that "then, one can increase the knowledge of the parts through the whole, and of the whole through the parts, in the same movement, producer of knowledge". What seems especially relevant for football, if we consider that, as Morin suggests, "the anthropo-social relationship is complex, because the whole is in the part, which is in the whole". It should be highlighted that from the relationship of the whole with the parts but result different states of complexity of the whole. The whole may be less than the sum of the parts, equal to the sum of the parts, or more than the sum of the parts. But only the organised whole can be more than the sum of the parts.

12 Algorithm: a number of rules and 'step-by-step' for mathematical procedures or to reach a conclusion (Stacey, 1995). It is therefore a finite sequence of instructions, clearly defined and non-ambiguous, that abide to logic commands overseen by an objective. It is important to highlight that although the concept of algorithm is commonly illustrated by the example of a recipe, there are algorithms whose essence and operationalisation is much more complex due to the dynamic of the process that they try to respond to, and by the consequent, constant need of 'revision and refuelling', even if paradoxically it has to be a processual regularity. Just like it happens with the Pattern Morphocycle.

colleague and friend Monge da Silva, who was the first person in Portugal to lecture things systematically in relation to Sport Training, that has to do with the understanding of two principles. <u>The principle of self-renovation of living matter and the principle or Law of Roux, Arndt-Schulz[13]</u>. And it strikes me that people who have a contemporary connection with faculties do not know any of that. The interpretation of the text, as it is, can be mutilating, but if you look at it through what we know from systems theory nowadays, you can understand how important that text is, and how it is a guarantee of what I told you earlier.

So, a little ago I was saying that facing the <u>need for some resting time </u>so that the team is again ready to develop the same dynamics, the same functionality and all that, it implied considering that the Morphocycle would be filled with effort, game performance, recovery, training on Thursday, recovery, match on Sunday. And having said that a formal framework would lead us to recognise the possibility of the existence of a single training session, even in what refers to training, without losing the profile or the adaptability matrix, and therefore, the specificity. This specificity, considering the way how we want to play, so the identity of our team even if still on a Thursday we can contemplate it, through repetitions with some intermittence, in the continuity that is independent of the central aspects, with the Principles or primary game criteria of the team being respected.

And I said that if something like this is presenting to most people, this sounds like sacrilege, how can you only train once a week?

But it is essential that regarding operationalisation that is recognised! So how can the Morphocycle emerge then with three acquisitive days, so it's not only one, it's three, and two days of recovery, and the Saturday also for recovery[14]? And this here is about solving an apparent paradox, like I had already mentioned to you, in what should still be a recovery period, to which extend, without losing that recovery, can I consider an acquisitive training, that can be acquisitive without at the same time compromising recovery? There are only two ways to do this. Knowing it is an essential aspect of the way of playing which we are interested in we have the guarantee that will affect an individual, the individual more precisely. And we also have the possibility that that potential individual growth supported by an indicator, which are the eccentric contractions for example, but having in mind some aspects of how we want to play. These will happen with the use of a bio-energetic support that is similar to the bio-energetic backing of the web, the more global game matrix, which is...and we are able to make this happen under conditional circumstances, conditional circumstances that lead to this happening with a dominance[15] of

---

13 Principle of Self-Renovation and Law of Roux, Arndt-Schulz: in this interview there are several references to this principle. So, for further clarification of these principles and laws, it is advisable to read the text mentioned by Professor Vítor Frade, titled 'The cycle of self-renovation and the Law of Roux, Arndt-Schulz'.

14 Dominantly: it is crucial that when we talk about acquisitive or recovery days we are not taking it too literally. This means that we are referring to what is dominant in those days, acquisition or recovery, having as a reference what is collective, but never exclusively one or other type, because there may be the possibility/need in days which formally are considered of recovery, to take into account the individual dimension of the acquisitive aspect. This is a call for attention that maybe be useful here but also later on this interview, especially with regards to the patterns of sub-dynamics implied on each Morphocycle day (pattern of muscular contraction, metabolic pattern, experienced complexity, etc.).

15 Propensities: those "conditional circumstances that lead to...", determined by the purposes of our

libro
futbol
.com
AL GOL SE
LLEGA LEYENDO

259

the emergence of the mechanisms or the alactic anaerobic metabolism. So, these are the conditions on both Wednesday and Friday, and Thursday, that identify the presence of the same matrix or of the same so-called physiological pattern, or even better, bio-energetic. And therefore, it is the guarantee of this happening without interruption every week, that not only allows me to maintain the same bio-energetic profile but also concerning what I have to do, it gives me the possibility of improving or at least not regressing because I know that the individuals...that I am giving each of them the possibility of improving, but also, and this is a fundamental aspect, not emphasising for lack of respect for the conditions, or the conditional circumstances over the appearance as a dominant emergence, *of the alactic anaerobic mechanisms, and that the adaptability, the direction of that adaptability changes. Therefore, it remains unchanged, as there is the need for all training to promote fatigue, but that fatigue must be the necessary condition, protecting the required time for the initial conditions to return without representing an anomaly. This will happen if I don't respect the breaks for the consecutive appearance of these conditions or of these conditional circumstances of alactic anaerobiosis. This leads me to say that the adaptability must be the consequence of the presence of the same bio-energetic pattern every day, because otherwise it is not specific. And this presence is only guaranteed with a perfect understanding of the Morphocycle.*

For me this is essential, and then we can return to the first question you asked, that had to do with the exercising times and with the break times. Because if I don't allow for break times, so if I don't respect a profile of intermittence I have no guarantee that the dominant mechanism that is present to support the effort will be, in fact, the alactic anaerobic mechanism[16]. So, it

---

way of playing, the emergence of a propensity that allows what we desire to effectively happen (criteria that support our Game Principles, and more precisely, those that we prioritise in a certain instant or training unit), and to happen as we want it to happen, respecting a determined eventual logic and abiding to the pattern configuration of the sub-dynamics of the specific day. As it can be verified in this explanation, we include in a connected way the three Methodological Principles of Tactical Periodization (Principle of Propensities – "conditional circumstances that lead to..."; Principle of Complex Progression – what in a certain moment is a priority; Principle of Horizontal Alternation in specificity – respect for the pattern of the training unit).

16 Metabolisms or Energetic Systems: reinforcing what it is said in the interview, Paulo Santos (undated) refers that "to understand the energetic needs of any sport, in terms of training and competition, it is essential to know the sport profoundly. The success of any motor task requires the conversion of energy to be performed efficiently, in a direct proportion to the energetic needs of the skeletal muscles involved in that activity. It will be important to mention that the energetic expenditure depends on various factors, among which we can refer the exercise typology, frequency, duration, intensity, dietetic aspects, environmental conditions for exercising (altitude, temperature, humidity), the athlete's physical condition, and her muscular composition with regards to fibres (type I and II)". We should remember that the metabolic systems are generally classified in three types: a) Anaerobic alactic system or phosphagen system (ATP and phosphocreatine – PCr): uses the immediate sources of energy supply, which are also the most powerful (highest energetic contribution per time unit), usually associated with performances that require high metabolic intensity and short duration); b) Anaerobic lactic system or glycolytic systems or glycolysis: uses carbohydrates as energetic source, with energy production being the result of glycogen unfolding (way of storing the carbohydrates in the cells) as lactic acid, in a process called glycolysis that occurs at the level of the cytosol without intervention of oxygen. In energetic terms, it is more efficient than phosphagens, because it provides a higher quantity of energy globally, but is less powerful, because it requires more time to act. It can be predominantly found in high intensity, while non-maximal performances, with a relatively significant duration (even if short). Although it can generate a great production of energy, it has, as a nefarious consequence, the accentuation of metabolic acidosis due to

is through the <u>breaks</u> that I guarantee that possibility of, once again, having the guarantee that the fuel will allow for a certain type of effort and no other. So, you have a formula 1 car, a way of playing like Barcelona, but that car, that way of playing, can only work if supported if having as a dominant support a certain metabolic mechanism and not any metabolism. Therefore, just like in a formula 1 car, if you use diesel as a fuel, there is no point having a formula 1 car. If you put fuel with little octanes,[17] it will also not serve you well, so the pattern of the physiological level, or of the bio-energetic level you are interested in, is guaranteed through the perfect understanding of the Morphocycle, which is something that in reality is not always, or very little respected. Because if you do not respect the possibility of providing enough time so that the metabolic web that is the result of the continuous demand of that metabolic coordination which is required for your way of playing, if you do not respect the time required to be again in good condition for it to emerge, what will happen, what will happen is that you may produce the effort, but you will do it at the expense of the dominance of the glycolytic mechanisms, and therefore with the presence of lactic acid in the circulation. <u>So, in the continuity, inclusively</u> the adaptability that will be generated will have to do with that, you keep producing the effort but not in the ideal conditions in which you would produce that effort it the support was the same. That is only possible depending on the <u>guarantee of an uninterrupted presence of the Morphocycle as I understand it.</u> So, on a Friday it is the same or even worse than on a Wednesday. I need to guarantee, I need to make sure that what I am doing...On the one hand, my interest is experiencing it. And that is why the situations are more small-sided, but notice that I say reducing without impoverishing. You will only not impoverish if you don't touch the metabolic coordination and if what I am doing is related with a possible gain of

---

the accumulation of lactic acid, which is counterproductive when the aim is to achieve quality performances. c) Oxidative or aerobic system: metabolic process that occurs at the level of the mitochondria, responsible for energy production with the intervention of oxygen (aerobic) through the mitochondrial oxidation of glucose (derivative stored as a result of carbohydrates), lipids (fatty acids) and also amino acids (proteins). It is the least powerful metabolic system, but at the same time the one that has more absolute capacity, being therefore commonly associated with efforts of a higher duration. It is essential to highlight that none of these systems operates in isolation, no matter what a type of performance requires predominantly. All systems are permanently involved, even if at different levels.

17 Fuel, Diesel, Octanes: this metaphor refers to the way how metabolic systems can interfere with performance. In Tactical Periodization, it is suggested that the metabolic system which is predominantly implicated in the emergence of a good way of playing (formula 1) in training and in competition, should ensure a great 'combustion' potential. There is a belief that what determines and differentiates the good ways of playing is the possibility of operationalising the desired action, adjusted to the circumstances, and that action can be operationalised through a variety of ways (with acceleration, slowly, in deceleration, at high speed, in the air, on the floor, static, changing speed, ...). Therefore, the metabolic support that 'feeds' such action, or better, that interaction, must allow for all this. And this variability is only allowed if the incidence or dominant stimulation in the training process aims at the alactic anaerobic metabolism., the only that respecting the recovery times will allow for the development of the other metabolic ways. The adaptability that the process should promote, through its continuous stimulation and consideration of the need of recovery, must potentiate and occur supported by the best fuel for the desired way of playing. And if the desired way of playing, just like a formula 1 car, requires curving, accelerations, braking, changing speed...if it encapsulates all that variability, then it demands the best possible fuel, in this case the more adjusted. And the more adjusted is petrol with many octanes (in football type formula 1 is the phosphagen system) without mixing other fuels when you have to fill the tank. A recurring and continuous need when one trains in the limit and that need for fatigue and recovery is recognised.

specificity. Here already with a capital S. Therefore, even using the analogy of fractal geometry, you can notice people proposing small-sided games without considering if the number of times that the individuals will intervene is related to the number of times those individuals will intervene during the match in their roles/positions.

And if it isn't, what does this lead to?

It results in, bringing this to a continuity, an expression that is not related to the fuel with higher octanes but in the use of the glycolytic mechanisms. To be fractal, what has to be dominant here (in the reduction) is the dynamic of the fractal[18]. Are you following me?! If so...that is why it is an important characteristic...the effort being followed by the necessary time for being fresh so that when it restarts the maximum fuel is anaerobic alactic. So, for me, this is key, essential, and this promotes inclusively the adherence to a certain type of playing. Therefore, where in fact the guarantee of what is essential to promote, by the spontaneity that is requires from me or any other, can be supported on the dominance of the request of anaerobic alactic mechanisms.

This is fundamental inclusively even, due to the following, because the energy is brought by the participation of triphosphate adenosine, but triphosphate adenosine, the ATP[19], can be implicated in the metabolic process A, or B, or C. It is clear that there is no energy if there is no ATP present, and its breakdown, its synthesis or re-synthesis. But we have seen that if I am working using the anaerobic lactic, the phenomenology involved is not the same, inclusively changing the participation of not only the ATP receptors but also of the enzymes involved in all this. The contextual alteration is fundamental not only because a certain adaptability is installed, but moreover, and nowadays we are certain of this, and this you will hardly hear in any sports faculty in the World being put like this...the ATP that exists in the interior of the cells, neural or non-neural, has two roles, one...So the one that exists internally in the cell has that role that is providing energy, but it has another that is related to signalling, transmitting information. Now see if it is not...it shouldn't be difficult to accept that the information to be brought in connection with other cells and with the external environment is not the same if the metabolisms involved are different. Once again, the relevance of specificity and more, when there is a need for tiredness, for fatigue in the cells so that there is self-renovation. And the self-renovation occurs bringing this particularity that has been activated, when is gestation time is respected, so that they can again be...appear

---

18   Fractal: the propriety of fracturing in similar models. The fractal dimension measures the constant degree of irregularity of a chaotic model (Stacey, 1995, p.547). "Fractality propose an uncentred ethnocentrism (as it unveils the centre in the periphery), it claims the local-global, the micro-macro (a global built from the emergence of the local and a local built from the evidence of globality). The fractality predicts that the micro is not opposed to the macro, it knows the macro contains the micro, but it is the micro who identifies it, who provides identity to the macro" (Cunha e Silva, 1999, p.62).

19   ATP: Triphosphate adenosine. The cells need to possess mechanisms for energy conversion. Therefore, they need the presence of a substance that has the capacity to accumulate the energy that comes from exergonic reactions (reactions that release energy). It is equally mandatory that this substance is posteriorly able of providing that energy to the endergonic reactions (that consume energy). That substance exists in our cells and is called adenosine triphosphate, commonly known as ATP. ATP is a labile chemical compost that is present in every cell. It is a combination of adenosine, ribose, and three phosphate radicals. The two last phosphate radicals are connected to the rest of the molecule through high energy connections.

improved, so that is why I say that it is self-renovation that leads to self-generation. So, <u>through fatigue</u>...and therefore this is related to the Principle of Self-renovation and the Law of Roux, Arndt-Schulz.

Now see, if...they even say that this circumstantial collapse state of the functionality of any atom or any organ, is a state of parabiose[20]. Because it is a moment when the circumstances or the reality regresses regarding functionality so that it can restructure to perform in better conditions if there is respect for time to allow for a delayed effect. As this is played, there needs to be a significant stimulation, a strong stimulation! If I don't respect the conditions for this emergence, the fatigue that arises is not the same, it's another, and that has very negative consequences in the organism, and that is why it should lead us to <u>reflect</u>...and I usually joke, <u>the way people usually train</u>, not respecting this logic, does not lead to parabiose but instead to 'paranecrose'[21]. And the indicators of this are the constant inflammations of the body, the constant pain, and that is a symptom of, how can I put it...organic injury, an injury of the issues. When this injury of the tissues occurs, the body in order to react accordingly provokes changes in the way it works with the ATP, and the ADP that results from the emptying of the ATP due to the restructuration of what is weakened originates, for example, that in the bloodstream the ADP, adenosine diphosphate and the mono-phosphate end up also connecting to receptors and the result of this is, for example, the ADP being connected to the platelets and the platelets, for the need of, let's say, recomposing the wound that was generated, creates clots that obstruct something that should be free. See here how this is relevant, the <u>specificity!</u> But more, all this implies understanding <u>proprioception[22]</u> to its ultimate significance, including the

---

20 Parabiose: process that illustrate the merger of living elements. It is used here, as being motivated by the qualitative training stimuli, and aiming at the articulation that occurs with this phenomenon, after the de-structuration generated, merging a certain generation linked to the stimulus that motivated it. It is a process of self-organisation that conceptualises the organism and its constitutive parts as dissipative structures which can aspire to increasing levels of complexity. Cunha e Silva (1999) argues that the systems that constitute themselves far from the equilibrium, as they require continuous energetic and matter supply for maintenance purposes, are called dissipative structures. This author, in consonance with the idea, conceptualises the 'moving body' and the 'sporting body' as dissipative structures, suggesting that these use the hostility of the environment, and as such, of the disorder that the latter contemplates, to overcome itself. To create a new form of internal order with increased complexity. He further proposes that the thermodynamics of non-equilibrium (a key concept in the way Professor Vítor Frade conceptualises football training) establishes the connection between order and disorder and also the possibility of emergence of structures (resulting from the parabiose) in the systems that are away from the equilibrium. He adds, reinforcing the need for training to be operationalised at the borders of chaos, with the consequent need for states of parabiose, that far from the equilibrium, in 'excitable' environments, we can observe a type of essential solidarity, an associative intelligence that leads the elements of the system to cooperate, with the objective of creating more complex structures that can make it viable, presenting them with new opportunities.

21 Paranecrose: phenomenon analogous to the description of parabiose, but whose effects, due to the qualitative difference at the level of the stimulus, due to a lack of respect for the recovery time, promotes the death of living elements and consequent loss of complexity by the system. Laborit (1971) suggests that "the death of the organism results on the death of the organ, but the most usual is that the death of the organ results in the death of the organism".

22 Proprioception: involves several roles of the nervous systems from which result the sensation of balance, position and movement of parts of the limbs and body (Habib, 2003). Marisa Gomes clarifies that "proprioception is a beautiful word but...it has to do with what you said about the academy kid. Proprioception is a capacity of the game, of being able to play, even when static, but being static in

eventual problem of the different mechanoreceptors as well[23]. Therefore, the importance of this <u>specificity</u> being guaranteed, and <u>guaranteed with regards to what?!</u> The framing that I want to see. Aspiring to play in a certain way <u>should not make me forget the present</u> because I get to the future depending on the trainability that I promote, and this involves the circumstances that are complex as hell! That is why I find a quote by Mark Twain amusing, which says that when a person's favourite tool is a hammer, then for him all problems will be nails. So, if we realise at a bare minimum that this is something complex, the tool must be complex too, with different degrees of complexity, but it must be complex! So, I return to my initial question, that I referred was already included in my doctoral application, the problem of causality.

I will tell you a story that happened very recently: I was watching a match between Benfica and FC Porto, under-15s, seating next to many Porto coaches, and a goalkeeper coach. And during the match, because Benfica had scored, Porto was playing near the opposing box, and the goalkeeper would adjust and position himself regularly on the limit of his own box so he would move, adapting sub-consciously to the circumstances. And the goalkeeper coach that was standing next to me starts shouting the name of the goalkeeper until he finally acknowledges the coach, who tells him not to leave the goal so often, because if... And that has a lot to do with the fact that "we should have assistant coaches, goalkeeper coaches, this and that", and how that can be a problem and makes me question that necessity at times. So, what happened? That interfered with the goalkeeper's spontaneity. How did we concede the two goals? Balls played to the middle of the centre-backs, on their back, the goalkeeper had to move from where he was to fight for the ball with the striker, and in both cases, the striker got there first and scored. Now, I ask, what if the goalkeeper coach had not shouted from the stand? Probably he would be at least a metre ahead, and he would not have conceded any of those goals.

It is not enough to talk about extreme sensitivity to the initial conditions[24]. These are expressions that we get from somewhere else, like fractals, but the reality is complex. So, I need to take into account the circumstances, and I consider these circumstances more or less depending on how I understand the logic of life, in this case, or the logic of reality. Therefore, on the one hand for the <u>acquisitive</u>, it cannot be any acquisitive. It has to be 'the' acquisitive. And it cannot be the acquisitive without the conditions for the acquisition of the acquisitive because otherwise that assimilation is not performed, and the conditions of the acquisitive imply that either in relation to the whole, or the

---

such a way that the player can intervene in the context, that is another expression of proprioception and proprioception is not only touching the ball, it's knowing how to touch the ball, it's doing so while considering the circumstances".

23 Mechanoreceptors: specialised receptors that can be found in the most diversified structures of the body (skin, muscles, tendons, ligaments, joint capsules, and very likely, in the bones too) and have the task of continuously sending information to the nervous system about the status of the body in each moment. The neuromuscular spindle and the Golgi Tendon Organ (GTO) are muscular receptors. There are also joint receptors like the Pacinian corpuscles, the Meissner corpuscles (both of fast adaptation), the Ruffini corpuscles and the Merckel receptors (slow adaptation). It is also important to mention the existence of skin receptors in different layers, like the corpuscles of Meissner and Pacini.

24 Extreme sensitive to initial conditions: "amplifying property of non-linear feedback mechanisms, meaning that minor changes may increase until a long-term change of behaviour is reached" (Stacey, 1995, p.548).

quasi-whole, or the individual, lead them to fatigue, to exhaustion, and allow time for the recovery to happen, so that they can be ready for that.

Roughly, this is what both the cycle of self-renovation and the Law of Roux, Arndt-Schulz refer to. They say that in any activity – they say physical activity, but it happens in any activity -, when we invest in it, it influences the organs, the systems, and the roles. I would even add, the individuals and with regards to football, the _individual in co-relation and co-difficulty,_ because there are the other guys, what makes it complicated. But it exerts on the individual, and if the activity has the symbolic side as significant, it has the side of previous intentions, of the intentionalised, meaning, the game criteria that we are look-ing for. Or, if you prefer, the Game Principles that we are looking for has over the Man as a psycho-biological unit, or even socio-psycho-biological because it is 'a society'. And what Tactical Periodization and the Morphocycle want is that this is considered, and that is considered _without excluding_ the capturing sensitivity of the individuals concerning the circumstances. And therefore this has to do with the first timing of expression of the parts of the body involved, therefore in the co-contractibility[25] that has to occur so that the movement of the body is fluid, and in how this occurs depending on the need to adjusted the circumstances to the surroundings and that many times is decodable in anticipation. But to be that it needs...it's not the problem of decision-making, because it can be wrong. It's a problem of choices, and the familiarisation with a context gives me that advantage, predicting, anticipating the decisions that I need to make and that I will do better when the body is used to it or when a somatisation has occurred. And this has to do with the second timing.

So, what do the first and the second principle tell us about reinforcement? What is the role, they call it functional load because they say there must be a stimulation, but they always do it in individual terms, they do it inclusively with each metabolism, saying that each of them has a different time of replen-ishment, they talk about the delayed effect of loads. But what we care about is the delayed effect of performance, our performance. The performance is a performance that demands a certain 'romance' among metabolisms. I need to know in advance which 'romance' I am looking for, and after finding that out and having this knowledge, I can make it happen. Therefore, this stimulation is a metabolic acceleration, they even call it a 'metabolic turmoil', that lead those things implicated to de-structure and restructure and therefore reappear improved. But these are the responsible for a very significant involvement, very strong and critical in the consumption of oxygen, with the internal respi-ratory processes of the tissues and with the...therefore associated to the oxi-dative phosphorylation and this acceleration of the activation of these things allows the human organism that trains, training under certain conditions, to perfect itself and self-renovate.

In the end, what they say is that this _self-renovation,_ is the way life and atoms exist, or those albuminoid bodies, as they say, the mode of existing or of existence consists in the constant renovation through themselves, of those implied bodies. Deep down, deep down, of the chemical components of their bodies, and an alteration occurs...sometimes there is only the need for a pro-

---

25 Co-contractibility: mechanism of muscular contraction in which more than one muscle receive an innervation message to contract, but in which the excitation is more intense for the agonists than for the antagonists. A contractile coordination that involves very importantly the mechanoreceptors and similarly its desired acculturation.

ton (H+) to change or a calcium or sodium ion so that things change radically. This was proven a long time ago through the labelling or the method of atom labelling. So, we can say that the <u>atomic composition of our body</u> renews itself endlessly and continuously or even perpetually. Now, that renovation is performed much faster that it was once thought, and that is why they say there is a kind of 'metabolic turmoil', but we have already seen, or we know that depending on the dominance of the metabolisms involved, a or b, time is not the same, we need to know when we do...That is why that I talk concerning recovery that I say that <u>recovery is achieved</u> by recovering with intermittent points where this metabolism, this metabolic web that results from the romance and the continuous 'marriage', is also activated, although shortened in its length. Its nature is the same, but the duration is different when prodding the same metabolism.

What is claimed is the opposite, look, this makes no sense to me, so you got tired due to a complex whole, and now you are acting on the aerobic metabolism and you are recovered!! Rubbish! What happens is that, and that is why I mentioned earlier on than when maximal exertion happens with fatigue resulting from it because the ATP or phosphocreatine stocks are temporarily emptied, in this state the aerobic activation is high, after it, depending on the great need for oxygen. The residual side of the lactic acid is suppressed or swept depending then on the arrival of oxygen, so during the break, that due to this existence is designated of anaerobic exercise, I don't know if it is. For me, it is not, because, in fact, I don't die after, I am resting and at that time what is happening is something totally different. Therefore, the metabolic processes develop rapidly in everything that is living matter in a constant self-renovation and that in this case, because it aims to be oriented, self-generative, and is intentional, <u>it is therefore essential that one knows what it is meant when in Tactical Periodization we discuss the Tactical dimension.</u>

The Tactical dimension only exists a priori as a theoretical configuration, a conceptualisation of what I aspire to, as a hypothesis. Because what is Tactical, what belongs to the Tactical, is what exists in Barcelona. Even when Barcelona is playing bad, you say that it is Barcelona playing, so it is <u>an intentionalised organisation</u> because they want to be in a certain way when they have the ball. They want to do things in a certain way, and when they don't have the ball they want to...that is the Tactical Dimension. <u>That is nothing that exists a priori,</u> it exists after as an <u>emergence</u>[26]. That is why it is said, "oh, the game model..."! No, the Game Model is nothing that I can say, it's this, it's that, no. That sets the boundaries of the Model's moderation because <u>the Model is when you want Barcelona playing</u> and say: "no, their game model is

---

26 Emergence: "emergence is a complex organisational structure that grows from simple rules. The emergence means unpredictability in the sense that small events cause great and qualitative changes in big events. The emergence is a law of nature to which human beings are submitted to" (Laughlin, 2005). Henry Atlan (2011) highlights that these phenomena can be observed in different scientific domains – epigenetic, physical-chemical, cognitive and in social sciences, because each cannot avoid an analysis to those complex systems. He adds that in these systems, a great number of elements interact with each other, in such a way that the global behaviour of the system cannot be predicted and understood from any of its elements. He classifies these as non-trivial emergence phenomena, characterised not only by the global results being larger than the sum of its constitutive properties, but also by the unpredictability of the result, at least in a detailed manner. Finally, he refers that it is a certain dose of serendipity, random disturbances, called noise by the theory of information and fluctuations in thermodynamics, that introduce an unpredictable novelty in those emergence phenomena.

a line of three and one loose guy...", But when they are doing it! It's a soma-tisation of certain values, certain categories, certain principles, certain criteria, and whatever.

Then, you can easily see that even within the Methodological Principles, and I get upset when some guys try to come up with more Methodological Principles, it's a lack of understanding that the Methodological Principle is one, but complexity is complex! And I must, without losing the unbreakable wholeness, 'breaking it down', keeping it present. And that is why I say that Specificity is related to the conjecture, it belongs to the theoretical, the con-ceptual, the values, it's a judgement of value, it's a way of playing that I choose. "No, we will play this way". It's an idea of playing that I extract from the conceptualisation of the game of football. The conceptualisation of the game of football has to do with the rules that football has so that it can be football. Otherwise, it's rugby, that belongs to the conceptualisation. From there I extract...it belongs to the axiology, it belongs to the values, it belongs to the judgement of value, it is a judgement of value that I have to make with regards to the way how I want to play. The Specificity is there but as a draft, because it is the only Specificity with a capital S when it happens as emer-gence. But even that way maybe with a capital S and between inverted com-mas, or better, with suspension points, because it won't stop growing at the level of the whole, at the level of quality uninterruptedly, and inclusively at the level of variability. That is why I say that the quality of the way of playing, then the option I have for the way of playing, occurs depending on the possibility of evolving at the same time the maximisation of redundancy. Or in other words, what is identifiable, what I said a while ago about Barcelona that even when playing badly, everyone can recognise that is Barcelona playing. With what? With the variability, the maximisation of variability. That is why the orienting principles must be present every week as context, as the background theme that allows me to improvise. It belongs to the meso and especially to the micro; I never have two equal matches, at the macro level, every match is the same because otherwise I...or almost the same, because otherwise, I cannot distin-guish Barcelona from Real Madrid, etc., etc., etc....

This means that...see...the importance or need for the Methodological Principle of Horizontal Alternation in specificity, I put specificity in lower case, because I alternate, giving contour to the Specificity, and inclusively having in mind the individual or considering the whole. But notice, how do I do that? Us-ing what contents? Contents that refer to the way how I want to play, contents that favour the emergence of what I am looking for, so they are propensities. And then, at the beginning of the season, I do it the same way as later? No. There is the Complex Progression. That is why I talk about a connective pat-tern, and this pattern appears when I respect the weekly Morphocycle without interruptions. So, this self-renovation or self-generation does not occur auto-matically as thought before, even if we know that a guy that spent two months sick or three in bed without walking when we finally got up, he could not manage to walk. Even if that was known, it was thought that it was some kind of natural law...no, you need...the processes of self-renovation are actioned, they are put to work. And for them to be actioned in a more appropriate man-ner without...there needs to be exhaustion, they need to be fatigued, and that is what the Law of Roux, Arndt-Schulz says. It is the value of the load, they said, the value of the stimulus is substantial, and it cannot be strong immedi-ately after without this happening. And it will only be achieved if the time for parabiose, and the phase of exaltation as they call it, or overcompensation, *occurs...Only through, they say the functional load, I call it performance. By the performance, or as they say, the functional load, resides the organism's excitation or, if you prefer, is the state of the whole organism. Again, the relevance of a correct understanding of the Methodological Principle of Horizontal Alternation in specificity, and it is so that nowadays everyone knows that what we have regarding neurological does not appear all at the same time, it is not born with us straight away. No, the neural plasticity, today we know that it is a reality, so what is happening is defining or influences that neural aspect. And today we know that even in the relationship between the myofibrils[27] and the neurons[28] and the information that passes to the brain, the heart, etc., etc... the glia[29] is very relevant, a kind of frontier of the nervous system, like the logic of participation and interference of the sympathetic and parasympathetic nervous systems. <u>Therefore</u>, the loss of specificity is the loss of all this.*

We can synthesise saying that either the glandular cell or the muscular fibre or the myofibrils or the nervous cell get worn when they work, when they are trained, when they are requested and especially when they are requested entirely, with an emotion linked to it. That is why the playing, the competition, is the essential nature of training. So, they are <u>worn, exhausted, fatigued.</u>

Even though for myself and for Tactical Periodization training means learning, it is about learning a way of playing, it is about learning in certain circumstances and only...that is why I initially told you about the <u>conception</u> people have of <u>learning,</u> either by reception or discovery, because by reception, it

---

27 Myology: the muscle is coated by a layer of connective tissue – epimysium – and there are fasciculi that, despite their small dimensions, are visible to the naked eye. Only microscopically can the functional units of the muscle be observed: the muscle fibres, which are also coated by sheath of the same connective tissue – endomysium. The muscular fibres may have different dimensions and each muscular fibre is enveloped in a membrane – the sarcolemma – and just like the other cells, it is composed by multiple organelles situated in the sarcoplasm (the cytoplasm of muscular fibres). This space is penetrated by a very dense net of small transversal tubules – t-tubules – that ensure the communication and transport of substances throughout the whole muscular fibre. The fibres possess a net of membranous channels as well – sarcoplasmic reticulum – whose main function is to release and store calcium ($Ca2+$) during all stages of muscle contraction and relaxation, respectively. The muscular fibres are also composed by numerous myofibrils, which are the contractile units of the muscle, and that are themselves composed by even smaller units – sarcomeres – with three bands (I band – light zone; A band – dark zone; H band – medium part of the A band). Within these bands we can also distinguish small protein filaments, ones thicker than others. The thinnest ones are actin and the thickest myosin. These are the two most important contractile proteins of the skeletal muscle. Myosin is composed by two intertwined filaments that end in a protuberance designated as myosin head. These structures, when in contact with actin, allow for the muscular contraction. Each muscular fibre is innervated by a motor nerve – motoneuron. The group of muscular fibres, together with the motor neuron that innervates them, is called motor unit. All the fibres of the motor unit have the same characteristics. They are all from the same type, which means that in one motor unit there are no different types of fibres. The skeletal muscle is characterised by the presence of different types of muscular fibres, that are usually classified in three types, depending on their metabolic profile and speed of contraction: type I (slow and oxidative), type IIa (fast oxidative-glycolytic) and type IIb (fast glycolytic). (Soares, 2005)

28 Neuron: "Main cellular unit for the transformation of information within the nervous system that normally is constituted by a cellular body (soma), dendrites and an axon" (Wolfe, 2004, p.183)

29 Glial cells: one of the two biggest types of nervous cells. The other is the neuron. The glial cells are present in a 10:1 ratio in comparison to the neuros and are also known as inter-neurons. They transport nutrients, allow for a rapid recovery of other nervous cells and can create its own communications network. Glia is the short term for 'neuroglia' (Jensen, 2002).

means that you...the primacy is in the frontal cortex, in the rationality, so the circuit to be established is very different if the primacy is in the brainstem[30]. The primacy is only in the brain stem when you are required to act, carrying the emotion with it, independently of you placing feelings in that after, or an understanding of the principles or the reasoning about this. So, the logic is not the same, and Damasio's recent book clarifies that well. This way of training and this way of playing <u>demand, when they occur,</u> the expenditure of highly energetic substances. The glycogen, for example, the phosphocreatine or cre-atine-phosphate and fundamentally the tri-phosphate adenosine acid (ATP). <u>Resting, recovery, the break is a sine qua non requirement,</u> and that is why I say that the break is more important than the effort itself, because only with the existence of the break, like I tried to explain, will I have the initial condi-tions for the desirable implication of the effort in this case.

That is why I told a while ago that understanding this is almost choosing a way of playing football. That is why I like Barcelona's way of playing so much. The resting after a drill, after exercising and...<u>but exercising what?!</u> With what?! And the <u>fatigue</u> that is not an ordinary resting state. It is, in fact, <u>a deliberate resting state.</u> It is not pragmatic, it's praxiological because the practice has logic and it is deliberate with regards to what we are looking for and depending on how it is brought to life. Therefore, the fatigued organ or organism <u>are converted during rest</u> in the accentuation of self-renovation if we wish, or self-renovate, self-generate as I like saying and this leads them, if the

---

30 Brainstem: structure usually presented as a primitive brain which deserves the attention of author and neuroscientist Antonio Damasio in his recent book 'Self Comes to Mind' – especially with regards to the construction of human consciousness. In this book, Damasio inverts all the existing paradigms that surround the role of consciousness, by presenting the brainstem as the key unit. He explains that "the brain does not start constructing consciousness, the conscious mind, at the level of the cerebral cortex, but at the level of the brainstem" (Damasio, 2010, p.41). "But contrary to tradition and conventions, I believe that the mind is not made in the cerebral cortex alone. Its first expressions emerge at the level of the brainstem. The concept that the mental processing has at the level of the brainstem is so little conventional that it does not even suffice to say it has little popularity...This concept, and the one that claims that the primary emotions occur in the brainstem are interconnected" (2010, p.103). The author clarifies that the brainstem does not play an exclusive role but is clear in stating that the human con-sciousness needs as much the cerebral cortex as it needs the brainstem. "The grand symphonic piece that is consciousness encompasses the foundational contributions of the brain stem, forever hitched to the body, and the wider-than-the-sky imagery created in the cooperation of cerebral cortex and sub-cortical structures, all united harmoniously, propelled to the future, in a continuous movement that can only be interrupted by sleep, anaesthesia, brain function or death." (Damasio, 2010, p.44). This book reinforces also the need for a permanent interaction between the non-conscious and conscious levels to live. More objectively, and in what regards football, these ideas reinforce the possibility of the con-comitant development of a 'know-how' and a 'knowledge about the know-how'. However, the relevance and the role of the brain stem highlights the need for a primacy of action in that aspiration, just like with survival. So, it is starting from the 'know-how' that players do, that we should trigger that knowledge about the know-how, the conscious realisation of what they are doing. In summary, it requires that in methodological terms the primacy is in the action, in doing, practicing, and not in the rationalisation, even if it does not ignore it at all. "There are two types of action control, conscious and non-conscious but the non-conscious control can be partially shaped by the conscious control. Human childhood and adolescence take the inordinate amount of time that they do because it takes a long, long time to ed-ucate the nonconscious processes of our brain and to create, within that nonconscious brain space, a form of control that may work, in a more or less reliable way, in accordance to intentions and conscious objectives. We can describe this slow education as a process of partial transfer of the conscious control to a nonconscious server, and not simply the offer of conscious control to the unconscious forces that can provoke chaos in human behaviour." (Damasio, 2010, p.332)

process is well driven, to accentuating its capacities and its potential, so referring to the animated operations of renovation and of its components. That is why I mentioned parabiose and paranecrose. 'Paranecrose' is something I invented, you cannot find this...

We can say and notice how this is relevant because it considers the oxygen important connecting it with an indexation; therefore the fatigued organism absorbs willingly, avidly, the oxygen, but where it absorbs the oxygen more willingly is precisely after an alactic effort. Now, the alactic effort is only alactic, especially if its more in its power than in its capacity if its duration is short. And then the absorption of oxygen is in fact, further to the substances that are nutrients, that are needed especially after the effort. And with this assistance, the <u>fatigued body recovers itself, restructures itself, re-functionalises itself,</u> replacing inclusively the substances used by new ones. All this is achieved, produced, operationalised, <u>modelled,</u> under the de-toning effect of oxygen. Oxygen that is, in fact, a key element for the re-synthesis and the reconstitution of phosphocreatine and ATP that are exhausted when the effort is performed. The reconstitution occurs, and if the text is conventional, if it has an analytical reading it says all this, <u>you only need to put on a different pair of glasses.</u> Therefore, the <u>reconstitution</u> does not only occur at the starting level, like a kind of natural law, therefore regularly, <u>going beyond</u> that reconstitution, the structuralism, and consequently that functionality. <u>But a matching functionality,</u> one that protects a certain logic and certain principles that is what Tactical Periodization aims to achieve by leading to the presence of three Methodological Principles and the emergence of a connective pattern through the realisation, or as I prefer to say, through <u>the weekly expression of the Morphocycle.</u> So, a super-reconstitution is obtained, as they put it, or a super-compensation, or a phase of exaltation as they also say and during this circumstance, there is more glycogen, more phosphocreatine in the muscle, as they say, more nitrogenated albumin[31]. And what else?! <u>The acquisitive Specific. As this is done</u> conditioned to the dominance of the acquisitive Specific, <u>the way in which it is articulated is not any, it's one...!</u>

That is why I get agitated when people talk about "the tension day, the strength day and the speed day". No, it is about bringing the muscular units, or the essential muscular groups to operate under certain conditions, but with the objective of doing something in more individual terms or in more collective terms, that has to do with the way I intend us to play.

Now look, when you add all this together, when this happens, when the existence of this process is protected, especially this addition of ATP, of the ATP reserves, therefore of the adenosine triphosphate acid... Thanks to this accumulation of new energetic loads, let's put it this way, the improvement of the fuel's octanes, <u>the exercising capacity is altered, and it is specifically</u>

---

31 Albumin: a protein with high biological value, the main protein of the blood plasma, synthesised in the liver through the hepatocytes. The replenishment of albumin is used, in the medicine, to treat severe burns and haemorrhages. It can also be used for the recovery of patients that underwent plastic surgeries like lipo-suction, because the albumin helps easing swelling. The normal concentration of albumin in animal blood is between 3.5 and 5 grams per decilitre and constitutes around 50% of plasmatic proteins. The albumin is fundamental for the maintenance of osmotic pressure, necessary for the correct distribution of bodily fluids between the intra-vascular and extra-vascular compartments located among the tissues. The main roles of albumin are related to the regulation of the following aspects: maintenance of osmotic pressure, transport of thyroidal hormones, transport of liposoluble hormones, transport of free fatty acids, transport of unconjugated bilirubin, competitive union with calcium ions and pH control.

changed, but during what?! During the stage that comes after the break time so that the reconstitution can occur, the <u>exaltation phase</u> as they call it. This is the stage that brings the organism, or brings the organ, or brings the atoms, or brings the added ATP, improved. <u>So, it's in that stage that I must focus on</u> the new stimulation, so it's in this moment that I need to focus. It is precisely this cycle that, like they call it and like they represented it through the cycle of self-renovation. But then the Law, or the so-called Law of Roux, Arndt-Schulz, says that if the functional load...and I say if the performance is not repeated the exaltation phase diminishes and disappears progressively. <u>Therefore, the importance of</u> continuity even in the biggest discontinuity. This <u>pattern of intermittence which guarantees</u> the existence not only in the alternation in the Morphocycle in a group of training units but also in the training units themselves is absolutely indispensable. That is why I said earlier on that the Law of Roux, Arndt-Schulz refers to the value of the functional load, <u>to the value of the performance</u> that triggers all the other processes that we mentioned earlier, but <u>all these processes must be linked to what we are looking for</u>.

They say this may be expressed in the following way: an excessively extreme excitation destroys the cellular functions, and it is extreme not only due to the, let's say, intensity of the load but also by not respecting the time required for reconstitution. So, they say, great excitation, great in the <u>optimal sense</u> are the ones that improve and allow us to overcome. The great is the <u>maximum relative intensity</u> so, with <u>maximum concentration,</u> they must be <u>playing,</u> and this is only maximum when I am <u>fresh, I</u> cannot find a better word than this. So, all the normal ones are of no interest, and the poor ones diminish. These <u>concepts</u> of extreme, great, normal and poor, these are <u>categories of the axiological framework,</u> and therefore <u>judgements of value</u> that I must identify concerning the way of playing that I choose. So, if they are categories they are judgements of value. And they can be extreme, great, and in this case the great ones, that is why I talk about maximum relative intensity, <u>are exerted over the scales of the</u> hypothetic Specificity, and therefore the maximised Specificity, either it is global, intermediate, individual or through the exaltation that Specificity to contribute towards a qualitative improvement of the emerging Specificity. <u>This should find support on</u> individualised repercussions, the Self-Eco-Hetero.

So, what is this? It is what I refer to when, regarding Tactical Periodization, I talk about the relationship between two dynamics, <u>the dynamic of the effort and the dynamic of performance.</u> Effort must be performance, it must characterise the performance, so that the effort is specific, within boundaries, convenient. And it is this <u>dominance of the performance dynamic</u> that leads me to <u>the dynamic of adaptability, but what? There needs to be another dynamic here, the dynamic of recovery,</u> because otherwise...there can be a lot of good will, but there is no recovery. That is why when Friday is used as it usually is, with a lot of goodwill – Hell has loads of that! And not only with long-term repercussions in the cells, because they have already been getting injured with the reaction of the organism, and many injuries are due to that and people cannot see it. Look, if you are familiar with or linked to the Principle of Horizontal Alternation in specificity, you are necessarily connected to the Principle of Propensities. Because it is with contents related to the way of playing, that I believe we can favour the appearance of contexts in which the relationship promotes a certain type of emergences, but it is also essentially marked out by the Principle of Complex Progression. This <u>recovery is achieved in connection with</u> the pattern of effort! So, to finish, we could say: performances, or as they say, functional loads, if they are repeated next to each other, it won't work. In such a way that the new efforts, if this happens, will be achieved before the processes of restoration allow the achievement of the initial and higher level, of a level that is better than the one we began with.

What is the conclusion when this happens? The outcome is that if I do not respect the Morphocycle (and that is why in the beginning I said that everything lies on the understanding of the Morphocycle), exhaustion will occur, the guys will say they are tired.

That is why it's very important that we recognise that we are colonised by a traditional way of thinking, by a traditional way of feeling, by a traditional way of reflecting, a traditional way of training, and these are cultural reinforcers[32] that lead several people to think and feel in the same way. So, the convention has its foundations in the concept of the athlete, it's about running more, running faster, running longer, and jumping higher, and even individually. The so-called universal biological principles can be all and nothing. The so-called rational principles of the game have no collective characteristics, the principle of penetration, where is the collective sense in that? Containment, what does that shit have to do with the pressing zone? And all that influences us consciously, and even worse subconsciously.

When this happens (alienating the freshness) I make an effort and go, but I go at the expense of other fuel that is not the one I should be interested in. Therefore, this system of reinforcers that any culture possesses, and the western has those that I was, in fact, saying were essential, and all that is not necessarily to throw in the bin, that's why I mentioned the example of the text. I grabbed it 40 years after to give them, and none knew about it, it was Chinese! I said: "look, this is all wrong and all right. It is all right if I use the glasses of Tactical Periodization, of systems theory, or the glasses of the second cybernetics, or the glasses of fractal geometry, etc., etc., etc....This is all right!" You only need to reconvert it.

We can say that it is fundamental to recognise that in a certain culture there is a system of reinforcers, and the individuals have preferential behaviours depending on those. They have preferential thought processes depending on those, they have preferential habits, preferential subconsciousness. Therefore, there are common reinforcers within a great number of people, and the so-called universal biological principles, overload, specificity, reversibility, adaptation, but these are notions or categories that...there is polysemy in here. It is all almost correct, without being correct. Even though the concept of load bothers me because for me the donkeys are the ones that have to deal with loads, right?! And football should be a pleasure...that is why it is difficult for people to imagine that if training three times a week is a pleasure, but under these conditions..." you don't have to train more", and in fact mostly due to the existing conventional reinforcers.

But we know that certain stimulating or stimulatory conditional circumstances that are continuously brought to life, under the same conditions or

---

32 On the topic of cultural reinforcers: "We cannot run our kind of life, in the physical and social environments that have become the human habitat, without reflective, conscious deliberation. But it is also the case that the products of conscious deliberation are significantly limited by a large array of nonconscious biases, some biologically set, some culturally acquired, and that the nonconscious control of action is also an issue to contend with". (Damasio, 2010, p.335)

under similar conditions, are 'stimuli' that are received by perceptual-sensorial mechanisms and by energetic mechanisms and by adaptation mechanisms, that with time, if the relationship between effort and recovery is protected, will lead to an adaptability. I don't know but many times, the understanding of people is low with regards to this, and that is why it is difficult to recognise... because what characterises the nature of playing, of competition...what is it? It's the multiple interactions. And more or less, more or less complex, this has to be always the dominant context, and I have to know that the causality linked to this is non-linear. I need to take this into account to propose, as I need to take this into account to think, that is why many times the quantification or the evaluation of what is happening can be done with probabilities, I need several times to notice a tendency or some tendencies, a regularity and all that.

I get back to the ATP because I have given out a text very recently to some of the staff at FC Porto and not only. And I would say that this is something that is out of the domain for 90% of the people, if not more, including those working in academia around the World. But there is a lot of evidence to back it up, even though it has been seeking acceptance for decades. It is about the effects of ATP, it being something else other than the supplier of energy and this something else is very important and especially for what we are interested in, the cooperative or coordinative synchronism within a whole that is the team that we have. But with regards to what I was mentioning in the Morphocycle, with regards to the importance of the Morphocycle, with regards to the importance of training and getting tired, recovering in order to get tired again and being able to get tired without getting to that point, meaning, to improvement, and so there is the cumulative and adverse effect.

So, the effects of ATP in the blood vessels, for example, that text that I gave referred key aspects, regarding the ATP's dual functionality. And it said that in the moment of contraction, in the moment of contraction of the vessels, the cells...so, it's a "stress", it's a tension that is exerted by the need to do something. The contraction occurs in the vessels, so who comes to assist us or the muscles so that they can work is the sympathetic nervous system. The cells of the sympathetic nervous system, at this moment, release ATP together with a neurotransmitter[33], so the ATP is also a neurotransmitter, something that will lead some people to say: "here we go, this guy is again inventing something", they cannot even be bothered to go and do some research. So, it gathers, together with the ATP, a neurotransmitter that is noradrenaline. The ATP connects to the receptors of the muscular cells that shape the walls of the vessels, causing a rapid contraction so that the blood can flow, etc.

But then, not only is this like this...this logic can be impeded if we are stressed or whatever. But if we know it is this way, and if we know that this is how the effort we aim for looks like it's about contracting and relaxing (in the blood vessels, dilating), so we can also help, getting the organism used to do this. And if we do not allow the tissues to get injured, we are doing even bet-

---

33 Neurotransmitters: biochemical messengers that allow the communication among neurons. Its typology is diverse, with more than 50 different types. Usually they act as an excitatory stimulus of a neighbouring neuron or as an inhibitor supressing the activation of the electrical impulse that travels from the cellular body through the axon (extension of the neurons that transports the impulses to the other neurons).

ter. _Dilation_ is the responsibility of epithelial cells[34], that under tension being under tension due to what one aims to achieve, release ATP as well. So, the ATP connects to certain p2y receptors, in the nearby epithelial cells and the blood vessel, or the arteries, relax due to that, and also due, it seems, to the nitric oxide[35], I think you say it like that.

For us, this is fundamental, very important because this has to do with what?

With the changes in the bloodstream, which is what must happen when we are working, and it must be smooth, it must be fluid as well. When these changes occur, there is a permanence tension, and that needs to be more and less, it's like the contraction, and then it has to do with the sodium and with the calcium[36]. Here when they produce that tension, in the epithelial cells, which coat therefore the walls of the vessels, they release ATP. When the ATP is released, it will activate the receptors in the nearby epithelial cells, so there are specific receptors to which the ATP is directed, and if it is ADP or AMP there will be others, and this is not irrelevant. When this happens, the ATP travels to the receptors of the respective cells and releases the nitric oxide that will allow the vessels to relax. If anything is impeding the fluidity of the process, then the system will break down. This happens when there is overtraining.

There is a functional oscillation in many teams, but that is why there should be a lot of reflection on Barcelona's way of training...see, in the traditional...

---

34 Epithelial cells: groups of cells that form a tissue called epithelium in a juxtaposed way. Its main functions are the coating of the external surfaces of the body, organs and internal cavities. In this interview, Professor Frade is referring to the epithelial cells that coat the walls of the blood vessels. The perfect union between the epithelial cells makes these cells efficient barriers against the penetration of invasive agents and the loss of bodily fluids. Nonetheless, they are selectively permeable to allow, for example, the necessary exchanges between the bloodstream and the cells of various tissues.

35 Nitric oxide: also known as nitrogen monoxide and azote monoxide, it is represented by the chemical formula NO1. It is a soluble gas, highly lipophilic, synthesised by the endothelial cells, macrophages, and a certain group of neurons in the brain. It is important for intra and extra-cellular signalling, and acts by inducing guanylyl cyclase, which produces cyclic guanosine monophosphate (cGMP), which among other effects, leads to the relaxation of the smooth muscle, provoking, as biological actions, the dilation of the vessels and bronchi.

36 Muscular contraction: for the muscle to contract, it needs a stimulus that comes from an impulse propagated through the motor nerve. When that impulse gets to the nerve endings, these produce a substance – acetylcholine (ACh) that acts as a facilitator in the transmission of that electrical impulse. This neurotransmitter connects to the receptors in the fibre membrane (sarcolemma) and, if the quantity of ACh is sufficient, an electric charge is created, and propagated throughout the whole fibre (action potential). This impulse is transmitted through the t-tubules and the sarcoplasmic reticulum to the interior of the cell. The arrival of the impulse leads to the release of the calcium stored (Ca2+) by the reticulum, which is directed to the interior of the cell. At rest, tropomyosin (one of the proteins that make the actin filaments) prevents the connection of the myosin heads to the actin, impeding consequently the possibility of contraction due to an absence of contact points. With the entrance of Ca2+, it connects to the troponin (one of the proteins that make the actin filaments), provoking the removal of the tropomyosin and allowing therefore the myosin heads to interact with the actin, starting the process of muscular contraction. This mechanism, multiplied by thousands of myosin-actin connections, promotes the shortening of the muscle and consequence production of mechanical work. The relaxation occurs when the Ca2+ is again pumped into the reticulum and the tropomyosin acts once again, preventing the contraction (Soares, 2005). The reference to sodium (Na) in this interview is due to this chemical element playing a role in the gradient differences that can be verified at a cellular level and also due to its relationship with the calcium gradients that are involved with the contractile mechanism.

people will say the following: "No, we need to stay away from an adaptability that is acting, and we need to recharge 'batteries' and whatever...". And then they don't understand why these oscillations happen, the loss of Specificity, which goes beyond the possible anomaly!

When this is not accomplished as it should be, and just like in training, for example, moving again to the Morphocycle, what happens is the possibility of damage to the cells, _and that is why I talk about 'paranecrose'_. This is when we feel pain and then inclusively take anti-inflammatory medication for that. And we know that nowadays there are some cases of sudden death caused by excessive use of anti-inflammatory medication.

So, when the cells are damaged, they spill ATP, they release ATP, ATP that is broken, broken down into ADP, the ADP connects to specific receptors, the p2y, but in the platelets. When this happens, in the organism there is the formation of clots that try to close the wound, to fight it...What does this lead to? The contraction and relaxation, if not accomplished through certain ways, can lead to the coagulation. Because most of the times, people that are coaching end up killing the guys! It is another significant advantage of Tactical Periodization. So, the blood coagulation happens, the ATP gets out of the cells in an injury and is broken down into ADP and then is reconnected, or links to the platelet receptors, these respond. And they respond to create a blood clot that starts circulating. This is disturbing either in the epithelial cells and in the muscular cells, therefore not only with a loss...imagine that there is not really a big problem, but there is a problem of intervention of something that is anomalous with regards to the Specificity, it's like you having something in between your teeth, it doesn't come out and you cannot chew properly, so you end up biting your tongue, etc., etc. But when this happens it may end up originating, for the reconstitution of the cells in the context, the cell pro-liferation that regards the reconstitution of what is damaged, and therefore the cells multiply, and the result may be, in a longer-term perspective or even medium, the re-narrowing or the narrowing down of the artery, something called stenosis.

This particularity of the metabolic functioning, circulatory of the ATP itself and now having in mind...I believe it is only respected by Tactical Periodiza-tion, even before I had understood these things, what ends up being amusing.

So, from that text that I gave, it is inclusively much more complex and much more detailed and mentions the ATP connections as signalling, or as signals that transmit messages to the exterior of the cell and that interferes positive or negatively for example, with the brain, in the brain, with learning, with memory, with the movement articulation. And curiously they say that when there is excessive signalling, of signals present, therefore once again there is the Specificity here protecting this, it may have a correlation with brain cases, for example with epilepsy or even some psychological issues. Inclusively with most sensorial organs, with the heart, etc., etc., etc. Curiously, _the immune system_ reacts and naturally, reacts 'a la longue', _reacts in accordance_ to the need of having to react regularly in a certain way, I don't know, I will spec-ulate, but probably the sudden deaths may also be related to that in some extent. Because _the immune system, when_ the ATP is requested', is released by the injured tissues, leading the immune cells to cause inflammation, which is a response that can even cause pain, once again here you can see the parabiose and the 'paranecrose'. The excessive and prolonged inflammation may dam-age the tissue, and examples referred here in the text like rheumatoid arthritis, etc., etc., etc. _The transmission of signals by the ATP also helps or can help the immune cells to kill the cells infected by anomalies, bacteria and others._ But see if on the one hand, _if there is a condition, if there is a kind of inversion and if this happens he has to intervene, but the inflammatory condition is not, or the damage of tissues does not occur, and the action of the immune system is advantageous, and it is indeed an important aspect._

I would tell you the following just to end, I would end as I started, it is the lack of understanding of the Morphocycle.

Why did I name it Morphocycle?

Why does it consider the recovery and the performance effort?

Why, and how is the sporting shape considered having the collective and the individual in mind?

Why must recovery be contemplated in a certain way?

What does the colour symbology mean?

So, I imagine that the emergence is the way how I want to play football, it emergences from realities in presence, so I recall two primary colours like blue and yellow that, when mixed, become green. Green is the emergence, it's the organisation. So if you imagine the fuel, and not only the fuel, and in this case the particular way of functioning of the muscular groups either in speed or under tension, which characterise the nucleus of regular performance, and how these indicators, or these aspects, when they occur just like that, _they demand the expression of bioenergetics and of a dominant relational pattern,_ conditional, among the various types of muscular fibres. This is the guarantee, when I happen to paint the blue with the blue – always -, the yellow with the yellow – always -, in the individual, without this becoming an anomaly with regards to the recovery, because it exists on Wednesday (Wednesday is the most fragmented day), on Friday...because you know, for example, the 100m world-record holder, he runs a 100m race, breaks the World record, rests for 30 minutes, and then he is ready to try and break it again. So, I don't interfere with the recovery, and at the same time I activate, catalyse a reality that I know that exists and that focusing on the individual will not disturb the recovery. Maybe it will even help me speed it up, and when it happens regularly, this blue and this yellow do a better job getting the green. _And this must be constant._ In the green of the week I am concerned with the Macro Principles and Sub-Principles, fundamentally with the macro, making the intermittence present there as well, and every time I reduce the activity I must not impoverish it, and this non-impoverishment contains all dimensions, the temporality of execution, the dynamic or the dynamism of the dynamic to bring to life.

And that is why I give you the example of a while ago, the guy, alright, proposes a 'small-sided activity. He does X minutes and is not concerned that the guy is intervening, he intervenes 20 times in a certain space, when in that space he would intervene 2 or 3 times in a real match? _It is obvious that the repercussions in metabolic terms, as a consequence for the adaptability are_ not the same. So, if throughout the time I don't have that in consideration, I will be tying, I will be placing a straitjacket. That won't happen if the Morphocycle is respected, but the Morphocycle does not arise from a vacuum. That is why I say that there are _two levels:_ a more conceptual, more theoretical level, *which belongs to the sphere of values, and that has to do with the way how I want to play. This is the way how I want to play, and I will I give birth to that? And the way how I will give birth to that is, when training, always training the same way?! Maybe yes, but what?! I contemplate all levels of complexity that this has?! Maybe not, then I will have to reduce this. And how can I reduce it without impoverishment? Well, but this is a whole with individuals! And how can I avoid losing the best of those individuals?! Then it is through...therefore, already <u>on the praxiological or operative side</u> or operational or phenomeno-logical, or methodological! How do I have to do this? Through the existence of the contemplation of the Specific in this weekly framework, repeating this way, and therefore systematic repetition but <u>the systematic repetition</u> is that of the Morphocycle! I think that's enough!*

Is it enough? No, it's not enough!

Not only, but the more-or-less high performance does not occur 'in vitro'! The quality of good football relies on a collective way of playing, with the lat-ter being achieved through <u>competition,</u> precisely the superior performance. A reality that contains as well, a club, directors, members, players, coaches, and the opponents, which can also be characterised in the same way! And the media, what are they in this problematic? So much 'sand' for such a 'big truck'! You don't need much more than common sense to understand that it is unavoidable to recognise the presence of a fundamental pre-condition that is part of the competition! Which? <u>The conflict.</u> Recognising it necessarily, also essential in structuring the psychologic of what is Human, relative to the per-sonality of individuals.

It is not possible to alienate the dominance of the presence of <u>conflict</u> in a latent context mixture and/or expressed in the <u>development of the eventual context</u> of trainability, and above all, of competition. So, the selfishness, the egocentrism, and even the egotism, or the tendential simulation of the indi-viduals in this competitive phenomenology, this is not fiction! And when this happens, it collides with what should be the consistency, the robustness, the cohesion, the fluidity, the empathy, or the mutual attraction, in the existence of a collective, with objectives to be reached as for such? This emotional pil-low, meaning the sentimentality, affectivity, empathy, synergy, all necessary, they become like the reason for the emergence of a <u>feeling of confidence</u> in the group even before its existence!

So, it is not a phenomenological framing 'in vitro'. The <u>conflictive</u> inherent to the eventual does not allow the one <u>leading, the coach</u>, to pretend that it is not present. In the village where I was born people used to say: "you must have them in their place!". The leadership style is another thing. Mourinho has one. Andre Villas-Boas has other. Guardiola, a different one. See for example how Mascherano (he was not bought as if he were a random player!) has been integrated!

Regarding these issues of affectivity, since long-time psychoanalysis has alerted that everyone, in different degrees, clearly ignores, or better, we are not conscious of many aspects related to what we feel, and therefore the way we see ourselves is never equal to how the others see us. To be at the TOP as a coach it is absolutely indispensable not to trick ourselves, otherwise, we will still be in the movie, but watching it upside down!

Therefore, even though a while ago I said it is not enough, it is good if I highlight that in the end, it is very handy not being mistaken with regards to what Tactical Periodization should be, what it is as a methodology! But then there is the fearful coach, the shitty coach, etc., etc., and then the one that can lead! And the latter does not do it...because if he did it like the Dalai Lama or Obama, or like Mother Teresa used to do...surely, he won't get there! And the same will occur, if as a coach he thinks like if the future to 'achieve', with regards to the way of playing that he wants to achieve, has no present. The future can only be 'pre-seen', it cannot be predicted, meaning that it can be prepared through periodization!

> ACKNOWLEDGEMENTS

Vitor Frade for everything (thanking through words for everything he has contributed to and for this book could require another book). But above all for his friendship.

Mauricio Pellegrino for the foreword, for the continuous lessons of football, humility, leadership, and above all for his advice and friendship.

Rui Faria for the foreword, for the attention and availability, and for the humanity that he shows in such an 'inhumane' world.

Jorge Maciel for his cooperation in this book (transcribing several interviews, conversations that we had, corrections, footnotes in 'The abyssal zone of Tactical Periodization', for his Tactical Periodization masterclasses, for his hospitality, friendship, etc., etc., etc.). Without his assistance this book would not have been possible.

Every and each of the interviewees and for their courtesy:

Carlos Carvalhal: manager of Sporting CP (Portugal) at the time of the interview.

Vitor Pereira: manager of Santa Clara (Portuguese Championship) at the time of the interview.

Jose Guilherme Oliveira: assistant manager of the Portuguese National Team during the 2010 South Africa World Cup at the time of the interview.

Marisa Gomes Silva: academy manager at FC Foz/Kick Off (Portugal) at the time of the interview.

Mara Vieira: coach at FC Porto youth academy and Feirense Ladies at the time of the interview.

Jose Tavares: coach at FC Porto youth academy at the time of this interview.

Miguel Lopes, Head of Dragon Force academy, which belongs to FC Porto, at the time of the interview, and Rita Santoalha, coach at Dragon Force Academy, who were also interviewed for the chapter on Youth Development which unfortunately ended up not being published in this book. Also, thanks to Miguel Lopes for the cooperation in the translation of the chapter 'The abyssal zone of Tactical Periodization'.

Joao Teixeira Fernandes, for his cooperation in the correction and improvement of the translation in the chapter 'The abyssal zone of Tactical Periodization'.

Domingos Paciencia: manager of SC Braga (Portugal) during the observation of his training sessions and to his assistant manager Miguel Cardoso, for his attention, permission to watch his training sessions, and for the conversations we kept, although at the end we did not managed to do the planned interviewed.

Rui Sa Lemos (coach at FC Porto's youth academy) and Nuno Faria (coach at Dragon Force) for their continuous assistance in each of my trips and for the hope they transmit and that influenced this book.

Ricardo Araujo, for his hospitality in each of my trips and for being always more than a 'distant cousin'.

Quique Hernandez, for giving me the opportunity to see and experience from the inside the reality of the world of professional football and for the 'master' he gifted me.

David Rodri, for his constant support, for his advice, and above all, for his friendship.

To all those who, in one or another way have contributed to make this book a reality. From those who have collaborated directly and that I have forgotten to mention (my apologies) to those who collaborated indirectly with their support, with their 'pushes', with their eagerness to read 'me' again, transmitted by all possible ways, with their interest shown by invitations for conferences, seminars, talks, by interviewing me or coming to watch my training sessions.

To my friends.

To my cousin Enric for always being a role-model.

To my Family, for being just like they are.

> ABOUT THE AUTHOR

Xavier Tamarit, holds a degree in Physical Activity and Sport Science from the University of Valencia (Spain, 2006). In 2012 completed the third level (UEFA PRO) of the Football Coaching Course.

He also attended the Sport Science and Physical Education Faculty of Porto University (Portugal, 2004-2005), studying in the Football Master's degree, with a specialisation in "Tactical Periodization" methodology.

Since 2012 he is the assistant of Mauricio Pellegrino, position that he held in Spain (Valencia CF 2012-2013, Deportivo Alavés 2016-2017 and Leganés 2018-2020), England (Southampton 2017-2018) and Argentina (Estudiantes de La Plata 2013-2015, Independiente de Avellaneda 2015-2016 and Vélez Sarsfield 2020-2021).

Between 2006 and 2012 he had various roles at Valencia CF: Women's First Team Head Coach, Head of Academy Coaching, U-15 Assistant Manager (League champions), among others.

He had other experiences in Levadiakos (Greece 2009-2010), Technical Assisant and Tactical Analyst with Aris Thessaloniki FC (Greece 2008-2009), and Fitness Coach at Juventude Barrio del Cristo (Spain, Regional Preferente 2006-2007).

CPSIA information can be obtained
at www.ICGtesting.com
Printed in the USA
LVHW080828261021
701547LV00002B/5